First World War
and Army of Occupation
War Diary
France, Belgium and Germany

41 DIVISION
122 Infantry Brigade
East Surrey Regiment
12th Battalion
1 May 1916 - 31 March 1919

WO95/2634/2

The Naval & Military Press Ltd
www.nmarchive.com
Published in association with The National Archives

Published by

The Naval & Military Press Ltd

Unit 10 Ridgewood Industrial Park,

Uckfield, East Sussex,

TN22 5QE England

Tel: +44 (0) 1825 749494

www.naval-military-press.com

www.nmarchive.com

This diary has been reprinted in facsimile from the original. Any imperfections are inevitably reproduced and the quality may fall short of modern type and cartographic standards.

© **Crown Copyright**
Images reproduced by permission of The National Archives, London, England, 2015.

Contents

Document type	Place/Title	Date From	Date To
Heading	WO95/2634/2		
War Diary	War Diary Of 12th Bn East Surrey Regt. May 1916 & June 16		
War Diary	Aldershot Le Havre	01/05/1916	03/05/1916
War Diary	Godcaesveldt	04/05/1916	04/05/1916
War Diary	Outersteene	05/05/1916	09/05/1916
War Diary	Steenwerck Ref Map. Sheet 36 1/40000	10/05/1916	28/05/1916
War Diary	Ploegsteert Trench Map 8 S.W. 30 M	29/05/1916	29/05/1916
War Diary	Ploegsteert	30/05/1916	31/05/1916
War Diary	Ploegsteert Ref. Trench Map 28 S.W. 1/20000	01/06/1916	31/07/1916
War Diary	Ploegsteert Ref. Trench Map 28 S.W.	01/08/1916	17/08/1916
War Diary	Thieushouck Ref. Map. 27 Belgium	18/08/1916	23/08/1916
War Diary	Mouflers Ref. Map. Lens. 11 Trench 2 1/100000	24/08/1916	05/09/1916
War Diary	Ref. Map. Trench B2 D 1/40000	06/09/1916	06/09/1916
War Diary	Albert Ref. Map. Trench 62 D 1/40000	06/09/1916	09/09/1916
War Diary	Fricourt Ref Map Trench 62 D. 1/40000	11/09/1916	15/09/1916
War Diary	Ref Map 57.c S.W 1/20000	15/09/1916	16/09/1916
War Diary	Albert Ref. Map. France 62 D 1/40000	17/09/1916	30/09/1916
Miscellaneous	Special Order Of The Day	02/09/1916	02/09/1916
Miscellaneous	Battalion Orders by Lieut Col. H.J. Walmisley-Dresser.		
War Diary	Albert Ref. Map France 62 D 1/40000	01/10/1916	02/10/1916
War Diary	France 57 C 1/10000	03/10/1916	10/10/1916
War Diary	Ref Map France Sheet 62D D27 D82	12/10/1916	16/10/1916
War Diary	Ref Map Abbeville 14 1/100000	17/10/1916	24/10/1916
War Diary	Map C 28 Ref Ms Av. 2.8	25/10/1916	28/10/1916
War Diary	Map Ref Of France Belgium 28 SW 1/2000 0.7 V 5.9-02 C. 6.8	29/10/1916	31/10/1916
Miscellaneous	Headquarters 122 Infantry Bde.	13/10/1916	13/10/1916
Miscellaneous	A Form Messages And Signals	14/10/1916	14/10/1916
Miscellaneous	Extract From Battalion orders By Lieut Col G. H. Kitching Comdg. 12th Bn East Surrey Regt.	14/10/1916	14/10/1916
Miscellaneous	41st Division	24/10/1916	24/10/1916
Miscellaneous	Headquarters 122 Infantry Bde	01/11/1916	01/11/1916
War Diary	St. Eloi Sector Sheet 28 O 1 And 2	01/11/1916	03/11/1916
War Diary	M5a 2.8 Ontario Camp	04/11/1916	07/11/1916
War Diary	Ontario Camp M 5a 2.8	08/11/1916	08/11/1916
War Diary	St Eloi Sector Sheet 28 O.1 & 2	09/11/1916	09/11/1916
War Diary	St. Eloi Sector	10/11/1916	12/11/1916
War Diary	St. Eloi Sector Sheet 28 O 1 & 2	13/11/1916	15/11/1916
War Diary	M5a25	16/11/1916	22/11/1916
War Diary	Diependaal Sub Sector From O1d 6 1/2.00-O2c8 1/2.9	23/11/1916	27/11/1916
War Diary	6w 7 & Q10 Camp. 5 5a 2.8	28/11/1916	30/11/1916
Miscellaneous	Headquarters 122 Infantry Bde.	01/01/1917	01/01/1917
Miscellaneous	Headquarters 122 Infantry Bde.	02/12/1916	02/12/1916
War Diary	Ontario Camp Sheet 28 M 5a 2.8	01/12/1916	02/12/1916
War Diary	St Eloi Sector Old And O 2c	03/12/1916	03/12/1916
War Diary	St. Eloi Sector 28 Old And 2 C	04/12/1916	09/12/1916
War Diary	Ontario Camp M 5a 2.8	10/12/1916	31/12/1916
War Diary	St. Eloi Sector	01/01/1917	31/01/1917
Miscellaneous	Headquarters. 122nd Infantry Bde.	01/03/1917	01/03/1917

War Diary		01/03/1917	28/03/1917
Miscellaneous	Headquarters. 122nd Infantry Bde.	01/04/1917	01/04/1917
War Diary	Reninghelst Ontario Camp	01/03/1917	31/03/1917
Miscellaneous	Headquarters, 122nd Infantry Bde.	01/05/1917	01/05/1917
War Diary	Reninghelst	01/04/1917	30/04/1917
War Diary	Nordausques	01/05/1917	26/05/1917
War Diary	Whitsunday	27/05/1917	31/05/1917
Miscellaneous	Headquarters. 122nd Infantry Bde.	01/07/1917	01/07/1917
War Diary	GHQ Line Between Voormezeele Scottish Wood	01/06/1917	04/06/1917
War Diary	Chippewa Camp	05/06/1917	06/06/1917
War Diary	Assaulton Dammstrasse	07/06/1917	17/06/1917
War Diary	Battle Of Waterloo	18/06/1917	19/06/1917
War Diary	Voormezeele	20/06/1917	25/06/1917
War Diary	By Dickebusch Lake	26/06/1917	30/06/1917
War Diary	Dickebusch Lake	01/07/1917	02/07/1917
War Diary	Near Vierstraat	03/07/1917	05/07/1917
War Diary	Roukloshille	06/07/1917	22/07/1917
War Diary	Wood Camp.	23/07/1917	23/07/1917
War Diary	Lock House	24/07/1917	30/07/1917
War Diary	Iron Bridge	30/07/1917	31/07/1917
Operation(al) Order(s)	12th Bn. East. Surrey Regt. Operation Order No. 104.	22/07/1917	22/07/1917
Operation(al) Order(s)	12th Bn East Surrey Regt. Operation Order No. 105.	23/07/1917	23/07/1917
Operation(al) Order(s)	12th Bn. East Surrey Regt. Operation Order No. 106.	28/07/1917	28/07/1917
War Diary	Canal Bank (o.5.c. 5.9)	01/08/1917	05/08/1917
War Diary	Bois Confluent	06/08/1917	06/08/1917
War Diary	Dezon Camp.	07/08/1917	10/08/1917
War Diary	Iron Bridge.	11/08/1917	13/08/1917
War Diary	Elzenwalla	14/08/1917	14/08/1917
War Diary	Boukloghille	15/08/1917	19/08/1917
War Diary	Zuypteene	20/08/1917	20/08/1917
War Diary	Zudausques	21/08/1917	31/08/1917
Operation(al) Order(s)	12th Bn East Surrey Regt. Operation Order No. 106	10/08/1917	10/08/1917
Operation(al) Order(s)	12th Bn East Surrey Regt. Operation Order No. 107	10/08/1917	10/08/1917
Operation(al) Order(s)	12th Bn East Surrey Regt. Operation Order No. 108	13/08/1917	13/08/1917
Operation(al) Order(s)	12th Bn East Surrey Regt. Warning Order No. 1	19/08/1917	19/08/1917
Operation(al) Order(s)	12th Bn East Surrey Regt. Operation Order No. 109	19/08/1917	19/08/1917
Operation(al) Order(s)	12th Bn East Surrey Regt. Operation Order No. 110	20/08/1917	20/08/1917
Operation(al) Order(s)	12th Bn East Surrey Regiment. Operation Order No. 114		
Miscellaneous	Headquarters, 122nd Infantry Bde.	01/10/1917	01/10/1917
War Diary	Zudausques	01/09/1917	14/09/1917
War Diary	Staple	15/09/1917	15/09/1917
War Diary	Fletre	16/09/1917	16/09/1917
War Diary	Chippewa Camp	17/09/1917	17/09/1917
War Diary	Ridge Wood	18/09/1917	18/09/1917
War Diary	Lock 8 Area	19/09/1917	19/09/1917
War Diary	Assembly Area	20/09/1917	20/09/1917
War Diary	Red Line	21/09/1917	30/09/1917
Miscellaneous	Battalion Temporarily Reduced To Lower Establishment		
Miscellaneous	Organisation Of The Infantry Battalion		
Miscellaneous	Table "A" Battalion Establishment (900 O.R's)		
Operation(al) Order(s)	Operation Order No. 157 by Major C.T. Williams Comdg. 12th. East Surrey Regiment.		
Operation(al) Order(s)	12th Bn East Surrey Regt. Operation Order No. 111.	13/09/1917	13/09/1917

Type	Description	Start	End
Operation(al) Order(s)	12th Bn East Surrey Regiment. Operation Order No. 112	13/09/1917	13/09/1917
Miscellaneous	12th Bn East Surrey Regt. Addendum to Operation Order No. 111.	13/09/1917	13/09/1917
Operation(al) Order(s)	12th Bn East Surrey Regiment Operation Order No. 113	16/09/1917	16/09/1917
Operation(al) Order(s)	Dagger Operation Order No. 117		
Operation(al) Order(s)	12th Bn. East Surrey Regt. Operation Order No. 115	26/09/1917	26/09/1917
Operation(al) Order(s)	12th Bn East Surrey Regt. Operation Order No. 116	27/09/1917	27/09/1917
Miscellaneous	Headquarters, 122nd Infantry Bde.	03/11/1917	03/11/1917
War Diary	La Panne	01/10/1917	15/10/1917
War Diary	Oost Dunkerke Bains	15/10/1917	17/10/1917
War Diary	Oost Dunkerke Bains	17/10/1917	22/10/1917
War Diary	Oost Dunnerke Bains	23/10/1917	29/10/1917
War Diary	Couderkerque Branche	30/10/1917	31/10/1917
Operation(al) Order(s)	12th Bn East Surrey Regiment. Operation Order No. 117.	06/10/1917	06/10/1917
Operation(al) Order(s)	12th East Surrey Regiment. Operation Order No. 116	14/10/1917	14/10/1917
Miscellaneous	12th East Surrey Regt. 122nd Infantry Brigade Warning Order No. 14.	25/10/1917	25/10/1917
Miscellaneous	12th Bn East Surrey Regt. Warning Order No. 16	23/10/1917	23/10/1917
Miscellaneous	12th Bn. East Surrey Regiment Defence Scheme.	27/10/1917	27/10/1917
Miscellaneous	12th Bn East Surrey Regt. Warning Order No. 11.	28/10/1917	28/10/1917
Operation(al) Order(s)	12th. Bn East Surrey Regt. Operation Order No. 119	29/10/1917	29/10/1917
Heading	WO95/2634/3		
Heading	12th Bn East Surrey Regt May 1916-Oct 1917 Mar 1918-1919 Mar		
Heading	12th Battn. The East Surrey Regiment March 1918		
War Diary	Italy	01/03/1918	02/03/1918
War Diary	France	03/03/1917	31/03/1917
Miscellaneous	First Army	26/02/1918	26/02/1918
Miscellaneous	Infantry Battalion. Provisional War Establishment.		
Miscellaneous	Headquarters. Third Army (A)	09/03/1918	09/03/1918
Heading	12th Battalion The East Surrey Regiment April 1918		
War Diary	Bucquoy	01/04/1918	01/04/1918
War Diary	Marieux	02/04/1918	02/04/1918
War Diary	Amplier	03/04/1918	03/04/1918
War Diary	Poperinghe	04/04/1918	04/04/1918
War Diary	School Camp	05/04/1918	07/04/1918
War Diary	Passchendaele Ridge	08/04/1918	11/04/1918
War Diary	Low Keep	12/04/1918	13/04/1918
War Diary	Mill Keep	14/04/1918	15/04/1918
War Diary	Goldfish Chateau Camp	16/04/1918	25/04/1918
War Diary	Dambre Camp	26/04/1918	30/04/1918
Miscellaneous	12th East Surrey's April 1918		
Operation(al) Order(s)	12th Bn. East. Surrey Regt. Operation Order No. 141.	07/04/1918	07/04/1918
Operation(al) Order(s)	12th Bn East Surrey Regt. Warning Order No. 1		
Operation(al) Order(s)	12th Bn. East Surrey Regt. Operation Order No. 139		
Operation(al) Order(s)	12th Bn East Surrey Regt. Operation Order No. 140		
Miscellaneous	122nd Infantry Brigade.	17/04/1918	17/04/1918
Miscellaneous	12th East Surrey Regt.	17/04/1918	17/04/1918
Miscellaneous	12th East Surrey Regt.	24/04/1918	24/04/1918
Miscellaneous	Headquarters. 122nd Inf Bde.	03/06/1918	03/06/1918
War Diary	Camp H. 4.a.	01/05/1918	02/05/1918
War Diary	Ypres	03/05/1918	17/05/1918
War Diary	Camp A. 30.c	18/05/1918	24/05/1918
War Diary	Ypres	25/05/1918	31/05/1918

Miscellaneous	12th East Surrey Regt.	03/05/1918	03/05/1918
Operation(al) Order(s)	Operation Order No. 2	06/05/1918	06/05/1918
Operation(al) Order(s)	Battalion Operation Order No. 98 by Lieut. Colonel. C. Hurdoch. Commanding "Dingle"	07/05/1918	07/05/1918
Miscellaneous	Administrative Instructions Reference Battalion Operation Order No. 95	07/05/1918	07/05/1918
Operation(al) Order(s)	12th Battn East Surrey Regt. Operation Order No. 3	10/05/1918	10/05/1918
Miscellaneous	12th East Surrey Regt.	11/05/1918	11/05/1918
Operation(al) Order(s)	12th Battn East Surrey Regt Operation Order No. 4	11/05/1918	11/05/1918
Miscellaneous	122nd Inf Bde.	15/05/1918	15/05/1918
Operation(al) Order(s)	Operation Order No 5	16/05/1918	16/05/1918
Miscellaneous	12th East Surrey Regt.	17/05/1918	17/05/1918
Operation(al) Order(s)	Operation Order No. 6 by Lieut. Col A.C. Brown DSO Comas 12th B East Surrey Regt	17/05/1918	17/05/1918
Operation(al) Order(s)	12th Bn. East Surrey Regt. Operation Order No. 7	24/05/1918	24/05/1918
War Diary	Ypres	01/06/1918	04/06/1918
War Diary	Watten	05/06/1918	05/06/1918
War Diary	Bayengham	06/06/1918	25/06/1918
War Diary	Robrouck	26/06/1918	26/06/1918
War Diary	Beauyaard	27/06/1918	30/06/1918
Miscellaneous	12th East Surrey Regt.	02/06/1918	02/06/1918
Operation(al) Order(s)	Operation Order No. 9. by Lieut Col. G. L. Brown D.S.O. Comdg 12th Bn East Surrey Regt.	02/06/1918	02/06/1918
Operation(al) Order(s)	Operation Orders No. 10 by Lt Col. G. L. Brown D.S.O. Comdg 12th Bn East Surrey Regt.	04/06/1918	04/06/1918
Miscellaneous	Headquarters 14th. Division "G"	07/06/1918	07/06/1918
Operation(al) Order(s)	Operation Order No. 15 by Lieut Col. G. L. Brown D.S.O. Comdg 12th Bn East Surrey Regt.	05/07/1918	05/07/1918
Miscellaneous	Second Army.	14/06/1918	14/06/1918
Operation(al) Order(s)	12th Bn East Surrey Regt. Warning Order No. 2	16/06/1918	16/06/1918
Miscellaneous	12th East Surrey Regt.	18/06/1918	18/06/1918
Operation(al) Order(s)	Operation Order No. 11 by Lieut. Col. G. L. Brown, D.S.O. Comdg 12th Bn East Surrey Regiment	19/06/1918	19/06/1918
Miscellaneous	12th Bn East Surrey Regiment. Battalion Exercise	21/06/1918	21/06/1918
Operation(al) Order(s)	12th Bn. East Surrey Regt. Operation Order No. 12	24/06/1918	24/06/1918
Operation(al) Order(s)	12th Bn. East Surrey Regt. Operation Order No. 15	26/06/1918	26/06/1918
Operation(al) Order(s)	12th Bn East Surrey Regt Operation Order No. 14	30/06/1918	30/06/1918
Miscellaneous	Organisation Training And Tactical Handling Of Lewis Guns.	31/05/1918	31/05/1918
Miscellaneous	Headquarters, 41st Division.		
War Diary	Reninghelst	01/07/1918	04/07/1918
War Diary	Laclytte	05/07/1918	15/07/1918
War Diary	Reninghelst	16/07/1918	20/07/1918
War Diary	Laclytte	21/07/1918	30/07/1918
War Diary	Reninghelst	31/07/1918	31/07/1918
Operation(al) Order(s)	12th Bn East Surrey Regt. In continuation of Operation Order No. 14	01/07/1918	01/07/1918
Operation(al) Order(s)	Operation Order No. 24 by Major C. T. William Comdg. 12th East Surrey Regt.	03/08/1918	03/08/1918
Operation(al) Order(s)	Operation Order No. 25 by Major C. T. William Commanding "Root"	06/08/1918	06/08/1918
Miscellaneous	12th. East Surrey Regt.	09/03/1918	09/03/1918
Operation(al) Order(s)	Operation Order No. 16 by Lieut Col. G.L. Brown D.S.O. Commanding 12th Bn East Surrey Regt.	04/09/1918	04/09/1918
Miscellaneous	Narrative Of Operations Carried Out By The 122nd Infantry Brigade Commanding Midnight	08/08/1918	08/08/1918

Operation(al) Order(s)	Operation Order No. 27 by Major C. T. Williams Comdg. Root.	09/08/1918	09/08/1918
Operation(al) Order(s)	Operation Order No. 28 by Major Ct Williams Comdg. 12th East Surrey Regt.		
Miscellaneous	41st Division "G"	14/08/1918	14/08/1918
Miscellaneous		11/08/1918	11/08/1918
Miscellaneous	Operation Orders by Major C.S. Williams Comdg. 12th Bn East Surrey Regt.	14/07/1918	14/07/1918
Miscellaneous	O C Company Reference Operation Order No.17.	15/07/1918	15/07/1918
Operation(al) Order(s)	Operation Orders No. 29 by Major C. T. Williams Comdg 12th East Surrey Regt.	15/08/1918	15/08/1918
Miscellaneous	12th. East Surrey Regt.	16/07/1918	16/07/1918
Operation(al) Order(s)	Operation Order No. 18 by Major CT. Williams Comdg Root	17/07/1918	17/07/1918
Operation(al) Order(s)	Operation Order No. 25 by Lieut Col G. L. Brown D.S.O. Comdg 12th Battn East Surrey Regt.	20/08/1918	20/08/1918
Miscellaneous	12th. East Surrey Regt.	22/08/1918	22/08/1918
Miscellaneous	Battn Order		
Operation(al) Order(s)	Operation Order No. 19. by Major C. T. Williams Comdg. 12th Bn East Surrey Regiment.	24/07/1918	24/07/1918
Operation(al) Order(s)	Operation Order No. 20. by Major C. T. Williams Comdg. 12th Bn East Surrey Regiment.	24/07/1918	24/07/1918
Operation(al) Order(s)	Operation Order No. 30 by Lieut. Col. G.L. Brown, D.S.O. Comdg. 12th. Bn. East Surrey Regiment.	25/08/1918	25/08/1918
Miscellaneous	Instructions For Holding The Line Battalion in Brigade Reserve.	28/07/1918	28/07/1918
Operation(al) Order(s)	Operation Order No. 21 by Major C. T. Williams Comdg. 12th Bn East Surrey Regt.	30/07/1918	30/07/1918
Operation(al) Order(s)	Operation Order No. 23 by Major C. T. Williams Comdg. 12th Bn East Surrey Regt.	31/07/1918	31/07/1918
Miscellaneous	12th Bn East Surrey Regt.		
War Diary	Reninghelst	01/08/1918	01/08/1918
War Diary	Wippenhoek	02/08/1918	03/08/1918
War Diary	La Clytte	04/08/1918	16/08/1918
War Diary	Reninghelst	17/08/1918	21/08/1918
War Diary	Wippenhoek	22/08/1918	25/08/1918
War Diary	Reninghelst	26/08/1918	28/08/1918
War Diary	Abeele	29/08/1918	29/08/1918
War Diary	Esquerdes	30/08/1918	31/08/1918
Heading	Headquarters, 122nd Infantry Bde.	01/10/1918	01/10/1918
War Diary		01/09/1918	30/09/1918
Miscellaneous	O C Company	01/08/1918	01/08/1918
Operation(al) Order(s)	Operation Order No. 32 by Lieut. Col. G. L. Brown, D.S.O.	01/09/1918	01/09/1918
Miscellaneous	12th East Surrey Regt.	02/09/1918	02/09/1918
Operation(al) Order(s)	Operation Order No. 33	02/09/1918	02/09/1918
Miscellaneous	Officer Commanding.	05/10/1918	05/10/1918
Operation(al) Order(s)	Operation Order No. 38 by Lieut. Col. G. L. Brown. D.S.O. Comdg 12th Bn East Surrey Regiment.	08/10/1918	08/10/1918
Operation(al) Order(s)	Operation Order No. 39 by Lieut. Col. G. L. Brown D.S.O. Comdg 12th Bn East Surrey Regt.	09/10/1918	09/10/1918
Operation(al) Order(s)	Operation Order No. 40 by Lieut Col G. L. Brown D.S.O.		
Operation(al) Order(s)	12th Bn East Surrey Regt. Operation Order No. 41	11/10/1918	11/10/1918
Miscellaneous	12th Bn East Surrey Regt. Administrative Instructions In Connection With O.O. No. 41	11/10/1918	11/10/1918

Miscellaneous	12th Bn East Surrey Regt. Warning Order.	13/09/1918	13/09/1918
Operation(al) Order(s)	Operation Order No. 34 by Major G. O. Searle Comdg 12th Bn. East Surrey Regt.	14/09/1918	14/09/1918
Miscellaneous	Very Urgent		
Operation(al) Order(s)	23rd Middlesex (Operation) Order No. 231		
Operation(al) Order(s)	12th East Surrey Regt. Operation Order No.	20/09/1918	20/09/1918
Operation(al) Order(s)	12th East Surrey Regt. Operation Order No.	22/10/1918	22/10/1918
Miscellaneous	Diary Of Operations.	21/10/1918	21/10/1918
Miscellaneous	12th East Surrey Regt.	24/09/1918	24/09/1918
Operation(al) Order(s)	Operation Order No. by Lieut. Col. G.L. Brown. D.S.O. Comdg 12th Bn East Surrey Regiment	25/09/1918	25/09/1918
Miscellaneous	Operation Order		
Miscellaneous	Operation Order by Lt. Col. G. L. Brown D.S.O. Comdg Advance Gourd.		
Miscellaneous	O.C. Coy.	14/10/1918	14/10/1918
Miscellaneous	Operation Orders 12th East Surrey Regt.	26/10/1918	26/10/1918
Operation(al) Order(s)	Operation Order No. 36 by Lieut. Col. G. L. Brown DSO. Comdg 12th Bn East Surrey Regiment.	27/09/1918	27/09/1918
Operation(al) Order(s)	Operation Order No 37 by Lieut. Col. G. L. Brown DSO. Comdg 12th Bn East Surrey Regiment.	28/09/1918	28/09/1918
Operation(al) Order(s)	15th East Hampshire Regiment Operation Order No. 145	31/10/1918	31/10/1918
War Diary		01/10/1918	30/11/1918
War Diary	Everbecq	01/12/1918	12/12/1918
War Diary	Herinnes	13/12/1918	13/12/1918
War Diary	Bierges	14/12/1918	14/12/1918
War Diary	Wanthierbraine	15/12/1918	16/12/1918
War Diary	Vieux Genappe	17/12/1918	17/12/1918
War Diary	Tilly	18/12/1918	18/12/1918
War Diary	Ligny	19/12/1918	19/12/1918
War Diary	Belgrade	20/12/1918	20/12/1918
War Diary	Pontillas	21/12/1918	21/12/1918
War Diary	Warnant	22/12/1918	31/12/1918
Operation(al) Order(s)	12th. Bn. East Surrey Regt. Operation Order No. 150.	01/11/1918	01/11/1918
Miscellaneous	12th East Surrey Regiment.	03/11/1918	03/11/1918
Operation(al) Order(s)	Operation Order No. 146 by Lieut Col. G. L. Brown DSO.	04/11/1918	04/11/1918
Miscellaneous	12th Bn East Surrey Regt. Warning Order No. 101	08/11/1918	08/11/1918
Operation(al) Order(s)	Operation Order No. 149 by Lieut. Col. G. L. Brown D.S.O. Comdg. 12th Bn, East Surrey Regt.	09/11/1918	09/11/1918
Operation(al) Order(s)	12th Bn. East Surrey Regt. Operation Order No.	17/11/1918	17/11/1918
Operation(al) Order(s)	122nd Infantry Brigade Operation Order No. 253	19/11/1918	19/11/1918
Operation(al) Order(s)	12th. Bn. East Surrey Regt. Operation Order No. 151	20/11/1918	20/11/1918
Operation(al) Order(s)	Operation Order No. 152 by Major C. T. Williams. Comdg. 12th, Bn. East Surrey Regt.	10/12/1918	10/12/1918
Miscellaneous	12th Bn East Surrey Regiment. 1st Amendment To Operation Order No. 152	11/12/1918	11/12/1918
Miscellaneous	12th. East Surrey Regt.	11/12/1918	11/12/1918
Operation(al) Order(s)	Operation Order No. 153 by Major C. T. Williams. Comdg. 12th Bn. East Surrey Rgt.	12/12/1918	12/12/1918
Operation(al) Order(s)	Operation Order No. 154 by Major C. T. Williams. Comdg. 12th East Surrey Regt.	13/12/1918	13/12/1918
Miscellaneous	122nd. Infantry Brigade Warning Order No. 111.	13/11/1918	13/11/1918
Operation(al) Order(s)	122nd Infantry Brigade Operation Order Number. 250	13/11/1918	13/11/1918
Miscellaneous	March Table to Accompany 122nd Infantry Brigade Operation Order No. 250		

Operation(al) Order(s)	R.A.M.C. Operation Order No. 75.by Colonel L. N. Lloyd C. R. G. D.S.O. A. M. S. A.D.M.S. 41st Division, Commanding Royal Army Medical Corps.	14/11/1918	14/11/1918
Operation(al) Order(s)	Operation Order No. 50 by Lieut. Col. G. L. Brown, D.S.O. Comdg 12th Bn East Surrey Regiment.	14/11/1918	14/11/1918
Operation(al) Order(s)	Operation Order No. 155 by Major C. T. Williams Comdg. 12th. East Surrey Regt.	15/12/1918	15/12/1918
Operation(al) Order(s)	Operation Order No. 156 by Major C. T. Williams. Comdg. 12th Bn. East Surrey Regiment.	16/12/1918	16/12/1918
Miscellaneous	Administrative Instruction No.1 Regarding March Of The 41st Division To Germany	16/11/1918	16/11/1918
Miscellaneous	Appendix "C" Medical Arrangement To Be Carried Out During And Prior To The March.		
Miscellaneous	Appendix "A" Composition of Billeting Parties.		
Miscellaneous	Sheet 2 Appendix "B"		
Miscellaneous	Appendix "B" Issued With 41st Division Administrative Instruction No. 1		
Miscellaneous	Tables Showing Composition Of Groups, Road Spaces And Times Required To Pass A Fixed Point, On Which All Calculations For The 41st Division Will Be Based.		
Operation(al) Order(s)	Operation Order No. 158 by Major C. T. Williams. Comdg 12th Bn East Surrey Regt.	18/12/1918	18/12/1918
Miscellaneous	41st Division Administrative Instruction No. 3 Regarding March Of Division Into Germany.	18/12/1918	18/12/1918
Map			
Operation(al) Order(s)	Operation Orders No. 159 by Major C. T. Williams. Commdg. 12th. Bn. East Surrey Rgt.	19/12/1918	19/12/1918
Operation(al) Order(s)	Operation Orders No. 160 by Major C. T. Williams. Comdg. 12th. East Surrey Regiment.	20/12/1918	20/12/1918
Heading	12th Bn East Surrey Regt Jan-Mar 1919		
War Diary	Warnant	01/01/1919	08/01/1919
War Diary	Marialinden	09/01/1919	31/01/1919
Miscellaneous	O.C. 12th East Surrey Regt.	26/01/1919	26/01/1919
Operation(al) Order(s)	122nd Infantry Brigade Operation Order No. 258	04/01/1919	04/01/1919
Miscellaneous	Table Of Relief To Accompany 122nd Inf. Bde. O.O. No. 258		
Miscellaneous	R.A.M.C. Warning Order No. 76 by Colonel. L. N. Lloyd C.M.G., DSO., A.M.S. A.D.M.S. Commanding Royal Army Medical Corps. 41st Division	04/01/1919	04/01/1919
Miscellaneous	41st Divisional Medical Administrative Instruction Relative To The Move To Germany	05/01/1919	05/01/1919
Miscellaneous	Administrative Instruction In Connection With 122nd Inf. Brigade O. O. 258	04/01/1919	04/01/1919
Miscellaneous	1st. Addendum To Administrative Instructions In Connection With 122nd Inf. Brigade O. O. 258	04/01/1919	04/01/1919
Miscellaneous	18th KRR Corps.	09/01/1919	09/01/1919
Miscellaneous	12th. East Surrey Regt.	06/01/1919	06/01/1919
Operation(al) Order(s)	122nd Infantry Brigade Operation Order No. 259	06/01/1919	06/01/1919
Miscellaneous	Table Of Permanent Guards Found By 122nd Inf. Bde.		
Operation(al) Order(s)	No. 161 Operation Orders by Lieut Col. G. L.Brown. D.S.O. Comdg. 12th. Bn. East Surrey Regiment.	06/01/1919	06/01/1919
Miscellaneous	122nd Infantry Brigade.	25/01/1919	25/01/1919
Miscellaneous	C Form Messages And Signals.	06/01/1919	06/01/1919
Miscellaneous	C Form Messages And Signals.	03/01/1919	03/01/1919
Miscellaneous	C Form Messages And Signals.	04/01/1919	04/01/1919
War Diary	Marialinden	01/02/1919	14/02/1919

War Diary	Hoffningstal	15/02/1919	28/02/1919
Operation(al) Order(s)	Operation Order No. 162 by Lieut. Col. G. L. Brown. D.S.O. Comdg. 12th. Bn. East Surrey Regiment.	01/02/1919	01/02/1919
Operation(al) Order(s)	122nd Infantry Brigade Operation Order No. 262	22/02/1919	22/02/1919
Miscellaneous	Administrative Instructions Reference 122nd Infantry Brigade. O.O. 263	22/02/1919	22/02/1919
War Diary	Volberg	01/03/1919	31/03/1919

move/2639C(e)4349(e)

joes/23C/s3+(e)

12 East S Vol 122/XLI 1.C 3 sheets

May 1916 & June/6
Dec '18

WAR DIARY
1/4th Bn East Surrey R

Army Form C. 2118

WAR DIARY
or
INTELLIGENCE SUMMARY

(Erase heading not required.)

Instructions regarding War Diaries and Intelligence Summaries are contained in F.S. Regs., Part II. and the Staff Manual respectively. Title Pages will be prepared in manuscript.

12th Bn. East Surrey Regt.   B. E. F.

Place	Date	Hour	Summary of Events and Information	Remarks and references to Appendices
Ailette & Le Havre	1/5/16	5.15 pm	Battalion parade for overseas. Strength 1018	
	2/5/16	1 am	Bn. arrived at Havre. Proceeded No. 6 Rest Camp.	
do	3-5-16	3.30 am	Bn. paraded for entrainment to Railhead	
Hedauvaelt	4-5-16	5 am	Bn. arrived. Marched to Billets at OUTTERSTEENE Strength as above.	
OUTTERSTEENE	5/5/16 6/5/16 7/5/16 8/5/16		Bn. in Billets. Strength as before — on 6th inst Strength 1019.	
	9-5-16	9 am	Bn. marched to Billets immediately West of STEENWERCK — Strength 1019.	
STEENWERCK Ref Map Sheet 36 40.c.0.0	10/5	7 am	Party of 50 including C.O. & Coy Commanders proceeded on Instructional Tour of 48 hrs. to the Trenches at PLOEGSTERT WOOD. Bn. in Billets — Work & Strength — normal —	
	11/5		Bath. in billets.	
	12/5	"	Party who proceeded to Trenches on 10th returned. Their places being taken by 10 others	
	13/5	"	Officers & No. Men unch. Bath. in billets.	
do	14/5 to 27/5		Bn. in Billets. Work = Several training, musketry & rifle marching including courses Officers & Senior N.C.O.s have visited the trenches for 2 days at different periods. Strength 1017. (32 officers, 985 rank & file.)	
do	28/5	2.30 am	Bn. paraded to march to new billet in Reserve at SOYER FM (B.6.a.3.5).	
PLOEGSTEERT Ref Map Sht 36 6 SW	29/5	6 am	Bn. moved out of Billets by companies to occupy trenches, relieving 7/8 Seaforth Highlanders. At Days. in firing line; B Coy Support; C Coy Reserve. Situation: CONVENT (U.27.d.32.) area. Bn. H. Qrs at Lawrences.	

Army Form C. 2118

WAR DIARY
or
INTELLIGENCE SUMMARY
(Erase heading not required.)

Instructions regarding War Diaries and Intelligence Summaries are contained in F.S. Regs., Part II. and the Staff Manual respectively. Title Pages will be prepared in manuscript.

12th Bn EAST SURREY REGT.   B.E.F.

Place	Date	Hour	Summary of Events and Information	Remarks and references to Appendices
PLOEGSTEERT	30-31/5		Bⁿ in Trenches. Situation as above (29th inst.). No enemy activity on our front. Work chiefly improvement of trenches & obstacles. Weather fine. One casualty occurred during the (31ˢᵗ) afternoon whilst the enemy was shelling Bⁿ Headquarters. No other damage done.	

Lieut Col.
Commdg 12ᵗʰ East Surrey Regt

6/1916.

Army Form C. 2118

WAR DIARY or INTELLIGENCE SUMMARY

(Erase heading not required.)

12th Bn. EAST SURREY REGT. B.E.F.

June 1916.

Instructions regarding War Diaries and Intelligence Summaries are contained in F.S. Regs., Part II. and the Staff Manual respectively. Title Pages will be prepared in manuscript.

Place	Date	Hour	Summary of Events and Information	Remarks and references to Appendices
PLOEGSTEERT Ref. Trench Map 28 S.W. 1/20,000	1st & 2nd June 1916		Bn. in Trenches [neighbourhood of CONVENT (U.27.6.8.2) vide Diary 29th May 1916] The enemy activity on our front, beyond occasional shelling of Bn. Hd. Qrs. & our R.F.A. in the vicinity, and slight machine gun activity during the night. Work — improvement of fire & communication trenches & rendering Bn. Hd. Qrs. bomb proof. Weather good: wind from W.S.W. to N.N.W. — 3 casualties on 1st inst.	
do.	3rd June		Bn. in Trenches. Enemy activity as for 1st & 2nd insts. Enemy Arty. placed 2 — 5.9 Shells within 20x of Bn. Hd. Qrs. — work as above — wind northerly & weather not so settled — 1 casualty.	
do.	4th	6 a.m.	Bn. relieved by 10th R. West Surrey Regt., & returned to Billets at SOYER FARM in reserve. A. coy at DELENNEL FM. B. coy at RODDEE FM. C. coy at FARM 1875, D. coy w/c Hd. Qrs. at SOYER FARM.	
do.	5th 6th 7th 8th 9th 10th 11th		Bn. as above (4th inst.) Work — chiefly fatigues for improvement of trenches & billets. No casualties. DELENNEL FARM has sustained occasional shelling.	
			Bn. in Trenches (neighbourhood of CONVENT (U.27.6.8.2) relieving 10th R. West SURREY REGT. — B & C coys in front line. A. coy in support, D. coy in Reserve near Bn. Hd. Qrs. at LAURANCE FARM. — Strength 1007	
do.		6 a.m.	As for 5th — 9th inst. Weather cold & rainy.	

Original

Army Form C. 2118
page 2

WAR DIARY / INTELLIGENCE SUMMARY

(Erase heading not required.)

Instructions regarding War Diaries and Intelligence Summaries are contained in F.S. Regs, Part II. and the Staff Manual respectively. Title Pages will be prepared in manuscript.

12th EAST SURREY REGT.   June 1916   B. E. F.

Place	Date	Hour	Summary of Events and Information	Remarks and references to Appendices
PLOEGSTEERT Ref. Trench Map 28 S.W. 1 20.00.0 do do do do do do	12th 13th 14th 15th 16th 17th 6am 18th 19th 20th		Bn in Trenches. No enemy activity beyond occasional shelling of our front and working parties behind our line. Work – improvement & repair of Trenches. Weather very bad. Some machine gun activity on both sides during the evening. Casualties 12th inst., but less machine gun activity. Draft of 10 men arrived from 3rd Bn. Bn in Trenches. Enemy artillery activity practically nil. Some Trench mortars known into our lines. Work as per 12th inst. At about 12 midnight (16th–17th inst.) the Gas alarm was sounded throughout the 41st Div., the alarm being communicated from further north where the gas attack one afternoon found to have been initiated by the Enemy. Some units of the Division suffered from it but the Bn did not experience any effects. The Bn transport lines back at de ROMARIN however got a slight amount of gas. Bn returned by 10th R.W. SURREY Regt. and proceeded back to billets at SOYER FARM in reserve. During period in Trenches Casualties were 9. The weather was bad throughout, with the exception of 18th inst. Bn in Billets. Working parties supplied to R.E. – Weather fine & sunny – Aeroplane & Art. activity on both sides – Bn in Billets. Work as per 18th inst. – Draft of 62 N.C.Os & men arrived from 3rd Bn.	H/Q H/Q H/Q H/Q H/Q H/Q H/Q

1875   Wt. W593/826   1,000,000   4/15   J.B.C. & A.   A.D.S.S./Forms/C. 2118.

WAR DIARY or INTELLIGENCE SUMMARY

Army Form C. 2118

June 1916   B.E.F.   page 3

Place	Date	Hour	Summary of Events and Information	Remarks and references to Appendices
PLOEGSTEERT Ref. June Map 28 SW 1/20000	21		Bn in Billets. Work as before. Weather excellent. A gas alarm was sounded at about 11 p.m. 22nd inst. — No gas however in our sector.	A/705
	22		Bn in Billets. SOYER F.M. shelled 8-9 p.m. T.M. H.E. Shells exploded in dining room causing 4 casualties.	A/705 7/705
	23			
	24	6 a.m.	Bn relieved 10th Queens in trenches. — LAURENCE F.M., Bn H.Q. G'n, A + D Coys in firing trenches, B. Coy. Support + C. in Reserve. LAURENCE FARM was shelled soon after relief was completed. Total strength 1081	
do	25		Bn in trenches. Repair workshop of trenches + C.T. — very little activity. Work = Enemy art. shelled Bn H.Q. G'n (LAURENCE F.M.) in morning. Wind in W. Scale. Weather excellent.	A/705
do	26		Bn in trenches. Weather rainy & cold.	
do	27, 28, 29		a.m. 26th inst. Enemy shelled Bn. H.Q. G'n heavily with shrapnel at H.E., being both 77 c.m. & 10.5 c.m.; also a shelling of 8.5 c.m.	
do	30		Bn in trenches. During the morning our trionizonal (4/1st) Artillery bombarded enemy's trenches + wire at selected points, cutting the latter. Enemy retaliated, damaging our trenches. at 9.15 p.m. Div. Art. commenced intense bombardment along our front. Gas emitted by own at 10 p.m. Raiding parties sent out to enemy's trenches — One party under Capt. Jessop + Lt. Fox, consisting of 34 N.C.O.s gunner, entered trenches & returned safely. 4 casualties. Gas experimented 12.20 p.m. — Total casualties: 1 K.G. R.S.M. + 1 Pte. * Major Tombruck (black) Stombart R.M.C., R.S.M. + 1 Pte. Running Hd Offrs Officer Struck by 8/6 4 pm shells	A/705 X 26

Army Form C. 2118
page 4

WAR DIARY
INTELLIGENCE SUMMARY
(Erase heading not required.)

Original June 1916

Place	Date	Hour	Summary of Events and Information 12th EAST SURREY Regt B.E.F.	Remarks and references to Appendices
do.	30th (cont.)		20 prisoners were captured by the raiding party, as the enemy had evacuated that part of his trenches.	77/to
d	1st July	6 a.m.	Bn. relieved by 18th Queens Regt. & returned to Billets at SOYER FM	77/20

3 July 1916.

Sutter Lieut Colonel.
Commanding 12th E. Surrey Regt

287
CB

Original
41 July
Army Form C. 2118
12th E Surrey
1916
vol 2
B.E.F.

WAR DIARY
or
INTELLIGENCE SUMMARY
(Erase heading not required.)

Place	Date	Hour	Summary of Events and Information	Remarks and references to Appendices
PLOEGSTEERT Rif Trench Map 28 S.W. 1 28.0.60	1st	5 a.m.	12th R. East Surrey Regt. Bn relieved by 10th R.W. Surrey Regt. (Queens), & returned to billets at SOYER FM.	H/Wo
	2nd		Bn in billets. Neighbourhood of SOYER FM heavily shelled by enemy (T.3, 5, 9 called) "82". during night 2nd – 3rd.	H/Wo
	3rd		Bn in Billets. Working parties covered. Heavy shelling on both sides during night 2nd – 3rd and 3rd – 4th. Weather improved.	H/Wo
	4th 5th		Bn in Billets. Considerable Art. activity on both sides	H/Wo
	6th 11.30 p.m.		do. Bn moved into new billets at GRANDE MUNQUE FARM, 2 coys & (T.20) HQ. Bn being in the Farm & 2 coys in PLOEGSTEERT WOOD about 600x N.E. of FM	H/Wo
	7th		Bn in billets.	H/Wo
do.	8th	10 p.m.	Bn in Trenches. Taking over a new line from 11th R.W. KENT REGT., north of PLOEGSTEERT WOOD, from 200 yds. N. of ANTON'S FM to LA DOUVRE R. "C" & "B" Coys in front line. A Coy in Subsidiary line, & "D" Coy at Batt. H.Q.	H/Wo
do.	9th 10th 11th 12th 13th		On 600 yds South of LE ROSIGNOL – no enemy activity of any note – Bn in trenches. Very slight enemy activity – Weather excellent. My Cuth action Bn in trenches. do do – At midnight 13th/14th. The Co (Lt Col. A.H. Lee) was wounded in the foot + evacuated to No 2 C.C. Hospital at BAILLEUL.	H/Wo do. H/Wo H/Wo 4 Sheet 289 H/Wo

3.C
4 sheet 289

WAR DIARY
or
INTELLIGENCE SUMMARY
(Erase heading not required.)

Army Form C. 2118

July 1916   12th EAST SURREY REGT.   B.E.F.

Place	Date	Hour	Summary of Events and Information	Remarks, and references to Appendices
PLOEGSTEERT	14th		Bn in trenches, as before. Our inform rather quieter, specially mrs -	A/140
Ref. Sheet 28 SW.1 20.000	15.		Bn relieved by 11th R. West Kent Regt. during the night 15/16. Considerable cannonading noticeable during the evening & night. During the period the Bn was in trenches our Cas: Lsr at times been very active. Several during the nights of raids have been carried out by the 123rd & 124th Inf Bdes.	A/141
	16		Bn in billets. HdQrs, A & B Coys at Gde. MUNQUE Fm, C & D Coys in Wood. Weather changing to rain & cold.	A/150
	17		Bn in billets - working parties, etc as usual. Weather improved. Coml in enemy's favour a "Gas Alert" ordered in fire trenches -	A/180
	18 19 20		Bn in Billets. Working parties as usual. Enemy Artl active on our Batteries in rear neighbourhood during this period -	A/10
	21 22		Bn in Billets. Working parties as usual. Honours awarded to Bn:- M.C. Capt Jessop; M.S.C. D.C.M. Sgt Donnelly; M.M. 14181 Sgt Calver, 15911 Pte Creswell, 16308 Pte Pye.	A/32 C.B.
	23 24 25		Bn in Billets. Working parties as usual.	A/32 C.B.
	26 27		Bn in Billets. Bn moved from Gde Munque HUNQUE at 7 A.m into fresh billets. H.Qrs SOYERS Fm; A Coy TILLEUL; B Coy SOYERS Fm; C Coy MAISON 75; D Coy DELEMELLE	A/32 C.B.

Army Form C. 2118

WAR DIARY
or
INTELLIGENCE SUMMARY

(Erase heading not required.)

Instructions regarding War Diaries and Intelligence Summaries are contained in F. S. Regs., Part II. and the Staff Manual respectively. Title Pages will be prepared in manuscript.

12 R East Surrey Regt.   July 1916   B. E. F.

Place	Date	Hour	Summary of Events and Information	Remarks and references to Appendices
Moe Osteen Bef. Trench Map 28 SW 1/20,000	27		La Grande Monque occupied by 10th (Ssv) Bn Pl Inniskilling Fusiliers	Hrs C/S
	28			
	29		Bn in Billets. Working parties as usual. Weather very fine & warm.	Hrs C/S
	30			
	31			

H.H. Graxer
Major
Commanding 12th East Surrey Regt.

1/8/1916.

Army Form C. 2118

WAR DIARY or INTELLIGENCE SUMMARY

(Erase heading not required.)

12 E Surrey   August 1916

Place	Date	Hour	Summary of Events and Information	Remarks and references to Appendices
Ploegsteert Retd Mar 22 S.W.	1 2 3		12th (S) Bn East Surrey Regt Bn in Billets. Working parties as usual. Weather fine & warm. At 5 a.m. Bn moved into Trenches U.28.c.2b.4. – U.28.a.1.2.9. with 12 3rd Inf Bde on right & 15th Bn Hants Regt on the left. "A" Coy holds right half of front line – Trenches Dundee Ave & Suffolk. "D" Coy holds left of front line – Trenches 109, 110 & gap. Fosse Support. "B" Coy holds the Suffolk Ave & "C" Coy the Reserve. Bn. Head Quarters at Maison 75. U.26.c.7.4. Everything very quiet. Patrol under Capt R. le Pelleau went out at 10.35pm from Trench 106, Bay 4, & worked up to Trench 108, Bay 3 & back again. Another patrol went out at 11pm under 2/Lt Walker from Trench 106 & advanced about 60 yards in front of our wire. Both patrols returned in 30 mins & reported everything quiet. Snipers active. quiet. Bn in Trenches. Altitude of Surrey quiet Weather very fine & warm. During night the 6–7 & 7–8 inst officers patrols went	H 5 (B) A D C 15 H.C. 4 sheet

1875 Wt. W593/826 1,000,000 4/15. J.B.C. & A. A.D.S.S./Forms/C. 2118.

WAR DIARY or INTELLIGENCE SUMMARY

Army Form C. 2118

12th (S) Bn EAST SURREY REGT.

August 1916.

Place	Date	Hour	Summary of Events and Information	Remarks and references to Appendices
PLOEGSTEERT Ref. Trench Map 28 S.W.	5/6/7		Out from BURNT OUT FARM to Subsidiary Saphead at 28.a.6.3½. Both the Saphead & Fort were found to be manned & the heads of about Ten Huns were seen.	#02 CB
	8		"B" Coy vacated Support Trenches & moved to LA CRÈCHE for the purpose of going through a Trench Warfare Course. They were relieved by 10th Queens. At 6.45 p.m. "C" Coy in right of line (hand) fire with 120 rifles commenced on enemy trenches about 200 yds right of THE FORT. On enemy retaliating over Stokes fire from T.T. 106 came into action, causing retaliation to become shorter. Our guns then opened fire until 8.45 p.m. when enemy became silent. Trench Mortars, Stokes etc were seen thrown into the air about 30 feet high in answer to our Stokes from Stores. We suffered no Casualties. The result of our Trenches –	H 02 CB
	9	5.30 a.m.	Bn returned to billets, being relieved by 10 Queens. Bn. H.Q. & Officers to J. Coy. I T.Lieut Emj. C Coy to TROBEQUE Fm; D Coy to DELLENELLE Fm.	H 02 CB

Army Form C. 2118

WAR DIARY
or
INTELLIGENCE SUMMARY

(Erase heading not required.)

Instructions regarding War Diaries and Intelligence Summaries are contained in F. S. Regs., Part II. and the Staff Manual respectively. Title Pages will be prepared in manuscript.

12th (S) Bn EAST SURREY REGT. August 1916.

Place	Date	Hour	Summary of Events and Information	Remarks and references to Appendices
PLOEGSTEERT Ref. Trench Map. 28 S.W.	10, 11, 12, 13, 14		BN in billets. Working parties as usual. Weather very warm & fine.	H.v.P.S.
	15		BN moved from Soyer Farm to LA CRECHE. Area A. 6.	
	16		BN moved from LA CRECHE to METEREN. area near X. 16-17.	
	17		BN moved from METEREN to FLETRE area X. 17. a. 5. 0; R. 51.a. 2.7; Q. 30.a.8.2.	H.v.P.S.
THIEUSHOUCK Ref. Map. 27. Ja. & Belgium.	18, 19, 20, 21, 22		BN in rest billets. Work:- BN marching, bayonet fighting, night operations, etc. BN strength – 40 officers, 934 other ranks	H.v.P.S.
	23		BN having entrained at BAILLEUL Station, started for LONGPRE at 11.28½	H.v.P.S.
MOUFLERS Ref. Map LENS II. France 1/80,000	24		BN arrived at LONGPRE at 10.a.m. After a half an hour & a half, marched to MOUFLERS where it went into billets. BN strength. 36 officers, 841 other ranks.	H.v.P.S.
	25		BN in billets. Work:- Attack & consolidation drill, Wood fighting, etc.	H.v.P.S.

Army Form C. 2118.

WAR DIARY
or
INTELLIGENCE SUMMARY

August 1916

12th (S) Bn EAST SURREY

Place	Date	Hour	Summary of Events and Information	Remarks and references to Appendices
MOUFLERS	26		R & C	
Ref. Map	27		Bn in Billets. MOUFLERS. area A.6. Work as above.	
LENS 11.	28		On Monday 28th inst. 'A' Coy (Capt Jessop's) moved to H.Q.	
France	29		4th Army Trench Warfare School, FLIXECOURT. Strength	
1/100,000	30		of Coy. 8 officers, 156 other ranks, including M.G. Detachment.	
	31			

H. C. Mallaney, Major
for I. Col. Comm'dg
12 E Surrey R.

WAR DIARY
INTELLIGENCE SUMMARY

12th East Surrey
Sep. 1916

Army Form C. 2118

Place	Date	Hour	Summary of Events and Information	Remarks and references to Appendices
MOUFLERS Ref. Map LENS 11. France 1/1,1000			12th (S) Bn EAST SURREY REGT.	
	1		Bn in Billets MOUFLERS area A.6. Work:- attaching & Consolidating trenches, bayonet fighting, s.c. Lt Col H.J. Walmsley-Dresser left for Paris on three days sick leave.	Hq PB
	2		Bn inspected by Major-General Jacobs C.B. Commanding 41st Division. Special order of the day. Major-General Jacobs, C.B. commanding 41st Division has expressed himself well pleased with all he saw at his Inspection today, was good enough to add that he & Per Zither conference that the 122nd Inf Brigade when called on would do it's duty. The Brigadier General Commanding trusts that all ranks will endeavour to show that this confidence is not misplaced. Signed George Thomas, Major B.S. 122 Inf Bde.	Hq PB
			Bn in Billets. MOUFLERS area A.6. Work as above at 10.30.a.m. on the 5th inst. the regimental transport proceeded to LONGPRÉ near AMIENS. Three Companies Young (B.C.A.Coy).	Hq PB
Ref Map France 62d 1/20,000	3 4 5			12 Inst Hq PB
	6		At 2.a.m. the Bn (less at LA FOLIE) proceeded with the rest of the 122nd Inf Bde to LONGPRÉ RAILWAY STATION, where it entrained & started for MERICOURT at 6.a.m, arriving at its destination at 10.a.m.	5C Hq PB

WAR DIARY
or
INTELLIGENCE SUMMARY

Army Form C. 2118

12(S) BN. EAST SURREY REGT.   SEPTEMBER 1916

Place	Date	Hour	Summary of Events and Information	Remarks and references to Appendices
ALBERT. Ref. Map. France 62D	6		At 11 a.m. the 122nd Infantry Brigade marched from MERICOURT L'ABBE to E.8.D.7.1. where it camped under canvas.	Hd.of C.B.
	7			
	8		BN in camp. E.8.D.7.1.	
	9		'A' Coy 72nd joined BN from FLEXICOURT. Coy. strength 8 offs, 156.O.R. Lt Feisnal Thomas, commg. XIV Army looks inspected 122 Inf. W/32	Hd.of C.B.
FRICOURT Ref. Map France 62D N.W. cor.	11		BN moved from E.8.D.7.1. to vicinity of FRICOURT. F.14.a. BN Strength: 36 officers, 777 other ranks.	Hd of P.S.
	12		BN in camp FRICOURT. F.14.a.	
	13			
	14	4.30.p.m	The BN proceed to take up disposition at the N.W. of DELVILLE WOOD. Battle strength 17 officers, 634 other ranks. The remainder of the BN proceed to the vicinity of FRICOURT.	Hd of C.S.
	15	2 a.m.	The BN had taken up its position at S. 11.D.0.8. The formation was lines of half platoons in file, 'A' Coy. on the right, 'D' Coy on the left. The half platoons were concealed in shell holes. On the right were the R.W. Kents + on the left the N.Z. Brigade + in front the K.R.R.C. The BN advanced at 6.15 a.m. + took the enemy's 1st + 2nd lines + trenches although it suffered severe casualties, losing nearly all its officers	

WAR DIARY or INTELLIGENCE SUMMARY

Army Form C. 2118

12th (S) Bn. EAST SURREY REGT. SEPTEMBER 1916

Place	Date	Hour	Summary of Events and Information	Remarks and references to Appendices
Ref Map 57 C.S.W. 1/20,000	15		Bn continued to advance to about 200 yards in front of FLERS & machine gunning trenches there. Casualties:- Roll of offrs killed & wounded :- Lt Col H.J. Walmisley-Dresser, died of wounds 17/9/16; Capt & adjt R.A. McCULLOCH wounded; Capt: F.D. JESSOP wounded, believed killed; Capt: J.L. BUCKMAN, killed; Capt: I.C. YORK-DAVIS, killed; Capt: A.D. GROOM, wounded; 2nd Lieut: J.W. STADDON, killed; Lieut C.C. FOX, killed; 2nd Lieut J.R. CHESTERS, killed; 2nd Lieut J.E.N. CROTHER, wounded; 2nd Lieut F. BEARD wounded; 2nd Lt J.W. EDWARDS wounded; 2nd Lieut S. STIMSON, wounded; 2nd Lieut H.T. PIKE, wounded; Lieut E.W.G. YOUNG, R.A.M.C. wounded; 2nd Lieut W.J. PARK was the only officer unwounded.	Offs 16; O.R. 286.
	16		Bn in reserve trenches. The King sent the Div.C. the following message:- "My congratulations to you & your brave troops on the brilliant success just achieved. Completest victory will ultimately crown our efforts and the splendid results of the fighting yesterday confirmed this belief" Geo R.I. About 5 pm Major H.S.L. Blathwayt himself from FRICOURT reinforcements of 6 officers & about 60 men & took over the command of Bn.	
ALBERT Ref Map France 62D 1/40,000	17		Bn in reserve trenches. Weather very wet & cold.	
	18	7 am	The Bn was relieved by a Bn of the K.O. Lanc. R. & proceeded to E.S.B.T.L. was in encamped.	
	19		Major C.H. KITCHIN, 15 Hants Regt took on command of Bn. Bn strength; offrs 29. O.R. 606.	

WAR DIARY
or
INTELLIGENCE SUMMARY

SEPTEMBER 1916

Army Form C. 2118

Place	Date	Hour	Summary of Events and Information	Remarks and references to Appendices
ALBERT Ref. Map France 62D 1/40,000	20 21 22 23 24		12th (S) B_N EAST SURREY REG^T. B_N in camp E.8.d.7.l. Re-organising. Weather wet + cold.	#10/FB
	25 26 27 28 29 30		B_N in camp E.8.d.7.l. Re-organising.	#24/26

H. de C. Blakeney, Major.

SPECIAL ORDER OF THE DAY

Major General Lawford C.B., commanding 41st Division has expressed himself well pleased with all he saw at his Inspection today and was good enough to add that he felt entire confidence that the 122nd Infantry Brigade when called on would do its duty.

The Brigadier General Commanding trusts that all ranks will endeavour to show that this confidence is not misplaced.

[signature]
Major,
Brigade Major,
122nd Infantry Brigade.

2nd September 1916.

SECRET.

BATTALION ORDERS
by
LIEUT.COL.H.J.WALMISLEY-DRESSER.

Ref.Maps 57c.S.W.
1/20,000 and special
Maps issued.

SITUATION.   1.   The Fourth Army in co-operation with the Reserve Army and the French is to attack and capture the enemy's system of defences up to and including the line MORVAL - LES - BOEUFS, GUEUDECOURT - HIGH WOOD.
The attack will be pushed home with the utmost vigour all along the line. The enemy's moral is known to be shaken, he has few if any fresh reserves, and it is considered that a combined and determined offensive will result a decisive victory.
The 41st Division will attack as the centre of the XV Corps attack, and will have on its right the 14th Division, and on its left, the New Zealand Division.
The 122nd Infantry Brigade will be on the left of the 41st Division, with the 124th Infantry Brigade on our right, and the New Zealand Brigade on our left.
The 123rd Infantry Brigade will be in Divisional Reserve.
The 122nd Infantry Brigade will attack in (4) four stages, with 15th Hampshire Regt and 18th King's Royal Rifle Corps in front line, and the 11th Royal West Kent Regt and 12th East Surrey Regt in Second line.

INTENTION.   2.   The 12th East Surrey Regt will attack in (4) four stages.
The attack on these 4 objectives will be carried out at the timings shewn on the attached Time Table.

ASSEMBLY.   3.   The Battalion will assemble in the Trenches known as Group D proceeding via Horse Track just North of MEAULTE-MONTAUBAN Road and MILK LANE.
One Officer and four guides from the 18th King's Royal Rifle Corps will meet the Battalion at POMMIERS REDOUBT on its arrival.
Companies will be taken to GREEN DUMP where a Staff Officer will meet them.
Companies will send in indents as soon as possible for S.A.A., Grenades, P.Bombs, S.O.S. Rockets, Flares.

APPROACH AVENUE. 4.   MILK LANE is allotted to 122nd Infantry Brigade.
Y and L Alleys, are not to be used.

FORMATIONS.   5.   The order of battle will be as follows :-
The Battalion will be on the left in the Second line, following behind 18th King's Royal Rifle Corps, with 11th Royal West Kent Regt, on the right.
The Battalion will advance in four waves on a four Company front, "A" Company on the right and "D" Company on the left, in columns of half platoons in file.
Distance between waves not to exceed 70 yards.

No. 2.

DIRECTING FLANK.	6.	The right of "A" Company will direct. The right of the 15th Hampshire Regt will direct the Brigade..
DIVIDING LINES.	7.	Between 122nd and 124th Infantry Brigades.

S.22.c.8.6 to
S.17.b.3.4. (inclusive to 124th Infantry Brigade).
LONGUEVAL - FLERS ROAD to Junction S.E.b.9.3.
T.1.a.4.8.
N.31.c.85.45.
N.31.b.15.15.
N.31.b.2.6.
Track to N.20.c.4.4.

Between 122nd and New Zealand Infantry Brigades.
S.21.d.8.7.
S.16.d.1.6.
S.11.c.0.4.
S.11.d.0.8.
Junction of PEACH and Tea Trenches (incl. to 122nd Infantry Brigade).
COFFEE LANE (inclusive to New Zealand Division).
M.36.d.3.3.
M.36.b.5.0. (inclusive to New Zealand Division)
M.31.a.2.5. (inclusive to New Zealand Division)
N.25.b.0.6. (inclusive to New Zealand Division)

ARTILLERY. 8. Our artillery will form creeping barrages. The attacking troops will advance immediately behind these barrages, and not more than 70 yards distance between waves.
An Artillery Liaison Officer will be with each Battalion Headquarters.

HOUR OF ASSAULT 9. At Zero hour which will be notified later, the
AND OBJECTIVES. leading waves of Battalions will be in position as close as possible to the creeping barrage. As each wave moves forward, its place will be taken up by the next troops in rear, and so on backwards.

FIRST OBJECTIVE. GREEN LINE.
Enemy's trenches 300 yards S. of FLERS - SWITCH LINE from junction of road (S.8.d.7.7.) to junction of COFFEE LANE (S.6.c.2.7.) Exclusive.
No halt will be made in TEA SUPPORT Trench but if necessary men must be left to deal with dug-outs.

SECOND OBJECTIVE. BROWN LINE.
Enemy's trenches running S.E. i.e. FLERS LINE from T.1.a.1.6. to M.36.d.6.4.

THIRD OBJECTIVE. BLUE LINE.
The village of FLERS to Road Junction N.31.a.8.5. (exclusive). The 122nd Infantry Brigade will capture FLERS.

FOURTH OBJECTIVE. RED LINE.
To establish line N.20.c.7.8. to N.20.c.3.6.to road Junction N.25.b.0.6. (exclusive).
The objectives in several cases consist of a double line of trenches, in which case, the trench furthest away is the objective, and steps must be taken to deal adequately with the intermediate trench.
These above objectives will be assaulted in accordance with the attached Time Table.

No. 3.

CLEARING UP.	10.	O.C. Companies will detail Mopping Up Parties to each Platoon. These parties will wear a yellow band round the left shoulder strap. P. Bombs will be extensively used
COMMUNICATION TRENCHES.	11.	O.C. "C" Company will arrange to dig forward a communication trench to join up with our first wave in the first objective.
STRONG POINTS.	12.	Strong Points will be constructed and garrisoned at the following places. North of FLERS BY ONE Platoon of "A" Company. N.26.b.25.75. RED LINE, one platoon "B" Company. Each garrison will have a Lewis Gun with it.
CARRYING PARTIES.	13.	O.C. A Company and O.C. D Company will each leave one platoon at GREEN DUMP, S.16.d.9.6. as carrying parties. The Officer in Command of the Carrying parties will report at Brigade H.Q. at 8 p.m. 14.9.16.
STOKES & MACHINE GUNS.	14.	Indirect covering fire (enfilade if possible) will be carried out to assist each advance, as the situation permits. Lewis Guns will be detailed to push beyond each objective gained to cease any tactical points not occupied by the enemy.
BOMBS.	15.	Every man will carry 2 Mills Grenades in his pockets. These should be regarded as a Reserve for use of Bombing Squads. They will not be thrown by the men carrying them, but should be dumped as required.
ROCKETS.	16.	Each Company will take with it 4 S.O.S. Rockets.
COMMUNICATION WITH AEROPLANES.	17.	Every Officer and N.C.O. and 50 men per Company will carry two red flares. These are to be lighted by the leading wave only at intervals of 20 yards on gaining each objective. Vigilant Mirrors are to be attached to the back of the coat of every tenth man. Panels and lamps will also be frequently used to report the situation.

VISUAL SIGNALLING & RUNNERS.	18.	VISUAL SIGNALLING.
		Visual Stations will be installed at the following points:-
		    S.16.c.1.9.
		    S.16.b.5.2.
		    S.16.d.6.1.
		    S.27.b.3.8.
		    POMMIER REDOUBT.
		RUNNERS.
		    The Signalling Officer will arrange to organize these into relays when necessary, each relay working between posts at intervals of about 300 yards.
		These routes should be clearly-marked.

No. 4.

PIGEONS.	19.	Each Battalion will be provided with 2 pigeons. The birds are only to be released for urgent messages if other means of communication fail. They are to be regarded as a reserve.
MEDICAL.	20.	Advanced Dressing Station, THE QUARRY. (S.22.c.2.6.) Divisional Collecting Station. Point F.6.a.2.0. MAMETZ - MONTAUBAN ROAD.
DUMPS.	21.	The position and contents of Dumps are shewn in Table attached.
BATTLE STOPS.	22.	Regimental Police Posts will be established as follows:- Junction of MILK LANE - YORK TRENCH. Junction of MILK LANE - CARLTON TRENCH. Junction of MILK LANE - ORCHARD TRENCH. They will take the numbers, names, and units of stragglers, and send those fit to return back to their units. A special mark will be put against those without arms. Divisional Collecting post at F.6.a.3.0.
PRISONERS OF WAR.	23.	An escort of 10% is sufficient.
WATCHES.	24.	Watches will be synchronised at Battalion H.Q. at 1.30 a.m. 15.9.16. 2nd Lieut. Edwards will report at Brigade H.Q. at midnight 14th/15th, for this purpose. He will take two watches with him.
REPORTS.	25.	The Report Centre will be immediately in rear of the Battalion during the advance. O.C. Companies will render Situation Report every clock hour after ZERO, and in addition any important event such as the capture of any objective.

14.9.16.

(sd) R.A.McCulloch,
Capt & Adjt.
"A" Battalion.

Copy No.1. File.
Copy No.2. C.O.
Copy No.3. 122nd Infantry Brigade.
Copy No.4. O.C. A Coy.
Copy No.5. O.C. B Coy.
Copy No.6. O.C. C Coy.
Copy No.7. O.C. D Coy.
Copy No.8. Signalling Officer.
Copy No.9. M.G. Officer.
Copy No.10. Transport Officer.
Copy No.11. Quartermaster.

APPENDIX.

TANKS.   Ten tanks Heavy Section, Machine Gun Corps, will co-operate in the attack, and will be in position in rear of our front line trenches by 4 a.m. on "Z" day.
These tanks will usually precede the Infantry. Their role is to destroy the hostile Machine Guns and Strong Points, and clear the way for the Infantry. The Infantry will follow behind the tanks, and should any Strong Point succeed in holding up the Infantry, they will call for a tank to assist them by using the signal "Enemy in sight" with the rifle. Should the tanks get in rear of the Infantry an escort of one N.C.O. and 10 men will be detailed by the nearest unit to remove any wounded which happen to lie in the path of the tank.
The escort will also protect the tank from close assault by the enemy Infantry, or from attack by explosive charges.
Should tanks become out of action our Infantry are on no account to wait for them, but will <u>advance at the hour arranged for the tanks</u>, in order that they may derive the benefit of the artillery barrage.
The following signals will be used from Tanks to Infantry and Aircraft:-

<u>Flag Signals</u>.
Red Flag   -   Out of action.
Green Flag -   Am on objective.
Other flags are inter-tank signals.

<u>Lamp Signals</u>.
Series of dash (T) - Out of action.
Series of 4 dots (H) - Am on objective.

SITUATION and CONTENTS OF DUMPS.

SITUATION.

Main Divisional Dump.........................F.7.a.0.3.
Right 122 Brigade Dump.......................S.23.a.6.6.
Left 122 Brigade Dump..(Known as GREEN DUMP) S.16.d.0.6.

CONTENTS.

Nature of Store.	Main Divnl.Dump.	Each Bde. Dump.
No.5 MILLS Grenades.	10,000	5,000
STOKES 3" bombs,	5,000	2,000
Red cartridges.	5,000	2,000
Green cartridges.	5,000	2,000
1" Very Lights.	4,000	1,000
1½" Very Lights.	2,000	500.
2" Trench Mortar.	1,000	250.
S.A.A. (boxes)	200	100.
P# Grenades.	1,000	500
Rifle Grenades.	4,000	1,000
Rockets S.O.S. and Sticks.	50.	25 ø
Flares, red.	400.	
Petrol Tins, 2 gallons.	1,000	400.

ø This includes those issued under Brigade Orders to units in the line.

Army Form C. 2118

WAR DIARY
or
INTELLIGENCE SUMMARY

OCTOBER 1916

12th (S) Bn EAST SURREY REGT.

(Erase heading not required.)

Place	Date	Hour	Summary of Events and Information	Remarks and references to Appendices
ALBERT Top Map France 62D 1/40,000	1. 2.		Bn in camp E.B.D.7.I. Re-enjuring.	
FRANCE 57C 1/10,000	3		At 2.30pm the Battalion, consisting of A. C. & D Companies and 15 men from B Company moves from the S.E. corner of MAMMETZ WOOD to relieve the 2nd Bn. N.Z. Rifle Brigade holding the portion of GIRD SUPPORT TRENCH with FACTORY CORNER. Guides met the Battalion at THISTLE DUMP at 4.30 P.M. and Companies proceeded to the front line in TURK LANE - FISH ALLEY passing via the required routes. Guides led the Battalion across the open, 600 yards south of FACTORY CORNER. Very heavy shelling was met with and in consequence Companies lost touch and suffered unnecessary casualties. Relief was w/ completed till 10.45 P.M. The disposition of the Battalion was as follows:- A Company - GIRD SUPPORT. B & C Companies - Strong Point. D Company - S.T. at FACTORY CORNER. C Company - FLERS SUPPORT.	Bn. strength 15 Off. 311 O.R. B.G. 50 O.R. Totals: MENTIE
Bn Rd TRANSPORT. S- MAMMETZ WOOD (S.19.d) Bn. H.Q. BROWN T. FLERS T. FLERS SUPPORT

Place	Date	Hour	Summary of Events and Information	Remarks and references to Appendices
	3		During the night there was continuous shelling along the whole front.	A/x C.B.
	4		During the whole day and night, enemy artillery was very active, especially in the vicinity of FACTORY CORNER. The Battalion experienced great difficulty in the position of Rations and Water. Salvage parties however were able to do a certain amount to cope with the situation, although greatly hampered by shell fire.	A/x C.B.
	5		To-day the enemy artillery slackened between noon and 6 P.M. Ration and Carrying parties took full advantage of this; in consequence all stores and supplies were able to reach the front line. Instructions were received that the Battalion was to be relieved tonight by the 26th Bn, Royal Fusiliers, when the Battalion would sigh a new line of trench as a "jumping off" trench for the attack on the 7th. The Sydney Martin was subsequently cancelled but we are now informed that the Battalion must take up their new position (when relieved) in FLERS TRENCH. B and D Companies were relieved at 10.30 P.M. C Company at 11 P.M. and A Company at 6 a.m. on the 6th inst.	A/x C.B.

WAR DIARY or INTELLIGENCE SUMMARY

Army Form C. 2118

Place	Date	Hour	Summary of Events and Information	Remarks and references to Appendices
	6		The Battalion occupied FLERS TRENCH.	H.of.B.
	7		Enemy shelled FLERS TRENCH very heavily during the morning. At 12.30 pm the Battalion prepared to vacate the trench when orders were received to support GOOSE ALLEY at once, and so to hold itself in readiness to support our attack. Moving by way of ABBEY ROAD to Flers the Battn. began to the attack at 1.15 P.M. On the 1.50 P.M. (Zero hour) GOOSE ALLEY was ordered at 1.15 P.M. Since the Battalion was unable to move until 2.10 P.M. when heavy shelling hit the Battalion, and it occupying the newly dug trench from where the 18"B" K.R.R.C. advanced to the attack. At 4.30 P.M. the Battalion moved forward to reinforce the 11 Bn. Royal West Kent Rgt. Being misdirected initially, was sent out and eventually got into the trench. Patrols led the Battalion to south now E. of EAUCOURT L'ABBAYE, a heavy enemy Barrage was encountered and the Battalion in pursuit in ramp of its original front line withdrew low. On reaching the 11th K. Royal West Kent Rgt, the Battalion consolidated and held the forward portion of Aut will. A small party who had been with were to be Battalion returned and holded communications to be dug.	

WAR DIARY
INTELLIGENCE SUMMARY

Army Form C. 2118

Place	Date	Hour	Summary of Events and Information	Remarks and references to Appendices
	7		Minor alt bombs [?] starts and enemy Patrols were repelled during the night. Many machine guns and Snipers were very active.	H.Q. C.B.
	8		The whole day an attempt to hush & [?] in the improving trenches. During the night, 30/7 the Battalion in the front line were withdrawn to the original front line (WIRED SUPPORT) to prevent eruption, and to facilitate the movement to the new trench. The Battalion was to have been relieved by the 23rd Bn. Middlesex Regt at 8 p.m. The relief did not commence till 1 a.m.; a Stopwatch barrage on our own original front line, lasting for about half hour with intervals of not more than ten minutes, prevented any movement of Troops - The relief was completed and the Battalion proceeded to by 3.30 a.m. the relief was known to SWITCH TRENCH.	
	9.		Reinforcements to the MAMETZ WOOD joined the Battalion at 5 P.M.	H.Q. C.B. H.Q. P.B.
	10		Weather Normal.	H.Q. C.B.

WAR DIARY or INTELLIGENCE SUMMARY

Army Form C. 2118

Place	Date	Hour	Summary of Events and Information	Remarks and references to Appendices
By Rly France Sheet 62D D 27 8 82	11		Battalion left SWITCH TRENCH for MAMETZ WOOD at 7.30 a.m. at 9.30 P.M. the Battalion left by train for DERNANCOURT wh came to arrive there at 11.45. At 4.0 P.M. orders were received to move off to RIBEMONT. The Battalion left DERNANCOURT at 7.12 and were settled in billets by 10.30 P.M. at RIBEMONT	CRCR
	12		Battalion generally re-organised. Battalion Strength 530.	CRCR CRCR
	13			
	14		Draft of 259 men arrived. See Appendix II	CRCR
	15		Draft of 191 men from Surrey Yeomanry arrived. Lt. Col. Lee DSO returned and resumed command of the Battalion. Lt. Col. Kitchening struck off Battalion Strength. 2Lt Pritchard - J.H.H. joined the Battalion for duty.	CRCR
	16		G.O.C. Division distributed medal ribbons to the following at 11.30 a.m. Meeting Bros. Bt. Park L.R. - 7539 C.S.M. Horseville B? D.C.M. 12816 4Cpl Carter W. - 16024 Pte Giles A. M.M. 17531 4Cpl Southall L.C. - 16066 Pte Butcher J.A. - 14327 Pte Hammond W. - 14848 Pte Budd P.S. - 6972 Pte Newton J. D.C.M. 17458 Pte Huggett P. - Further honours to men who were wounded and unable to receive them :-	CRCR

WAR DIARY or INTELLIGENCE SUMMARY

Army Form C. 2118

Place	Date	Hour	Summary of Events and Information	Remarks and references to Appendices
	16		MM 6681 Sgt McGuire C – 12953 Pte Tonks G – 16110 Pte Clew W. Gee Bugote to spbn to the Battalion and Carried it on at Sgms work during the Brigade Athletics of the previous week.	CMGR
	17		Battalion left Billets at RIBEMONT for MERICOURT-RIBEMONT Railway Station, where it entrained at 12:02 hrs and route for OISEMONT.	CMGR
HQ WH RIBEMONT	18		Battalion arrived at OISEMONT at 8am and route marched to Billets at HOPPY on the road 6 miles. Here Capts. Buckle HS, 2nd Worters OE and 2Lt Edwards RE. joined the Battalion for duty. Lt-Col Lee DSO took on command from 2Lt. 1/12 Inf Bde to take over of Brig-Gen Torring, and Major H&C Blakeney assumed Command of 2B/2L Battalion.	CMGR
	19		Battalion spent the day in Co-party training and reorganising its new drafts. Capt W. Hope proceeded on leave.	CMGR
	20		Battalion left HOPPY at 8:23, entrained at 12:30 to Pont Remy Station, where GOEDERSVELDE	CMGR
			1062 Ors. Hers Guide and led the way to the Billeting Area at INGLES by 2pm.	
	21			

Army Form C. 2118

1/4th Bn East Surrey Regt.

WAR DIARY
or
INTELLIGENCE SUMMARY
(Erase heading not required.)

October 1916

Place	Date	Hour	Summary of Events and Information	Remarks and references to Appendices
	22	11.6	Ordered (Company) Training was carried on. On the 23rd the Battalion did a route march of 6½ miles. Route (ECKE – THIOUROCK – FLETRE – CAESTRE – ECKE)	over
	23			over
	24		The Battalion left ECKE at 11.30 A.M. to march to GODEWAERSVELDE. Owing to the Billeting Area being scarce and only 2 Companies could be Billeted at first C and D Companies being left at ECKE. Later in the day however Billets were found for C and D Companies and the Battalion was reported in Billets at 6.30 P.M. the same evening	over
Map C.28	25.		The Battalion marched to new Camp at RENINGHELST	over
Ref. M.5. a.2.8.			at 7.30 A.M. and arrived at ONTARIO CAMP at midday – Batt. Strength on march GODEWAERSVELDE: {Officers 45 + MO } { O.R. 1014 }	over
	26.		Training in Camp – Men were practised in the use of the New Box Respirator	over
	27.		Battalion was inspected by (Genl. Sir Hubert) C.O. Plumer (G.C.M.G. – K.C.B.) the G.O.C. Division who pitched the camp. (Sir Maurice I) Officers ( )	over
	28.		Battalion on orders to relieve the 20th Bn. Durham Light Infantry in Trenches the following Day. Lt. Steven C.O. proceeded in Charge	over 29th

WAR DIARY
INTELLIGENCE SUMMARY

(Erase heading not required.)

Army Form C. 2118

Place	Date	Hour	Summary of Events and Information	Remarks and references to Appendices
Hdp Rd Trenches BELGIUM 28 SW 20,60 07b59 – 02 C.6.B.	29		Battalion left ONTARIO CAMP at 10 a.m. en route for Trenches to relieve to Battalion at DICKEBUSCH and the relief was complete at 6.30 P.M. The Battalion occupies the line. 07b59 – 02C6B. Disposition of Companies – FRONT LINE and CRATER – C. Coy. R. Line. Right Coy. B. Left Coy. D. Coy in Reserve at N6 65t. The Support line is not held being under water for the most part. The main line of Defence is the "R" line which is held by two Companies.	C.P C.R.
	30		Day passes with no incident of any importance. Enemy's attitude quiet. The CRATER at 02 C.5½ at present is but cistern is being built up, drained, and terraced under RE Supervision.	CdWR
	31		Another Quiet day – Capt.n W Heyer returned from leave.	CPad

H.re E. Stallenney Major
Com'd'g 12 E. Surv. R.

SECRET

Headquarters
122 Infantry Bde

Herewith War Diary for month
of September 1916

H. Raymond
Lt. Adj
12/Bn East Surrey Regt

15 Oct 1916

"A" Form.
MESSAGES AND SIGNALS.

Army Form. C.2121

Prefix	Code		Words	Charge	This message is on a/c of:	Recd. at	m.
Office of Origin and Service Instructions.			Sent		Service.	Date	
			At...............m. To By		(Signature of "Franking Officer.")	From By	

TO	JACKAL		X

Sender's Number.	Day of Month.	In reply to Number.		AAA
SC 64	14th			

Following	wire	from	15th	Corps
timed	7.15 a.m	aaa	aaa	the
following	wire	from	the	Commander
in	Chief	begins	aaa	following
gracious	telegram	received	from	The
King	aaa	I	congratulate	you
and	my	brave	troops	on
the	brilliant	success	just	achieved
aaa		have	never	doubted
that	complete	victory	will	ultimately
crown	our	efforts	and	the
splendid	results	of	the	fighting
yesterday	confirmed	this	belief	aaa
George	R.I	aaa	Addressed	all
units	and	formations	that	Division
aaa				

From: JAY

Place:

Time: 9-25 AM

Extract from Battalion Orders
by
Lieut. Col. C.H. Kitching
Comdg. 12th Bn. East Surrey Regt.

14. X. 1916

917. SPECIAL. The 41st Division has now shown its value as a fighting unit, and may well be proud of the part it has taken in the battle of the SOMME.

We must uphold and increase this reputation and that already gained for work, smart turnout, and good behaviour. During the ensuing months, every effort should be made to prepare for further active operations against the enemy; in order that all ranks may have full advantage over him when next met with.

(Sd) H.C. Reynard.
2/Lieut & Adjt.
12th Bn. East Surrey Regt.

Above, Certified True Copy.

APPENDIX I.

4th Army. No. 335(G.S.)

41st Division.

I desire to place on record my appreciation of the work done by the 41st Division, during the battle of the SOMME, and to congratulate all ranks on the brilliant manner in which they captured the village of FLERS on Sept. 15th. To assault three lines of strongly defended trench system, and to capture the village of FLERS as well, in one rush, was a feat of arms of which every officer, non-commissioned officer and man may feel proud.

It was a very fine performance and I offer my best thanks for the gallantry and endurance displayed by all ranks.

The work of the Divisional Artillery in supporting infantry attacks and in establishing the barrages deserves high praise, and I trust that in some future time it may be my good fortune to have this fine division again in the Fourth Army.

(Sd) H. Rawlinson
General
Comdg. 4th Army.

H.Q. 4th Army
27 Oct. 1916

Above Certified True Copy.

122/4

122/4   94/16

Vac 6

Headquarters
122" Infantry Bde.

Herewith Original copy War Diary
for this past Battalion for the month of
October

[stamp: 12th BATTALION, EAST SURREY REGIMENT. No..... Date.....]

C. Colclough Major
12/Bn East Surrey Regt

1st Nov 1916

Army Form C. 2118

WAR DIARY
or
INTELLIGENCE SUMMARY 12 E Surrey Regt

Vol 7

(Erase heading not required.)

NOVEMBER

Place	Date	Hour	Summary of Events and Information	Remarks and references to Appendices
ST. ELOI SECTOR Sheet 28 O1 and 2	1st		Enemy shelled BOIS CONFLUENT 1 killed 6 O.R. wounded	ever.
do.	2nd		2 Lts. A.V. Reimer, H.S. Todd, J. Ashton attached for duty to 18th K.R.R.C. O.O. for relief by 20th D.L.I. received. 2 Lt G/G. Read took over duties of Brigade Intelligence Officer.	C.O.C.R.
do.	3rd	4.17 P.M.	12th East Surrey Regt. reported relief complete. Battn. returned via MILLEKAPELLEKEN FARM — OUDERDOM — RENINGHELST to ONTARIO CAMP (M 5 a 2.8) Battn. settled in camp. Casualties mail. During return Major A&C Blakeney was thrown from his horse and sustained injuries in the head. Capt. W. Hagen assumed command. Lieut. L.S. Beautify returned from 2nd Army Sniping School and 2.S. took over the one Lt of Battn Sniping & Intelligence Officer.	QKQR

7.C
10 Nov

WAR DIARY or INTELLIGENCE SUMMARY

Army Form C. 2118

Place	Date	Hour	Summary of Events and Information	Remarks and references to Appendices
M5a2,8 ONTARIO CAMP	4th		Kit and rifle inspections, and training in use of small box respirators. Capt. J.A.C. Mc Calman appointed Area Commandant, BOESCHEPE Area. 2Lt. H.P. Railey proceeded to 228th Field Coy. R.E. for instruction in R.E. work.	L.S.B.
do.	5th		Battn. on duty; almost all of the unit being on working parties. Lieut. F. Grant R.A.M.C. took over the duties of Medical Officer from Capt. W.F. Wilson R.A.M.C., on leave.	L.S.B.
do.	6th		Bathing in the morning. Small box respirators tested with lachrymose gas in the afternoon. Major Blakeney returned from hospital and assumed command from Capt. Hogan.	L.S.B.
do.	7th		Quiet day; heavy rain. 2Lt. Edwards temporarily took over the duties of D.S.O. L.S.B. duties of Divisional Salvage Officer.	L.S.B.

WAR DIARY
or
INTELLIGENCE SUMMARY

(Erase heading not required.)

Army Form C. 2118

Instructions regarding War Diaries and Intelligence Summaries are contained in F. S. Regs., Part II. and the Staff Manual respectively. Title Pages will be prepared in manuscript.

Place	Date	Hour	Summary of Events and Information	Remarks and references to Appendices
ONTARIO CAMP M5a.2.8	8th		Lt.-Col. M. Lee, D.S.O. returned from acting as Brigadier-General and assumed command of the Battn. Battn. on duty, finding working parties. 2 Lt. A.V. Reinto returned from duty with 18th K.R.R.C.	Z.S.O.
ST. ELOI SECTOR Sheet 28 O.1 + 2	9th		The Battn. relieved the 20th D.L.I., leaving ONTARIO CAMP at 8.30 A.M. and marching by way of OUDERDOM — MILLEKRUISSE — DICKEBUSCH — Order of relief; Lt. Headquarters, C Coy. in reserve in farm at N6a 8.5, B Coy. in left reserve, D Coy. in right reserve, A Coy. in front line and No. 1 CRATER. Trench strength, 756. Relief complete at 4.20 P.M. Capt. F.C. Clatt attached as Drainage Officer, from 20th D.L.I. The enemy was very quiet, only a few shells being fired at long intervals; indirect fire at night on BOIS CONFLUENT. Casualties nil.	

WAR DIARY
or
INTELLIGENCE SUMMARY
(Erase heading not required.)

Place	Date	Hour	Summary of Events and Information	Reference to Appendices
ST. ELOI SECTOR	10th		Quiet day, except between 2.0 & 3.0 P.M. when our Trench Mortars in BOIS CONFLUENT bombarded the enemy front line under cover of artillery fire. The enemy retaliated slightly but caused no damage. Casualties nil. Advantage taken of the fine weather to continue drainage work.	BOIS
do	11th		Quiet during daytime. At 10 P.M. Lieut. CO Stocks and 2Lt. J.F. Walton took out a patrol of 4 O.R. to reconnoitre the enemy wire on left of No. 16 crater. On arriving there they were heavily bombed and fired at with M.G's, and on one of the party (Stretcher bearer) were sent for and on their arrival the party was again fired upon by M.G.'s sustaining more casualties and being thus forced in consequence Lieut. Stocks is now reported missing believed wounded, 2Lt. Walton wounded and missing and 4 O.R. all missing. 2 Lt. J. Baker took command of B Coy.	K.S.O.
do	12th		Enemy most active during the day, sniping at No. 16 crater Sap and enfilading a portion of Trench 02.2 from their left, causing one casualty, a Sergeant killed. One other rank killed by indirect fire near DEAD DOG FARM	K.S.B.

Army Form C. 2118

WAR DIARY
or
INTELLIGENCE SUMMARY
(Erase heading not required.)

Instructions regarding War Diaries and Intelligence Summaries are contained in F. S. Regs., Part II. and the Staff Manual respectively. Title Pages will be prepared in manuscript.

Place	Date	Hour	Summary of Events and Information	Remarks and references to Appendices
ST. ELOI SECTOR Sheet 28 O.1&2	13th		Another quiet day. No enemy artillery activity. No activity being put over by own artillery. Very little attention on the enemy's line in front of No. 1 Crater, several shells falling short close to our front line.	
		8.5 P.M. to 10.40 P.M.	2nd Lt. W.R. Miller took out a patrol of 6 O.R. from Trench O.1.2 to reconnoitre the ground in front. The ground was found to be firm, covered with long grass and free from shell holes. Casualties nil. No shots ordered.	L.S.B.
do.	14th		A very clear day, excellent for observation, but there was little activity. Gas alert stood on. Casualties nil. 2nd Lt. J.D. Walker returned from hospital and took over again the duties of Signalling Officer.	L.S.B.
	15th		A Coy. was relieved in the huts live by D Coy. for the River line. The relay task place at 3am. Quiet day.	C.O.R.

Army Form C. 2118

WAR DIARY
or
INTELLIGENCE SUMMARY
(Erase heading not required.)

Instructions regarding War Diaries and Intelligence Summaries are contained in F.S. Regs., Part II. and the Staff Manual respectively. Title Pages will be prepared in manuscript.

Place	Date	Hour	Summary of Events and Information	Remarks and references to Appendices
MS 28	16th		Battalion in reserve in Trenches. 4 & 20 B.L.I. - Relay to reports complete at 8 PM and kitchen in settled in Billets at ONTARIO CAMP.	CoKer
	17th		Battalion on fatigue - Battery and carrying work.	CoKer
	18th		Lt. H.C. REYNARD proceeded on leave. Lt. R.W. ANEMY TIKAU joined Battalion.	
	19th		2d F.B.B. DOWLING proceeded on a 8 mths Course to TENBIG (PLM) - 1. 2d PRITCHARD proceeded on a Course at the D.T.W.S. 2d O.S. TO for relief received. Lt. Col. Sir T.L.N. MORLAND LCB, DSO, Commdg 5th Corps presented medal ribbons at 10.45 to the foll. Officers and men of the Battalion. Militia Crest Lt. H.S. OPENSHAW — 12552. Militia Medal. Nurse. 14252 Sjt SIMPSON G.W. — 12771 L/Cpl DAWES J. — 16124 Pte WILLIAMS E. 16224 Pte COOMES P.C. — 12797 L/Cpl MORRIS E. Lt. H.S. OPENSHAW returned from leave and assumed Command. J.B. Conspicuous	CoKer
	20th			

WAR DIARY
or
INTELLIGENCE SUMMARY

Army Form C. 2118

Place	Date	Hour	Summary of Events and Information	Remarks and references to Appendices
	20th		To the Captains who were asked to proceed to Wulverghem & Battery, B & C Sg the one the Ordnance Stores and A & B Engineers and for Short Trench Mortar memory. In the position B & C Sgs did a Short Trench Mortar	Order
	21st		Quiet Day.	APPA
	22nd		brigade msg. Battalion orders for the Relief issued —	tr.
Dickebusch Sub. Sectr. from O.18.b.00 — O.2.c.81.9	23rd		The Battalion relieved the 20th Bn D.L.I. in the DIEPENBAAL Sub-Sectr. the relief being completed at 4.45 P.M. Disposition of Companies as:	Ord
			FRONT LINE. Right — 2 Platoons S B Coy Left — 2 Platoons ¾ D Coy CRATER No 1. 1 Platoon ¾ A Coy. RESERVE LINE. Right — 2 Platoons ¾ B Coy Left — 2 Platoons ¾ D Coy RESERVE 2 platoons at N6 = 8 6½ A Coy less 1 Plat The relief passed off without incident and no casualties were suffered.	

WAR DIARY
or
INTELLIGENCE SUMMARY
(Erase heading not required.)

Army Form C. 2118

Place	Date	Hour	Summary of Events and Information	Remarks and references to Appendices
	24th		No activity worth noting. Major-Gen. S.T.B. LAWFORD C.B. visited Bn HQ	GRCN.
	25th		Quiet day. 2nd Lt PACK proceeded to his Machine Gun Course at ETAPLES. 2nd Lt BEAUFOY was relieved of Command of D Coy by 2nd Lt R.A.V. BREARY owing to temporary indisposition. The former Brigade O.O. for the Relief by the 2nd D.C.L.I received by Bn. 1.O.R. D. Coy.	GRCD.
	26th		Lt Col POTTER D.A.A.& Q.M.G. 41st Divn. visited trenches with the Brigade Major. Mining was suspected to be going on under D Coy. MG and TOII. So a mining officer was sent for and proceeded to find time for the purpose of listening — He's opinion was that it was improbable that the enemy was mining at that spot at the present time. A further report is he promised after investigation.	GRCL.
	27th		Quiet Day	

Army Form C. 2118

WAR DIARY
or
INTELLIGENCE SUMMARY
(Erase heading not required.)

Instructions regarding War Diaries and Intelligence Summaries are contained in F.S. Regs., Part II. and the Staff Manual respectively. Title Pages will be prepared in manuscript.

Place	Date	Hour	Summary of Events and Information	Remarks and references to Appendices
	27		Brigade Orders No 8 Army Intent happened. It was decided to relieve the Right Company up to the front line by B D Trench and the left Company on the front line by MIDDLESEX LANE to wind up by 21 Regent remained the same.	Green
CAMERIE CAMP N? A - 8	28		2nd Bn DURHAM LIGHT INFANTRY relieved front E sector to trenches right the Castle by 4.30 PM. Send down for a relief a a pt. Showered and covered any it moved Battalion was reported present in Camp at 8.30 PM	Open
	29		Large Inter Platt in called for which relief the Battalion and Camp Games both the same game to the remainder of the Battalion	Open
	30		Bn Battalion and Baltic dates Intellign Plas took no duties	Open

1875 Wt. W593/826 1,000,000 4/15 J.B.C. & A. A.D.S.S./Forms/C. 2118.

Secret 97/8.

Headquarters
122nd Infantry Bde

Herewith Original copy War Diary for
Batt under my command for month of December
1916.

[Stamp: 12th BATTALION, EAST SURREY REGIMENT. No........ Date........]

H.E. Waldren Major
Comdg 12/Bn East Surrey Regt

1st Jany 1917

[Stamp: 122nd INFANTRY BRIGADE No. 168 Date 1/1/17]

Headquarters
122 Infantry Bde

Herewith Original copy War Diary
for month of November for the Batt under
my Command.

[signature]
Lieut Col
Comdg 12/Bn East Surrey Regt

2° Dec 1916

WAR DIARY or **INTELLIGENCE SUMMARY**
(Erase heading not required.)

Army Form C. 2118

Vol 8

DECEMBER 1916

Place	Date	Hour	Summary of Events and Information	Remarks and references to Appendices
ONTARIO CAMP SHEET 28 M5 a 2.8	DEC. 1st		Quiet day. Training continued.	L.S.D.
	2nd		Training continued. Boxing contest in afternoon.	L.S.D.
ST. ELOI SECTOR O1d and O2c	3rd		Battn. relieved 20th D.L.I. Left ONTARIO CAMP at 8.15 A.M. and proceeded by OUDERDOM — MILLEKAPELLEKEN FARM — DICKEBUSCH. Disposition. A Coy. Front and reserve lines on the right. C Coy. Front, support and reserve lines on the left. B Coy. Reserve line near P.&O. Trench D Coy. Reserve farm at N 6 a 8.6 Relief complete at 2.0 P.M. Trench strength 698. 2/Lt. J.A. Rogers proceeded on leave. Casualties nil.	L.S.D. 8.C 11 what

WAR DIARY or INTELLIGENCE SUMMARY

Army Form C. 2118

Place	Date	Hour	Summary of Events and Information	Remarks and references to Appendices
ST. ELOI SECTOR 28 O 1 d and 2 a	4.12.16	8.0 A.M. to 1.0 P.M.	Enemy artillery unusually active; field gun fire distributed over all the Batt'n front; reserve and C.T's. Increased rifle fire and M.G. fire on P.40, trench. Casualties. 2 Lt. J.W. Barron "wounded remaining on duty". 2.O.R. wounded.	L.S.B.
		night	Work continued as reported in front line.	
do.	5.12.16	4 A.M. to 5 A.M.	6 "fishtails" with artillery support damaged trenches O2.3 + O2.4, causing 5 casualties in C Coy.	
		2 to 2.30 P.M.	Some place again bombarded with fishtails; no damage. Enemy artillery again unusually active, and several times stopped by retaliation with howitzers and field guns. 2 Lt. D. Walker proceeded on leave. Work on front line as usual. Casualties. 5 O.R. wounded.	L.S.B.
do.	6.12.16		Quieter day, except from midnight till dawn, during which time many fishtails were fired at our left causing damage to CRATER LANE, but no casualties.	

Date	Hour	Summary of Events and Information	Remarks and references to Appendices
6.		Wet in Front line. Continued.	L.S.B
7.		Misty Day, raining in front of R. line during morning. Put me in afternoon and enemy artillery were active again, using heavie shells on R Line and field guns on Front line — No damage. Capt. C.N. PRIDHAM returned from leave and resumed command of D Coy. Casualties. 1. O.R. killed by rifle bullet in No 1 CRATER.	L.S.B
8.		Quiet by day. Between 3 PM & 5 PM when an artillery bombarded the near of the enemy lines and he retaliated with rifle gun and heavy shells on our front and Reserve lines. No material damage was done. Casualties Nil.	L.S.B
9.		Battalion relieved by 20th B. D.L.I. relief reported complete at 3.15 AM. Settled in (ONTARIO CAMP MS.a 2.8) by 8 AM. Casualties Nil. 2 Lt AT LIBBY returned from leave.	Effr. L.S.B

Army Form C. 2118

WAR DIARY
or
INTELLIGENCE SUMMARY
(Erase heading not required.)

Instructions regarding War Diaries and Intelligence Summaries are contained in F.S. Regs., Part II. and the Staff Manual respectively. Title Pages will be prepared in manuscript.

Place	Date	Hour	Summary of Events and Information	Remarks and references to Appendices
ONTARIO CAMP MSa.2.8	10.12.16		Promotions. Temp. Lt. C.O. Slocke, Temp. 2Lt. D. McBolhin, Temp. 2Lt. H.C. Raynard } To be temporary captains dt/16.9.16. Temp. 2Lt. J.A. Rogers - To be temporary lieutenant dt 17.9.16	L.S.D.
do.	11.12.16		Working party of 350. Church parade and cleaning up for remainder.	L.S.D.
do.	12.12.16		Training continued. Particular attention paid to the making of everything bolted mine, Lewis Gun fired on 30 yards range at Brigade Trench Warfare School.	L.S.D.
			Heavy snow. Work confined to lectures in huts.	L.S.D.

1875 Wt. W593/826 1,000,000 4/15 J.B.C. & A. A.D.S.S./Forms/C. 2118.

Place	Date	Hour	Summary of Events and Information	Remarks and references to Appendices
	13ᵗʰ 14ᵗʰ		Training continued in Camp. 2ⁿᵈ Lt BEAUFOY went to a Sound Ranging Course to the First Army Company Battalion who are for the relief in trenches by the 20ᵗʰ D.L.I were warned	G/Cr.
	15ᵗʰ		The Battalion relieved the 6ᵗʰ Bn. DURHAM LIGHT INFANTRY in trenches, the relief being completed by 1.30 P.M. 2ⁿᵈ Lt. C. R.G. REAH returned from leave 2/Lt B. F. DODD returned from hospital and remained at the Transport Lines under the M.D.'s orders.	G P C R
	16ᵗʰ		Quiet day. Brig.-Gen. TOWSEY visited trenches (and expressed his satisfaction at the work that was being done on them, especially the wiring.	G P G O
	17ᵗʰ		The weather was strongly misty, witnessing to a fog. Trends however, and made Observation practically impossible for the day. Advantage was taken of the day to pushing up a good deal of wire in the daytime.	G/Cr.

WAR DIARY
or
INTELLIGENCE SUMMARY

Army Form C. 2118

Place	Date	Hour	Summary of Events and Information	Remarks and references to Appendices
	17.		CRATER LANE was shelled in two places by Trench Mortars, but no very serious damage done. 2Lt WINDER H.E. returned from the Div'nal T.W. School; also he had been undergoing a course.	G.H.Q.
	18.		A Rather bad day for Observation. The enemy were quite active during the afternoon, with their artillery and Rifle Grenades, on the left. and Ete a late their Machine Guns, sweeping the road behind Bn. H.Q. Captain H.S. WALKER returned from Course. 2Lt WALKER returned from leave. Cpl Griffiths I.O.R.	G.H.Q.
	19.		An unusually quiet day; the enemy showing practically no artillery activity. The C.O. reconnoitred the G.H.Q. line in the afternoon from the BRASSERIE to VIERSTRAAT; the portion of the line that would in case of an attack on his opposite number, be taken up by the Battalion. L-Cpl MARTIN of the X Corps visited the CRATER unit Lt-Col. NORTH 9th 20 "D.L.I" 123 Bde Brigade operation orders for relieving the Battalion by 123 Bde in trenches received.	G.H.Q.

Place	Date	Hour	Summary of Events and Information	Remarks and references to Appendices
	20th		Quiet day except for the fact that at 10 a.m. a short 5.9 shell landed in the RESERVE FARM area, killing one O.R. and wounding 2 Lt. WINDER H.E. and 4 O.R. Major H de C BLAKENEY left trenches for the purpose of proceeding to BAISIEUX to transact P.R.I. business. 2 Lt. F.R. MATTHEWS took on duty of Battalion Transport Officer vice 2 Lt. ETBW MYERS, who reported in trenches for duty with D Coy. 2 Lt. WALTER LEE returned home, which originated much aerial activity on both sides. 2 Lt. LEE returned from Transport Course and went to C. Coy.	CdCn
	21st		Nothing of interest happened. There was a strong wind blowing and the weather was showery. A quiet day was reported by the front line Companies.	CdCn
	22nd		The Battalion was relieved in trenches by the 20th L.I., the relay taking place without casualties and being completed by 2.40 p.m. In the morning Captain POLLOCK of the 2nd Army School at WISQUES visited trenches for the purpose of looking round.	CdCn

WAR DIARY
INTELLIGENCE SUMMARY

(Erase heading not required.)

Army Form C. 2118

Place	Date	Hour	Summary of Events and Information	Remarks and references to Appendices
ONTARIO CAMP. M5 a 2.8.	22nd		The Battalion arrived reported present in Billets at ONTARIO CAMP at 8.30 P.M., after which a Rum Issue was ordered.	A.P.C.R.
	23rd		A quiet day was spent in cleaning and getting ready for the medal distribution tomorrow by the Divisional Commander.	APCR
	24th		The Battalion paraded at 8 A.C. (that is less Companies, the remainder being on working parties) to march to CHIPPAWA CAMP, where the Parade was to take place — Medal ribbons were distributed to the following: MILITARY MEDAL :- Ssr McKENZIE and L/Cpl KITCHING of B Company. Lt.-Col. LEE. D.S.O. proceeded to WISEVES to a Divisional Conference. Lt OPENSHAW accompanied him. The latter taking Commanding Officers Course. Lt BLAKENEY took on Command of the Battalion.	CPCR.
	25th		The Day in chiefly spent in getting up Xmas Dinner for the men, which took place at 2.o.c. There was no alarm, and the day passed quietly.	CPCR

WAR DIARY or INTELLIGENCE SUMMARY

Army Form C. 2118

Place	Date	Hour	Summary of Events and Information	Remarks and references to Appendices
	26.		Major H de C BLAKENEY to HAZEBROUCK to preside at a F.G.C.M. Captain A.S. WALKER assumed command of the Battalion in his absence. The G.O.C. held an inspection of the Battalion in the lines at 7.30 p.m. 2Lt B.F. TODD proceeded to TICQUES Musketry Camp for duty there. 2Lt WALKER proceeded to the ST ELOI Gmp Artillery for a tour of duty.	G.P.G. 2.
			Came in the working of the S.O.S.	G.G.R.
	27.		2Lt MILLER and 2Lt R.C. BAKER proceeded to BERMICOURT for duty with the H.M.G.C. Battalion provided working parties.	G.G.R.
	28.		Quiet day, work was in progress about the Camp. Battalion was for the relief was warned -	
	29.		The Battalion relieved the 20th D.L.I. in trenches, the relief passed without incident though there was a certain amount of shelling. At the region of the BRASSERIE 2Lt WALKER rejoined the Battalion for duty, also 2Lt ASTON and 2Lt TODD, who has been attached to the 18th K.R.R.C, owing to the shortage of officers in that Battalion.	G.G.R.

WAR DIARY
or
INTELLIGENCE SUMMARY

(Erase heading not required.)

Army Form C. 2118

Place	Date	Hour	Summary of Events and Information	Remarks and references to Appendices
	30.	—	Quiet Day. There was no artillery shoot by us in the afternoon, but the day was in the main fairly quiet state. There were a few patrols made communication between the front line in a water-logged condition, this rendering the front line and the R. line a problem. The water however in rather clear by dusk and work proceeded as usual.	C/PER
	31.		Quiet Day and clear for observation. Two O.R's were wounded in the CRATER by a sniper firing obliquely from the left. Covering the inundation & ystray, to trenches are in a markedly good condition and water patrols carried forward with their work. At 6p.m. CAPT - BARNETT command'g the 122 Bde visited the Coy's work, with the Brigade Major in the afternoon.	C/PER

H.O. C. Stott Maj.
Comm'g 12 S. Serv. Bn.

Army Form C. 2118.

WAR DIARY
or
INTELLIGENCE SUMMARY.
(Erase heading not required.)

12 E Surrey Regt
Vol 9

9.C
8 March

Instructions regarding War Diaries and Intelligence Summaries are contained in F. S. Regs., Part II. and the Staff Manual respectively. Title pages will be prepared in manuscript.

Place	Date	Hour	Summary of Events and Information	Remarks and references to Appendices
St ELOI SECTOR	1917 Sept 1st	5.45 P.M.	A quiet day. till 5.45 P.M. when there was considerable Artillery activity on the front of the Enemy. This did no damage to our trenches and only resulted in 1 O.R. being killed. 2 Lt BARROW was slightly wounded. Lt McMORRIS joined the Battalion for duty, and took on the duties of Pioneer Officer.	Ext A.M.
	2nd		There was considerable activity on both sides all day, in addition to which it being a clear day, there was considerable aerial activity. Bn HQ= received two long "strafes" and some shrapnel in the morning and in the afternoon there was repeated shelling. The Bn was relieved by the 2nd Bn D.L.I; relief being completed without Casualty.	Ext A.
	3rd		Relief reported Complete by 2 P.M. The Bn was afterwards proceeded to Billets at ONTARIO CAMP at 1 P.M.	Ext B.
	4th		Major H de BLAQUIERE attended conference of C.O's. at Bde HQ at 10 A.M. Working Parties occupied the greater part of the Battalion. The weather was bad and 50 inspections were held of the men left in Camp as to kit and equipment generally.	
	5th		The Bn went to the Baths. Major H.d.C BLAQUIERE went at 10 A.M. to preside over F.G.C.M.	

Place	Date	Hour	Summary of Events and Information	Remarks and references to Appendices
	6.		Major General S.T.B. LAWFORD, C.B. Commanding 41st Division and Lt Col H.H. LEE, D.S.O. Commanding the "111" Inf Bde, inspected the Battalion doing training.	
	7.		Relief moved — Working parties were called for from the Bn, which occupied most of the Battalion. The remainder of the men going on Church Parade.	
	8.		The Bn. relieved the 20th Bn. D.L.I. in trenches the relief being reported complete by 2.30 a.m. In the evening six dummy figures were placed in NO MANS LAND and attacked by wires to the front line trench. These are in preparation for a dummy raid which is to take place in the 9th W.	
	9.		Our Trench Mortars cut the enemy wire between O.3a.35.95 and O.2c.55.10, the enemy doing little retaliating. At 6:55 P.M. the figures which had been placed in NO MANS LAND were pulled up from the front line trench and at 7.00 P.M. (Zero hour) our batteries opened fire on the enemys trenches. Smoke was to have been set over by us, but owing to the direction of the wind, this was not possible. The Bombardment which was intensive lasted for 30 minutes, during which time, the enemy did not retaliate. After the bombardment a very quiet night passed.	

WAR DIARY
or
INTELLIGENCE SUMMARY.
(Erase heading not required.)

Army Form C. 2118.

Place	Date	Hour	Summary of Events and Information	Remarks and references to Appendices
	10th		Quiet day. A Dummy figure was placed out in NO MANS LAND and a party of bombers under 2/Lt HARDING lay in wait for any enemy who should come and investigate it. No enemy did come however.	G.P.G.R.
	11th	10-15 AM	BOIS CONFLUENT was shelled with 4.2 but no casualties resulted. A fit. Pung about all day, which made Flanders impossible. Advantage was however taken of this to put out wire during the day.	
	12th		QUEEN VICTORIA STREET was damaged by shrapnel shells in the morning, not seriously however; working parties were sent out to repair the damage but it was repeated in a short time. 2Lts. LAZENBY S. HUTCHINSON A.V. and PUTTUCK RN. joined the Battalion for duty.	CPCR
	13th		A very quiet day. BOIS CONFLUENT was shelled during the morning and a few light trench Mortars fell just behind the front line. There were flurries where new communication trenches the Reserve and the two line dittiwe - orders for relief in trenches by the 20th B. D.L.I were received	CPCall
	14th		The B[n] was relieved in trenches by the 20th "B" DURHAM LIGHT INFANTRY, the relief being reported complete by 2.30 PM	

WAR DIARY
or
INTELLIGENCE SUMMARY.
(Erase heading not required.)

Army Form C. 2118.

Place	Date	Hour	Summary of Events and Information	Remarks and references to Appendices
	15th		300 men of the Battalion were sent to supply R.E. working party.	allen.
	16th		2/Lts MAINES R.N. STENNING B.C. DUNCAN A.T. and Lt. BAKER A.V. joined the B.n. for duty.	allen.
			R.E. were arranged for the men, which had to be available, owing to the note supplies not being available, to provide them.	allen.
	17th		Lt.Col. H.P. LEE D.S.O. returned to the Battalion Brigade – relieved F.W. TOWSEY. who having resumed Command of the Brigade, on his return from leave. Lt Col LEE did not take over command of the Battalion however, but was proceeding on leave the following day. Battalion had Outpost Schemes by Companies. Lt Col. LEE D.S.O. proceeded on leave –	allen.
	18th		2/Lts PRITCHARD and WOOLARD and 5 O.R.s were wounded by the premature explosion of trench hand grenade at the Bomb'g P.d. 75 O.R.s for Carrying were called for the R.E. for R.E. working parties. Company training in General on other remainder. Training was carried on throughout the day.	allen.
	20th		The Battalion went to the Battg. R.R. trenches were held whilst the men returned	allen.

Army Form C. 2118.

WAR DIARY
or
INTELLIGENCE SUMMARY.
(Erase heading not required.)

Instructions regarding War Diaries and Intelligence Summaries are contained in F. S. Regs., Part II. and the Staff Manual respectively. Title pages will be prepared in manuscript.

Place	Date	Hour	Summary of Events and Information	Remarks and references to Appendices
	21st		The Battalion relieved the 2/7th D.C.L.I. in trenches, relief being reported complete by 4:30 P.M. The relief was a late one owing to the thick snow which lay on the ground. A short night was passed.	CoPCoA
	22nd		Our T.M. Mortars trench Mortars were active, there were however satisfactorily dealt with by our 18 pdrs., the rest of the day passed without incident.	Culm.
	23rd	12·15 AM	T.O.11 came into some light shelling, no damage was caused however – At 11·30 AM T.O.11 and to Rdt of P.O.C.T. were bombarded by 4·2. The latter being treated to five pieces. This was on a retaliation on our Medium Trench Mortary which had sent rounds at the enemy line Minute T.O.21. into good effect. Our Stokes guns had also been putting shells into CRATER No. 2. Captain H.S. OPENSHAW returned from Company Commander Course at WISQUES. A fine day led to much aerial activity. Two German aeroplanes were brought down by hostile anti-aircraft fire, one crashing in flames in the enemy support line opposite BOIS CONFLUENT. Otherwise an uneventful day passed.	CoMCoA
CoPCoA

WAR DIARY or INTELLIGENCE SUMMARY

Army Form C. 2118.

Date	Hour	Summary of Events and Information	Remarks and references to Appendices
25.		Fine weather. Continuing with hard frost and low temperature. RESERVE FARM was shelled at 11 in during the morning, receiving no less than thirteen direct hits. One O.R. was killed. A good deal of Grenatte - batting work was carried on during the day, a Belgian battery of light Field Guns being put out of position. Lt BAKER was attached to B Coy and 2/Lt BAYLEY reported for duty to B Coy.	CRCR
26.		A fine day, which gave rise to considerable aerial activity on both sides. At 11.30 am a portion of QUEEN VICTORIA ST. was blown in, but we suffered no casualties. Lt R.A.V. BREARY proceeded to transport lines in order to attend Company Commanders Course at WISQUES. Lt BAKER assumed command of his Company. 2/Ls. BENNETT and VANNER joined the Battalion for duty, the former rejoining sick at the transport lines under M.O.'s orders. As latter proceeded to B Coy.	GRCR
27.		Quiet day. Bois CONFLUENT received a few shells in the afternoon. Lt BREARY returned from the transport line, missing transport line being slightly better.	GRCR.
28.		The Bn was relieved in trenches by the 20th Bn D.L.I., relief being complete by 2.30. Two Machine Gunners were put in DICKYBUSCH on the way to	

2353 Wt. W2544/1454 700,000 5/15 D. D. & L. A.D.S.S.-Forms/C. 2118.

WAR DIARY
or
INTELLIGENCE SUMMARY.
(Erase heading not required.)

Army Form C. 2118.

Place	Date	Hour	Summary of Events and Information	Remarks and references to Appendices
	28.		Camp. Attained the relay hound. H. interior inidents 2ud C.P. COOPER joined the Bn. for duty and was posted to B Company.	Regr.
	29.		120 men were called for for R.E. fatigue parties at 10 a.m. As Brigade Grenadier. Lt. Col. 1. CAREY-BARNARD D.S.O. inspected No 15 Platoon, and the Divisional Commander Brig-Gen? F.W. TOWSEY C.M.G. inspected the same men again at 3 P.M. Major H. de C. BLAKENEY and 2ud C.P.G. REAH proceeded to St ELOI Group HQ for attachment to the R.A. Cpl. Wilkins assumed Command of the Bt.	Even.
	30.		Battn. and Fd hospitals. Nguen the day.	
	31.		The whole Battalion with specialist exception were set on R.E. fatigue parties.	Gpgr

H. de C. O'Mallsery Major
Comd: 12 E. Surrey?

R30/10.

Headquarters
122nd Infantry Bde.

Herewith Original copy War Diary
for month of February for Battalion under
my command.

[Stamp: 12th BATTALION, EAST SURREY REGIMENT. No........ Date: March 1917]

H. Yhu Lieut Col
Comdg 12/Bn East Surrey Regt

Army Form C. 2118.

WAR DIARY
or
INTELLIGENCE SUMMARY.
(Erase heading not required.)

XII A Survey Pos'
Vol 10

10.C
6 sheets.

Date	Hour	Summary of Events and Information	Remarks and references to Appendices
1st		B. R.A.V. BARRY proceeded to WISQUES to take a Company Commanders Course. Companies carried out training according to the weekly B'n Training Scheme. Major H de C BLAKENEY returned from attached to R.F.A. Group H.Q. and resumed Command of the B'n.	APCR
2.		B'n did working parties. Lt Col. H.H. LEE D.S.O. returned from leave and assumed Command of the 12th Bn Rif Bde in the absence of Brig Gen'l F.W. TOWSEY. C.M.G.	APCR
3.		B'n relieved the 20th B'n D.L.I. in trenches. The relief passed off without casualties. Coy reports complete by 2·30 P.M.	APCR
4.		Quiet day in trenches. P. & O. C.T. was shelled with heavy T.M's. There were no casualties. A Considerable amount of Crater-butting work was in progress throughout the day. Very poor visibility. Frost continuing. A party of R.E. working in R.14 were shrapnel fire in the morning - there were no casualties however and the trench was not damaged.	APCR
5.		A very quiet day. A German Sniper was very active and killed a Sergeant in the Sap leading to CRATER No 1. In the afternoon Bos HOOSE was shelled with light shrapnel. Our 18th'rs silenced a trench mortar which was very active against the B'n on our right.	APCR
6.			APCR
7.			APCR

WAR DIARY
or
INTELLIGENCE SUMMARY.
(Erase heading not required.)

Army Form C. 2118.

Instructions regarding War Diaries and Intelligence Summaries are contained in F.S. Regs., Part II. and the Staff Manual respectively. Title pages will be prepared in manuscript.

Place	Date	Hour	Summary of Events and Information	Remarks and references to Appendices
	7		Apart from Coats Battery there was little shelling. VOORMEZEELE was shelled with light shrapnel. 1 O.R. was killed by enemy sniper located yesterday. Our 18ch we directed on to the supposed spot but failed to hit it, owing to the observation of the spot being not from a forward enough O.P.	CWR
	8		At 10.30 A.M. CRATER LANE was heavily shelled with MINENWERFER. The portion just between the front line and the Support's being thrown in. Working parties were trying in it and it was possible within a few hours. The day was very clear and gave rise to a good deal of aerial activity on both sides. Lt. Col. H.H. LEE D.S.O. resumed command of the B⁰ on return from Gen⁹ J.W. PONSOR C.M.G. from the Division.	O. W.
	9		Artillery activity on both sides was below normal all day. There was desultory shelling of SCOTTISH WOOD areas. We did a shoot with 18hrs on the enemy supply train in the front line, many found destruction owing to the hard nature of the ground. However, the shells did not burst well and the sniper was not put out of action.	CWR
	10		The B⁰ was relieved in trenches by the 20⁰B⁰ D.L.I. The relief having been carried out with no casualties to an officials numbers from an enemy sniper. B⁰ was reported present in billets at ONTARIO CAMP at 8.30 P.M. 2/Lt. G.P. COOPER. proceeded to MONT DES CATS for Smith's course.	CWR

WAR DIARY
or
INTELLIGENCE SUMMARY.
(Erase heading not required.)

Army Form C. 2118.

Place	Date	Hour	Summary of Events and Information	Remarks and references to Appendices
	11.		The C.O. made an inspection of the H.Q. Coy. Voluntary church parade. Working parties for the majority of the Bn.	CRCR
	12.		Baths for the Bn. The C.O. proceeded to ABEELE to No 6 Squadron R.F.C. to witness an exhibition of Contact patrol work with Italian aeroplanes and Infantry in the attack. 2 Lt S. LAZENBY proceeded to TERDIGHEM to undergo a Bombing Course.	CRCR
			2 Lts VENNER, HUTCHESON, BENNET, STENNING, SAMUELS proceeded to ABEELE to attend a course at the Div. Trench Warfare School. 2nd Lt ASTON proceeded to POPERING to take up the duties of draft Conducting Officer there.	
	13.		The C.O. inspects B. Coy. 2 Lt Mc WALTER assumed Command of D Coy vice Lt BAKER returned transferred to A Coy. A tactical Conference was carried out by Composite in the afternoon. The Bn. Coys. for a route march in the morning route WESTOUTRE - MONT ROUGE - KASTEL MOLEN -	CRCR
	14. 15.		The C.O. inspects C. Coy & The Bn. did training in Camp. Major General S. T. B. LAWFORD. C.B Commanding the 10th Division inspected the Camp. accompanied by the Brigadier. The Companies were doing manual exercises and training about the Camp.	CRCR
	16.		Large working parties took the whole Bn. Rainy odds issued	CRCR

WAR DIARY
or
INTELLIGENCE SUMMARY
(Erase heading not required.)

Army Form C. 2118.

Place	Date	Hour	Summary of Events and Information	Remarks and references to Appendices
	17.		The Bn relieved the 20th Bn. DURHAM LIGHT INFANTRY in trenches. The Battalion on its right was heavily shelled in the evening but beyond a few stray shells hit the BEAD DOG in the area. This did not affect us much.	W/Ch.
	18th		A very quiet day. We did some good shooting with our light field guns.	a/w
	19th		A very foggy day kept to guns quiet. It also prevented any observation from O.P's	a/w
	20th		At Hr 9.0 C.T. was shelled however no damage was done and the retaliation from it was swift and sure and silenced the hostile battery. VOORMEZEELE Extn received a few light shells but they did no damage. Anthr. fine day for observation.	Cttes
	21st		At 4:30 A.M. CRATER LONG and the R Line near it was shelled with light shells and the former was badly knocked about. It was rendered passable however by the evening. Our artillery was letting some along CRATER No.2. at this time and the shelling of CRATER LONG may have been retaliation for this.	ARR.
	22nd		The Bn was relieved by the 20th D.L.I. The relief was a late one becauce of the enemy's short shrift which was to take place. He shown did not however take place owing to this incident. The Bn was, at present, in Camp the night. Two Coys. had hardly partiers, to these two had kit inspections	CPLR.
	23.			W/Ch.

WAR DIARY
or
INTELLIGENCE SUMMARY.

Army Form C. 2118.

Place	Date	Hour	Summary of Events and Information	Remarks and references to Appendices
	24		Working Parties were called for from the Bn. Captain REYNARD represented the C.O. at the Conference of Commanding Officers at Bde HQ, Lt-Col LEE DSO being unfit to attend to duties	CofCR
	25.		The Battalion in reserve in attending Church Parade and going to the Butts. Captain R.A. McCULLOCH returned to the Bn for duty and took on the duties of Adjutant vice Captain REYNARD — Lt RAV BREARY returned to duty from attending a Company Commanders Course at WISQUES.	CofCR
	26		Small working parties were called for and the men who are not battle yesterday were rested to day — Training in the Area in General at by the Remainder.	CofR
	27		The 6th relieved the 20th Bn B.L.I in trenches. The relief passed of without incident. Situation in front normal.	CofR
	28		Lt AT LIDOR was sent to hospital having had a fall from his horse. Captain AW HEWLETT — A quiet day in trenches, with fair visibility	CofR

Headquarters
122nd Infantry Bde

Herewith original copy War Diary for the Battalion under my command for month of March 1917.

1st April 1917

[signature] Lieut Col
Comdg 12/Bn East Surrey Regt

WAR DIARY
or
INTELLIGENCE SUMMARY.

Army Form C. 2118.

12 E Surrey Regt
March 1917.
Vol XI

11.C
8 sheets

Place	Date	Hour	Summary of Events and Information	Remarks and references to Appendices
LENNICLET ONTRO CAMP.	MARCH 1917			
	1.		Quiet day. 2Lt McWATER took over the duties of acting Adjutant vice Captain R. REYNARD. Captain R A McCULLOCH proceeded to RENINGHELST to take on the duties of acting Quartermaster vice Lt A.T. LIBBY.	APEN
	2.		A good deal of Counter-battery work was going on during the day. 2Lt DUNCAN was killed by a enemy sniper. 10 OR killed.	APEN
	3.		Quiet day. Excellent for aeroplane.	
	4.		Artillery seemed to be registering as there was steady shelling on trenches in the whole sector. A good deal of artillery activity on both sides and much aerial activity owing to the good day. Casualties 2 OR.	APEN
	5.		Bn was relieved in trenches by the 20th Bn DURHAM LIGHT INFANTRY, Lt Col H H LEE DSO proceeded to Bn HQ there to meet the Army Commander. Captain HS WATKINS assumed Command of the Bn in his absence as handed over to our opposite number. The C.O. held a Conference of Company Commanders. Brig Gen' F.W. TOWSEY CMG visited the Camp and expressed his Satisfaction at its condition.	APEN
	6.		C Coy paraded for inspection by the CO. in the new organisation Y Company.	
	7.		Lieut GCC REASN proceeded to 12th 1 Bde HQ, to take on the duties of Intelligence	

WAR DIARY
or
INTELLIGENCE SUMMARY.
(Erase heading not required.)

Army Form C. 2118.

Place	Date	Hour	Summary of Events and Information	Remarks and references to Appendices
Renninghelst			Officer 2Lt J ASTON took over the duties of Bn. Intelligence Officer and Asst. Adjutant	J.A.
Unknown Camp	8		Day's Training in Camp. C.O. inspected practice of proposed raid. Orders received (6.0.pm) for Bn. to Stand to in case of need to support XVIth Div. where lines had been raided by enemy. Order cancelled 7.0 pm.	J.A.
	9		Day's training in Camp. C.O. inspected practice of proposed raid.	J.A.
	10		C.O. held conference of Coy Commanders at 1.30 pm. Brig-General W.Toursey C.M.G. inspected Transport at 2.30 & was pleased with its condition. 2nd Lt W.G.Robinson joined the Battalion.	J.A.
	11		Battn relieved the 20th Battn DURHAM LIGHT INFANTRY in trenches. Relieved 1.0 & 2.0 pm. Two of our aeroplanes brought down over VOORMEZEELE. Intermittent enemy shelling during afternoon - 1 casualty at RESERVE FARM. C.O. made tour of trenches at 10.0 pm. Patrol under 2nd Lt PUTTOCK examined enemy wire.	J.A.
	12		Brig. Genl. F.W.Toursey. C.M.G. made a tour of the trenches in the morning, accompanied by the C.O. Our T.M.s & 18 pdrs cut wire in front of enemy front line 2.0 pm — 3.30 pm. Enemy shelled back areas in morning & front line + P & O Trench in afternoon. 2nd Lt VANNER, SAMUELS & STEMMING report back for duty after course, & 2nd Lt BENNETT at Transport. Patrol under 2nd Lt BAYLEY examined enemy wire.	J.A.

WAR DIARY
or
INTELLIGENCE SUMMARY.
(Erase heading not required.)

Army Form C. 2118.

Place	Date	Hour	Summary of Events and Information	Remarks and references to Appendices
	13		C.O. accompanied by Adjutant visited line during morning. Major L.A. HICKSON (West Kent Regt) assumed to take up duties of 2nd in Command. 2 shrapnel shells fell at 1.30 p.m. near RESERVE FARM. Our 18 pr, Stokes Guns & TMs cut enemy's wire successfully in front of trenches O.11, O.12, O.21, O.22 from 12.20 p.m. – 1.20 p.m. Our front line badly damaged in two places by enemy T.M. One of our aeroplanes flew along enemy front line at 3.40 p.m. firing low down with M.G. Patrol out at night under 2nd Lt PUTTOCK. 2nd Lt W.R. GURRIN joined Battn.	J.A.
	14		Considerable enemy shelling of RESERVE FARM & HQ neighbourhood with 77 mm about 12.0 noon. Intermittent trench mortars 0.15. damaged by Minnenwerfers. 6.0 – 10.0 p.m. Considerable hostile M.G. & rifle fire along our front. Our guns gave intense bombardment 10.30 p.m. Advance parties under Lt PUTTOCK seen & fired on by enemy – 2 O.R. wounded. Enemy was evidently prepared for raid under 2nd Lt CLIFF & 2nd Lt TODD. OC Raid judged attempt impossible, + it was not carried out. Enemy artillery slight on our front line, causing some damage. 2 O.Rs (wounds) in front line + 6 O.Rs in Craters during afternoon bombardment. MAJOR BLAKENEY arrived as Transport O.	J.A.
	15		Very quiet day, clean. 2 air fights in afternoon. C.O. left for Transport at 2.30 p.m., after handing over Command at Battn to Major HICKSON. Lt Col B.L. ANLEY Div! GSO 1 found our trenches, viewed damage done on previous day + appreciated work of repair done by the Battn.	J.A.

Army Form C. 2118.

WAR DIARY
or
INTELLIGENCE SUMMARY.
(Erase heading not required.)

Place	Date	Hour	Summary of Events and Information	Remarks and references to Appendices
	16		Very quiet day. A good deal of sniping. Major HICKSON inspected line in morning + evening.	J.A.
	17		Bn. was relieved in trenches by 20th DURHAM LIGHT INFANTRY. During relief there was considerable enemy shelling on C.T.s, but no casualties. 2nd LT R.D. BROWN & RUSSELL joined Bn. Lt R.A.V. BREARY & 2nd LT PUTTOCK proceeded to LE TOUQUET on Lewis Gun Course.	J.A.
	18		Voluntary Church Parade 10.0 a.m. Working parties. C.O. attended conference at 41st Divl HQ. at 5.0 p.m. 2nd LT A. HEMSLEY joined Bn.	J.A.
	19		A ceremonial Company of 250 under Capt. WILLIAMS attended Ceremonial Parade at 10.0 a.m. at CHIPPEWA CAMP under Maj-Genl S.T.B. LAWFORD, C.B. for distribution of awards + distinctions lately gained in the Division. Capt. McCALMAN rejoined Bn. M.O. Capt. BINNEY proceeded on leave, handing over to Capt. HARRISON. C.O. held conference of Coy Commanders at 5.0 pm. Training Day in Camp - Gale + heavy rain. 2nd LT J.M. HUTCHISON joined Bn.	J.A.
	20		At 3.0 pm. Col. MALONEY A.S.C. Transport Officer inspected Bn. Transport, + expressed himself very pleased with turnout + smartness, + Brig. Genl P.W. TOWSEY, C.M.G. sent his congratulations. Major BLAKENEY proceeded to BOESCHEPE to take up duties of Area	J.A.
	21		Commandant + Town Major. 2nd LT ASTON, I.O. made special reconnaissance of routes to front line under orders from Brig-Genl. A.D.S.S.	J.A.

Army Form C. 2118.

WAR DIARY
or
INTELLIGENCE SUMMARY.
(Erase heading not required.)

Instructions regarding War Diaries and Intelligence Summaries are contained in F. S. Regs., Part II. and the Staff Manual respectively. Title pages will be prepared in manuscript.

Place	Date	Hour	Summary of Events and Information	Remarks and references to Appendices
	22.		In the morning & afternoon the C.O. and old Coys paraded & inspected them. During the day the Batn was sent in detachments to Divisional Gas School for instruction in anti-Gas Shell measures. At 5.0. p.m. a conference of Coy Commanders was held at H.Q. M.B.O. a special performance of the Brigade Pantomime ALADDIN was given for the batn. in the YMCA. REVINGHURST. 2/Lt A.N. HOWITT rejoined Batn. 2/Lt LEE evacuated with measles.	J.A.
	23.		Batn relieved 2nd Bn DURHAM LIGHT INFANTRY in trenches. Relief reported complete 1.15. p.m. RESERVE FARM having been burnt down the previous day, C. Coy was accommodated in dugouts in MIDDLESEX LANE & Mc GEE TRENCH. The C.O. accompanied by I.O. inspected OPs, BUS HO & RESERVE LINE in afternoon. The Adjutant went round line during night. Capt H.S. WALKER being temporarily attached to Brigade Trench Warfare School as Assistant Commandant, 2nd Lt P.B.B. DOWRING took over command of C. Coy. Capt WILLIAMS took over duties of 2nd in Command / 2nd Lt TODD taking command of A Coy.	J.A.
	24.		Heavy firing heard in direction to S.E. 4.0 a.m. — 5.15. a.m. At 9.15. a.m. an enemy aeroplane was brought down in NO MANS LAND by our anti-aircraft guns. Hell to left of enemy craters. At 1.30 p.m. our TMs bombarded enemy front line with about 10 shells + again at 2.35. At 4.0. p.m. our artillery heavily bombarded enemy support + reserve lines in front of our position. About 4.30 p.m. our heavy guns began bombarding enemy	J.A.

Army Form C. 2118.

WAR DIARY
or
INTELLIGENCE SUMMARY.
(Erase heading not required.)

Instructions regarding War Diaries and Intelligence Summaries are contained in F. S. Regs., Part II. and the Staff Manual respectively. Title pages will be prepared in manuscript.

Place	Date	Hour	Summary of Events and Information	Remarks and references to Appendices
			Lines in front of Left Battalion. Enemy retaliated, Heavy firing continued till 8.0 pm At 2.15 pm enemy did some damage near Tp of P & O Trench with 4.2 shells. Some 77mm shells fell near R. line in BOIS CONFLUENT. At 5.30 pm enemy leaving bombarded our right sector with trenchmortars, TMs & fishtails, continuing till 6.10 pm. Telephone wire to HQ & Battery was cut & considerable damage done to front line Trench. 2nd LT BENNETT sent to BRASSERIE suffering from shell shock. Brig-Genl F.W. TOWSEY CMG inspected line during morning, & also the C.O. visited front line about same period.	
	25		Enemy patrol driven off by Lewis guns about 12.30 a.m. Shortly after 1 Sergt & 1 OR of wiring party wounded. C.O. visited line 1.0 – 5.30 a.m., & at 2.30 pm went to visit BRIGADIER & ARTILLERY GROUP COMMANDER. Patrol under 2nd LT BROWN went out 9.20 pm.	J.A.
	26		Quiet day. C.O. visited line 11.30 a.m. & 9.45 pm. TM bombardment of enemy first line 9.30 pm. Some retaliation on our R. front. Little damage.	J.A.
	27		Quiet day. Our Stokes guns & TMs fired about 30 rounds on enemy front at 4.0 pm. Enemy TMs replied with about 12 rounds near Sp of P & O Trench. No damage. Brig-Genl F.W. TOWSEY CMG visited Sector in morning. C.O. visited line in afternoon +	J.A.

WAR DIARY
or
INTELLIGENCE SUMMARY.
(Erase heading not required.)

Army Form C. 2118.

Instructions regarding War Diaries and Intelligence Summaries are contained in F. S. Regs., Part II. and the Staff Manual respectively. Title pages will be prepared in manuscript.

Place	Date	Hour	Summary of Events and Information	Remarks and references to Appendices
	28		Held conference of Coy Comm^{rs} at 4.0 p.m. Lt R.A.V. BREAREY reported at Batin HQ on arrival from Lewis Gun Course at Le Touquet.	J.A.
			Maj-Genl S.T.B. LAWFORD. C.B. visited line in morning & again in early afternoon. C.O. made tour of trenches in morning. Aircraft activity during day. At 2.0.p.m. bombardment of enemy front line with Stokes guns. He replied on O.11 & P.O. Trench with minenwerfers, TMs & Fighballs. A little damage done. 1 O.R. sent down with severe shell shock. 2nd Lt CLARK proceeded to join R.F.C. at HESDIN.	
	29		2nd Lt BENNETT returned from BRASSERIE to A Coy. Lt A.J. ROGERS reported from hospital. C.O. visited line at 3.0. am. Brig Genl F.W. TOWSEY. C.M.G. visited sector in morning. Quiet day.	J.A.
	30		Batin relieved in trenches by 20th Bn DURHAM LIGHT INFANTRY. Relief reported complete 1.30 pm. C.O. in afternoon visited our supporting Battery C. 187.	J.A.
	31		Lt Gent Sir T.L.N. MORLAND. KCB. KCMG. DSO came to Corps nailed Camp in morning, & also Col H.H. RATTRAY ADMS & Major L.N. THURSTON - DADMS. Lt Col. H.H. LEE. DSO. returned from leave during afternoon & resumed command of Batin. Lt A.V. BAKER rejoined Batin. A.B & C Coys on fatigues all day.	J.A.

Headquarters
122nd Infantry Bde.

Herewith original copy War Diary
for Battalion under my command for the
month of April 1917

[Stamp: 12th BATTALION, EAST SURREY REGIMENT. No... Date 1 May 1917]

[signature] Lieut Col
Comdg 12/Bn East Surrey Regt

WAR DIARY or INTELLIGENCE SUMMARY

Army Form C. 2118.

12 E Survey Regt
Vol 12
APRIL, 1917.

Place	Date	Hour	Summary of Events and Information	Remarks and references to Appendices
RENINGHELST	1		Church Parade in morning. Battn rest in afternoon. Capt R.A. McCULLOCH relinquished duties of Q.M.T., being evacuated sick.	J.A.
	2		Conference of C.O.s at Brigade HQ under Brig-Genl F.W. TOWSEY. C.M.G. at 10.0 a.m. Batta for Battn & parades under Coy arrangements with special reference to the attack. 2nd Lt R.W. GURRIN proceeded on duties with R.E.s.	J.A.
	3		Capt H.S. WALKER proceeded to STEENWOORDE on a 3-days course, 2nd Lt T.B.B. DOWLING taking command of C. Coy in his absence. The Adjt. Lt T.B. McWALTER proceeded on leave. 2nd Lt A.R. PUTTOCK returned from course. Conference of C.O.s at Brigade HQ at 5.0 p.m. Day Training in Camp. Heavy blizzard night of 2/3 & in morning.	J.A.
	4		Battn parade in morning before C.O. Major L.H. HICKSON, 2nd in command, evacuated sick with measles. Conference of officers at 2.0 p.m.	J.A.
	5		Battn relieved 20th Bn DURHAM LIGHT INFANTRY in trenches. Relief reported complete 1.50 p.m. Capt C.T. WILLIAMS took over duties of 2nd in Command, Lt J.A. ROGERS taking command of A. Coy. Heavy firing & raid to S. at 8.45 p.m. Enemy shelled our R. line & P&O Trench till 10.15 p.m. 4 O.R. killed & 1 wounded. From 11.0 p.m. — 11.25. our guns cut wire opposite our R. sector. Capt H.S. DOWNSHAW remained at Transport Lines, 2nd Lt W.G. ROBINSON taking our B. Coy.	J.A.

WAR DIARY
or
INTELLIGENCE SUMMARY.
(Erase heading not required.)

Army Form C. 2118.

Place	Date	Hour	Summary of Events and Information	Remarks and references to Appendices
	6 (GOOD FRIDAY)		Heavy artillery fire all day. HQ + R. Line shelled about midday, as well as other points in section. 4.0 – 4.20 p.m. T.M. bombardment on both sides. 1 OR killed, 1 wounded in morning. Brig-Gen. F.W. Towsey. C.M.G. visited line during morning. Capt. J.A.C. McCALMAN proceeded to WISQUES on Coy Comm[d]s course, 2/Lt H.P. BAILEY taking command of D. Coy. Capt. BINNEY, R.A.M.C. returned from leave, taking over duties from Capt. W. HARRISON, R.A.M.C. Patrol went out at 11.45 p.m. under Lt. A.V. BAKER.	J.A.
	7		Considerable artillery activity throughout day. Our guns bombarded enemy lines heavily at intervals in preparation for Dummy Raid in evening. Enemy retaliated on various points of our sector, doing some damage to trenches. At 7.50 p.m. one of our aeroplanes flying over our front line dropped green verey + all guns opened an intense bombardment. At the same time smoke bombs were discharged from our front line. Very heavy firing also began in direction of BLUFF where 47 E Div[n] was carrying out actual raid. Enemy retaliated heavily all over our sector. R. Lines, Q. Victoria St + Craters Lane suffered most, many places in these trenches being blown in. At 10.45 p.m. enemy blew a camouflet in Q. Victoria St Sap	J.A.

Army Form C. 2118.

WAR DIARY
or
INTELLIGENCE SUMMARY.
(Erase heading not required.)

Instructions regarding War Diaries and Intelligence Summaries are contained in F. S. Regs., Part II. and the Staff Manual respectively. Title pages will be prepared in manuscript.

Place	Date	Hour	Summary of Events and Information	Remarks and references to Appendices
			All was quiet by 11.0.p.m. Our casualties 1 OR killed, 5 wounded. C.O. visited line at 11.30 p.m. Capt H.S. Walker returned from course + resumed command of C. Coy on following day. 2nd Lt W.G. Robinson, R.N. Haine, + A. Hensley proceed on Divl Trench Warfare Course at Abeele. 2nd Lt F.J. Harding returned from Course Mortars at Terdeghem.	Appendix attached Divl Commdg letter. Ap. 12. J.'A.'
	8 (Easter Sunday)		Brigr Genl F.W. Towsey C.M.G. visited our line at 3.0. am. Quiet day. About midday + during night 8/9 enemy dropped a few 4.2. shells at intervals about Bus Ho − Q. Victoria St and Much aerial activity on both sides 2nd Lt F.A. Samuels proceed on Divl Gas Course. C.O. visited OPs in morning, Brigade HQ. in afternoon.	J.'A.'
	9		In the morning Majr Genl S.T.B. Lawford. C.B. Divl Commander + Brigr Genl Clemson visited the sector. Also Col. Clark, commg 32nd Battn Royal Fusiliers + other officers of 32nd R.F. preparing to taking over sector later. About 10.30 am. enemy fired Rifle Grenades + Trakads near Top of P & O Trench, + about 3.30. blew in front line in R. sector with Minenwerfers, killing 3 OR + wounding 1. It also blew COL. B.L. ANLEY in our lines at intervals during night.	J.'A.'
	10		Fairly quiet day. Some shelling of Fort + R. lines. At 7.0. pm. front line + Voormezeele Extension C.T. badly knocked with 5.9s. on bay of 0.23 known	J.'A.'

Army Form C. 2118.

WAR DIARY
or
INTELLIGENCE SUMMARY.
(Erase heading not required.)

Instructions regarding War Diaries and Intelligence Summaries are contained in F. S. Regs., Part II. and the Staff Manual respectively. Title pages will be prepared in manuscript.

Place	Date	Hour	Summary of Events and Information	Remarks and references to Appendices
			in. 3 OR killed 2 wounded. 1 OR killed wiring. Disturbed night - left front line suffered most.	
	11		Enemy artillery active during morning. Q.Victoria St & Crater Lane shelled in Afternoon. Quiet. C.O. into line early morning. HQ shelled about 5.0.a.m.	J.A.
	12		5.0.a.m. H.Q. shelled again. Batt'n relieved in trenches by 32nd Bn. Royal Fusiliers. Relief reports complete 2.43.pm.	J.A.
	13		Rest day for Batt'n. C.O. attended Conference at Brigade HQ 5.30.pm. Capt W. HAGEN returned from 41st Div'l HQ & assumed command of D. Coy. Lt T.B. McWALKER returned from leave & resumed duties of Adjutant.	J.A.
	14		Day's training in Camp. Gale.	J.A.
	15		Voluntary Church parade 10.0.a.m. 2nd Lt A.G. HOWETT returned from 122 Brigade HQ & was posted to B. Coy.	J.A.
	16		Day's training in Camp. In morning C.O. tested some officers in tactical schemes. Conference of officers under C.O. 5.0.pm. Batt'n went to Baths during day.	J.A.
	17		Major I.A. HICKSON returned from hospital. Stormy night. Capt C.T. WILLIAMS relinquished duties of 2nd in Command, handing over to Major HICKSON	J.A.

T2134. Wt. W708 – 776. 500000. 4/15. Sir J. C. & S.

WAR DIARY or INTELLIGENCE SUMMARY.

Army Form C. 2118.

(Erase heading not required.)

Instructions regarding War Diaries and Intelligence Summaries are contained in F.S. Regs., Part II. and the Staff Manual respectively. Title pages will be prepared in manuscript.

Place	Date	Hour	Summary of Events and Information	Remarks and references to Appendices
	18		& reassuming command of A. Coy. 2nd Lt S. LASENBY returned from Signalling course. C.O. inspected Coys practising new scheme of attack. Blizzard during day. Capt H.S. OPENSHAW returned from leave. Lt BREARY & 2nd Lts ASTON, TODD, & DOWLING were detailed to accompany 11th Bn Royal West Kent Regt, who proceeded to ST ELOI sector to take up trenches formerly occupied by us. 2nd Lt ASTON returned in the evening, the others on the following day. Battn mostly on working parties. Football match v. 18th RRRE in afternoon. Score 2–2. Snow & sleet. 2nd Lt A.M. ENGLAND joined Battn.	J.A.
	19		Day's Training. B & D Coys proceeded to MIC MAC CAMP (H 31 b central) A, C, & HQ Coys remained at ONTARIO CAMP. 2nd Lt V.L. CLIFT returned from leave. 2nd Lt L.H. JENNINGS joined Battn. 18/4/17.	J.A.
	20		2/Lt D. WALKER proceeded to GANSPETTE near ST OMER in charge of 122 Brigade Signalling Party. In evening enemy raid on 11th R.W.K.s in our old sector.	J.A.
	21		Route march for A & HQ Coys in morning. C.O. proceeded to RECQUES in N.W. of ST OMER, to reconnoitre future training ground, returning in evening.	J.A.
	22		Rest day of Battn. Football match. Battn v. 26th Battn R.F. Score 2–2. 2nd Lt S. LASENBY proceeded to 15th Bn HAMPSHIRE Regt as temp Signalling Officer	J.A.

WAR DIARY
or
INTELLIGENCE SUMMARY.
(Erase heading not required.)

Army Form C. 2118.

Instructions regarding War Diaries and Intelligence Summaries are contained in F. S. Regs., Part II. and the Staff Manual respectively. Title pages will be prepared in manuscript.

Place	Date	Hour	Summary of Events and Information	Remarks and references to Appendices
	23		At 11.0 a.m. 2 enemy aeroplanes flew low over our camp, but in spite of A.A. gunfire, escaped. Many aeroplanes over us again all evening. C.O. attended Conference at Brigade HQ. 5.0.&pm. Football match v. Br. Queens Royal West Surrey Regt. Result Lost. 1-0. Major L.H. HICKSON relinquished duties of 2nd in command & proceeded to take up command of 7 Bn. Royal West Kent Regt.	J.A.!
	24		Bn. D Coys returned from MICMAC to ONTARIO CAMP. Day occupied in preparation for departure to Brigade Training Area at RECQUES. CO held conference of officers at 2.0 p.m. & Brig. Gen. F.W. TOWSEY C.M.G. held address all officers of 123rd infantry Brigade at 5.0.pm. A large number of ORs on command rejoined Batn. 2nd Lt J.M. HUTCHISON evacuated sick. 10.0pm very heavy firing heard to WNW.	J.A.!
	25	9.0 10.0	Bn. (less Mess, 29 officers and 935 Men Rank and file marched sophie transport) from RENINGHELST to STEENVOORDE enroute to RECQUES. On having dinners and billeted by 2.0 P.M. the Divisional Commander Major General S.T.B. LANFORD, and Brigade Commander Brigadier General F.W. TOWSEY both inspected their highest admiration	

WAR DIARY
or
INTELLIGENCE SUMMARY.

(Erase heading not required.)

Army Form C. 2118.

APRIL 1917.

Place	Date	Hour	Summary of Events and Information	Remarks and references to Appendices
	25.		advancing of our Infantry forward and the general harrying of Orleans and rebels. 2nd Lieut J Nelson Intelligence Officer proceeded to Bezard on telephone	✓
	26.		Battalion acted at STEENVOORDE. Commanding Officer made enquiry killed.	✓
	27.		Battalion marched from STEENVOORDE to LEDERZEELE and WULVERDINGHE A good march of 15-17½ miles. Falling out nil. The march compares very favourably. Battalion provided the mounts and splendid condition and spirit. En route passed the Corps Commander who expressed great satisfaction.	✓
	28.		Battalion marches from LEDERZEELE and WULVERDINGHE to NORDAUSQUES LE PANNE and QUEMBERGHE and the traning and Church Parades. Training except for K1 Inspection noted.	✓ ✓
	29.		Parade Ammunition at 5.15am. In trucks for Ammunition Inspection.	✓
	30.		Slight Operation 9pm - under 2am Genume Series - bombing our to and forward up on hostile positions no news nearly perhaps any dawn	✓

Condyt/Sn Cost Surrey Regt
[signature] Lieut Col

MAY: 1917.

Army Form C. 2118.

WAR DIARY
INTELLIGENCE SUMMARY.
(Erase heading not required.)

E. Knapp
Major
Commanding 12th Bn. East Surrey Regt.

No 13

Place	Date	Hour	Summary of Events and Information	Remarks and references to Appendices
NORDAUSQUES	1–14		Battalion continued training for coming offensive in Training Area. 2nd Lt L.A. ROSSITER joined Battn. on May 3rd. On May 9th Battalion Sports were held. 2nd Lt F.I. HARDING proceeded on course to WISQUES on May 12th. Lt J.A. ROGERS proceeded on another course to WAREHAM on May 12th. 2nd Lt B.F. DODD proceeded on May 14th to take up duties of Adjutant at Divisional Trench Warfare School. Battalion left Training area & marched from NORDAUSQUES to LILLERS in WULVERDINGHE & LEDERZEELE.	J.A.
	15			
	16		Battn. resumed march & reached STEENVOORDE.	
	17		Battn. marched via POPERINGHE & RENINGHELST to MICMAC CAMP near DICKEBUSCH.	

Army Form C. 2118.

WAR DIARY
or
INTELLIGENCE SUMMARY.
(Erase heading not required.)

Instructions regarding War Diaries and Intelligence Summaries are contained in F.S. Regs., Part II. and the Staff Manual respectively. Title pages will be prepared in manuscript.

MAY 1917.

Place	Date	Hour	Summary of Events and Information	Remarks and references to Appendices
12TH BN EAST SURREY REGT	17		Battn marched, starting early, from STEENWOORDE viâ POPERINGHE & RENINGHELST to MICMAC NORTH CAMP [Sheet 28 NW. H.31.b.] Relief taken of 122 Brigade returning to their old camps at CHIPPEWA & ALBERTA. 1st Lt McWALTER was evacuated sick, & 2nd Lt R.A.V. BREAREY took on duties of Adjutant. 2nd Lt J. ASTON (I.O.) returned from leave.	J.A.
	18		C.O. attended Conference at Brigade HQ at 5.0. pm & at 8.30. held a meeting of Coy Commanders.	J.A.
	19		Battn relieved 20th DURHAM LIGHT INFANTRY in our original sector St ELOI (R) - Relief completed 11.35. am. Trenches found somewhat damaged owing to retaliation for DURHAMS' raids on two preceding nights; however the whole state of trenches improved. 2nd Lt PALK proceeded on leave. C.O. visited line 10. pm. Weather Sunny.	J.A.
	20		C.O. visited line 6.0. am. Very quiet day - much aerial activity in Summy weather. Air fight between about 6 of our & 6 of enemy planes 10. am. One of our brought down in enemy lines. Capt McCALMAN proceeded to BOULOGNE enroute for Rest camp. 2nd Lt HUTCHISON proceeded to join R.F.C. Between 7.15 & 8.30. pm enemy shelled our Rt line esp. BUS HOUSE with 5.9s. 1 OR wounded.	J.A.
	21		Brig-Gen F.W. TOWSEY CMG. visited sector the early morning. C.O. visited Brigade HQ.	J.A.

Army Form C. 2118.

WAR DIARY
or
INTELLIGENCE SUMMARY.
(Erase heading not required.)

Instructions regarding War Diaries and Intelligence Summaries are contained in F. S. Regs., Part II. and the Staff Manual respectively. Title pages will be prepared in manuscript.

Place	Date	Hour	Summary of Events and Information	Remarks and references to Appendices
	22		Foggy day. Our artillery continued bombarding enemy lines, esp. back areas & craters. In afternoon enemy artillery bombarded our lines at intervals with 7.7's & 5.9's. no damage. At 9.40.p.m. a heavy enemy bombardment opened on their section on our R & L, & continued till 10.35.p.m. A few shells were dropped in our lines. To the great regret of all ranks Lt Col H.H. Lee. D.S.O., feeling that his health, which had been poor for many months past, was not such as to enable him to undertake the strain of the coming offensive, gave up command of the battn. & proceeded to RENINGHELST. Major E. KNAPP. MIDDLESEX REGT. assumed command. Maj-Genl S.T.B. LAWFORD. C.B. visited the sector during the morning. Capt. H.S. WALKER proceeded to BOESCHEPE on short course of wireless. Rainy morning. clear afternoon. Our guns continued steady bombardment of various points in enemy lines. Very little retaliation. At 8.0.a.m. a man was seen in NO MANS LAND, (followed by a German). The German was shot by 2d LT PUTTOCK. Shelter crawled to our parapet & was pulled in. He turned out to be L.Cpl. FAULKNER, of 1/4 SOUTH LANCS	"A"

WAR DIARY or INTELLIGENCE SUMMARY

Army Form C. 2118.

Place	Date	Hour	Summary of Events and Information	Remarks and references to Appendices
	23		R.E.'s who were captured 4 days before in an enemy raid succeeded on our R. + had lived 2 days without food in shell-holes behind enemy front-line & got over in the night. At 5.15 pm one of our aeroplanes fell steeply nearly ground on our lines but righted her-self & drew over DEAD DOG (Bn HQ) & flew away westward. Our artillery continued shooting on + off all night on enemy lines & back areas. Quiet on our sector. C.O. visited line 4.0 – 6.0 p.m. Sunny day, bright wind. Aircraft visible 5 of our planes down 7 A.m. Our artillery continued bombardment of enemy lines. Little retaliation. Enemy fired two apparently no in very (a) condition, trains almost gone. C.O. went down to Div. HQ in RENING HEIST. Capt WALKIE returned from BOESCHEPE Center- -naire firing by our guns all night.	J.A.¹
	24		Bright weather. Our artillery firing at intervals all day, v.p. heavy shelling of enemy craters + front-line in O.2.C. 12.0 noon – 2.30 pm. Very slight retaliation 20 5.9 shells on Bos Confluent & 530. Air fight ensued 7.45 pm 4 of our planes v. 35 Huns. 2ⁿᵈ L.T. RAY BREARLY proceeded on leave, 2ⁿᵈ L.T. CLIFT to-day on duties of acting Adjutant. 10.30 pm heavy bombardment began on our R. Shelled after enemy began to bombard our sector with 5.9s + 77s on R. + 5.9s + futiles, minnenwerfer	J.A.¹

T.2134. W. W708–776. 50000. 4/15. Sir J. C. & S.

Army Form C. 2118.

WAR DIARY
or
INTELLIGENCE SUMMARY.
(Erase heading not required.)

Instructions regarding War Diaries and Intelligence Summaries are contained in F. S. Regs., Part II. and the Staff Manual respectively. Title pages will be prepared in manuscript.

Place	Date	Hour	Summary of Events and Information	Remarks and references to Appendices
	25		& shrapnel on our L. CRATER LANE damaged near front line - 2 ORs wounded. all week Eng 11.0 p.m. Intermittent bombardment of enemy back areas continued all night. C.O. visited line after 1.0 a.m.	J.A.
			Very sunny. Our artillery bombarded enemy line & back areas at intervals all day. Hardly any retaliation on our sector. Enemy parapets badly knocked in front line. Much aeroplane activity. C.O. visited line in afternoon. A patrol under 2ⁿᵈ Lt PUTTOCK attempted to enter enemy front line but found it too full of water, owing to raid on Craters at 1.30 a.m. by Battn on our Right - (18ᵗʰ KRR) Quiet night but for after 7.75 - 1 O.R. wounded	J.A.
	26		9 - 11.0 am area about S.14 shelled with 4.25 - no casualties but some damage near Nine Sap. Battn relieved by 23ʳᵈ Bn MIDDLESEX REGT. Relief complete 12.25 p.m. Battn marched back to ALBERTA Camp, RENINGHELST. Lt ROGERS returned from revolver course in England. Very hot.	
WHITSUNDAY	27		C.O. attended Conference of Battn Commanders at Brigade HQ. 9.30 a - went on Train to front in ARRAS sector. Most of Battn on working parties. Remainder attended Church Parade 11.0 p.m. 2ⁿᵈ Lt BROWN proceeded on course to POPERINGHE. 2ⁿᵈ Lt J. ASTON proceeded on	J.A.

WAR DIARY
or
INTELLIGENCE SUMMARY.
(Erase heading not required.)

Army Form C. 2118.

Place	Date	Hour	Summary of Events and Information	Remarks and references to Appendices
	28		Course to BOESCHEPE. 2nd Lt HEMSLEY ~~proceeded on course~~ to POPERINGHE. Lt A.V. BAKER appointed Capt. 2nd Lt TODD returned from Bombing Course. Battn on working parties.	
	29		Battn on working parties + baths.	J.A.
	30		Battn on working parties. Capt WILLIAMS 2nd in Command, proceeded to ARRAS Sector for a day's tour. C.O. attended Conference at Brigade HQ. 2nd Lt ASTON returned from BOESCHEPE. Our transport shelled out of MIC MAC camp during night & removed to CHIPPEWA.	J.A. J.A.
	31		Battn relieved 11th Bn Queen's ROYAL WEST SURREY Regt in G.H.Q line in front of SCOTTISH WOOD. Relief reported complete 2.15 p.m. Sunny day. Heavy bombardment of enemy lines still continuing. Enemy retaliation somewhat heavier on back areas with H.E. & gas shells during night.	J.A.

Headquarters
122nd Infantry Bde.

Herewith original copy War Diary for the month of June for the Batt'n under my command.

G Williams
Capt
Comdg 12/Bn East Surrey Reg't

WAR DIARY
of
INTELLIGENCE SUMMARY.
(Erase heading not required.)

Army Form C. 2118.

June 1972 E Surrey Regt

Instructions regarding War Diaries and Intelligence Summaries are contained in F. S. Regs., Part II. and the Staff Manual respectively. Title pages will be prepared in manuscript.

Place	Date	Hour	Summary of Events and Information	Remarks and references to Appendices
GHQ Farm between VOORMEZEELE & SPOILBANK WOOD	1		Weather fair. Our bombardment of enemy lines continued. Hot much retaliation by enemy except for counter-battery work. Enemy wire in particular, along his front opposite No 1 & No 2 Sub Sectors reported much damaged.	J.'A'.
			C.O. held conference of Coy Commanders & HQ officers 10.0–12.30 to explain details of raid & of coming offensive. Warm day. Continued bombardment of enemy lines. Raid on enemy front & support lines from 08a.48 to 02c.7.1d by party of 3 officers & 68 ORs of our battalion. Very successful. O.C. Operations Capt W. HAGEN; O.C. raid 2nd Lt A.G. HOWITT; O.C. 'A' party 2nd Lt H.S. TODD. Barrage began 9.45 pm. Raiding party entered enemy front line 10.0 pm & returned 10.30 pm. Trenches found demolished. The following were taken:– 2 UNTEROFFIZIERS & 5 ORs of 44 E.I.R. 2nd (EAST PRUSSIAN) Division, 1 MG, 1 Telephone, several rifles & some equipment. Our casualties 5 ORs slightly wounded. A dugout with a dozen men in who would not surrender was also bombed & the inmates probably killed. Our guns kept up heavy bombardment all night.	J.'A'. Ref. Map 28 S.W. 2 See Appendices I & 2
	3		Continued bombardment. Special practice barrage on enemy lines on Divisional front 3.0–3.30 pm. Warm day; very hot for the enemy. 2nd Lt H.S. TODD	J.'A'. 1st what

14.C

WAR DIARY
or
INTELLIGENCE SUMMARY.
(Erase heading not required.)

Army Form C. 2118.

Place	Date	Hour	Summary of Events and Information	Remarks and references to Appendices
	4		proceeded on leave home. 2ⁿᵈ Lt D.WALKER proceeded to RENINGHELST in connexion with his duties with Brigade HQ in the coming offensive. Heavy bombardment continued. Very slight retaliation. We learn from examination of prisoners taken on June 2 that enemy front & support lines & CTs are terribly damaged. Brig. Genl P.W.TOWSEY, C.M.G. visited the sector at midday. 2ⁿᵈ Lt F.B.B. DOWLING proceeded to no 2 Training Camp, ETAPLES, to relieve Lt C.N. PRIDHAM, who is returning to the Battn. The Battalion during this tour has been employed on working parties, chiefly at night. 1 OR wounded.	J.'A.'
CHIPPEWA CAMP	5		The Battalion was relieved at 8.0.a.m. by one company of the 26ᵗʰ Bn R.F., + marched out to CHIPPEWA CAMP A. (M.6.a.4.7). Coming out, the M.O., Capt. W.N.BINNEY, R.A.M.C. was badly wounded in the foot by a shell near SCOTTISH WOOD. The C.O. attended a Conference at Brigade HQ (MCMAC CAMP) at 4.30. 2ⁿᵈ Lt A.F. DODD + Capt J.A.C. McCALMAN returned from courses, + 2ⁿᵈ Lt W.J. PALK from leave. Bombardment continued becoming very heavy after 10.30.p.m.	J.'A.' Ref. Belgium + France 28.S.W.
	6		C.O. promoted to Lt Col. Conference of Coy Commanders 10.0. a.m. to settle final details of coming offensive. At 12.0. noon Inspection of Battn by Major Genl	J.'A.'

WAR DIARY
or
INTELLIGENCE SUMMARY.

(Erase heading not required.)

Army Form C. 2118.

Place	Date	Hour	Summary of Events and Information	Remarks and references to Appendices
			S.T.B. LAWFORD. C.B. commanding A.1st Div: accompanied by Brig.-Genl. F.W. TOWSEY. CMG. commanding 122 Brigade. Last preparations for attack. Capt H.H. PRENTISS. RAMC. joined Battn as M.O. 2nd Lt J. ASTON proceeded to HQ of 140 Inf Brigade at LOCK HOUSE as liaison Officer for the following day. The following was the List of Officers for the Attack. H.Q - C.O. Lt Col E. KNAPP. 2nd in Command. Capt H.S. WALKER. Adjt. 2nd Lt V.L. CLIFT. A.Coy. O.C. 2nd Lt W.G. ROBINSON B.Coy. O.C. Capt H.S. OPENSHAW " W.J. PALK 2nd Lt B.F. DODD " R.N. HAINE " A.G. HOWITT " A.W. ENGLAND " W.A. YANNER C.Coy. O.C. Lt J.A. ROGERS D.Coy. O.C. Capt A.V. BAKER " 2nd Lt L.W.B. RUSSELL 2nd Lt A.R. PUTTOCK " A. HEMSLEY " F.A. SAMUELS " L.A. ROSSITER The Battn moved off at 9.0 p.m. following the new overland route by MICMAC.	

Army Form C. 2118.

WAR DIARY
or
INTELLIGENCE SUMMARY.
(Erase heading not required.)

Instructions regarding War Diaries and Intelligence Summaries are contained in F.S. Regs., Part II. and the Staff Manual respectively. Title pages will be prepared in manuscript.

Place	Date	Hour	Summary of Events and Information	Remarks and references to Appendices
Assault on DAMMSTRASSE	7		CAMP N.E. of DICKEBUSCH & fence between ENGLISH & SCOTTISH WOODS to concentration area in front of OLD FRENCH TRENCH in I 32 d & I 33 c & d.	Appendix 3.
			A desultory bombardment was in progress as the troops moved up & important ately the enemy was dropping shells, as he had daily done of late at intervals about I 32 d & 3.3. close to the point where the R.A.P. & Batln dump had been sited. About eight 4.25 fell & caused some casualties in D. Coy., & in the rout, & was much congested with the troops of the 123 Brigade & those of our own. By 1.30 a.m. the Brigade was in position waiting for zero hour. The scheme of operations was as follows:- The II.nd Army was to capture the MESSINES RIDGE & the enormously strong enemy positions alongst, which had been held by the Germans for nearly 2½ years, along a front of 9 miles from Mt SORREL on the N. to LA DOUVE BROOK on the S. The objective of the 41st Division was the DAMMSTRASSE & the woods & positions beyond it up to BLACK LINE. The first objective (BLUE LINE) was to be taken by the 123 Bde, with 124 Bde acting on their R; the second (BLACK LINE) by the 122 Bde, the 124 Bde at the same time continuing forward with them	APPENDIX 4.

WAR DIARY
or
INTELLIGENCE SUMMARY.
(Erase heading not required.)

Army Form C. 2118.

Place	Date	Hour	Summary of Events and Information	Remarks and references to Appendices

On the L. of the 41st Divn was the 140 Bde (47th Divn) consisting of the 6th, 7th, 8th, 15th Battns, London Regt, whose objective was the ground immediately S. of the CANAL. On our R was the 19th Divn. After the capture & consolidation of the BLACK LINE, a period of about 8 hrs was to elapse, then the 24th Divn was to advance through us on to the GREEN LINE, the extreme objective. At Zero hour 20 mines were to be sprung along the entire Army front & the intense bombardment to begin.

At 3.10 a.m. the great mine, charged with over 50 tons of Amunal, which had been driven by the Canadian Tunnellers, was blown at St ELOI beneath Nos. 2, 3 & 4 craters, causing a terrific explosion, killing many of the enemy & demolishing the occupants of their lines. At the same instant every gun & howitzer opened intense fire on the enemy trenches & batteries. Under this fearful barrage the four assaulting waves went over (accompanied by Tanks). By 5.0.a.m. every position on the DAMMSTRASSE has been gained by the 123 Brigade, & a fair number of prisoners were coming back. There was hardly any resistance, except on our left at the WHITE CHATEAU, which caused some delay to the 140 Brigade.

WAR DIARY
or
INTELLIGENCE SUMMARY.
(Erase heading not required.)

Army Form C. 2118.

Place	Date	Hour	Summary of Events and Information	Remarks and references to Appendices
			At 5.10.a.m. the 122 Brigade moved forward under some hostile barrage & by 6.0 a.m. were in position on the DAHNSTRASSE, found in worse for the barrage. At 6.30. the worse moved up close under our barrage. At 6.50. this began to move forward by 50 yd leaps, & our men pressed on behind it, clearing the enemy dugouts & trenches in PHEASANT WOOD & DENYS WOOD & taking many prisoners, who were too demoralised to offer more than a very slight resistance. The C.O. established Batt. HQ in a shellhole in PHEASANT WOOD, using as a battle sign a piece of paper stuck on a twig, on which he sketched a DAGGER, the code name of the Battn. The BLACK LINE was occupied according to timetable by 7.15 a.m. Unfortunately, as the troops went forward in foot of the enemy's line in OBSCURE SUPPORT to by themselves in the Barrage appeared to drop back, & a good many casualties was thus caused by our own fire. The line was soon consolidated & & advance posts & 1 O.P. established by 8.30 a.m. when our contact aeroplane came over. The enemy continued to shell the area intermittently, with H.E., causing some casualties. Their bombardment now slackened,	Appendix 5

WAR DIARY
or
INTELLIGENCE SUMMARY.
(Erase heading not required.)

Army Form C. 2118.

Place	Date	Hour	Summary of Events and Information	Remarks and references to Appendices
			Though our guns still kept up a considerable shelling of the positions in the GREEN LINE area. Indeed, but for the barrage, our troops might have gone a good way further & captured some of the battle field guns. A battery was seen half left abandoned, but the gunners returned & fired their pieces away, moving at some 500 yds distance across our front. "B" Coy opened on them with Lewis guns & rifles, but without effect. 2ⁿᵈ Lᵗ D. WALKER, with 2ⁿᵈ Lᵗ L.H. JENNINGS, who was in charge of the Brigade Advanced Signal party, came up behind the troops & established a post at DAMMSTRASSE, doing excellent work in keeping up communications with Brigade HQ in VOORMEZEELE SWITCH Trench. Later 2ⁿᵈ Lᵗ R.W. GURRIN brought up a party with material for consolidation. At 3.10. pm opened an intense bombardment of the GREEN LINE, while the 24ᵗʰ DIVⁿ came up & through the positions we had won, passing on to the final objectives. By 5.0. pm there has all been gained. The enemy kept up an intermittent shelling of our positions during the evening & night, but did little damage. A thunderstorm broke about 6.0. pm, with a heavy shower of rain.	

Army Form C. 2118.

WAR DIARY
or
INTELLIGENCE SUMMARY.
(Erase heading not required.)

Place	Date	Hour	Summary of Events and Information	Remarks and references to Appendices
			The 12th Bn EAST SURREY REGT took 268 prisoners (44th I.R. 2nd Div. & 139 I.R. 24th Div., German IVth Army) 6 MGs & 2 Trench Mortars besides much smaller material. 6 officers were wounded - Capt BAKER, 2nd Lts ROBINSON, PALK, PUTTOCK, VANNER & ENGLAND. 23 ORs were killed, 160 wounded (of whom 7 died soon after) & 6 missing. Messages of congratulation were later received from the Corps Commander, the Divl General & the Brigadier General.

Thus on this glorious day the IInd Army drove the enemy out of positions, immensely strong by nature & every resource of military art, which he had occupied for 2½ years, from which he commanded observation of all our movements & preparations. At least 30,000 of his troops must have been put out of action, over 7300 prisoners were taken, 51 guns, 242 MGs, & a vast amount of other military stores & equipment. Our total casualties did not total 16000, & every objective was taken in 14 hours. At very few points was there serious resistance, & the two counterattacks the enemy attempted were dispersed with heavy losses by our artillery fire almost before they left | APPENDIX 6 |

Army Form C. 2118.

WAR DIARY
or
INTELLIGENCE SUMMARY.
(Erase heading not required.)

Place	Date	Hour	Summary of Events and Information	Remarks and references to Appendices
Their Trenches.			The wonderfully successful result of these operations was chiefly due to the vast preponderance of our Artillery, the concentration of which was 30% greater than any previously known. By this means the hostile trenches were pulverised for a fortnight with H.E., the wire destroyed, the guns silenced or shattered, the dugouts smashed in, & the troops demoralised. All this was made possible by the magnificent work of the R.F.C. The staff work too was admirable. In short, it was the cooperation of all arms of the service in harmonious working that effected this splendid victory, the most striking yet gained over the armed might of Germany.	

WAR DIARY
or
INTELLIGENCE SUMMARY.
(Erase heading not required.)

Army Form C. 2118.

Place	Date	Hour	Summary of Events and Information	Remarks and references to Appendices
	8		The 122 Brigade this morning was moved out of the positions it had won & went back to OLD FRENCH TRENCH where it remained till the night of Jan 12th. The 12th EAST SURREYS were relieved by the 7th Bn NORTHANTS REGT. Major Genl. S.T.B. LAWFORD C.B. & Brig-Genl F.W. Towsey. C.M.G. visited the Baton. Capts WILLIAMS, McCALMAN & HAGEN came up from Divl. Reinforcement Camp, & also Lt R.A. BREAREY from leave & 2nd Lt R.D. BROWN from sniping course. 2nd Lt J. ASTON returned from duties with 140 Inf. Brigade. The Battalion was occupied in salvage & clearance of the battlefield. A few 4.2s fell near the Bivouacs about 7.0.p.m — no casualties. Heavy firing about 10.p.m — enemy counterattack on our forward positions. Batteries were moving forward throughout the day. 1 R.F.A battery & 2 6pdr guns established close to B2. The following promotions in connexion with raid of June 2 were announced. 2nd Lt A.G. HOWITT - M.C. Sergt MADDISON D. Coy. Sergt HAYSTON C. Coy. } M.M. Corpl. COGHLAN D Coy. Pte. RICHARDSON B Coy.	J.A.

Army Form C. 2118.

WAR DIARY
or
INTELLIGENCE SUMMARY.
(Erase heading not required.)

Place	Date	Hour	Summary of Events and Information	Remarks and references to Appendices
	9		Battn still resting + on Salvage duties. Roads were under construction up to DAMMSTRASSE, + batteries moving forward. Desultory bombardment at intervals. A few shells again fell by our lines about 7.0 pm. C.O. attended conference at Bde HQ at 2.30 pm. Conference of Coy Commanders at 10.30 am. In the afternoon Coy Commanders & some other officers went up to inspect position occupied by 7th Bn LONDON Regt in O.2) German line with a view to coming relief. Reorganisation of Battn proceeds. Lt C.N. PRIDHAM rejoined Battn.	J.A.
	10			
	11		Reorganisation continued. 2nd Lt J. ASTON visited our new front line in OPAL RESERVE + WHITE CHATEAU with Bde I.O. 2nd Lt R.W. GURRIN proceeded to Xth Corps Infantry School. Great heat still continuing.	J.A.
	12		Conference of Coy Commanders 2.30 pm. At 11.0 pm. Battn moved off to occupy new position in OAK SUPPORT & OAK TRENCH (O4 a & c), relieving 7- Bn. LONDON Regt. Bn H.Q. moved to Sap in CANAL Bank at O3 b 9.9. Relief reported complete 3.30 am 13/6/17.	J.A.
	13		Battn in support of 16th Bn KRRC + 11th Bn R.W.Ks. Quiet day. Enemy attempted unsuccessful counterattack on N. of CANAL. Lt R.A. BREAREY pro-	J.A.

WAR DIARY
or
INTELLIGENCE SUMMARY.
(Erase heading not required.)

Army Form C. 2118.

Place	Date	Hour	Summary of Events and Information	Remarks and references to Appendices
	14		-ceeded to POPERINGHE with 1 Sergt & 10 men for execution of a private of D. Coy for desertion. 2⁰ Lt ASTON & 28 ORs & HQ Coy was sent to TRANSPORT lines at HALLEBAST (N 3 a central). 2⁰ Lt F.J. HARDING arrived at Transport from WISQUES. Quiet day. At 7.30 p.m. frontline Battn carried out a minor operation driving the enemy out of OLIVE & OPTIC TRENCHES & OBLIQUE ROW, inflicting considerable loss & suffering some. Our battn did not move. Casualties from shellfire 1 OR killed, 7 wounded. Lt BREARY returned to Bn HQ. 2/Lt A. HEMSLEY proceeded to IInd Army Signal School.	J.A.
	15		Quiet day. Some shelling. Enemy counterattack on our new front line positions in evening, apparently on a large scale. Our Artillery frustrated this by barrage, & only a small bombing attack materialised, which was easily repulsed. A 5.9 fell at entrance to HQ Sap, & a dump nearby was also blown up. Casualties 5 ORs wounded (1 of whom died later).	J.A.
	16		Our new transport Camp at HALLEBAST was shelled, & transport forced to move back again to CHIPPEWA CAMP. 2/Lt J. ASTON with 5 observers returned to Bn. At 10.0 p.m. Battn moved up & relieved 11th Bn. ROYAL WEST KENT Regt. in front	J.A.

WAR DIARY
or
INTELLIGENCE SUMMARY.
(Erase heading not required.)

Army Form C. 2118.

Place	Date	Hour	Summary of Events and Information	Remarks and references to Appendices
Support lines.	17		HQ were established in ex enemy strong point in cellars of WHITE CHATEAU. Coys were disposed as follows — D Coy in OBLIQUE ROW, B Coy in OPTIC TRENCH O5d0202 — O5d46, including Bombing Post + Block established in OBLIQUE TRENCH, which was still in The enemy's hands. C Coy were in OPAL RESERVE O5c22.12 — O5c42.5, D Coy from O5c42.5 — O5c67. These Trenches were still much damaged but were gradually strengthened, & a CT run forward to front line. Relief reported complete 3.0 am 17/6/17. Casualties 1 OR killed, 6 wounded. Enemy kept up considerable shelling of our area. At 11.0 am a shell entered WHITE CHATEAU, wounding 3 ORs. Enemy continued to shell OBLIQUE TRENCH + OPTIC SUPPORT & various shelters to our front with small parties, which were strengthened at night. Enemy aeroplanes were constantly over us in large numbers. Our artillery continued bombardment of enemy areas. The Brigadier visits the line in the early morning, + the CO. at noon. At dusk a bombing raid was made on OBLIQUE TRENCH, but was at once observed + the party had to return, with 2nd Lt R.D. BROWN wounded, 1 OR killed + 1 wounded. 2nd Lt HSTEDD returned from leave. 2nd Lt F.R. MATTHEWS proceeded on leave, + Lt R.A. BREARY took	Appendix 7.

WAR DIARY
or
INTELLIGENCE SUMMARY.
(Erase heading not required.)

Army Form C. 2118.

Place	Date	Hour	Summary of Events and Information	Remarks and references to Appendices
	18		Over duties of Transport Officer. Casualties for day. 1 off. wounded. 2 ORs killed, 8 ORs wounded.	JA
(Battle of WATERLOO)			WHITE CHATEAU + support lines were shelled from about 12.30 am onwards. Enemy aeroplanes very active again on our lines. They were after casualties. Enemy aeroplanes very active again early morning flying very low over our front line, specially during in early morning. A special fighting squadron about noon at firing own with MGs. engaged enemy bringing down two of their machines. WHITE CHATEAU was heavily shelled from 9.45 am – 12.45 pm making egress + ingress difficult. D. Coy lines shelled in evening – Capt. W. HAGEN wounded in ankle. At 4.0 pm our lines were a heavy shower of rain with thunder, which flooded the trenches with mud. 2nd Lt L.A. ROSSITER proceeded on course to WISQUES. Casualties for day - 1 Officer wounded. 2 ORs killed, 6 ORs wounded.	
	19		Shelling continued during night + morning. Enemy aeroplanes again very active in early morning. The trenches were in a very bad state all day after the rain. Considerable shelling with 7.7s during afternoon. The Battn. was relieved at night by 20th Bn DURHAM LIGHT INFANTRY – 123 Bde. Reliefs reported	JA

T.J.134. Wt. W708–776. 500000. 4/15. Sir J. C. & S.

WAR DIARY or INTELLIGENCE SUMMARY

Army Form C. 2118.

Place	Date	Hour	Summary of Events and Information	Remarks and references to Appendices
VOORMEZEELE	20		Complete 3.35 am 20/6/17. dark night. Casualties 1 OR wounded. Letter received from Mayor of Bermondsey. Batln in VOORMEZEELE SWITCH TRENCH & MIDDLESEX LANE, HQ in VICTORIA ST close to VOORMEZEELE. 2nd LT F.J. HARDING returned to Batln with rest of HQ Coy. New QM joined Batln, Hon LT & QM W.W. EASTER — late RSM 23rd Bn MIDDX REGT. The Brigade C of E Chaplain — Capt C.H. SCHOOLING, C.F. unfortunately killed by a large shell in DICKEBUSCH. Rain fell during day. Weather much cooler after intense heat, which lasted since end of April. 2 Observation Balloons brought down by enemy planes 5.0 pm. Capt H.S. WALKER proceeded on leave.	Appendix 8 J.A.
	21		CO left conference at HQ at 10.0.am. Batln reorganized. Rain again. Much canal activity. Batln on working parties at night. Some shelling. Working parties. Rainy day.	J.A.K
	22		Some working parties. Enemy shelling of VOORMEZEELE Area continued. Lt Col E. KNATP. C.O. proceeded on leave. 2nd Lt R.F. DODD appointed Assistant Adjutant. Capt C.T. WILLIAMS assumed command of Batln. 4 observation Balloons brought down by enemy aeroplanes. More enemy shelling of our area.	J.A.
	23		Lt. Capt. 11 RWK acting Brig-Genl. holds our lines.	J.A.

Army Form C. 2118.

WAR DIARY
or
INTELLIGENCE SUMMARY.
(Erase heading not required.)

Instructions regarding War Diaries and Intelligence Summaries are contained in F. S. Regs., Part II. and the Staff Manual respectively. Title pages will be prepared in manuscript.

Place	Date	Hour	Summary of Events and Information	Remarks and references to Appendices
	24		Brigade Churchparade - C of E - near Brigade HQ. - EIZENWALLE CHATEAU. Intermittent shelling by enemy round VOORMEZEELE. 2nd Lt R.M. HAINE proceeded with Wiring party to BERTHEN. 1 Observation balloon brought down by enemy. Working parties.	J.A.
	25		Battn again on wiring parties. 2nd Lt J.A. ROGERS went down to 22nd LONDON Regt in evening to take over camp. - Enemy shelling continued. 3 O.R.s wounded in D Coy.	J.A.
by DICKEBUSCH LAKE	26		Battn relieved 22nd Battn LONDON REGT in dugouts in banks of DICKEBUSCH LAKE - (H 28 d central) for working duties during several days - Col. Cope, acting Brig. Genl, visited camp. - Aerial activity.	J.A.
	27		Battn on working parties - 2 Observation Balloons brought down closely by enemy aeroplanes in afternoon.	J.A.
	28		122 BRIGADE moved for rest to BERTHEN area, but 12th Bn EAST SURREYS & 15th Bn HAMP-SHIRE REGT remained in reserve for working parties. Capt. J.A. Mc CALMAN proceeded to IInd ARMY School of Musketry to witness platoon attack. Heavy thunderstorm rain 8.30 p.m.	J.A.
	29		Battn on working parties.	J.A.
	30		Battn on working parties. Heavy rain. The following awards for gallant	J.A.

WAR DIARY
or
INTELLIGENCE SUMMARY.
(Erase heading not required.)

Army Form C. 2118.

Place	Date	Hour	Summary of Events and Information	Remarks and references to Appendices
			conduct in the assault of June 7 were announced:—	
			Cpl. W. Mallett — C. Coy ⎫	
			L/Cpl. R. Collins — D. Coy ⎪	
			L/Cpl. J. Dare — C. Coy ⎬ Military Medal.	
			Pte. A. Pegg — A. Coy ⎪	
			" A. Floyd — B. Coy ⎪	
			" W.J. Thompson — C. Coy ⎪	
			" W. Southwood — C. Coy ⎪	
			" W.J. Varrow — D. Coy ⎭	
			During the month 6 ORs arrived on drafts.	
			Chhious Capt.	
			Comdg. 12/En East Surrey Regt	

Army Form C.2118

12E Surrey Rft
N00/5

a.D. 15.C
8chst

WAR DIARY
or
INTELLIGENCE SUMMARY.
(Erase heading not required.)

JULY: 1917:

Instructions regarding War Diaries and Intelligence Summaries are contained in F.S. Regs., Part II. and the Staff Manual respectively. Title pages will be prepared in manuscript.

Place	Date	Hour	Summary of Events and Information	Remarks and references to Appendices
DICKEBUSCH LAKE	1		Battn. on working parties. Major H.deC. BLAKENEY would there over command of Battn.	J.A.
			2nd Lt. MATTHEWS returned from leave & resumed duties of Transport Officer. LT.R.A.V. BREARLEY returned to Battn. & assumed command of D Coy. 1 O.R. wounded on working party.	J.A.
	2		Fine day. Battn. on working parties	J.A.
Near WIERSTRAAT	3		Battn. moved in morning to new camp. H.Q. at N10 a 3.8., ABC Coys at N3 b 2.4, D Coy at BURGOMASTERS FM. Major C.C. CLIFTON joined Battn, taking duties of 2nd in command.	J.A.
	4		Battn. on working parties. H.M. The KING passed in car at 8.30 am on way to visit line	J.A.
	5		Battn. on working parties. Capt. C.T. WILLIAMS proceeded on C.O's Course to ALDERSHOT.	J.A.
ROUKLOSHILLE	6		Battn. left for Training area at 9.0 am, marching via HALLEBAST, LA CLYTTE, LOCRE & BAILLEUL to ROUKOSHILLE, which was reached at 2.15 p.m. H.Q. established at farm at R.31.d.4.1. 2nd Lt HAINE rejoined Battn. Air raid by enemy planes during night on BAILLEUL.	J.A.
	7		Battn. resting. Battn. Brig-Genl. F.W. TOWSEY. C.M.G. visited camp. Severe Thunder-storm with heavy rain during night. New Draft arrived.	J.A.
	8		Church parade at Bde HQ 11.0 am. interrupted by heavy rain. Battn. resting	J.A.
	9		Training began. Brig-Genl F.W. TOWSEY. C.M.G. visited camp during morning-	

WAR DIARY
or
INTELLIGENCE SUMMARY.
(Erase heading not required.)

Army Form C. 2118.

Place	Date	Hour	Summary of Events and Information	Remarks and references to Appendices
	14		C.S.M. MADDISON. M.M.	
			Sergt. MAYSTON M.M.	
			Cpl COGHLAN M.M	
			Pte RICHARDSON M.M.	
			Pte VARROW M.M.	
			Pte THOMPSON M.M.	
			Sergt LATIMORE Mentioned in despatches	
			Sergt BURGESS Mentioned in despatches	
			Bath Route March 2.0. p.m. The CRUMPS 41st Divisional Concert Party gave an entertainment to the Battn at 6.30. p.m.	
			The Divl Commander gave a garden party at Div HQ, BERTHEN, to all officers of the 41st Divn. The Battn beat the 18th Bn KRRC 3 goals — 2.	J.'A'
			Officers' Promotions from London Gazette — 12th July.	
			Capt C.T. WILLIAMS (Spec Res) to be Temp. Major.	
			Temp Sec Lt D. WALKER to be Temp. Lt	
			Temp Sec Lt V.L. CLIFT to be Temp. Lt	

Army Form C. 2118.

WAR DIARY
or
INTELLIGENCE SUMMARY.
(Erase heading not required.)

Instructions regarding War Diaries and Intelligence Summaries are contained in F.S. Regs., Part II. and the Staff Manual respectively. Title pages will be prepared in manuscript.

Place	Date	Hour	Summary of Events and Information	Remarks and references to Appendices
	10		Batln Training. Lt R.A.V. Breary & Hon Lt & Qr W.W. Easter evacuated sick. The following awards for the operations on July 7th were announced - Lt Col E. Knapp. D.S.O. 2nd Lt F.A. Samuels. M.C. C.S.M. Hill - B. Coy. D.C.M. 2nd Lt H.P. Bailey - (T.M.B.) M.C. 2nd Lt F.A. Samuels proceeded on leave.	J.A:
	11		Batln on Musketry & General Training. Baths.	J.A:
	12		Batln Parade 11.0 a.m. - General training during day. Inter-Coy Football Competition won by C. Coy. - Brig-Genl P.W. Towsey C.M.G. visited Camp during morning. Bailleul shelled about noon, causing casualties to civil population.	J.A:
	13		Inspection of Batln 9.20 a.m. by Major Genl S.T.B. Lawford. C.B. comm'g 41st Division, accompanied by Brig-Genl F.W. Towsey C.M.G. comm'g 122 Inf. Brigade. After the inspection + some exercises the following decorations were presented - 2nd Lt A.G. Howett. M.C. C.S.M. Hill. D.C.M. M.M.	J.A:

WAR DIARY
or
INTELLIGENCE SUMMARY.
(Erase heading not required.)

Army Form C. 2118.

Place	Date	Hour	Summary of Events and Information	Remarks and references to Appendices
	15		Temp. Sec. Lt. A.G. HOWETT tbc Temp Capt. 2nd Lt R.N. HAINE proceeded to join 122nd TMB for Temporary attachment. 2nd Lt R.W. GURRIN returned from course. 2nd Lt C.R. HAYNES joined the Batln. Inter--Coy football competition won by C. Coy. Capt A.G. HOWETT. M.C. assumed command of D. Coy.	J.A.
	16		Batln. Church parade 9.30 a.m. Rest day.	J.A.
			Batln. in training. Batln. beat 11th ROYAL WEST KENT Regt. 2-1 winning Brigade Inter-Batln. Competition. 2nd Lt F.J. HARDING proceeded on course to 2nd Army Signalling School.	J.A.
	17		Batln. in training. 2nd Lt W.J. PALK M.C. returned from Hospital. Brig-Genl. F.W. TOWSEY. C.M.G. visited camp during morning. Major H. DEC. BLAKENEY. C.O. held conference of Company Commanders at Batln HQ on coming offensive at 11.0. a.m. Lt C.N. PRIDHAM resumed command of B. Coy. 2nd Lt BEARD evacuated sick.	J.A.
	18		Capt H.S. OPENSHAW proceeded on leave. B. Coy proceeded to RIDGE WOOD for attachment to 228 Field Coy. R.E. Major C.C. CLIFTON returned sick to ENGLAND. Capt A.W. PUTTICK.M.C. Royal West Kent Regt. assumed duties of 2nd in Command. Batln in Training Route March 2.0.pm - 5.0.pm.	J.A.

Army Form C. 2118.

WAR DIARY
or
INTELLIGENCE SUMMARY.
(Erase heading not required.)

Instructions regarding War Diaries and Intelligence Summaries are contained in F. S. Regs., Part II. and the Staff Manual respectively. Title pages will be prepared in manuscript.

Place	Date	Hour	Summary of Events and Information	Remarks and references to Appendices
	19		Major H. De C. BLAKENEY. proceeded on leave. Major R. PENNELL. K.R.R.C. assumed duties of C.O. Batln Sports were held during the afternoon. 2nd Lt E. AUCUTT joined the Batln	J.A.
	20		C.O. held conference of Batln officers at HQ. 9.30 am. Capt H.H. Prentice. R.A.M.C. evacuated sick. Capt R. HERDMAN. RAMC. Took over duties of M.O. Batln in training inspection by C.O. 2.0. pm. when the following were presented with cards from the G.O. Comm'g 41st Divn in recognition of services on June 7th :— Capt H.S. WALKER Capt A.G. HOWETT. M.C. Lt V.L. Clip 2nd Lt A.W. ENGLAND Sergt HAMBLETON. D Coy Lance Sergt FERNEY B Coy L. Cpl BARTLETT D Coy L. Cpl LYNFORD C Coy	J.A.
	21		2. O Rs of B Coy wounded in trenches. Batln in training. C.O. attended Conference at Brigade HQ in morning. 3 ORs of B Coy wounded	J.A.

Army Form C. 2118.

WAR DIARY
or
INTELLIGENCE SUMMARY.
(Erase heading not required.)

Instructions regarding War Diaries and Intelligence Summaries are contained in F. S. Regs., Part II. and the Staff Manual respectively. Title pages will be prepared in manuscript.

Place	Date	Hour	Summary of Events and Information	Remarks and references to Appendices
	22		Battn. Church Parade 9.30.a.m. Conference of Coy Commanders at HQ 10.30.a.m. 1 O.R. wounded (attached to 228 Field Coy).	J.A.
WOOD CAMP.	23		Battn. moved from LA ROUKSHILLE at 8.0.a.m via BERTHEN & WESTOUTRE to WOOD CAMP (M 5 d central). 2nd Lt. Astin went up to LOCK HOUSE to reconnoitre position to be occupied by Battn. next day. 1 O.R. wounded.	R.B. for J.A.
LOCK HOUSE	24		Conference of Coy Commanders at 9.15 a.m. Battn. moved up to Lock House area - by Coys. (Battn. 500 strong) - Battn. strength - remainder left in WOOD CAMP. Disposition H.Q. & C. Coy. LOCK HOUSE (O.3.C.2.8.) A Coy Canal end of ECLUSE TRENCH. & B Coy in trenches at O.4.a.18. D Coy in our old R line at O.1.d.9.3. Our Artillery continued bombardment of ENEMY lines. ENEMY guns quieter than late during the day, though still a considerable number of shells or batteries in our area. 1 O.R. wounded	R.B. for J.A.
	25		Some evening parties. Continued bombardment by our guns at intervals, night & day. Enemy reply not heavy. Capt. Walker & 2nd Lt. Astin reconnoitred forward position in afternoon. 1 O.R. wounded.	R.B. for J.A.
	26		Continued intermittent bombardment. Heavy shelling by enemy of WHITE CHATEAU & forward area. - C.R., Capt. Walker & M.O. went up to reconnoitre in morning. 2nd Lts. Todd, Haynes, Alcott & Sanders took reserves up to reconnoitre the position for their respective Coys. for Y-Z night. Conference of Officers H.Q. dugout 6 p.m.	R.B. for J.A.

WAR DIARY or INTELLIGENCE SUMMARY.

(Erase heading not required.)

Army Form C. 2118.

Place	Date	Hour	Summary of Events and Information	Remarks and references to Appendices
	27		2nd Lt ASTON seriously wounded near OPTIC TRENCH. 2nd Lt STENNING reported died of wounds. Battn. engaged chiefly on working parties. Casualties 2 O.R. wounded (accidentally)	L.R.
	28		Artillery duel continued. Area near CANAL shelled heavily by ENEMY during evening. 2nd Lt ROSSITER re-joined Battn from Course at WISQUES and assumed duties of Intelligence Officer. 2nd Lt PACK (Sick) proceeded to transport lines. LOCK HOUSE area received several gas shells during the night. Casualties = nil.	L.R.
	29		Continued artillery duel. Heavy enemy shelling of our back areas in the neighbourhood of SPOILBANK. Thunder storm during the morning which made observation difficult throughout the day. Orders received for BATTN. to move to advanced position next day. Casualties = nil.	L.R.
	30.		Battn. moved to advanced position – H.Q. leaving LOCK HOUSE during the morning. Companies moved up to assembly area leaving old position at 11 p.m. Our artillery was active throughout the day on enemys forward & back areas. The enemy shelled both banks of the CANAL in neighbourhood of IRON BRIDGE intermittently during afternoon & evening. The C.O. + 2 Lt. ROSSITER reconnoitred our enemy area during the evening. Casualties – 1	L.R.
IRON BRIDGE	31		At 3.50 a.m. our artillery barrage opened a BRIGADE attack on HOLLEBEKE commenced. The Battn. remained in trenches allotted – OPAL RESERVE, NEW SUPPORT LINE, OBLIQUE	L.R.

WAR DIARY
or
INTELLIGENCE SUMMARY.

Army Form C. 2118.

Place	Date	Hour	Summary of Events and Information	Remarks and references to Appendices
	31		Rem # 1 Coy in O.G.1. The Batt. was practically employed throughout the day on carrying parties up to the advancing troops. At 4 p.m. "B" Coy under Capt HOYITT moved forward in attack enemy troops which was still holding out in HOLLEBEKE and was successful in gaining his objective & establishing a line in front of HOLLEBEKE. Major BLAKENEY and Capt. OPPENSHAW report from leave yesterday & one with the TRANSPORT LINES. Total PRISONERS passing through Collecting Station 64, including 4 officers. Casualties reported - 7. (misging).	L.R.

SECRET   Copy. No. 1.

12th Bn. East Surrey Regt.
OPERATION ORDER No. 104.
Ref. Map Sheets, HAZEBROUCK 5A, 27 S.E., and 28 S.W.

1. The 12th Battn. East Surrey Regt. will move to the WESTOUTRE AREA tomorrow 23rd inst. Route :- PIEBROUCK - BERTHEN, - WESTOUTRE. The Battn will occupy WOOD CAMP at M.5.d.central.

2. The vacated Camps will be taken over by a Unit of the 69th Infantry Bde on the 23rd inst. Receipts for all Tents, Bivouacs, Stores etc. will be obtained and forwarded to Orderly Room as soon as possible.

3. O.C.Companies are responsible that the Camp and surroundings are left perfectly clean. A certificate to this effect will be forwarded to the Orderly Room.

4. All Packs, which must be clearly marked with the owners number, name and company, will be stacked near the road outside Company Billets by 6 a.m. These will be conveyed to the new Camp by Motor Lorry.

    Officers Valises, Mess Baskets, and other stores will be stacked outside E Company Billets by 7 a.m. sharp. These will be collected, commencing at "C" Company at this hour.

    The Maltese Cart will be outside the Medical Inspection Room by 7 a.m.

    Lewis Gun Limbers will be sent to Companies by 6 p.m. tonight. They will be loaded and returned to Transport Lines.

5. Water Bottles will be filled overnight.

6. The Battn. will parade in column of route in three's on the ROUKLOSHILLE - NOOTE BOOM road facing East, ready to move off by 8 a.m, the head of the column to be at cross roads R.34.c.3.4.

7. Order of march :- H.Q., "A", "C", "D". Transport and Baggage Wagons will follow in rear of the Battn.

8. Dress :- Fighting Order.

9. An interval of 200 Yards between "A" and "C" Coys will be maintained after moving off from the starting point. The normal clock hour halts will be observed.

10. Watches will be synchronised before moving off.

11. Rear Party, consisting of 1 C.Q.M.S. & 2 men per Company, (1 N.C.O. & 2 men from H.Q. Coy) under Lieut. Rogers will take charge of all stores left behind, and will obtain receipts as required under para. 2 above.

12. ACKNOWLEDGE.

Issued at ....3.p.m   (sd)   V.L.Clift.   Lieut. & A/Adjt.
Date. 22nd July 1917.

    Copy No.1.   Filed.
    "   2.   C.O.
    "   3.   2nd in command.   Copy No. 8.   Transport Offr.
    "   4.   O.C. "A" Coy.   Copy No. 9.   R.Q.M.S.
    "   5.   O.C. "B" Coy.   Copy No.10.   Medical Offr.
    "   6.   O.C. "C" Coy.   Copy No.11.   Signalling Offr.
    "   7.   O.C. "D" Coy.   Copy No.12.   Intelligence Offr.
                                                 Copy No.13.   R.S.M.

SECRET.   Copy No......

12th Bn East Surrey Regt.
OPERATION ORDER No.105.
Refce. Map. Sheet 28 S.W.
@@@@@@@@@@@@@@@@@@@@@@@@@@@@@@@@

1. The 12th Battn. East Surrey Regt. will relieve the 8th Battn. London Regt. in Support to the Right Sub-Sector, to-morrow, Tuesday 24th inst.

2. Order of Relief will be as follows:-
B Coy, A Coy, H.Q. Coy, C Coy, D Coy.

3. Parade. B Coy will march from Ridge Wood in time for the leading platoon to arrive at O.I.a.3.0½ at 4.30 p.m. where they will be met by a guide.
The remaining Companies will parade on their own grounds and march off as follows:
- A Coy.   2.10 p.m.
- H.Q. Coy. 2.25 p.m.
- C Coy.   2.40 p.m.
- D Coy.   2.55 p.m.

Movement will be by platoons at 500 yards interval.
Dress: Fighting Order. Waterbottles will be filled before moving off.
Route: WOOD CAMP - CROSS ROADS M.5.a.2.2. - OVERLAND TRACK to MICMAC CAMP - HALLEBAST CORNER - N.3.d.5.9. - RIDGE WOOD to O.I.a.3.0½.

4. Disposition.
- Battn. H.Q.   LOCK HOUSE.
- A Coy.   ECLUSE TRENCH (I.32.a.)
- B Coy.   OLD BRITISH FRONT LINE from OAK DUMP to NORFOLK BANK.
- C Coy.   DUGOUTS IN LOCK HOUSE BANK
- D Coy.   BOIS CONFLUENT and OLD FRENCH TRENCH from O.I.d.0.6. to O.2.a.0.I.

5. Guides. One Guide per Company will be stationed at O.I.a.3.0½ by 4.30 p.m.

6. Trench Stores. All Maps, Aeroplane Photographs and Trench Stores will be taken over by ingoing Companies and receipts forwarded to Battn. H.Q.

7. Baggage. All Packs will be stacked near Battn. H.Q. Guard by II.0 a.m.
Officers Valises, Mess Baskets and Company Stores will be stacked in the same place by 2.0 p.m.

8. Companies will report completion of relief by B.A.B. Code, No.3.

9. Marching Out States will be rendered to Orderly Room by 10.0 a.m. to-morrow.

10. ACKNOWLEDGE.

(Sd) V.L.Clift. Lieut & A/Adjt.

Issued at ....m
23rd July 1917.

Copy No.I Filed.   Copy No.2 C.O.   Copy No.3. 2nd in Commd.
--   4 O.C. "A".   --   5 O.C. "B"   -- No.6. O.C. "C"
--   7. O.C. "D"   --   8 Transport Officer.
--   9. R.Q.M.S.   --   10 Medical Officer.
--   II Sig. Offr.   Copy No.12 Int. Offr. Copy No.13 R.S.M.

SECRET.   Copy No. 1

12th BN. EAST SURREY REGT.

OPERATION ORDER. NO. 106.
                                                 28.7.17.
ASSEMBLY.

1. The 12th Bn East Surrey Regt. will assemble on 'Y/Z' night in accordance with the following instructions. All Companies will be in their Assembly Areas by Zero minus One Hour.

2. Battalion Headquarters will be established by 12 noon on 'Y' Day at
    O.4.b.I.4.

3. Battalion Headquarters will be marked by Code Name, 'DAGGER', painted on a canvas screen in large letters.

4. Completion of Assembly will be reported to Battn. H.Q.

5. The Battalion will assemble in the first instance as follows:-
    A, C & D Companies in OLD GERMAN FRONT LINE, from O.3.b.7.0½ to the CANAL. A Coy on the right, D Coy on the left.
    B Coy will remain in OLD BRITISH FRONT LINE.
    The above assembly will be carried out in the following order: "C", "A", "D" Companies. Head of "C" Coy will cross OLD BRITISH FRONT LINE at II p.m.

6. From the above positions Companies will move to the following positions in time to be assembled in them by Zero minus One Hour:-
    "A" Coy - OPAL RESERVE.
    "B" Coy - OLD GERMAN FRONT LINE.
    "C" Coy - New Support Trench, in front of OPAL RESERVE
    "D" Coy - OBLIQUE ROW.

7. ACKNOWLEDGE.

                                    V. L. Clift,
                                    Lieut & A/Adjutant.

Copy No. 1. File.
 --   -- 2. C.O.
 --   -- 3. O.C. "A" Coy.
 --   -- 4. O.C. "B" Coy.
 --   -- 5. O.C. "C" Coy.
 --   -- 6. O.C. "D" Coy.
 --   -- 7. Sig. Officer.

Army Form C. 2118.

WAR DIARY
or
INTELLIGENCE SUMMARY.
(Erase heading not required.)

12 E Surrey Rg
9/10/16

16.c
8 sheet

Place	Date	Hour	Summary of Events and Information	Remarks and references to Appendices
CANAL BANK (O5.c.5.9.)	Aug. 1.		Companies have now moved to forward area as follows – A & C Coy OPTIC SUPPORT. B & D in front of HOLLEBEKE extending along to FORET FARM. Much rain during the last two days and trenches in very bad condition. 2nd Lt. SAMUELS found FORET FM. when he reconnoitred with a patrol before "B" moved into position – to be unoccupied by the Enemy. Enemy continued indiscriminate shelling of our forward and back areas throughout the day. Major BLAKENEY left Transport lines & proceeded to LINES OF COMMUNICATION.	Appendix I Map. HOLLEBEKE 1/10,000 attached. R.R.
	2.		The C.O. & Capt. Walker reconnoitred the line near HOLLEBEKE and on our back areas. The trenches occupied by A & C Coys are in exceptionally bad condition. B Coy are in front with the left of the 1st HOVAL NTH LANCS. REGT in the region of FORET FM. Lt. Col. KNAPP, D.S.O. rejoined the Batt'n. at Transport lines today.	R.R.
	3.		Enemy artillery continued active at intervals throughout the day on our forward areas in the neighbourhood of HOLLEBEKE and OPTIC TRENCH. An enemy observation was found in HOLLEBEKE showing way to his Néry left aligned and was forwarded to Brigade H.Q. Strong front at FORET FM. was completed and our forward line consolidated. Capt. OPPENSHAW took details covering from Transport lines supplied carrying party for Battn. relieved.	R.R.
	4.		A quieter day. Enemy artillery less active through WHITE CHATEAU WOOD received attention from his heavy guns at intervals. Our support line Coys. (A & C) are now greatly depleted chiefly owing to sickness caused by inclement season & bad condition of trenches. 2nd Lt. ADCOTT reported sick.	R.R.
	5.		After a heavy barrage lasting four hours the enemy assaulted our position in HOLLEBEKE and FORET FM. Owing to very heavy mist S.O.S. signals which had been sent up from the front line could not be seen at H 3.30 a.m. & A.M.G. 1/Coy. arrived at Battn H.Q. saying that the enemy were advancing.	R.R.

A5834 Wt. W4973/M687 750,000 8/16 D.D. & L. Ltd. Forms/C.2118/13.

Army Form C. 2118.

WAR DIARY
or
INTELLIGENCE SUMMARY.
(Erase heading not required.)

Instructions regarding War Diaries and Intelligence Summaries are contained in F. S. Regs., Part II. and the Staff Manual respectively. Title pages will be prepared in manuscript.

Place	Date	Hour	Summary of Events and Information	Remarks and references to Appendices
	5.		HOLLEBEKE and adjoining on OPTIC TRENCH. All our lines from Battn. H.Q. were "dis". The S.O.S. was sent up from our H.Q. & a runner dispatched to the HANTS REGT. H.Q. & to Brigade H.Q. The our was still = heavy & our S.O.S. was not seen. Under Major Pennell the H.Q. Coy. turned out & advanced towards HOLLEBEKE. We joined up with a Coy of the HANTS REG. in NEW SUPPORT LINE & continued to advance further about 200 yds of HOLLEBEKE where we were held up by known M.G. fire & snipers. We proceeded a few German who were forward of their line where we made prisoners. Prisoners asserted that they could not approach further & two were unable to ascertain from them any information as to the numbers or strength of the enemy attacking. We went now on touch with another Coy of the HANTS. Regt. on our left who had occupied trenches on the left of HOLLEBEKE. A patrol went out on the right but was unable to get into touch with other troops. The patrol was fired on by enemy M.G. & snipers. A few Germans were seen to be retreating. They were fired on by Major Pennell who also led some forward as they approached. We ascertained from them main body. (The clean of the enemy was in command.) Sgt. PRIORS a strong fighting patrol of HOLLEBEKE was reported 5,173.25 slightly forward of the whole line was then pushed forward a further 5,173.25 slightly forward of the line we held prior the attack on HOLLEBEKE. We PRIDHAM then 17th coveted the line we held prior the attack on HOLLEBEKE. We PRIDHAM then 17th coveted of the EAST SURREYS (about 25 O.Rs.). We opposed it have two many prisoners in D of B Coy. the mass being so strong our effects were successfully before they could give any alarm. In this hurry the Battn. (about 90 strong) moved to Battn. CONFLUENT had the details under Capt COPPENSHAW moved up the line as a Platoon of a Company & (came) from Pack Regt. in the Brigade. Figures are undoubtedly	

(A7592) Wt.W12839/M1293. 75 000. 1/17. D. D. & L., Ld. Forms/C.2118/14.

WAR DIARY
or
INTELLIGENCE SUMMARY.
(Erase heading not required.)

Army Form C. 2118.

Instructions regarding War Diaries and Intelligence Summaries are contained in F. S. Regs., Part II. and the Staff Manual respectively. Title pages will be prepared in manuscript.

Place	Date	Hour	Summary of Events and Information	Remarks and references to Appendices
	5		an to casualties at present but we have heard of the following among Officers. Capt HOWITT killed. 2nd Lt GORRIN died of wounds. Missing believed prisoner. 2nd Lt SAMUELS. 2nd Lt JENNINGS wounded ? 2nd Lt HAYNES. Lt Col KNAPP, D.S.O. assumes Command of Battn.	
BOIS CONFLUENT.	6.		A few O.R's have reported having attached themselves to the STAFFS Regt. during the attack on MONS FORET FARM. We have received some news but shelling & traffic covering casualties. Slight aerial activity on both sides but rain at intervals prevented much flying. 2nd Lt TODD proceeded to transport lines sick. Orders received for Battn to move from BOIS CONFLUENT.	
	7.		CAMP. Casualties killed- 2 O.R. wounded 1 O.R. Maj. Genl ST.B. LAWFORD C.B. visited B.H.Q. at 9.15am. At 11.30 a.m. Battn moved from BOIS CONFLUENT. Motor buses met the Battn on the BRASSERIE & proceeded to DEZON CAMP. 2nd Lt CLIFT proceeded to hospital sick. Capt. McCARNAN reported sick. Casualties to Battn from 24th July to 4th Aug:– KILLED-23, DIED OF WOUNDS-7, WOUNDED 115, MISSING-54, SICK-125	
DEZON CAMP	8.		Battn employed throughout the day on reorganisation of Companies, mending clothing, baths, etc. Lt-Genl Sir T. L.N. MORLAND K.C.B. etc. inspected the Battn at DEZON CAMP at 11 a.m. 2nd Lt ROSSITER sick.	
	9.		Temporary re-organisation of Companies into Platoons, sections etc.- inspection of Gas Helmets. Orders received for Battn to move to forward area tomorrow. Platoon & Company Commanders will reccee their routes. Capt. OPPENSHAW & 60 O.R's to re-enforce OBLIQUE ROW by 6 p.m. tomorrow.	
	10		DOWLING rejoined the Battn. from Base Training Depot at ETAPLES. 2nd Lt's. Battn moved from DEZON CAMP to forward area, by motor bus to BRASSERIE. Battn marched from BRASSERIE via MORTED GRANGE, BUS HOUSE, SHELLEY DUMP, SPOILBANK. Disposition in forward area as follows. Battn H.Q. IRON BRIDGE, 2 officers & 64 O.Rs OBLIQUE ROW, 1 officer & 64 O.Rs OPTIC TRENCH 50 O.Rs WHITE CHATEAU. 2 officers & 15 O.Rs. will report to O/C 11th Royal W22191 W. M9250/M293 75,000 1/17. D.D. &Co.,Ltd. CAMP & will relieve a Company of the HANTS. REGT. at FORET FM.	

WAR DIARY
or
INTELLIGENCE SUMMARY.

(Erase heading not required.)

Army Form C. 2118.

Place	Date	Hour	Summary of Events and Information	Remarks and references to Appendices
IRON BRIDGE	10		Details left behind moved to Transport lines.	NB
	11		The day passed without event. At dr WALTER relieved LT. ROGERS, the latter proceeding to Transport lines. Casualties. 1 O.R. Killed	NR
	12		At dawn there was much shelling from forward area, but afterwards the day was quiet. There was much aerial activity on our side which appeared to silence the Enemy guns. 2/Lt. ROGERS proceeded to Counts' Sanctuary at 2nd Army Central School. WISHUES. Casualties nil	NR
	13		At dawn there was again the usual shelling of Battn H.Q. Camp in for some attention from the Enemy Heavy Guns. The Battn. was relieved by the 2 Comp. of the 12th Surrey Regt & 2 Comp. of the 15 HANTS REGT, on the night 13/14, the relief commencing at 9.30 p.m. The relief went with ad S Coy. going out when enemy commenced gas shell bombardment on STRAY BANK and the RATION TRACK. Casualties 5 O.Rs. wounded.	NB
ELZ WALLA	14		On the way down from the line Battn. Bugles until 9.15am at WILTSHIRE CAMP in the neighbourhood of ELZ WALLA. At 4.15 p.m. Battn (about 250 strong) marched via BIRKEBUSCH LAKE to HALLABUSTE CORNER where it bivouaced by entry lorries to billets at POUKLOSHILLE arriving there at 1.15 a.m. Casualties 1 O.R. Killed (there was at OAK DUMP on the journey down from the trenches in early morning.)	NB
POUKLOSHILLE	15		Battn. employed on reorganisation, foot inspection, Lists & Knapsack the day. The M.O. Capt HERDMAN. C.B & again Field Ambulance and Capt. HARRISON assumed duties of M.O 17th Battn 2 Lt. RUSSELL proceded to Lewis Gun Courses at LE TOUQUET. LT LIBBY posted to B Coy, Lt. MC WALTER to E Coy and Lt B REARDEN "A" Coy, 2nd Lt JOLLY to D Coy.	NB
	16		The C.O. inspected the Battn. at 11.30 a.m. In the afternoon at 3pm Brigadier General TOWSEY C.M.G. inspected the Battn. incorporating all ranks on the recent operations in HOLLEBEKE. The following officers joined the Battn. and were posted to Companies as shown :-	NB

Army Form C. 2118.

WAR DIARY
or
INTELLIGENCE SUMMARY.
(Erase heading not required.)

Place	Date	Hour	Summary of Events and Information	Remarks and references to Appendices
	16		2nd Lt HUTCHESON to "C" Coy 2nd Lt WHITE, G.L. " A " Lt WHITE, R.E. " C " 2nd Lt HALL, N.G. " D " 2nd Lt DUNKLEY " B "	
	17		The Battn. paraded for ceremonial parade at 9.30.a.m. & marched to the neighbourhood of METEREN where the Corps Commander congratulated the Brigade. The Corps Commander spoke of the splendid work that had been done in the recent operations & particularly the fighting around HOLLEBEKE. The Brigadier. He warmly congratulated all ranks on the recent fighting around HOLLEBEKE. The Divisional Commander congratulated & thanked the Brigade for the work that has been done. The Corps Commander then awarded the following decorations to the undermentioned N.C.Os and men for gallantry in the field on dates shown:— Military Medal. 14908 Sergt. Baker J. 31.7.17 31704 Pte. Brussler A. 31.7.17 25582 " Scott H. 5.8.17 25414 " Dance O. 31.7.17 16218 " Manley H. 31.7.17 25468 " Brodough A. 5.8.17 15838 " " 5.8.17	
	18		In the morning the Battn. was inspected by the Army Commander in the neighbourhood of METEREN. 2nd Lt. C.J.W. FAITH joins the Battn. for duty and is posted to "B" Coy.	
	19		The Battn. paraded for Divine Service (C.of E.) at Battn. H.Q. at 9.30 a.m. Orders received for	

WAR DIARY
or
INTELLIGENCE SUMMARY.

(Erase heading not required.)

Army Form C. 2118.

Place	Date	Hour	Summary of Events and Information	Remarks and references to Appendices
			Batn. to move to EBBLINHEM area tomorrow. 2/Lt. B.F. DODD proceeded the Batn. to act as billeting Officer in the new area. 2/Lt. T.H. LLOYD joins the Batn. for duty and is posted to "D" Coy. The undermentioned N.C. Os. and men have been awarded the MILITARY MEDAL for gallantry in the FIELD in date stated :-	
			No. 16312 Sergt. DICKSON, H. 31.7.17	
			" 12471 Corpl. SAVANT, S.J. 31.7.17	
			" 5157 L/Cpl. BOLTON, E.E. 31.7.17	
			" 25419 Pte. GEORGE, T. 31.7.17	
			" 25207 " HOARE, A. 5.8.17	
ZUYDTEENE	20		The Batn. paraded at 5.30 a.m. and marched to ZUYPTEENE, via CAESTRE, HONDEGHEM, and STAPLE, where we remained in billets for the night 20/21, arriving at ZUYPTEENE at 11.30 a.m. on the morning of the 20th. 2/Lt B.F. DODD proceeded to ZUDAUSQUES in the afternoon to act as billeting Officer for the Batn. in the new area. Orders received for Batn. to move to ZUDAUSQUES tomorrow. Boetians from Batn. Underwent "The Commanding Officer wishes to convey to all Ranks his appreciation of the d killing way in which they carried out the march today."	
ZUDAUSQUES	21		The Batn. paraded at 4.15 a.m. + marched from ZUYPTEENE to NIEPPE where we were met by motor lorries which conveyed us to billets at ZUDAUSQUES, arriving there about 11.40 a.m. Batn. H.Q. were established at CHATEAU du MIR CARME (W.1.d.7.5.)	

(A7038). Wt. W12839/M1293. 75,000. 1/17. D. D. & L., Ltd. Forms/C.2118/4.

Army Form C. 2118.

WAR DIARY
or
INTELLIGENCE SUMMARY.
(Erase heading not required.)

Place	Date	Hour	Summary of Events and Information	Remarks and references to Appendices
In the FIELD	21		The under mentioned men have been awarded the MILITARY MEDAL for gallantry No. 11483 Pte LYNCH, D. " 16078 " TUSTIN, C.T. " 12361 " TURNER, C	APa
	22	9.30 am	Battn. paraded at 9.30 am. & ran under Company arrangements until 10.30 am. At 10.30 am the Commanding Officer's Class was as formed consisting of all Officers, N.C.O's & a few selected Private Soldiers, and Training was carried out under instruction by the Commanding Officer, the remainder of the Battn. was under the Adjutant. In the afternoon the Commanding Officer 2nd Lt. RUSSELL rejoined Battn. from LE TOUQUET	APa
	23		Minutes a lecture to this class by the Commanding Officer 2nd Lt. RUSSELL rejoined Battn from LE TOUQUET. The Battn. carried out Range Practice at CARRE de MARNE (Q.14.L.3.7.). Rain at intervals during the morning.	APb
	24		Battn paraded for Ceremonial Parade, and marched to Divisional Parade Ground at W.22.b. when the 41st Division was inspected by the Commander-in-Chief. Rain at intervals during the morning.	APa Appendix II Inspection by Commander in Chief
	25		Battn continued training under Company Commanders	

WAR DIARY
or
INTELLIGENCE SUMMARY.
(Erase heading not required.)

Army Form C. 2118.

Instructions regarding War Diaries and Intelligence Summaries are contained in F. S. Regs., Part II. and the Staff Manual respectively. Title pages will be prepared in manuscript.

Place	Date	Hour	Summary of Events and Information	Remarks and references to Appendices
Camp	26		Battn. paraded for Divine Service (C.of.E.) at 11.15 a.m. Rest day	
	27		Battn continued training. Musketry, Drill, Bayonet fighting, Community Singing, Clean up. Much rain during the afternoon training.	
	28		Training interrupted through incessant rain during the morning. Extract from Battn. Orders "Yesterday" Sept. Lt. V.L.CLIFT to be ADJUTANT vice A/Lt.T.B.M.C.WALTER who relinquishes appointment at his own request & resumes Regimental duties a/2.4.5.17.	
	29		Rain at intervals throughout the day. Battn continued training.	
	30		Battn training during the morning. Brig-Gen.TOWSEY,C.M.G. visits Battn.H.Q. Lt. BREARY left Battn. to proceed to R.F.C. The following awards decorations have been awarded to the undermentioned officers and N.C.O.	
			The Military Cross T/Capt. H.S.WALKER. 31/7 - 5/8/17.	
			T/Lt. D.WALKER. 31/7 - 1/8/17.	
			T/2nd Lt. A.M.MACKINTOSH 31/7/17. (attached T.M.B.)	
			The Distinguished Conduct Medal No. 11910 Sergt. G.D.PROSSER. 5/8/17.	
	31		Ranges allotted to Battn. will continues rain interrupted firing during the morning.	

SECRET.   Copy No............

12th Bn East Surrey Regt.
OPERATION ORDER No.106.

1. The Battalion will move to the Forward Area to-morrow, Friday, 10th August, 1917., at a time to be notified later.

2. <u>Disposition.</u>

   Battalion Headquarters BROKEN BRIDGE (O.4.b.2.4).
   1 Officer & 64 O.Rs.   OPTIC TRENCH.
   2 Officers & 64 O.Rs.   OAK ROW.
   50 O.Rs.   WHITE CHATEAU.

   Platoons forming Composite Company under CAPTAIN POWLES will rejoin their Units on the 10th August, 1917.
   O.C. Composite Company will detail the platoon of CAPTAIN OPENSHAW and 60 O.Rs to occupy OBLIQUE ROW by 6 p.m. on 10th August.
   2-Officers and 75 O.Rs will relieve D Company of the 15th Hampshire Regiment in the front line in front of FORRET FARM (O.11.d.5.9).
   Platoons occupying OBLIQUE ROW, OPTIC TRENCH, O.11.d.5.9, and WHITE CHATEAU, will come under O.C. 11th Royal West Kent Regt, for tactical purposes.
   The 11th R.W.Kent Regt Hqrs will be at O.5.c.5.9.

3. <u>Parades.</u> The 2 Officers and 75 O.Rs detailed to proceed to the Front Line will parade with the 11th R.W.Kent Regt at WOOD CAMP (M.5.d.Central) to-morrow, at a time to be notified later.
   Further parades, movement, order of relief, dress, route, guides, will be notified later.

4. <u>Trench Stores.</u> All maps, aeroplane photos, and trench stores will be taken over by ingoing Companies, and receipts forwarded to Battn.H.Q.

5. Platoons will report completion of relief by Runner.

6. Marching Out States will be rendered to Orderly Room at a time to be notified later.

7. ACKNOWLEDGE.

                             (sd) B.F.Dodd,
                                  2nd Lieut & A/Adjt,
                                  12th Bn East Surrey Regt.

Copy No.1.   Filed.
"   " 2.   C.O.
"   " 3.   2nd-in-Comd.
"   " 4.   Intl.Officer.
"   " 5.   Sig.Officer.
"   " 6.   M.O.
"   " 7.   R.Q.M.S.
"   " 8.   R.S.M.
"   " 9.   Capt.Openshaw.
"   " 10. Capt.Walker.
"   " 11. Lieut.Rogers.
"   " 12. Lieut.Pridham.

SECRET.   Copy No. 1.

12th Bn East Surrey Regt.
OPERATION ORDER No. 107.
(IN CONTINUATION OF OPERATION ORDER No. 106 d/9.8.17).

10th August, 1917.

1. **MOVE.** The Battalion, less one Company of 2 Officers & 75 O.Rs, will move off from present Camp by lorries at 4.30 p.m.
   The Company of 2 Officers & 75 O.Rs will parade at 4.15pm and march to WOOD CAMP (M.5.d.Central) arriving there at 5.45 p.m. They will report to O.C. 11th R.W.Kent Regt.
   All lorries will stop at the BRASSERIE where parties will de-bus.

2. **PARADES.** The Battalion will parade at 4.15 p.m.

3. **DRESS:-** Fighting Order.

4. **ROUTE.** The Battalion will march from the BRASSERIE by the "W" Route via MOATED GRANGE - BUS HOUSE - SHELLY DUMP - SPOIL BANK.

5. **ORDER OF RELIEF.** Hdqrs.   BROKEN BRIDGE. (O.4.b.2.4).
   2 Officers & 64 O.Rs.   OBLIQUE ROW.
   1 Officer & 64 O.Rs.   OPTIC TRENCH.
   50 O.Rs.   WHITE CHATEAU.

6. **MOVEMENT.** All movements will be by platoons at 500 yds distance.

7. **PACKS ETC.** All packs will be stacked on the road leading into the Camp by 3 p.m.
   Officers Valises, Mess Baskets, and Company Stores, will be stacked in the same place by 2.30 p.m.

8. Marching Out States will be rendered to Orderly Room by 1 p.m.

9. **RATIONS.** Rations for consumption on the 11th inst will be carried. Rations for platoon of the 12th E.Surrey Regt attached to the Composite Company will come up in the ordinary way.
   O.C. Composite Company will arrange that these be drawn from OAK DUMP as before.

10. **DETAILS.** Details remaining behind will parade in full marching order at 4.15 p.m. and will be marched to the Transport Lines.

11. **CORRECTION TO BAB CODE No.3.** The following code letters and correction numbers will be brought into use at midnight 9th/10th August :-
    Xth Corps - S = plus 70.

12. **ACKNOWLEDGE.**

(sd) B.F.Dodd, 2nd Lt & A/Adjt,
12th Bn East Surrey Regiment.

Copy No. 1. Filed.
"   "   2. C.O.
"   "   3. 2nd-in-Comd.
"   "   4. Capt.Walker.
"   "   5. M.O.
"   "   6. Lieut.Rogers.
"   "   7. Lieut.Pridham.
"   "   8. Int.Officer.
"   "   9. Sig.Officer.
"   " 10. Transport Officer.
"   " 11. R.S.M.
"   " 12. R.Q.M.S.

SECRET.

Copy No...... 1

12th Bn East Surrey Regt.

OPERATION ORDER No. 108.

13th August 1917.

1. **MOVE.** The Details and Transport less Two Travelling Kitchens and One Water Cart, will proceed to the FLETRE Area, via WESTOUTRE and BERTHEN, to-morrow 14th inst, and will be located in the same billets at LE ROUKLOSHILLE.

   Two Travelling Kitchens and One Water Cart will proceed in advance and prepare dinners for the Battalion on arrival at Battn. Hqrs. They will leave present Camp at 8.0 a.m. and proceed via WESTOUTRE and BERTHEN.

2. **PARADE.** Details and Transport will parade on the LA CLYTTE-RENINGHELST Road, facing South, at 10.10 a.m.

3. **DRESS.** Fighting Order.

4. **PACKS & BAGGAGE.** All Surplus Baggage and Packs will be loaded on Motor Lorries at 7.0 a.m. The R.S.M. will detail a party for this purpose. 1 N.C.O. and 3 men will accompany each lorry to the new Area.

5. **OFFICERS' STORES.** Officers' Valises, Mess Baskets etc will be stacked at the Quartermaster's Stores by 9.0 a.m.

6. **MARCH DISCIPLINE** The usual clock hour halts will be observed.

7. **BILLETS.** All huts, tents etc will be left scrupulously clean. The Orderly Officer will inspect these before moving off, and report to the Adjutant.

8. **REAR PARTY.** The R.S.M. will detail a Rear Party of 1 N.C.O. and 3 men who will take charge of the present Camp until the arrival of the incoming unit, from whom they will obtain a certificate to the effect that the Camp and Wagon Lines are clean.

(Sd) V. L. Clift,

Lieut & A/Adjutant.

12th Bn East Surrey Regiment.

Copy No. 1 Filed.
"   "   2 O.C.Details.
"   "   3 Capt. McCalman.
"   "   4 Transport Officer.
"   "   5 R.S.M.
"   "   6 R.Q.M.S.

12th Bn EAST SURREY REGT.

WARNING ORDER No.1.

Copy No...1...

1. The Battalion will march to the EBBLINGHEM area to-morrow.

2. Approximate distance of march is twelve miles.

3. Approximate hour of starting 6 a.m.

4. There will be no long halt.

5. Orders for march will be issued later.

(sd) V.L.Clift,

Lieut & A/Adjt,

12th Bn East Surrey Regt.

Issued at................
19th August, 1917.

Copy No. 1. File.
 "   " 2 O.C. A Coy.
 "   " 3. O.C. B Coy.
 "   " 4 O.C. C Coy.
 "   " 5 O.C. D Coy.
 "   " 6 Transport Officer.
 "   " 7 A/Quartermaster.

SECRET.   Copy No.......... 1

                        12th Bn EAST SURREY REGT.

                        OPERATION ORDER No. 109.

1. MOVE.   The Battalion and Transport will move to the EBBLINGHEM
                    area to-morrow, 20th inst.

2. PARADE.   The Battalion will parade on the road outside Battn. H.Q.
                    at 5.30 a.m. in the following order :-
                    H.Qrs., A Coy, B Coy, C Coy, D Coy, Transport.
                    The head of the column to be level with Battn.H.Q. facing
                    WEST.

3. DRESS.   Fighting order.

4. PACKS &   All packs and surplus baggage will be stacked near the
   BAGGAGE.   Road outside Company billets by 5 a.m. Each Company
                    will detail 1 N.C.O. and 2 men as guard over above. They
                    will load the motor lorries and accompany them to the
                    new area. The Regtl.Sgt.Major will detail a guide to
                    meet three motor lorries at X.3.c.05.45 at 6 a.m. and
                    direct them to Battn.H.Q. 2nd Lieut.C.F.W.Faith will
                    act as O i/c Lorries.

5. OFFICERS   Officers Valises and Mess Baskets will be stacked near
   STORES.   the road outside Company billets by 5 a.m.

6. MARCH   Company Commanders are reminded that march discipline
   DISCIPLINE.   must be rigidly enforced. The usual clock hour halts
                    will be observed. Cigarette smoking is prohibited
                    except during halts.
                    An interval of 50 yards will be maintained between Coys.

7. BILLETS.   All barns and tents occupied as billets must be left
                    scrupulously clean.

                                    (sd)   V.L.Clift,
                                           Lieut & A/Adjt,
                                        12th Bn East Surrey Regt.

   Issued at............
   19th August, 1917.

   Copy No. 1. Filed.   Copy No. 2. C.O.
    "   "   3. 2nd-in-Comd.   "   "   4. O.C. A Coy.
    "   "   5. O.C. B Coy.   "   "   6. O.C. C Coy.
    "   "   7. O.C. D Coy.   "   "   8. Signalling Officer.
    "   "   9. Transport Officer.   "   " 10. Medical Officer.
    "   " 11. Intelligence   "   "   " 12. R.S.M.
    "   " 13. R.Q.M.S.

Copy No...8...

12th Bn East Surrey Regt.

OPERATION ORDER No.110

Reference Map. Sheet 27.

1. The Battalion will move to the ZUDAUSQUES Area tomorrow 21st inst.

2. The Battalion will march to LE NIEPPE (approximate distance 5 miles.
   Starting point :- Road junction t.13.d.8.2.
   Order of march :- H.Q., C, D, A, B, head of column to pass starting point at 7.15 a.m.
   The Battalion will march in column of three's
   Mounted Officers will ride to LE NIEPPE; Grooms will take horses at this point and await arrival of the Transport Column.
   On arrival at LE NIEPPE, the Battalion will embus. It will be told off in parties of 25, all ranks. These parties will be formed up on the left hand side of the road (facing West), 15 yards between parties.

3. Transport. Attached personnel, Pioneers, Quartermasters Staff, etc., will parade at Transport Lines (O.14.a.central) at 7.30 a.m. They will proceed by march route under the Transport Officer via AIQUES - St.OMER & St.MARTIN, to ZOUDAUSQUES. After St. Martin, the shortest route will be taken to the new area at ZOUDAUSQUES.
   Head of column to pass cross roads LE NIEPPE at 9.25 a.m.
   Normal halts will be observed.
   There will be a halt on route for watering and feeding, to be arranged by the Brigade Transport Officer.
   A guide will meet the party at ZOUDAUSQUES CHURCH.

4. Valises, Mess Baskets etc., will be stacked at Billets ready for collection by Regimental Transport at 6 a.m.
   All Packs and surplus stores will be stacked by the same hour ready for collection by Motor Lorry. Loading arrangements as before.
   2nd Lieut. Todd will be O.i/c Lorries.

5. Billets must be left scrupulously clean.

6. The Commanding Officer wishes to convey to all ranks his appreciation of the excellent way in which they carried out the march today.

(sd)   V.L.Clift.   Lieut. & Adjt.,
                      12th Bn East Surrey Regt.

Issued at 7.30 p.m.
20th August 1917.

Copy No.1 File.   Copy No.2   C.O.
"   " 3 2nd in Comd.   "   " 4   O.C. "A" Coy.
"   " 5 O.C. "B" Coy.   "   " 6   O.C. "D" Coy.
"   " 7 O.C. "C" Coy.   "   " 8   Signalling Offr.
"   " 9 Intelligce Offr "   " 10 Transport Offr.
"   " 11 Medical Offr.   "   " 12 R.Q.M.S.
"   " 13 R.S.M.

7. continued.
The Table shewn in para 10 gives the reallotment of men left behind when the Battalion goes into action. Of the total of 100 it will be seen that 64 come from the Platoons. The total drain on the strength of Platoons may therefore be placed at about 175 to 180 per Battalion.

8. A considerable proportion of the men left behind when the Battalion goes into action might actually be included in the numbers of those at classes and courses or on leave. In order, however, to make as ample provision as possible, the difference in total strength between the maximum and the minimum strength (going into action) has been placed at 192 other Ranks, excluding 100 O.R's detailed in para 10.

9. The following are the principal alterations made in Battn. Headquarters :-
5 Stretcher Bearers are added making 1 N.C.O. and 8 O.R's in all.
4 Grooms are added.
To prevent a drain on Platoons, 1 N.C.O. and 12 O.R's will be attached to Battn. Headquarters to man the 4 Lewis Guns for Anti Aircraft purposes. These men will be struck off the fighting strength of their Platoons.
The principal alteration in Company Headquarters is the addition of 2 Runners.

10. The new allotment to be left behind when the Battalion goes into action is as follows :-

(a) Battn. Headquarters.
C.S.M.	2.
Signallers	4.
Runners	1.
Sergt Instructors	5.
Total	12.

12.

(b) Each Company.
Sergt.	1.
Corpl.	1.
L/Cpl.	1.
Signallers	1.
Runners.	2.
Total	6

24.

(c) Each Platoon.
Riflemen (R.B.)	1.
Riflemen (Scout & Sniper)	1.
Lewis Gunners	2.
Total	4

64.

TOTAL 100.

TO BE RETURNED TO BATTN. HDQRS. WHEN THE BATTN. GOES INTO THE LINE.

SECRET.   Copy No:......

12th Bn EAST SURREY REGIMENT.

OPERATION ORDER No.114.

Reference Maps ZILLEBEKE 1/10.000 and SHREWSBURY FOREST.

1. **INTENTION.** The 41st Division will take the Offensive at an early date, in conjunction with the 23rd Division on the Left and the 39th Division on the Right. The 21st and 53rd Divisions will be in reserve.

2. **ORDER of BATTLE.** Order of Battle within the 41st Division :-
   Right............124th Brigade.
   Left.............122nd Brigade.
   Reserve..........123rd Brigade.

   Order of Battle within 122nd Brigade:-
   Right....18th Bn K.R.R.C. & 12th East Surrey Regt.
   Left.....15th Hants Regt. & 11th R.W.Kent Regt.

   Left Battn. of 124th Brigade will be 21st Bn King's Royal Rifle Corps for 1st two objectives and 26th Bn Royal Fusiliers for 3rd Objective.

3. **DIRECTION of ATTACK, OBJECTIVES and BOUNDARIES.**
   The general direction of Attack in the 122nd Brigade will be 93 degrees T.B.
   There will be three objectives:-
   1st Objective.........RED LINE.
   2nd Objective.........BLUE LINE.
   3rd Objective.........GREEN LINE.

4. **METHOD OF BRIGADE ATTACK.**
   (a) The attack will be made in depth and on the "leap-frog" principle.
   (b) The attack on the RED and BLUE Lines will be made by the 18th Bn.K.R.R.C. on right and 15th Bn Hants Regt on left. Each of these Battalion will be on a two-Coy front: the leading two Companies of each Battn. will attack and consolidate the RED LINE and the remaining two Companies will pass through these and attack and consolidate the BLUE LINE.
   (c) The 12th Bn.East Surrey Regt. on the right and the 11th Bn. Royal West Kent Regt. on the left will assemble on a two Coy front in rear of the BLUE Line after its capture, behind the 18th Bn.K.R.R.C. and 15th Bn Hants Regt respectively. They will then pass through the 18th Bn.K.R.R.C. and 15th Hants Regt and their two leading Companies will attack and consolidate the GREEN LINE. The remaining two Companies of each of these Battns will consolidate on a line 200 - 300 yards in rear of the GREEN LINE.

5. **DISPOSITIONS & FORMATION of the BATTALION.**
   The 12th Bn East Surrey Regt. will form up with "A" Coy on the Right, and "B" Coy on the left in front. C Coy on the Right and D Coy on the Left in rear, each Company will be on a two platoon front.

6. **ASSEMBLY.** The Battalion will assemble with its front resting on a tape at right angles to the line of advance. Battn. flanks will be marked by notice boards and the dividing line between right and left Companies will be marked by a tape.
   Information concerning routes to, and times for, assembly will be published later.
   The marsh by BOD IN COPSE may prevent the right and left Coys from maintaining contact in the assembly. As <u>each</u> wave moves forward to the assault it will <u>at once</u> obtain contact on clearing the marshy ground.

Headquarters
122nd Infantry Bde

Herewith original copy of the War Diary for the Battalion under my command for the month of September 1917. Please

[Stamp: 12th BATTALION, EAST SURREY REGIMENT. No......... Date..........]

1st October 1917

[signature]
Major
Comdg 12/Bn East Surrey Regt

12 E Surrey
17 C
6 sheet

WAR DIARY
or
INTELLIGENCE SUMMARY
(Erase heading not required.)

Army Form C. 2118.

Place	Date	Hour	Summary of Events and Information	Remarks and references to Appendices
ZUDAUSQUES	Sept. 1		In the morning Battn. was inspected by Brig. Genl. TOWSEY C.M.G. in new attack formation which took place over Battn. Shell-hole Training Area. Fine day. 36th Batt Strength 736 37 offs 698 o.r.	
	2		Battn paraded for Divine Service 11:15 a.m. Fine day. NSN	
	3		Battn continued training in attack over Shell-hole Area. 2nd Lt. W. D. WALKER promoted Lt. on Wireless Course at Signalling School at ZUYTPEENE. NSN	
	4		Battn carried out an attack over Bayenghem Shell-hole area in the morning. Fine day. Inter-Coy football match in afternoon. NSN	
	5		Battn continued training. During the day Major PUTLER, Capt WALKER, 2nd Lieut TOLLEY & 2nd Lieut WHITE R.E. made tour of Battle-area reconnoitring area in the neighbourhood of SHREWSBURY FOREST & reconnoitred the line. NSN	
	6		Battn in training under Coy arrangements. NSN	
	7		Battn attack scheme under practice was carried through today. Lt-Col KNAPP DSO, Capt OPPENSHAW, Lieut CLIST, 2nd Lieut RUSSELL & 2nd Lieut HALL reconnoitred the line in the neighbourhood of SHREWSBURY FOREST. 2nd Lieut JOHNS R.E. from the Battalion to joined 6th Div. Engrs. NSN	
	8		Battn continued training. Sports in the afternoon. The intervention of ferry rain at...	

Army Form C. 2118.

WAR DIARY
or
INTELLIGENCE SUMMARY.
(Erase heading not required.)

Instructions regarding War Diaries and Intelligence Summaries are contained in F. S. Regs., Part II, and the Staff Manual respectively. Title pages will be prepared in manuscript.

Place	Date	Hour	Summary of Events and Information	Remarks and references to Appendices
ZUDAUSQUES	Sep 7		Battalion this day at our posted to Companies as follows:-	
	8		2nd Lieut. MUTCH. W.D. "A" Coy. Batt Strength	
			2nd Lieut. FISHER. C.H. "B" Coy. 469 OR	
			2nd Lieut. JOHNSON N.T. "D" Coy. 34 Officers	
				19th
	9		Battalion paraded at 8am & marched to assembly area W.12.a & ward ground for practice attack. 19th	
	10		Battalion in training under Coy arrangements. 19th	
	11		Battalion paraded at 7-45am & marched to Division at training area, they there carried 19th out a practice attack from the assembly area W.12.a	
			The undermentioned Officers joined for duty this day.	
			Capt. R. Z.N.BROOK C.Compy	
			2nd Lieut. H.C.WARD D.Compy 19th	
	12		Battalion in training under Coy arrangements	
			Battalion paraded at 9 p.m. & carried out practice forming up on tape for attack 19th	

WAR DIARY
or
INTELLIGENCE SUMMARY.
(Erase heading not required.)

Army Form C. 2118.

Place	Date	Hour	Summary of Events and Information	Remarks and references to Appendices
	Sep 13		Battalion in training under Coy arrangements. Conference of Coy Commanders at B.H.Q.	10h.
J.D.BUSQUES	14		Battalion marched to STAPLE via ST. MARTIN, ARQUES & LE NIEPPE. 2nd LIEUT W.D. MUTCH proceeded to BATTLE AREA to reconnoitre route to FORMING UP AREA.	A.M.
STAPLE	15		Battalion moved to FLEATRE via CAESTRE. Batt Stg H.Q. J.9220R 410. Officers	10h.
FLETRE	16		Battalion moved to CHIPPEWA CAMP via WESTOUTRE & RENINGHELST	10h.
CHIPPEWA CAMP	17		Battalion moved to RIDGE WOOD. Conference of Coy Commanders at Battalion Headquarters	10h.
RIDGE WOOD	18		Battalion moved to LOCH 8 AREA via TOWSEY'S TRACK. Batt Stg H.Q.	10h.
LOCH 8 AREA	19		Conference of Coy Commanders at 11 A.M. under Lt. Col. KNAPP. D.S.O. Battalion moved up by Coys to assembly point J.19d. via TOWSEYS TRACK at 11.PM. Batt Stg H.Q. for Battle. 44y.OR. 18 Officers. Casualties 2.O.R. wounded.	10h.
ASSEMBLY AREA	20		Battalion arrived at ASSEMBLY AREA at 3.A.M. B Coy forming up position on left flank of Batt front. A Coy on RIGHT FLANK. Both A & B on front tape. D Coy Rear in position on LEFT FLANK & C Coy on RIGHT FLANK on second tape. On the left flank of Battalion was posted the 11th ROYAL WEST KENTS. On our RIGHT FLANK the 26th FUSILIERS 12th BRIGADE Heavy MG. fire during the night B. 19 & B. 20 from our own Rear between the hours of 9 P.m. & 1 a.m.	

WAR DIARY or INTELLIGENCE SUMMARY

Army Form C. 2118.

Place	Date	Hour	Summary of Events and Information	Remarks and references to Appendices
ASSEMBLY AREA	Sept. 20		During the advance our Artillery continued to contain Enemy Strong Point. Enemy replied heavy. We had 3 casualties during the advance before Zero Hour. Our Barrage started promptly at Zero Hour & remained for 3 minutes 150 yards in front of our Jumping line. Following the 18th K.R.R. to from up close in rear of. The Barrage then moved towards the RED LINE at the rate of 200 yards in forming line at the rate of 50 yards in 6 minutes until it reached a line 200 yards beyond the RED LINE. Our Battalion (12 East Surreys) proceeded close behind the 18th K.R.R. & reinforced them when held up at a STRONG POINT at J.19.a.9.5. After being held up at this point for a short time dispersed the enemy with RIFLE GRENADES & proceeded to advance to the BLUE LINE where we had to form a defensive Flank on our right owing to the 12th Brigade on our Right Flank being unable to gain its objective thirty being on Hand open to machine gun fire & snipers. We proceeded to consolidate the position we had attained throwing out STRONG POINTS in front with Machine Guns under the charge of 2nd Lieut. WARD. Our Casualties during the day were 100 o.R. & 13 officers officers.	

Army Form C. 2118.

WAR DIARY
or
INTELLIGENCE SUMMARY.
(Erase heading not required.)

Instructions regarding War Diaries and Intelligence Summaries are contained in F. S. Regs., Part II. and the Staff Manual respectively. Title pages will be prepared in manuscript.

Place	Date	Hour	Summary of Events and Information	Remarks and references to Appendices
	Sept			
RED LINE	21		Battalion continued to hold line although heavily shelled by enemy artillery	
			Enemy sniper on strong point on our Right Flank caused many casualties throughout the	WD
			day, also our working parties were busy active casualties on our own	
			Lieuts Beaumont & Ration Parties. Casualties during the day were officers	
			Lt. Col. Knapp DSO wounded. OR. 60 Bandsmen & OR Ranks & Lieut	WD
			Bombardier 85 OR. 41 Officers	
	22		Battalion continued to hold line. Enemy artillery very active.	
	23		Battalion was relieved by the 13th Royal Sussex Regt at 1 am & moved by TOWSERS TRACK to	
			RIDGE WOOD. Casualties June 20th & 23rd inc 284 OR & 13 Officers	WD
			At 4.30 pm Battalion moved to CAESTRE entraining at OUDERDOM at 7.45 pm	
	24		Battalion in training. Inspected by Brig.Gen. Tanner CMG.	WD
	25		Battalion inspected by Brig.Gen. Tanner CMG	WD
	26		Battalion employed throughout the day on reorganization of companies. Baths & Coy.	WD
	27		Battalion employed on Kit-Inspection, Reorganization & Rifle inspection	WD
	28		Battalion moved to UXEM by Motor Lorry arriving at 11 am	WD
	29		Battalion moved to LA PANNE via ADINKERKE arriving at FURNES CAMP N° 22 L 55 at 11 am	WD
	30		Battalion paraded for Divine Service at 9.30 am Service held at YMCA LA PANNE	WD

Bart Strength 19 OR 289/R

signature, Lt. Col., MAJOR.
COMDg. 12th BATT. EAST SURREY REGT.

A.

BATTALION TEMPORARILY REDUCED TO LOWER ESTABLISHMENT
(900 OTHER RANKS).

```
Battalion H.Q.   Fighting Portion .............. 72.
                 Serjeant Instructors .........  6 (a)
                 A.A. Lewis Gun Section .......  13 (b)
                 Administrative ...............  61
                                                       152
4 Company H.Q.   Fighting portion @ 23 ........ 92
                 Administrative @ 4 ...........  16
                                                       108
16 Platoon H.Q. @ 3 ..............................  48
                                                      308    308
                                  (d)
32 Rifle Sections; minimum 7, maximum 11 .........       224    352
                                  (d)
16 Lewis Gun Sections; minimum 11, maximum 15 ...        176    240
                                                         708    900
```

Battalion H.Q.

Fighting portion :

Serjeant Major	1
Orderly Room Clerks	1
Serjeant Drummer	1
Provost Serjt. & Police	5
Scout Serjt. & Corporal	2
Signallers	25
Stretcher Bearers	9
Pioneers	11
M.O. Orderly	1
Serjt. Cook & Cooks	3
Sanitary	1
Runners	5
Batmen	7 72

Administrative:

Q.M.S. and storemen	3
Orderly Room Clerks	2
Cooks	2
M.O. Orderly	1
Transport establishment	28
C.O's Groom	1
Grooms for 8 mounted Officers	4
Water Duties	5
Sanitary	2
Shoemakers	5
Tailors	3
Butcher	1
Postman	1
Batmen	3 61

Company H.Q.

Fighting portion :

C.S.M.	1
Signallers	7
Stretcher bearers	4
Gas	1
Cooks	2
Runners (e)	4
Drummers (f)	2
Batmen (f)	2 23

Administrative:

C.Q.M.S.	1
Groom	1
Sanitary	2 4

Platoon H.Q.

Platoon Serjeant ...	1
Runner	1
Batman (f)	1 3

(a) 1 Musketry, 1 P. & B.T., 1 Bombing, 2 Lewis guns, 1 gas.
(b) Separate provision made as a temporary measure only until Battalions can be raised to higher establishment.

/ (c)

ORGANISATION OF THE INFANTRY BATTALION.

1.   As a result of the fighting in March and the early part of April, it became necessary arbitrarily to reduce the battalion from 968 other ranks to 900 other ranks. It is imperative, therefore, to revise the organisation of the battalion, with a view to laying down an establishment which will enable the organisation to be maintained on a tactically sound basis.

A reduced establishment has therefore been drawn up as shewn on the attached table A (other ranks only), designed to admit of battalions going into action with rifle and Lewis Gun Sections complete at their minimum — that is to say, as effective tactical units — while allowing a wide margin for maintenance.

2.   It is essential to allow a wide margin between the maximum and the minimum of the rifle and Lewis Gun Sections, so as to ensure as far as possible that the normal deductions from fighting strength can be met without reducing sections below the minimum necessary for tactical efficiency. The maximum represents the War Establishment (as temporarily reduced for the time being). The minimum represents the actual fighting strength at which a battalion will go into action; the battalion should take into action that actual number of men, — no less and no more.

3.   The minimum number necessary for tactical efficiency in a rifle section is placed at one leader and six men.

The minimum number necessary for tactical efficiency in a Lewis Gun Section of two guns is placed at one leader and ten men. This latter is less than the number required to fight the two guns separately. But the principles on which the double Lewis Gun Section must be based are, that Lewis Guns must be fought in pairs if the utmost tactical efficiency is to be secured: that the section should be able to ensure having one gun always in action; and that the possession of the second gun may enable double fire power to be developed when fleeting opportunities offer in specially favourable circumstances.

4.   In providing for the indicated increase in the Lewis Gun Sections, and in providing the necessary margin between the maximum and minimum of both rifle and Lewis Gun Sections, it is impossible at present to maintain the existing number of rifle sections in a platoon. It becomes necessary, therefore, to reduce the platoon to two rifle sections and one double Lewis Gun Section.

5.   The average number of men sick, and on Brigade, Divisional and other employ, appears to amount normally to about 50 per Battalion. The average number of men absent from a battalion at any one time at classes and courses, and, when normal leave is open, on leave, appears to amount to about 90. Of the above total of 140, about four-fifths may be assumed to be a drain on the strength of the platoons.

The table shewn below in para. 7 gives the re-allotment of men left behind when the battalion goes into action. Of the total of 100, it will be seen that 64 come from the platoons. The total drain on the strength of the platoons may therefore be placed at about 175 to 180.

No allowance is made for attachments to Field Companies, which must not be permitted except as indicated in S.S.135, Section XII, 7.i.; and no allowance is made for attachments to Light Trench Mortar Batteries, since the establishment of the latter units is now under reconsideration.

A considerable proportion of the men left behind when the battalion goes into action might actually be included among those at classes and courses or on leave. In order, however, to make as ample provision as possible, it will be noted that the difference in total strength between the maximum (reduced establishment) and the minimum (strength on going into action) has been placed at 192 other ranks.

6. The following are the principal alterations made in battalion headquarters:-

Five stretcher bearers are added, bringing the total of battalion headquarters up to 1 N.C.O. and 8 other ranks.

Four grooms are added (for eight mounted officers).

So long as it is necessary to keep battalions on the reduced establishment (900 other ranks) it is considered desirable to add one N.C.O. and 12 other ranks as personnel for the four Lewis Guns allotted to battalions as anti-aircraft armament, thus avoiding the necessity of drawing on the platoons for these men.

The principal alteration in company headquarters is the addition of two runners; this is also designed to meet the need for providing batmen for surplus officers.

7. The revision of the establishment necessitates a revision of the allotment of other ranks to be left behind when the battalion goes into action. The new allotment will therefore be as follows :-

(a) Each Battalion.

    C.S.M.   2
    Signallers.   4
    Runner.   1
    Musketry Instructor. 1
    Lewis Gun Instructor. 2
    Bombing Instructor. 1
    Gas Instructor.   1
                            12   12

(b) Each Company.

    Sergeant.   1
    Corporal.   1
    Lance-Corporal.   1
    Signaller.   1
    Runners.   2
                             6   24

(c) Each Platoon

    Rifleman
      (Rifle Bomber)   1
    Rifleman
      (Scout & Sniper)   1
    Lewis Gunners.   2
                             4   64

                         Total   100

(b) (c) When circumstances admit of raising Battalions to higher establishment it is proposed to add a third rifle section to each platoon, making 48 rifle sections in all.

C (d) If raised to higher establishment, with three rifle sections and one double Lewis Gun section per platoon, the maximum of the rifle sections will be reduced to 10 and the maximum of the Lewis Gun sections to 14.

(e) Includes batmen for surplus officers.

(D) (f) Also act as runners.

TABLE "A"

BATTALION ESTABLISHMENT (900 O.R's)

Battalion Headquarters.		Minimum Strength	Maximum Strength
Fighting portion............72.			
Sergt Instructors..........6.			
A.A.Lewis Gun Section......13. (a)			
Administrative portion ....61.		152.	
Company Headquarters.			
Fighting portion..........23.			
Administrative portion....4. 27.			
4 Companies		108.	
Platoon Headquarters. 3.			
16 Platoons.		48.	
		308.	308.
Rifle Sections (1 N.C.O & 6 O.R)			
32 Sections. (b).		224	(c) 352. 11 per section
Lewis Gun Sections (1 N.C.O.& 10 O.R)			
16 Sections. (d).		176	(c) 240. 15 per section
TOTALS		708	900.

Battn. Headqrs. Fighting portion

Sergt Major.......................1	
Orderly Room Clerks.............1	
Sergt Drummer 1	
Provost Sergt & Police 5	
Scout Sergt & Corpl 2	
Signallers 25	
Stretcher Bearers 9	
Pioneers 11	
M.O.Orderly 1	
Sergt Cook & Cooks 3	
Sanitary 1	
Runners 5	
Batmen 7	72.

Battn.Headqrs. Administrative.

Q.M.S.& Storemen........3.	
Orderly Room Clerks ...2.	
Transport Establishment 28.	
O.C's Groom ....1.	
Grooms.................4.	
Water Duties..........5.	
Cooks.................2.	
MO Orderly ....1.	
Sanitary ....2.	
Shoemakers ....5.	
Tailors ....3.	
Butcher ....1.	
Postman ....1.	
Batmen ....3.	61.

Company Hdqrs. Fighting portion

C.S.M........................1.	
Signallers ....7.	
Stretcher Bearers ....4.	
Gas ....1.	
Cooks ....2.	
Runners ..(d).................4.	
Drummers .(d).................2.	
Batmen ...(d).................2.	23.

Company Hdqrs Administrative

C.Q.M.S. ....1.	
Groom ....1.	
Sanitary ....2.	4.

Platoon Hdqrs.

Platoon Sergeant ....1.	
Runner.......................1.	
Batman .(d).................1.	3.

NOTES.
- (a) Separate provision made as a temporary measure only until Battalions can be raised to a higher establishment
- (b) When circumstances admit. of raising Battalions to higher establishment it is proposed to add a third rifle section to each platoon, making 48 rifle sections in all.
- (c) If raised to higher establishment, with three rifle sections and one double Lewis Gun section per Platoon, the maximum of the Rifle Section will be reduced to 10 and the maximum of the Lewis Gun Sections to 14.
- (d) Also act as Runners.

OPERATION ORDERS No.157
by
MAJOR C.T.WILLIAMS
Comdg. 12th. East Surrey Regiment

1. The Battalion with Transport will parade at 11.50 to-morrow in the following order:-
    H.Qr's - Drums - A. D. - Band - B. C. Coys.
    Head of column, at a point 500 yards S. of where track leaves road opposite Glassworks. Column facing S.
    Dress - Full Marching Order.

2. The Battalion will be located on night of 18th/19th. in SOMBREFFE Area.

3. Billeting parties as usual will report to 2/Lieut. W.S.HALL at Glassworks at 07.15. They will meet the Staff Captain at SOMBREFFE Church at 08.00.

4. Lorries will be as usual. 2/Lieut. A.C.COWLIN is detailed as Officer in xxxxx charge of lorries, he will collect blankets from Companies commencing 10.30.

5. Blankets will be stacked on main road outside billet by Companies at 10.00.

6. Officers valises Mess Kit etc will be stacked outside Company H.Qr's ready for collection by 10.00.

7. Each Company will detail 5 men who are unable to march in the column to parade at 10.00 under the Orderly Officer for the 19th. inst. They will proceed by devious routes to new area avoiding the main road.

8. Companies will take advantage of the late hour in starting for cleaning up and having their platoons thoroughly inspected.

SECRET.

12th Bn EAST SURREY REGT.

OPERATION ORDER No.111.

13-9-17.

1. The Battalion will march to STAPLE to-morrow, 14th Septr, 1917.

2. The Battalion will parade in column of route in the following order on the road from BRASSERIE to W.3.a.8.4, head of column to be at W.3.a.8.4 ready to move off at 9.15 a.m.

    Headquarters.
    Band.
    A Company.
    B Company.
    C Company.
    D Company.

Dress:- Fighting order.

3. Route:- ST.MARTIN - ARQUES - LE NIEPPE.

4. Packs & Stores. All packs and stores will be packed ready for collection by motor lorry as follows :-
 1st Journey. H.Qrs packs & Qnr.Stores, to be stacked at Qnr.Stores.
 2nd Journey. A & B Coys packs at B Coy H.Q.
 3rd Journey. C & D Coys packs at the BRASSERIE.
All the above stores will be stacked by 8.30 a.m.

5. Loading Parties. Three guards of three men each as hereunder stated will take charge of all stores at each of the above dumps, reporting in each case by 7.30 a.m.

 Qmr.Stores:- No.14349 L/C Brown. A Coy.
     No.6297 Pte Dance. D "
     No.14107 " Payne. H.Q. Coy.

 B Coy.H.Q.:- No.14344 Pte Brookes. A Coy.
     No.12272 " Huntingford. B Coy.
     No.14857 " Rham. B Coy.

 BRASSERIE :- No.10534 Pte Andrews. C Coy.
     No.12291 " Halliday. D "
     No.782 " Trigg. D "

The above mentioned men only will proceed by motor lorry.

6. Officers Valises and Mess Baskets. All Officers Valises will be stacked outside Company billets by 6.30 a.m. for collection by G.S.Wagon commencing with C Company.
Mess baskets will be stacked outside Company billets by 7.30 a.m. Collection by Mess Cart will commence with H.Qrs. Coy.

7. Marching out states will be rendered to Orderly Room by 7 a.m. to-morrow.

       (sd) V.L.Clift,

        Capt & Adjt,

       12th Bn East Surrey Regt.

SECRET.

12th Bn EAST SURREY REGIMENT.

OPERATION ORDER No.112.

14th September, 1917.

Reveille 7.30 a.m.   Sick Parade 7.45 a.m.
Breakfasts 8.15 a.m.

1. The Battalion and Transport will march to the LE ROUKLOSHILLE AREA to-morrow, 15th September, 1917.

2. The Battalion will parade in mass on the field behind CREVE-COEUR FARM at 10.10 a.m. Dress:- Fighting Order.

3. Route:- HONDEGHEM STATION - CAESTRE - FLETRE.

4. Packs & Stores. All packs and stores will be stacked near the entrance to CREVE-COEUR FARM by 8.30 a.m.

5. Officers Valises & Mess Baskets. These will be stacked as above by 9 a.m.

6. Loading Parties. The men detailed in Operation Order No.111, Para. 5, will act as loading parties to the above stores.
2nd Lieut. RUSSELL will be O i/c Lorries.

7. Normal halts will be observed on the march. There will be no long halt.

(sd) V.L.Clift,

Capt & Adjt,

12th Bn East Surrey Regiment.

12th Bn EAST SURREY REGT.

ADDENDUM to OPERATION ORDER No.111.

8. Normal halts will be observed on the march. In addition there will be a one hour's halt when head of Brigade reaches level Railway Crossing at FORT ROUGE, 1¼ miles EAST of ARQUES.

(sd) V.L.Clift,
Capt & Adjt,
12th Bn East Surrey Regt.

13.9.17.

SECRET.

12th Bn East Surrey Regiment.

OPERATION ORDER No.113.

16th September, 1917.

1. The Battalion and Transport will march to the MURRUMBIDGEE AREA to-day 16th September, 1917.

2. The Battalion will parade in column of route in three's on the ROUKLOSHILLE-NOOTE BOOM ROAD facing EAST by 12.45 p.m. ready to move off. The head of the column will be outside "B" Company's Headquarters.
   Order of march:-   Headquarters.
                      "B" Company.
                      "C" Company.
                      "D" Company.
                      "A" Company.
   An interval of 50 yards will be maintained beyween Companies.

3. Route:- PIEBROUCK - BERTHEN - WESTOUTRE - and OVERLAND TRACK.

4. Packs and Stores. All packs and stores will be stacked outside Billets by 11 a.m.

5. Officers Valises and Mess Baskets. These will be stacked as above by 11.30 a.m.

6. Loading Parties. The men detailed in Operation Order No.111, Para 5, will act as Loading Parties to the above stores. 2nd Lt.RUSSELL will be O i/c Lorries.

7. Normal halts will be observed on the march. There will be no long halt.

(sd) V.L.Clift,

Capt & Adjt,

12th Bn East Surrey Regiment.

No. 2.

No. 6 (Contd)

No. 7. METHOD OF BATTALION ATTACK. Each Company will be on a two platoon front and will advance in columns of sections until the BLUE LINE is reached. Here the platoons of A and B Coys will extend to Battle Formation. C and D Companies will continue to advance in column of sections until they are within 200 - 300 yards in rear of GREEN LINE, where they will extend and consolidate.

At Zero hour the barrage will form about 150 yards in front of the Assembly Area. The Battalion will conform to the movements of the 18th Bn K.R.R.C., a distance of about 50 yards being maintained between Battalions until the 18th Bn K.R.R.C. attack the BLUE LINE. After the BLUE LINE has been captured by the 18th Bn K.R.R.C. "A" and "B" Companies will pass through them and form up as close under the barrage as is possible. When the barrage moves forward they will follow it, attack and consolidate the GREEN LINE.

No. 8. MOPPING UP. Each assaulting wave from the time it moves forward under the barrage is responsible for its own mopping up. Supporting and reserve platoons will examine all shell holes and dug-outs as they pass them, to ensure that no enemy are left in our rear: it is not sufficient guarantee of safety that the 1st wave has passed over them.

The following known possible points of resistance will be dealt with the 18th Bn K.R.R.C. as follows :-
J.20.c.10.00 M.G. Post.
J.20.c.10.15 Ruins.
J.20.c.30.35 Ruins.
J.20.c.84.40 Ruins.
J.20.d.05.10) Dug-outs &
J.20.d.25.10) M.G. Posts.
J.20.d.15.30) about JAVA TRENCH.

The following known possible points of resistance will be dealt with by platoons of the 12th Bn East Surrey Regt.
J.2p.d.80.05. Battn.H.Q. Dug-outs. left leading platoon of A Coy.
J.27.a.20.95. M.G. & Ruins. The then left leading platoon of A Coy
J.21.c.25.25. M.G. & Ruins. The left leading platoon of B Coy.

Leading platoons not engaged by these points of resistance must assist by fire in their capture, and support and reserve platoons must be ready to engage them instantly if the leading wave is held up.

No. 9. CONTACT WITH OTHER TROOPS. Each wave will keep contact with the corresponding wave on its flanks. Special men will be told off for this purpose. Particulars care must be taken on the right flank which is on the Brigade Boundary.

At all times, both during movement and consolidation, Commanders must ensure that their flanks are adequately protected.

After A and B Companies have passed through the 18th Bn K.R.R.C. subsequent to the capture of the BLUE LINE, C and D Coys must keep touch with them. Troops already on their objectives will give all assistance to those passing through to enable them to keep direction by saying whether they are the right or left of their Coys or Battn.

No. 10. ARTILLERY BARRAGE. (a) At Zero hour the barrage will form about 150 yards in front of our front line where it will remain until Zero plus 3 mins. while the Infantry form up close under it. At Zero plus 3 mins. the barrage will move forward covering the first two hundred yards at a rate of 100 yards in 4 mins and then proceeding at a rate of 100 yards in 6 mins. until it reaches a line 200 yards beyond the RED LINE. On this line the barrage halts for approximately 45 mins.

(b) On moving forward the barrage will advance at a rate of 100 yards in 8 mins until a line 200 yards beyond the BLUE LINE is reached. On this line barrage halts for approximately 2 hours.

No. 3.

X in 8 minutes to a line 200 yards

No.10 (Contd) ARTILLERY BARRAGE. (c) On resuming the advance, barrage will move forward at a rate of 100 yards X beyond the GREEN LINE, on which line the protective barrage forms. Infantry posts will be pushed forward to a maximum distance of 100 yards in advance of the final line selected for consolidation.
(d) The portion of the creeping barrage nearest our own Infantry will be known as barrage "A", and this barrage will, on lifting off the RED, BLUE and GREEN LINES, contain a proportion of Smoke Shell to indicate that the respective Objectives have been gained.
(e) Barrage "A" will pause 200 yards beyond the RED, BLUE and GREEN LINES.
(f) An 18-pdr barrage 200 yards beyond the GREEN LINE. This barrage will continue till Zero plus 8 hours 3 mins, with a pause of 30 mins from Zero plus 5 hours 18 mins to Zero plus 5 hours 48 mins, and a pause of 1¾ hours from Zero plus 6 hours 3 mins to Zero plus 7 hours 48 mins.
(g) A barrage in depth of all natures of Hows up to 9.2" Hows and 60-pdr guns beyond the 18-pdr barrage. This barrage continues until Zero plus 9 hours 3 mins, with a pause of 1 hour from Zero plus 5 hours 33 mins to Zero plus 6 hours 33 mins, and a pause of 1 hour from Zero plus 7 hours 18 mins to Zero plus 8 hours 18 mins.
This barrage searches forward to a depth of 1,500 yards and at intervals by lifts of 100 yards.

No.11. CONSOLIDATION. The captured ground will be organised for defence in depth as follows :-
(a) A front zone of defence, with outposts and strong points to the rear of then about the line of the GREEN LINE.
(b) A support zone of defence, with strong points at intervals, about the line of the BLUE LINE.
(c) A zone of posts, about the line of the RED LINE, covering crossings of the BASSEVILLE BEEK.
(d) A reserve line to be dug and wired on our present front line.
Each assaulting wave will consolidate its own objective and supporting and reserve platoons will consolidate in rear of the leading waves.

No.12. HEADQUARTERS & COMMUNICATIONS.
(a) Headquarters at Zero hour will be as follows :-
122nd Brigade Hdqrs)
122nd M.G.Coy.   ) HEDGE STREET TUNNELS.
122nd L.T.M.B.   )

18th Bn.K.R.R.C.   ) Dug-outs near J.25.a.3.9.
12th Bn East Surrey Regt)

15th Hants Regt.   )
11th R.W.Kent Regt.)   "   "   J.19.c.50.15.

31st Bn K.R.R.C.   "   "   J.25.a.1.3.

(b) Signal communications will be on the same lines as on 7th June 1917.
Brigade Forward Parties will be formed to go forward with the attack.

No.13. LIGHT SIGNALS. The following Light Signals will be used within the Brigade during the attack only:-
(a) To be fired by an Officer only (as long as there is one at the taking of the objective):-
Single white Very light fired towards our original line to signify as objective gained.
(b) To be fired by any rank:-
Single Red Very light, fired in direction of suspected point of resistance holding up attack, for information of immediate supports.

No.4.

No.13. **LIGHT SIGNALS (Contd).** Contact Aeroplanes will call for flares by firing a white light and sounding a KLAXON Horn. Leading Infantry will light flares approximately at the following times when called for by the aeroplane:-
On the RED LINE, Zero plus 45 mins, on the BLUE LINE, ZERO plus two hours and 5 mins, on the GREEN LINE Zero plus 4 hours and 50 mins.

No.14. **KIT.** Dress and equipment to be worn by all ranks as laid down for the operations of 7th June 1917, except that bombers will carry 100 rounds of S.A.A. and only 5 bombs.
150 rounds of S.A.A. and 2 grenades per man (100 rounds S.A.A. and 5 grenades for bombers) and S.A.A. for Lewis Guns will be drawn as soon as the Battalion arrives in RIDGE WOOD AREA and will be taken up on the men when the Battalion moves into the line.

No.15. **DATES & TIMES.** The day on which the operation will be carried out will be called the "Attack Day". Actual date will be notified later to all concerned.
Zero hour will be the exact moment at which the barrage opens. After this hour references to times will be given in hours and minutes, am. or pm; e.g. 7.30 p.m. **not** Zero plus so many hours.
Until zero hour is known times will be referred to as zero plus or minus so many hours and minutes.

No.16. **SECRECY.** All ranks taking part in the operation must be thoroughly acquainted with the whole plan. At the same time the necessity of keeping the information to themselves, especially if taken prisoner, must be impressed upon them.
All papers dealing with the operation will be returned to Battn. Hdqrs in sealed packets before the Battalion goes into the line.
If it is ordered that any papers dealing with the operation be destroyed they will be burnt by an Officer.

No.17. **APPENDICES.** Maps for attack and assembly, diagram of formations, barrage tables, instructions for signal communications, assembly, synchronization and liason, and necessary extracts from administrative instructions will be issued later.

(sd) V.L.Clift,
Capt & Adjt,

Issued at 12 noon
17th September, 1917.

12th Bn East Surrey Regt.

Copy No. 1 C.O.
" No. 2 2nd in Command
" No. 3 Adjutant.
" No. 4 Asst.Adjutant.
" No. 5 File.
" No. 6 War Diary.
" No. 7 O.C. A Coy.
" No. 8 O.C. B Coy.

Copy.No. 9. O.C. C Coy.
" No.10. O.C. D "
" No.11. Signalling Officer.
" No.12. Intelligence Officer.
" No.13. A/Quartermaster.
" No.14. Transport Officer.
" No.15. Medical Officer.
" No.16. Spare.

DAGGER
Operation Order No 117

1. The Battalion will move by platoons at 100 yards distance from LANKHOF CHATEAU to Assembly Area at J 19 d 22 :-
Order of march B - A - D - C - HQ Coy
The first platoon of B Coy will leave at 11 p.m. so as to pass Track Junction J 19 a 10 at 1 a.m. Sept 20 1917

2. An Advance party of 1 OR per platoon under 2Lt MUIR will leave at 7 p.m. in order to be at Track Junction at 9 p.m.
They will reconnoitre Assembly Area & eventually guide their platoons to Assembly Area by "B" Track

3. Route LANKHOF CHATEAU via TOWSEY'S TRACK & "B" TRACK.

4. Water for refilling of water bottles will be at LANKHOF CHATEAU at 9 p.m.

B.T D.L.S. White
A/Adjt

SECRET.   Copy No. 1.

12th Bn. East Surrey Regt.

OPERATION ORDER   No.115.

The Battalion will move to the DUNKERKE AREA to-morrow, 27th September, 1917.

1. The Battalion will parade in column of route at W.2.a.1.2 at 6 a.m. to-morrow, in the following order :-
   - Headquarters.
   - "A" Company.
   - "B" Company.
   - "C" Company.
   - "D" Company.

   and will then proceed to Q.31.b.3.4 for embussment.
   Dress:- Full marching order.
   Rations. Rations for the day will be carried on the man.

2. No one will embus until orders have been given by the Adjutant directing embussing.

3. On arrival at destination short of UXEM :-
   (a) Personnel will not debus except under orders of the Adjutabt directing embussing.
   (b) After debussing the Battalion will form up at once, if possible clear of the road, and will not move off until the busses are clear.
   (c) A guide will then meet the Battalion which will then march off to UXEM.
   A distance of 200 yards will be maintained between Companies on the march.

4. O.C. "D" Company will detail one Officer to accompany a bus which will collect Officers Valises, Mess Baskets, and cooking utensils. This bus will proceed to Companies in the following order :-
   - "D" Company.
   - "C" Company.
   - "B" Company.
   - "A" Company.
   - Headquarters.

   Companies will detail one man per Company to remain at their billets and accompany this bus. These men will act as loading party.

5. O.C. Companies will ensure that when billets are vacated they are left in a scrupulously clean condition. A certificate to this effect will be rendered to the Adjutant on arrival at the starting point.

                                    (sd) B.F.Dodd,
                                         2-Lt & A/Adjt,
                                    12th Bn East Surrey Regiment.

Issued at.....
26th September, 1917.

    Copy No. 1. File.   Copy No. 6. O.C. A Coy.
     "   No. 2. C.O.   "   No. 7. O.C. B Coy.
     "   No. 3. 2nd-in-Comd.   "   No. 8. O.C. C Coy.
     "   No. 4. Adjutant.   "   No. 9. O.C. D Coy.
     "   No. 5. Medical Officer. "   No.10. R.S.M.

SECRET.   Copy No. 6

12th Bn EAST SURREY REGT.

OPERATION ORDER No.116.

1. The Battalion will move to   LA PANNE to-morrow, 26th September, 1917.

2. The Battalion will parade in column of route at I.6,c,4,4, at 6 a.m. to-morrow in the following order :-
    Headquarters.
    "A" Company.
    "B" Company.
    "C" Company.
    "D" Company.
    Transport.
    Dress:- Full marching order.

3. Normal halts will be observed on the march.

4. Distances of 200 yards will be maintained between Companies.

5. Officers Valises, Mess Baskets, and cooking utensils will be stacked outside Company billets by 5 a.m.
   Companies will detail one man per Company to remain at their billets in charge of Company kit. These men will act as loading party.

6. O.C.Companies will ensure that when billets are vacated they are left in a scrupulously clean condition. A certificate to this effect will be rendered to the Adjutant on parade.

                                        (sd) B.F.Dodd,

                                            2-Lt & A/Adjt,

                                        12th Bn East Surrey Regiment.

Issued at........
27th September, 1917.

Copy No. 1. File.
 "   No. 2. C.O.
 "   No. 3. 2nd-in-Command.
 "   No. 4. Adjutant.
 "   No. 5. Medical Officer.
 "   No. 6. O.C. A Coy.
 "   No. 7. O.C. B Coy.
 "   No. 8. O.C. C Coy.
 "   No. 9. O.C. D Coy.
 "   No.10. Transport Officer.
 "   No.11. A/Quartermaster.
 "   No.12. R.S.M.

Headquarters
122nd Infantry Bde

R26/22.

Herewith Original copy of War Diary for the month of October for the Battalion under my command

C. F. Stallard
Lieut. Col.
Comdg 12/Bn East Surrey Regt

[Stamp: 12th BATTALION, EAST SURREY REGIMENT. 3 November 1917 No....... Date.......]

Army Form C. 2118.

12 E Surrey
Vol 18

WAR DIARY or INTELLIGENCE SUMMARY.
(Erase heading not required.)

Instructions regarding War Diaries and Intelligence Summaries are contained in F. S. Regs., Part II. and the Staff Manual respectively. Title pages will be prepared in manuscript.

Place	Date	Hour	Summary of Events and Information	Remarks and references to Appendices
LA PANNE	1917 Oct 1		Battalion in training under Coy arrangements. Relieved every given by Coy Commanders on Trench Routine and Routine. W9M Major C.T.H.WILLIAMS assumed duties of Second in Command W9M.	
	2		Battalion inspected by Divisional Commander at V.24.d.9.5. afterwards carrying out a Route march. Bathing Parades were carried out by Coys. Major B.W.PUTTICK.M.C. assumed command of Battalion on 21-9-17. Capt H.S.WALKER.M.C. assumed duties of acting Second in Command on 21-9-17. 2nd Lieut. B.E.DODD assumed duties of acting Adjutant on 19-9-17. Major R.T.WILLIAMS rejoined the Battalion this day for duty W9M.	
	3		Battalion in training under Coy arrangements. N.C.O's Class started encounter training by R.S.M. Lieut ROGERS proceeded on leave this day. W9M Major A.W.PUTTICK.M.C. rejoined 1st Line of Trench P. to L. taken over by Battalion in NIEUPORT SECTOR	7.a
	4		Battalion in training under Coy arrangements. Baths are allotted to Battalion at N.23.c. Band D Coys 300 Strong & 3.6 Officers proceeded to R.32.6 on working party under Major R.T.WILLIAMS 2nd Lieut W.H.IZZARD assumed duties of Signalling Officer this day W9M.	B.C 7 that
	5		Battalion in training under Coy arrangements. Capt M.S.WALKER.M.C. reconnoitred Line of Trenches P. to L. taken over by Battalion in NIEUPORT SECTOR 2/Lieut R.V.RENYER to be acting Capt from this date W9M	

WAR DIARY or INTELLIGENCE SUMMARY.

Army Form C. 2118.

(Erase heading not required.)

Place	Date	Hour	Summary of Events and Information	Remarks and references to Appendices
LA DANNE	1917 Oct 6		Battalion in training under Coy arrangements. Bombing & Grenade Throwing practices were carried out. 2/Lieut C.H.FISHER assumed temp Command of J.A. Coy from this day	
	7		Capt H.S.WALKER M.C. assumed duties of Acting Adjutant. W.Th. Battalion paraded for Divine Service. Lieut A.B.WRIGHT joined the Battalion this day & posted to A. Coy. W.Th.	
	8		Battalion in training under Coy arrangements. W.Th.	
	9		Battalion in training under Coy arrangements. Miniature Range work & practices carried out. W.Th.	
	10		Baths were allotted to Battalion at ST IDESBALDE. Battalion paraded Cake under Coy arrangements. Decorations were awarded to the following NCO's & men of the Battalion. Bar to Military Medal No 14531 L/c L.E.Douthall Military Medal No 4493 C.Q.M.S. W. Barnes " " " 15876 Pte L. Greaves " " " 14608 Pte E. Lomas " " " 9338 Sgt L. Harwood " " " 25303 " F. Davey " " " 14448 Pte H. Kenyon " " " 12824 " T. Cunningham " " " 33947 " E. Hindley W.Th.	

WAR DIARY
or
INTELLIGENCE SUMMARY.
(Erase heading not required.)

Army Form C. 2118.

Place	Date	Hour	Summary of Events and Information	Remarks and references to Appendices
	1917			
LA PANNE	OCT 11		Bogies being taken into Coy areas ground 6. 2/LIEUT L.A. GOODING joins the Battalion	
	12		Two Coys reported to C Company. NRL	
			Battle Coy formed at 9am under C.O. & proceeded in Push Bank via D.BERGHE & BRAY DUNES Rd. 2/LIEUT LEWIS Indisposed from a result of Deep Sea School the day. NTR.	
	13		Battalion in training. TEMP Coy arrangement 2/LIEUT R.H. HAINE rejoined the Battalion this day. 7/2 Indicating 2nd/LIEUT to EYLISS' from 1-9-17 Supplement to London Gaz. Sept 13-10-17.	
			Battle Coy through R.29 Officers 53Y OR's NTR.	
	14		Bombardments started heavy shells on Y.M.C.A Hut LA PANNE at 10-15 A.M. NTR	
	15		Battle Coy paraded at 8-30 am and marched to OOST DUNKERKE BAINS via COXYDE to R.P. over dunes on Coast DEFENCES on a Front reaching from R.32.a to R.23 & R.25 incl SKILL OOST DUNKERKE. NRL	
OOST DUNKERKE BAINS	15		Battn relieved from 10th Batt QUEENS REGT. Relief completed at 1pm. LT & S/LT RYAN joined the Battn this day. LIEUT B.F. DODD proceeded on Cour this day. NTR.	
"	16		Situation report normal. Occasional shelling in vicinity of NIEUPORT BAINS. Kmg trace NTR.	
"	17		Situation report normal. 2nd/LIEUT G.P. COOPER & R.K. WATTS joined the Battn this day. 7 our parties to B. D. Coys. LT. COL A.W. PUTTICK M.C. relinquished Command of Batt from this date.	

LIEUT. COL. C.F. STALLARD. M.C. assumed command of Battalion from this date. NTR.

WAR DIARY
or
INTELLIGENCE SUMMARY.
(Erase heading not required.)

Army Form C. 2118.

Place	Date	Hour	Summary of Events and Information	Remarks and references to Appendices
OOST DUNKERKE BAINS	17		LIEUT COL H.W. PUTTICK M.C. 11th ROYAL WEST KENTS was transferred to the 15th Bn HAMPSHIRE REGT.	
"	18		Situation report normal. Enemy aeroplanes active during the morning, occasional shelling	
			of OOST DUNKERKE BAINS & NIEUPORT BAINS. 2nd/LIEUT L.L. LINFORD joined the Battalion for duty this day	
"	19		Situation report normal. Enemy machine gun active during the day. Interm't Bombt: shelling of	
			OOST DUNKERKE BAINS & NIEUPORT BAINS. The following Officers joined the Battalion the day	
			for duty: — CAPT A.R. KEDSELL A.Coy, LIEUT R.F. COPP A.Coy, LIEUT R.C. EDGAR B.Coy,	
			LIEUT E.B. GILLETT D.Coy, LIEUT E.H. BARRY A.Coy, LIEUT G.C. DAVENPORT B.Coy, LIEUT L. DAWSON C.Coy.	
			Casualties (1) (202483 PTE A.H. HILLS's wounded)	
"	20		Situation report normal. Occasional shelling by Enemy of OOST DUNKERKE BAINS	
			Battalion relieving the 416 June. S.S.& O.R.2 The following Officers & men receiving Decorations	
			Military Cross Capt W.L.A. HARRISON R.A.M.C. D.C.M. N° 490 C.S.M. LOVE	
			" 2nd/LIEUT H.D. MUTCH " N° 25434 SGT R.W. MAYSTON	
			" 2nd/LIEUT C.H. WARD " N° 32704 PTE A. TRUSSLER	
"	21		Situation report normal. Wind E. & S.W. Dangerous.	
"	22		Situation report normal. Occasional shelling by enemy of OOST DUNKERKE BAINS & NIEUPORT BAINS	

WAR DIARY
or
INTELLIGENCE SUMMARY.
(Erase heading not required.)

Army Form C. 2118.

Place	Date 1917	Hour	Summary of Events and Information	Remarks and references to Appendices
OOST DUNKERKE BAINS	OCT 23		Situation report received. Occasional shelling by enemy of Oost Dunkerke Bains & Nieuport Bains	
			Act/Capt. TODD proceeded on leave. Casualties (1) 161154 Pte. C.D. Cooper wounded) 19th	
	24		Situation report received. Occasional shelling by enemy in vicinity of Oost Dunkerke Bains & Coxyde 19th	
	25		Situation report received. Enemy aircraft & Artillery active throughout the day.	
			Lieut G.G. DAVENPORT to opposite Lewis Gun Officer from this day. Lieut A.C. EDGAR as opposite "Musketry" Officer from this date 19th	
	26		Situation report received. Enemy Artillery active in Dunes. E of Oost Dunkerke Bains for some hours during day & night. Casualties Nil. Lieut G.P.C. REAM to C. Act. Captain from 20-7-17. 19th	
	27		Situation report received. Enemy artillery fairly active throughout the day in Oost Dunkerke Bains & Nieuport Bains. Battalion strength 16 Officers & 665 O.R.s 19th	
	28		Situation report received. Enemy artillery fairly quiet throughout the day. Casualties Nil. Divine Service in Concert Room, Oost Dunkerke Bains. 19th	
	29		Battalion relieved by 1st South African Infantry Brigade. Relief complete at 5.30 p.m. Battalion proceeded by Louvie Inter Coxyde Bains to Coudekerque Branche via Le Panner, Dunkerke. Act/Capt. A.B. REINER resumed duties with Battalion from Divisional Ypres Barracks. 19th	

Army Form C. 2118.

WAR DIARY
or
INTELLIGENCE SUMMARY.
(Erase heading not required.)

Instructions regarding War Diaries and Intelligence Summaries are contained in F. S. Regs., Part II. and the Staff Manual respectively. Title pages will be prepared in manuscript.

Place	Date	Hour	Summary of Events and Information	Remarks and references to Appendices
COUDEKERQUE BRANCHE	1917 Oct- 30		Battalion employed throughout the day on re-organization Kit & Rifle inspection. LIEUT DODD R.E. AS'T ADJUTANT returned from Leave this day.	
	31		Battalion paraded under the Commanding Officer at 10 a.m. & proceeded on Route March returning at 1 P.M. A/CAPT TODD returned from Leave this day. 2/LIEUT C.L.WHITE returned to Battalion from Divisional Depot Battalion. 2/LIEUT T.M.LLOYD returned to Battalion from Divisional Gas Course. 2/LIEUT C.F.W.FAITH assumed duties as O.C. "D" Battalion from "Twenty-one'd Bn."	

C.J. Stallard
LT.-COL.,
COMDg. 12th BATT. EAST SURREY REGT.

SECRET.   Copy No. 1

13th Bn EAST SURREY REGIMENT.

OPERATION ORDER No.117.

Ref:- Sheet 11 S.E. (BELGIUM & FRANCE) 1/20.000.

---

1. The Battalion, less Transport, will move on the 7th October, 1917, to the ST. IDESBALDE Area and form part of the Reserve Brigade to the NIEUPORT BAINS SECTOR.

2. The Battalion will parade at W.22.b. on the right side of the Main Road facing North in full marching order at 9.15 a.m. in the following order :-
   Headquarters, "A" Coy, "C" Coy.

3. Route. By Coast Tracks.

4. Normal halts will be observed on the march and a distance of 200 yards will be maintained between Companies.

5. Blankets, Stores, etc. Blankets, Stores, etc. will be stacked outside the Qur.Stores by 8 a.m. The Regtl.Sgt.Major will detail a guard.

6. Officers Valises, Mess Baskets etc. Officers Valises, Mess Baskets, etc. will be stacked outside Company Messes by 8 a.m.

7. Transport. The Battalion Transport will move on the 7th Octr, 1917, from the present Camp to Camp at W.16.b.5.7. Head of Transport to pass Cross Roads at W.16.c.8.7 at 9.15 a.m.

8. Route:- Via DE ZUIDPANNE.

9. Normal halts will be observed on the march and a distance of 200 yards will be maintained between Units.

10. O.C.Companies will ensure that when billets are vacated they are left in a scrupulously clean condition. A Certificate to this effect will be rendered to the Adjutant on parade.

                                    (sd) H.S. Walker,
                                    Capt & A/Adjt,
                                    13th Bn East Surrey Regt.

Issued at 12.30 p.m.
6th October, 1917.

Copy No. 1. File.
"   No. 2. C.O.
"   No. 3. 2nd-in-Command.
"   No. 4. Adjutant.
"   No. 5. A/Adjutant.
"   No. 6. Intelligence Officer.
"   No. 7. Signalling Officer.
"   No. 8. Medical Officer.
"   No. 9. O.C. A Coy.
"   No.10. O.C. B Coy.
"   No.11. O.C. C Coy.
"   No.12. O.C. D Coy.
"   No.13. Transport Officer.
"   No.14. A/Quartermaster.
"   No.15. A/R.S.M.

SECRET.   Copy No...1..

12th EAST SURREY REGIMENT.
OPERATION ORDER. No.114.

Map Reference. Sheet 11 S.E. 1/40.000. and Sheet 19 1/40.000.

1. **INFORMATION.**   The 122nd Infantry Brigade will relieve the 124th
                     Infantry Brigade in the COXYDE BAINS Coast Defence
                     Sector on the 14th & 15th October, 1917.

2. **INTENTION.**   The 12th Bn. East Surrey Regt. will relieve the 10th Bn.
                     Royal West Surrey Regt. in the Right Battalion Sector,
                     EOLIAN ROAD, R.24.c. to R.31.Central, to-morrow, 15th
                     October, 1917.

3. **INSTRUCTIONS.** The Battalion and Transport,(less R.E. Detachment) will
                     parade in column of route on the road adjoining Camp
                     facing North at 8 a.m., the head of the column being
                     opposite the Guard Room.

   (a) Order of March.   Headquarters.
                              "C" Company.
                              "A" Company.
                              Transport.
   An interval of 200 yards will be maintained between
   Companies and Transport.

   (b) Route.   Via COXYDE - COXYDE BAINS - OOST DUNKERKE BAINS.

   (c) Disposition. "C" Company will hold the Right Sub Sector from
                    R.23.b.90.15 to R.27.c.90.75, and will furnish Posts
                    Nos. 1 - 15 (a) inclusive.
                    "C" Company Headquarters will be at R.32.c.45.25.
                    "A" Company will hold the Left Sub Sector from
                    No.15 (b) Post at R.27.d.10.75 to R.33.b.1.9, and will
                    furnish Posts Nos.15 (b) - 18 inclusive.
                    "A" Company Headquarters will be at SURREY CAMP R.32.b.4.9.
                    Transport and Qmr.Stores will take over from opposite
                    number.

   (d) Relief.   The Relief will be complete by 1 p.m. completion being
                 notified to Battalion Headquarters in the usual manner.

   (e) Trench Stores. Companies will take over all Plans, Aeroplane
                      Photographs, and Trench Stores, from the Company they
                      relieve. Receipts for same will be forwarded to Orderly
                      Room.

4. **REPORTS.**   Reports will be sent to Battalion Headquarters at
                     R.27.c.6.4.

                                              (sd) H.S.Walker.
                                                   Capt & A/Adjt
                                              12th Bn East Surrey Regiment.

Issued at..........
14th October,1917.

Copy No. 1. File.   Copy No. 2. War Diary.
  " No. 3. C.O.   " No. 4. 122nd Infantry Brigade.
  " No. 5. 2nd-in-Command.   " No. 6. Adjutant.
  " No. 7. O.C. A Company.   " No. 8. O.C. B Company.
  " No. 9. O.C. C Company.   " No.10. O.C. D Company.
  " No.11. Medical Officer.   " No.12. Intelligence Officer.
  " No.13. Signalling Officer.   " No.14. Transport Officer.
  " No.15. A/Quartermaster.   " No.16. R.S.M.
  " No.17. 10th R.W.Surrey Regt.

S E C R E T

12th East Surrey Regt.
15th Hampshire Regt.
11th Royal West Kent Regt.
18th Kings Royal Rifle Corps.
122nd Machine Gun Company.
122nd Trench Mortar Battery.

122nd INFANTRY BRIGADE WARNING ORDER No.14.

1.- 122nd Infantry Brigade will probably relieve the 124th Infantry Brigade in the NIEUPORT BAINS SECTOR on the 31st and night 31st October/1st November, being relieved by the 123rd Infantry Brigade in COAST DEFENCE SECTOR.

2.- Relief of Machine Gun Companies and Light Trench Mortar Batteries will take place 24 hours in advance of the remainder of the Brigade.

3.- On relief the 18th Bn. King's Royal Rifle Corps will hold the front line in the Left Sub-sector, with the 15th Bn. Hampshire Regiment in Support.

The 11th Bn. Royal West Kent Regiment will hold the front line in the Right Sub-sector, with the 12th Bn. East Surrey Regiment in Support.

4.- Officers Commanding Units will make arrangements to send Officers to reconnoitre the positions which they are to take over, before the relief takes place. Not more than 4 should be sent at any one time.

Officers visiting the front line positions will report at Headquarters 124th Infantry Brigade before going round the line.

5.- ACKNOWLEDGE.

6.- There will be a Conference of Commanding Officers at Brigade Headquarters at 2.15 p.m. to-morrow, 26th instant

J.E. Snell
Captain.
Brigade Major.
122nd Infantry Brigade.

25-10-17.

SECRET.   Copy No. 1.

12th Bn. EAST SURREY REGT.

WARNING ORDER No. 14.

1. INTENTION.   The 122nd Infantry Brigade will probably relieve
                 the 134th Infantry Brigade in the NIEUPORT BAINS
                 SECTOR on the 31st October, 1917, and night of
                 31st October/1st November, 1917.
                 The 122nd Infantry Brigade will probably be relieved
                 by the 133rd Infantry Brigade in COAST DEFENCE
                 SECTOR.

2. DISPOSITIONS. The 11th Bn. Royal East Kent Regt will hold Front
                 Line in RIGHT sub Sector (Bn.Hdqrs. at M.20.b.8.4)
                 with the 12th Bn. East Surrey Regt in Support
                 (Bn.Hdqrs. at K.3.a.9.1).
                 The 16th Bn. King's Royal Rifle Corps will hold
                 Front Line in LEFT sub Sector with the 15th Bn.
                 Hampshire Regt. in support.

3. INSTRUCTIONS. O's C. Companies will arrange to reconnoitre the
                 positions which they are to take over, and also
                 the Front Line, and will also detail Officers to
                 do the same.
                 Not more than one Officer per Company will visit
                 the Front Line at any one time.
                 Before visiting the Front Line Sector all Officers
                 will report to Headquarters, 134th Infantry Brigade,
                 at R.24.a.6.6.

                                             (sd) H.S.Walker,

                                                  Capt & A/Adjt,

                                           12th Bn East Surrey Regiment.

Issued at..........
24th October, 1917.

Copy No. 1. File.   Copy No. 2. War Diary.
 "   No. 3. C.O.   "   No. 4. 2nd-in-Command.
 "   No. 5. Adjutant.   "   No. 6. O.C. A Company.
 "   No. 7. O.C. B Coy.   "   No. 8. O.C. C Company.
 "   No. 9. O.C. D Coy.   "   No.10. Medical Officer.
 "   No.11. Intelligence Officer.   "   No.12. Signalling Officer.
 "   No.13. Transport Officer.   "   No.14. A/Quartermaster.
 "   No.15. R.S.M.

SECRET.   Copy No......

                        13th Bn. EAST SURREY REGIMENT.

                              DEFENCE SCHEME.

Map Reference - Sheet 11 S.E. 1/20,000.
----

1. FRONTAGE.   The Battalion is responsible for the COS? DUNKERQUE
                    RIGHT SECTION from ROUTE EOLIENNE to R.31.Central
                    exclusive.

2. DISPOSITIONS.   C Company will hold Front Line from R.33.b.8.3 to
                    R.37.d.0.8. with Company Headquarters at R.35.c.5.0.
                    A Company will hold Front Line from R.37.c.9.8 to
                    R.31.b.7.3. with Company Headquarters at R.32.a.8.3.
                    H.Q. Details at R.37.c.8.8. will form Support under
                    2nd Lieut.Hutch, M.C.
                    B and D Companies at SURREY CAMP (R.30.b.=.9) will
                    form Reserve.

3. ALARM POSTS.   O's C. Companies will ensure that every man knows
                    exactly where the Alarm Post is.
                    O's C. Companies are responsible that the men under
                    their command are a fighting force ready to turn out
                    at once on the Alarm to counter attack if necessary.
                    Particular attention to be paid to Lewis Guns and
                    filled magazines for same.
                    Dress:- Fighting Order.
                    In case of an Alarm O's C. B and D Companies will
                    assemble on Alarm Post and will await further orders.
                    They will send one Runner per Company to Battn.Hdqrs.

4. ALARM SIGNALS.   Sentries are responsible for the look out on the beach.
                    Alarm of impending Hostile landing will be given as
                    follows :-
                            Telephone. Signaller at Post will give Alarm by
                                calling H.Q.Coast Defence and Buzzing
                                "Raid near - Post - Section, repeating
                                same to Battn.Hdqrs. In case of a jamb
                                on line reports to Brigade will be sent
                                strictly in rotation. Post 16 will have
                                precedence of 17, 17 over 16, and so on.
                            Naval Lookout Posts burning White and Green Flares.
                            Ships at Sea sending up Green and White Rockets or
                                three Green "Very" Lights in succession.

5. COMMUNICATIONS. G.O.C. Coast Defence is in telephonic communication with
                    Battn.Hdqrs. and Battn.Hdqrs. is in communication with
                    Companies; Companies with Posts.
                    Visual between Battn.Hdqrs. and Brigade; C Company and
                    Battn. Hdqrs.

6. LOOK-OUT POSTS. The number of Look-Out Posts by day per Company will
                    not exceed two; exclusive of any A.A.Sentries. But
                    during misty weather sentries as for night will be posted.

7. WORK.   Companies are responsible for the upkeep of the Trenches
                    and Posts in their Sections, for the repair of the belt
                    of wire in front of their position, and for the
                    provision of adequate shelter for their Posts.

8. AMMUNITION.   13 boxes of S.A.A. will be at the disposal of each
                    Company in the Line, 24 magazines per Lewis Gun to be
                    kept filled.
                    Rifle Grenades. 2 boxes per Company will be kept at
                    Company Headquarters.
                    Gun Ammunition. 37 and 47 mm guns will each have 300
                    rounds per Gun.

No. 2.

9.	GAPS IN WIRE.	All permanent gaps will be provided with wired knife rests which will be placed across the gaps half an hour after Sunset, and removed before Sunrise.
10.	SITUATION REPORTS.	1. Situation Reports - as in trenches - will be rendered to Battn. Hdqrs. by 5.45 a.m. and 5.45 p.m. daily. 2. All unusual occurrences and anything of interest noticed will invariably be reported AT ONCE, to Battn. Hdqrs.
11.	BEACH ORDERS.	Eastwards of Board at Point W.o.b.6.c. the Beach by day will be under Military Control, and all Posts and Sentries will stop anyone going on the Beach anywhere, except :- (a) Our own airmen, if forced to land, when all possible assistance will be rendered by Coast Defence Troops. (b) Intelligence Officers carrying a Green flag on the handle bars of bicycle. (c) Signal linesmen (by day or night) wearing two Red Runner arm bands in addition to the Blue and White Signal arm bands. (d) General Officers on duty, and Officers accompanying them, and O's C. Coast Defence Battalions in their own area.
12.	CARE OF DEFENCES.	No troops are allowed to cross the wire entanglement at any Point except where gaps are cut, or to walk over any of the Defences, except on duty.
13.	NIGHT ORDERS.	1. By night the Beach everywhere will be under Military Control during the hours of darkness. During this time the whole of the Coast lying between the wire entanglement and the Sea will be treated as NO MAN'S LAND, and persons entering it will be liable to be fired on. The sole exception will be LA PANNE SECTION where every person will be challenged twice, and if possible apprehended. If such person endeavours to evade apprehension after being challenged, he will be fired on as in other sections. 2. There will be no firing by night, except in case of a hostile landing, or under circumstances as indicated in Para. 1.
14.	SENTRIES.	All Sentries will at all times use their discretion in opening fire, particular care will be taken not to fire on British or Allied aeroplanes that have to make a forced landing.

(sd) H.S. Walker,
Capt & A/Adjt,
13th Bn. East Surrey Regiment.

Issued at........
27th October, 1917.

Copy No. 1. File.
" No. 3. 123nd Inf. Brigade.
" No. 5. Adjutant.
" No. 7. O.C. A Coy.
" No. 9. O.C. C "
" No.11. Hdqrs. Coy.

Copy No. 2. War Diary.
" No. 4. C.O.
" No. 6. 2nd-in-Command.
" No. 8. O.C. B Coy.
" No.10. O.C. D "
" No.12. R.S.M.

SECRET.

12th Bn EAST SURREY REGT.

WARNING ORDER, No. 11.

1. A Unit of the South African Infantry Brigade will relieve the Battalion in the present sector, on the 29th inst.

2. The Battalion will proceed to SYNTHE AREA on relief.

3. Detailed orders will be issued later.

(sd) H.S.Walker,
Capt & A/Adjt,
28th October, 1917.   12th Bn East Surrey Regiment.

SECRET.   Copy.No. 1

12th Bn. EAST SURREY REGT.
OPERATION ORDER. No.11.

1. The 123nd Infantry Brigade will be relieved in the Coast Defence Sector by the South African Infantry Brigade, 9th Division, on October 24th, 1917.
   The 12th Bn. East Surrey Regt, will be relieved in the present Sector by a Unit of the South African Infantry Brigade, and will move to billets vacated by South African Infantry Brigade at COUDEKERQUE BRANCH.

2. Billeting Parties. Billeting parties consisting of one N.C.O. per Company under 2nd-Lt.LLOYD will rendezvous with cycles at CROSS ROADS, COXYDE BAINS (T.6.a.9.6) at 8 a.m. and will report to Captain REAH.

3. Guides. One guide per Company including Hdqrs will be detailed to report at Brigade Hdqrs. at 10 a.m. 24th inst, to meet advanced billeting parties of the relieving Unit.

4. Relief. Relief will commence immediately on arrival of incoming Unit. When relief is complete the Battalion will rendezvous at the embussing point Cross Roads, COXYDE BAINS, (T.6.a.9.3). On arrival of Companies at embussing point they will immediately report to the Adjutant. All moves will be by Platoons at 200 yards distance.

5. Dress:- Full marching order.

6. Rations. The unexpired portion of the day's rations will be carried on the man.

7. Cleanliness of Billets. O/C.Companies will ensure that billets and Posts are left scrupulously clean, and will render certificates to this effect to the Adjutant at the embussing point.

8. Marching Out States. Marching out states will be rendered to the Orderly Room by 6 a.m.

9. Trench Stores. Companies will hand over to the relieving Unit all plans, aeroplane photographs, and trench stores, together with all maps of the Fourth Army area, and will obtain receipts for same which will be forwarded to Orderly Room.

10. Blankets. All blankets will be rolled in bundles of 10 and stacked outside billets ready for collection by the Regtl. Transport at 7.30 a.m. The Transport Officer will arrange to convey these, together with surplus stores, to COXYDE BAINS - ST.IDESBALDE ROAD, near T.6.a.4.0, by 8 a.m. Where they will be stacked by side of road to await lorry which will be allotted by embussing Staff Officer. A party of one man from each Coy will be detailed to proceed with blankets and to act as loading party.

11. Valises, Mess Baskets etc. Officers Valises, Mess Baskets, etc. will be stacked outside billets ready for collection by Regtl. Transport at 9.30 a.m.

12. Lewis Guns. The Transport Officer will arrange to collect Lewis Guns of B and D Companies. A and C Companies will carry Lewis Guns.

13. Transport. Transport will proceed by road to PETIT SYNTHE ARD. passing starting point Cross Roads, COXYDE BAINS, (T.M.a.9.6) at 12.35 p.m.
    Route:- COXYDE BAINS - COXYDE - KERKEP.NNS - LE PANNE - ADINKERKE - DUNKERKE.
    Halts of 10 minutes will be made at each clock hour.
    The usual distance between Units will be kept.
    Horses should be watered and fed before starting.

No. 4.

14. Reports. Reports will be sent to Battn.Hdqrs. up to 12 noon, and after that hour to COXYDE BAINS Cross Roads. On arrival in the new area Companies will immediately report by runner when they are settled in billets.

(sd) H.S. Winkler,

Capt. & A/Adjt,

13th Bn East Surrey Regt.

Issued At 2.10 a.m.
6th October, 1917.

Copy No. 1. File.
" No. 2. War Diary.
" No. 3. C.O.
" No. 4. 2nd-in-Command.
" No. 5. Adjutant.
" No. 6. O.C. A Company.
" No. 7. O.C. B "
" No. 8. O.C. C "
" No. 9. O.C. D "
" No.10. Medical Officer.
" No.11. Intelligence Officer.
" No.12. Signalling Officer.
" No.13. Transport Officer.
" No.14. A/Quartermaster.
" No.15. R.S.M.

300g/365ml (3)

300g/365ml (3)

41ST DIVISION
122ND INFY BDE

12TH BN EAST SURREY REGT
MAY 1916-~~DEC 1918~~ OCT 1917
MAR 1918 — 1919 MAR

ITALY 1917 NOV — 1918 FE

122md Inf.Bde.
41st Div.

Battn. with Bde. returned to France from Italy 1/5.3.18.

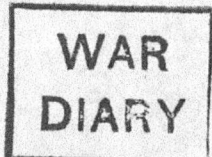

12th BATTN. THE EAST SURREY REGIMENT.

MARCH

1918

WAR DIARY
or
INTELLIGENCE SUMMARY.

Army Form C. 2118.

12th Bn. East Surrey Regt.

Place	Date	Hour	Summary of Events and Information	Remarks and references to Appendices
Italy	March 1st 1918		Half the Battn. A & C Coys paraded at the cross-roads in TOMBOLO and marched to CARMIGNANO arriving at 10.35 AM. Entraining was then carried out, the train leaving at 11.51 AM	
			At midnight MILAN was reached after passing through VICENZA VERONA and BRESCIA	
	2nd		MODANE was reached at 1.15 pm via TURIN. The rate of advance of the train being	
			at MODANE station was 6w [illegible] = 30 franco	
France	3rd		GRAY was reached at 5 p.m. via AMBÉRIEU	
	4th		AMIENS was reached at 10 p.m. via CHALONS SUR MARNE, EPERNAY and ESTRÉES	
	5th		At 3.30 am MONDICOURT was reached & at HQ Coys detrained and marched to HALLOY and LWFD. Second half of Battn. arrived at MONDICOURT and moved	
			to the loft at HALLOY. A/Capt TODD MC admitted to hospital this day	
	6th		The Bn. paraded under Coy arrangements and carried out disciplinary affairs. Box Respirator inspection also. In the afternoon the C.O. inspected all billets	
	7th		The Battn paraded at 9.30 and route march to MARIEUX at [illegible] miles. Officer Ether and Drum marched at [illegible] and the C.O. 2 in C and Adjt. inspected the beet part of a Brigade column on the afternoon the Battn marched back to billets under the Adjt.	

5 sheets

Army Form C. 2118.

WAR DIARY
or
INTELLIGENCE SUMMARY.
(Erase heading not required.)

Instructions regarding War Diaries and Intelligence Summaries are contained in F. S. Regs., Part II. and the Staff Manual respectively. Title pages will be prepared in manuscript.

Place	Date	Hour	Summary of Events and Information	Remarks and references to Appendices
France	March 8th		The Battn paraded under the C.O. at 9am and marched to CROUCHES returning via DOULLENS MAIN ROAD distance approximately 8 miles BATTN STRENGTH 12 O. 273 O.R's	10TH
	9th		The Battn paraded at 9-30 am under the CO and marched to PAS returning via MONDICOURT orders were taken distance about 9½ miles.	AH
	10th		The Battn paraded at 9-30 am for DIVINE SERVICE in conjunction with the R.W.K. Regt Holy communion was celebrated at 10-30 am	AH
	11th		Battn paraded at 9-30 am for tactical scheme, D Coy spent the morning on the range, officers of A.B.&C. coys paraded on road S of LA LARDE for tactical scheme	AH
	12th		Battn paraded at 9-30 am (training) in triangle of BAILEY-AMPLIER-GAUMESNIL. The range was allotted to C Coy (in 2½) HARD ME proceeded to England on leave in the day	AH
	13th		Battn. Holiday allotted to Battn A Coy paraded at 9-30 am for training	AH
	14th		Coy. Cap. paraded at 9-30 am Tactical scheme, A Coy worked on the range	AH
	15th		B.C & D Coys paraded for Tactical scheme at 9-30 am. A Coy were allotted the range (the Coy was billeted in Orpheus ?)	AH
	16th		Coy paraded for route march at 9-30 am via LE HUID HONTEBISE FORT MONDICOURT distance 9 miles	AH
	17th		Battn Holiday Divine Service at Mess Room at 10-30 am and at each woonded ortho	
	18th		The Battn paraded at 9-30 am for tactical scheme. Coy officers range. Lt Col Elliott assumed command of the Battn in the day on receiving draft of 40 O.R's	

(A7853) Wt. W869/M1672 350,000 4/17 Sch. 52a. Forms/C/2118/14 D.P. & L., London, E.C.

WAR DIARY
or
INTELLIGENCE SUMMARY.
(Erase heading not required.)

Army Form C. 2118.

Place	Date	Hour	Summary of Events and Information	Remarks and references to Appendices
France	Mch 19th		Battn. under orders to move at any moment. 2/Lt Hall W.S. returned from England	A.S.H
	20th		off leave on this day. Battn received draft of 21 O.R's	
			A Echelon transport moved at 11am and proceeded to ACHIET LE GRAND. Lt Col Stallard M.C. and 2/Lt T.H. LLOYD proceeded on leave to England.	A.S.H.
	21st		Battn paraded at 4pm and marched to MONDICOURT PAS where they entrained for ACHIET LE GRAND. Capt Russell proceeded on leave to England but was called back owing to leave being cancelled.	A.S.H
	22nd		Battn detrained at ACHIET LE GRAND at 2am and marched to SAVOY CAMP, paraded again at 1pm and proceeded to take up a line in front of SAPIGNIES Battn. again moved at 4pm and dug in on a line astride the BAPAUME-VAUX road but were moved to the line in front of SAPIGNIES again where A & B coys took up a line on a ridge overlooking MORY forming a defensive flank on the right and left flanks of the 6th & 4th Corps	
	23rd		At 7am A & B coys were moved to a line behind MORY with C & D coys in support, Bn H.Q. established in track originally held by A & B coys, the Germans entered MORY on this day but were then held up, the rest of the day was fairly quiet, there was considerable aerial activity.	A.S.H
			LT MATTHEWS was reported missing on this day.	A.S.H.

WAR DIARY or INTELLIGENCE SUMMARY

Army Form C. 2118.

Place	Date	Hour	Summary of Events and Information	Remarks and references to Appendices
France	Mar 24th		Enemy shelling throughout the day in Batt. area, considerable aerial activity on the part of the enemy, very little seen of our aeroplanes throughout the day. At 6 p.m. the Batt. received orders to fall back to a line in front of SAPIGNIES. The withdrawal took place immediately after dark, the Batt. dug in on a line behind FAVREUIL A,B & C coys in front line, D Coy taking up a line on the BAPAUME-ARRAS road. A letter of appreciation was received from G.O.C. 41st Divn for the good work done on the 23rd March.	A.3.1
	25th		At 3:30 am a party of Dults under 2 officers retired through our lines and at 4:30 am it was discovered that both flanks of the Batt. were open; D Coy having received orders to conform to the movements of [?] Right flank fell back the rest of the Batt. with the exception of the C.O. and C Coy withdrew to the ridge at SAPIGNIES by 5:30 a.m. The enemy commenced an attack on the line held by C Coy and a few machine gunners but were repulsed and held up until 10:30 a.m. when the C.O. finding that the enemy were getting round Lth flanks as well as attacking frontally gave orders to retire only the C.O. and 1 N.C.O. survived this stand by C Coy gave great assistance to its troops who were then digging in a line in front of BIHUCOURT and who saved to guns at ACHIET-LE-GRAND which but for this stand would have been captured. The rest of the Batt. under Capt. WALKER	

Army Form C. 2118.

WAR DIARY
or
INTELLIGENCE SUMMARY.
(Erase heading not required.)

Instructions regarding War Diaries and Intelligence Summaries are contained in F. S. Regs., Part II. and the Staff Manual respectively. Title pages will be prepared in manuscript.

Place	Date	Hour	Summary of Events and Information	Remarks and references to Appendices
France	Mar 25th cont		Pushed to fill a line between SAPIGNIES and BIHUCOURT but without to the BIHUCOURT line at 4pm when they dug in on a line to effect. The Hampshires tried a stand was made. The Batt. also suffered a counter attack made by the Huns on BIHUCOURT WOOD. LIEUTS DAVENPORT, COPP & LINFORD and GOULDING were wounded, 2/LT WARLAND wounded & missing and 2/LIEUT JOHNS & LT DAWSON missing.	DSM
	26th		At 1am the Batt. received orders to withdraw to BUCQOY and arrived there at 3.30 am resting in a field S of village until 8 am when they moved to a line N of GOMMECOURT taking up the line at 9 am, the day was very quiet.	DSM
	27th		O.R. 1 and the Batt. moved to ELENVILLERS where they rested in a field S of the village, this day was quiet and the Batt rested	DSM
	28th		At 11am the Batt. moved to a line S of GOMMECOURT via FONQUEVILLERS, considerable enemy shelling of back areas. MAJ WILLIAMS applied to the Batt. on the line on this day.	DSM
	30th		Fairly quiet all day, at 11pm the Batt. moved via GOMMECOURT and relieved the 7th MANCHESTER REGT. Batt. in support to the line Batt. in front of BUCQOY	DSM
	30th		Except for occasional shelling by the enemy the day was fairly quiet, very little aerial activity	DSM
	31st		Our guns active in morning intermittent shelling by the enemy, otherwise quiet. 2/Lt Marsh proceeded on special leave to England	DSM

A.H. Bevers Lt Col.

CONFIDENTIAL.

O.B./1919.

First Army.
Third Army.
Fourth Army.
Fifth Army.

    The attached revised establishment for an Infantry Battalion has been approved subject to the provisos mentioned below (authority War Office letter No. 79/82 (S.D.2.) dated 16th February, 1918.).

    (1) The appointment of a Serjeant Drummer is not yet approved, but meanwhile a Serjeant may be authorised instead.

    (2) The appointment of a Serjeant Tailor is not yet approved.

General Headquarters,
26 February, 1918.

Lieutenant-General,
C. G. S.

BRIGADE MAJOR,
122nd INFANTRY BRIGADE.

INFANTRY BATTALION.

PROVISIONAL WAR ESTABLISHMENT.

DETAIL.	Officers	W.Os	S.Serjts & Serjts	Drummers	Rank & File	Total	Riding	Draught	Heavy Draught	Pack	Total	Bicycles
Hd.Qrs. (excl. att'd).	9	2	16		111	138	6	28	9	7	50	9
Hd.Qrs. (attached).	1		1			2	1				1	
Four Companies.	24	4	32	16	784	860	4				4	
Total Battn.(ex.attd).	33	6	48	16	895	998	10	28	9	7	54	9
Total Battn.(in.attd)(a)	34	6	49	16	895	1000	11	28	9	7	55	9

COMPOSITION IN DETAIL.

(i) Personnel, Horses and Mules.

Headquarters.-

DETAIL.	Officers	W.Os	S.Serjts & Serjts	Drummers	Rank & File	Total	Riding	Draught	Heavy Draught	Pack	Total	Bicycles
Lieut.Colonel.	1					1	1				1	
Major.	1					1	1				1	
Adjutant.	1					1	1				1	
Assistant Adjutant.	1					1						
Quartermaster.	1					1	1				1	
Lewis Gun Officer.	1					1						
Scout Officer.	1					1						
Serjeant Major.		1				1						
Quartermaster Serjt.		1				1						
Qr.Mr's Storemen.					2	2						
Orderly Room Serjt.(b)			1			1						
Orderly Room Clerk.(c)			1			1						
Clerks for Orderly Room.					2	2						
Serjeant Drummer.			1			1						
Provost Serjt. and Regimental Police.			1		4	5						
Scout Serjt. and Scout Corporal.			1		1	2						
Signalling Officer.	1					1						
Signallers.			1		24(d)	25						9
Serjeant Instructors -												
Musketry.			1			1						
P. & B.T.			1			1						
Lewis Guns.			2			2						
Bombing and Rifle bombing.			1			1						
Gas personnel.			1			1						
Stretcher bearers.					4	4						
Orderlies for Medical Officer (e).					2	2						
Pioneer Serjeant and Pioneers.			1		10(f)	11						
Serjt.Cook & Cooks.			1		4(g)	5						
Transport.-												
Transport Officer.	1					1	1				1	
Transport Serjeant.			1			1	1				1	
Drivers 1st Line transport (including spare) (h)					27	27		28	9	7	44	

INFANTRY BATTALION.

PROVISIONAL WAR ESTABLISHMENT.

DETAIL	PERSONNEL						HORSES					Bicycles
	Officers	W.O's.	S.Serjts & Serjts	Drummers	Rank & File	Total	Riding	Draught	Heavy Dft.	Pack	Total	
Runners					4	4						
Water Duties (1)					(d)5	5						
Sanitary Duties					(d)3	3						
Shoemakers			1		4	5						
Tailors			1		2	3						
Butchers					1	1						
Postman					1	1						
Batmen					10	10						
C.O's. Groom.					1	1						
Total.	9	2	16		111	138	6	28	9	7	50	9
Attached:-												
R.A.M.C.	1					1	1				1	
Armourer A.O.C.			1			1						
Drivers A.S.C.(train transport)					4	4				8	8	
Total Headquarters. (including attached)	10	2	17		111	140	7	28	9	7	51	9
Company.-												
Headquarters.-												
Major or Captain (j)	1					1	1				1	
Captain (2nd in Command)	1					1						
Company Serjt.Major		1				1						
Company Qr.Mr.Serjt.			1			1						
Drummers				4		4						
Signallers					(k)7	7						
Scouts					4	4						
Gas personnel					1	1						
Stretcher bearers					4	4						
Cooks					2	2						
Sanitary Duties					2	2						
Privates (l)					2	2						
Batmen (m)					2	2						
Groom					1	1						
Total Coy. Hd.Qrs.	2	1	1	4	25	33	1				1	
To be distributed among platoons or used for headquarters duties as required.												
Serjeants.			3			3						
Corporals					(n)3	3						
Total			3		3	6						

INFANTRY BATTALION

PROVISIONAL WAR ESTABLISHMENT (Continued)

Detail	\multicolumn{6}{c}{PERSONNEL}				
	Offrs.	W.Os.	S.Sjts. & Sjts.	Drummers.	Rank & File.	Total.
Four Platoons each.						
Headquarters.-						
Subaltern Commanding...	1					1
Platoon Serjeant......			1			1
Private. (l).........					1	1
Batman. (m)..........					1	1
Total Platoon Hd.Qrs..	1		1		2	4
Four Sections.-						
Rank and file.					40(o)	40
Total COMPANY.........	6	1	8	4	196	215

(ii) TRANSPORT.

1st Line.	Vehicles.	Drivers.	Draught Horses.	Heavy Dr. Horses.	Pack Mules.
Headquarters.-					
Bicycles for Signallers...	9	-	-	-	-
Carts, Maltese, for medical equipment.......	1	1(p)	1	-	-
" Officers mess	1	1	1	-	-
" Water............	2	2	4	-	-
Wagons, limbered G.S. for S.A.A	3	3	6	-	-
" " " grenades .	1	1	2	-	-
" " " tools...	2	2	4	-	-
Pack Mules for S.A.......	-	2	-	-	2
Spare animals	-	2	2	1	1
Spare drivers	-	2	-	-	-
4 Companies.-					
Wagons, limbered G.S. for Lewis guns and ammunition (1 per Company).....	4	4	8	-	-
Pack Mules for ammunition (1 per Company).....	-	4	-	-	4
Travelling Kitchens (1 per Company). (q)......	4	4	-	8	-
Train.					
Wagons G.S. for baggage stores and supplies.	4	4 (r)	-	8	-
Total......	27	27	28	9	7

INFANTRY BATTALION.

PROVISIONAL WAR ESTABLISHMENT. (Continued).

(a) Battalions which have an authorised establishment of pipers will have one serjeant-piper and 5 pipers in addition. A battalion of Foot Guards will have two drill serjeants in addition. (Warrant Officers, Class II).

(b) Attached to General Headquarters, 3rd Echelon.

(c) The orderly room clerk may be of the rank of corporal, in which case he will be deducted from the serjeants and added to the rank and file.

(d) Includes a corporal.

(e) Two men (one a lance-corporal) trained for the duties will be placed under the orders of the Medical Officer. The private drives the cart for medical equipment.

(f) Includes 1 saddler.

(g) Includes 1 for Officers' Mess.

(h) Includes two cold-shoers.

(i) Category 'B'.

(j) One Company is commanded by a Major, and 3 Companies by Captains.

(k) Includes a corporal or a lance-corporal.

(l) Act as runners.

(m) Also act as runners.

(n) Two Companies will each have two corporals and one additional private instead of a third corporal.

(o) Includes two corporals (If no corporal is included in the Company Signallers, one platoon will include three corporals - see note (k).)

(p) Medical Officer's orderly.

(q) Battalions which do not possess travelling kitchens will have in lieu 4 limbered G.S. wagons with 4 drivers and 8 draught horses.

(r) Provided from the Divisional Train.

NOTES.
1. Of the 50 corporals in a battalion 8 may be lance-serjeants and of the privates 41 lance-corporals.

2. Drummers are fully trained soldiers and available for ordinary duties.

Third Army A/A/8473
A.G. AG/3837 (G)

Headquarters
Third Army (A).

With reference to G.H.Q. letter No.O.B./1919 dated 28-2-18 forwarding revised establishment for an Infantry Battalion instructions have been ~~received~~ issued for the number of supernumerary Officers with such battalions to be reduced to 10.

Infantry Battalions will therefore be allowed to demand up to 43 Officers per Battalion made up as follows -

33 as per Establishment, plus the 10 supernumeraries.

The number of Officers that can be demanded for Pioneer Battalions will be as follows:-

23 as per Establishment, plus 14 Supernumeraries, making a total of 37 Officers.

All previous instructions on this subject are cancelled.

(sd) H.E.PRYCE-JONES
Lt.-Col.A.A.G.
for Adjytant General.

G.H.Q.
9-3-18.

2

12th East Surrey Regt.
15th Hampshire Regt.
18th Kings Royal Rifle Corps.

For information.

Lieut.
A/Staff Captain.
15-3-18.   122nd Infantry Brigade.

41st Division.
122nd Infantry Brigade.

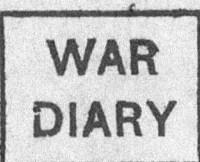

12th BATTALION

THE EAST SURREY REGIMENT

APRIL 1918

12th Battalion East Surrey Regt.

Army Form C. 2118.

WAR DIARY
INTELLIGENCE SUMMARY.
(Erase heading not required.)

Vol 24

Place	Date	Hour	Summary of Events and Information	Remarks and references to Appendices
			April	
BUCQUOY	1.4.18		The day on the whole was quiet. At 9 p.m the Battalion was relieved by the 1/6th Hampshire Fusiliers. On relief the Battalion marched to the point on the BIENVILLERS-SOUASTRE ROAD, where it embused at 11.30 p.m for the THIEVRES area. 2/Lt W.D MUTCH, M.C. proceeded on special leave to the United Kingdom. The leave was extended by W.O. to 26.4.18	A/R
MARIEUX	2.4.18		The Battalion debused in the early morning at THIEVRES and marched to an aerodrome at MARIEUX. Here it rested until 1 p.m. when it moved via SARTON and ORVILLE to AMPLIER arriving at 2.30 p.m. Here the Battalion was billeted.	A/R
AMPLIER	3.4.18		The Battalion paraded at 6.30 a.m and marched to THIEVRES where it embused for FREVENT arriving at 1 p.m. On arrival the Battalion detrained and proceeded to POPERINGHE.	A/R
POPERINGHE	4.4.18		The Battalion detrained at POPERINGHE at 4 am and marched to billets in RUE DE FURNES. At 6 p.m it moved to SCHOOL CAMP arriving at 7.30 p.m. 2/Lt C.H WARD and 2/Lt C.W.F. FAITH reported from English leave	A/R
SCHOOL CAMP	5.4.18		The Battalion was under Company arrangements for this inspection, baths and relaxing	A/R
SCHOOL CAMP	6.4.18		The Battalion was inspected by the G.O.C. 8th Corps, Major Williams commanded the Battalion in the absence of the C.O. who was awaiting the Section of the line being taken over by him. Capt RUSSELL M.C. (attached) left the Battn. this day to join the 10th Royal West Kent Regt. A draft of 102 O.Rs joined the Battn. this day. Battalion strength 33 Officers 864 O.Rs.	A/R
SCHOOL CAMP	7.4.18		A voluntary parade service was held at 9.30 am. At 4 p.m. the Battalion marched to QUINTON STATION and entrained. His light railway at 6 p.m for BERRY FARM. Three guides were met from the 1st GUERNSEY L.I. whom the C.O. & Adjutant went on ahead. The relief was completed at 10.45 a.m the A & D Companies in the front line with C & B. Battn. H.Q at INDIGO DIA 6 7 5 6. On this day Major C.F. STALLARD M.C. proceeded to join the 10th Royal W. Kent Regt as 2nd in Command. The following casualties were noted:- from BASE a/Capt H. STODDART transferred to ENGLAND sick 23/3/18 a/Lt G.B. GILLETT transferred to ENGLAND sick 23/3/18 2/Lt. J.A LINFORD transferred to ENGLAND wounded 28/3/18 2/Lt. G.C. DAVENPORT transferred to England wounded 27/3/18 2/Lt. J.A GOLDING transferred to ENGLAND wounded 28 3/18. A draft of 97 O.R joined the Battn.	A/R
PASSCHENDAELE RIDGE	8/4/18		Situation quiet throughout the day. Heavy mist made observation abs/la	A/R	2 Affs
PASSCHENDAELE RIDGE	9/4/18		B Company took 3 prisoners and D Company 1. These men had lost their way while on patrol and wandered into our lines. Enemy shelled Both H.Q and Supt. Intermittent shelling all day. Observation was poor. A draft of 15 o.R. joined the Battn. this day. Casualties this day 1 O.R. wounded	A/R	2AC 3 Anny
PASSCHENDAELE RIDGE	10/4/18		Situation very quiet throughout the whole day. Heavy mist made observation quite impossible. A draft of 13 O.R joined the Battn. Casualties this day 1 O.R. wounded.	A/R

MVE DIV?4

Army Form C. 2118.

12th Battalion East Surrey Regt.

WAR DIARY
or
INTELLIGENCE SUMMARY.

(Erase heading not required.)

Instructions regarding War Diaries and Intelligence
Summaries are contained in F. S. Regs., Part II.
and the Staff Manual respectively. Title pages
will be prepared in manuscript.

Place	Date	Hour	Summary of Events and Information	Remarks and references to Appendices
PASSCHENDAELE RIDGE	11.4.18		A creeping barrage of light calibre shells was put on the outpost line at 5.30 am, followed by 4.2 and 5.9 on the ridge lasting for an hour. The day was clear and observation good. 2/Lt C.H. WARD was badly turned whilst acting as observing officer at IBERIAN. Casualties the day O.R. 1 killed, 4 wounded.	O/R
LOW KEEP	12.4.18		The Battn was relieved at 1 a.m. by the 2/6 N. STAFFORDSHIRE Regt. 59th DIV. The Battn. entrained at IBERIAN for ST JEAN & marched to MAIDEN CAMP. During the day H.C.O. and Coy/Coy Commanders reconnoitred a line through SQUARE FARM and LOW FARM. The Battn. marched to this line at 6 pm and dug in during the night in anticipation of a hostile attack from the morning front line. A & C Companies in front, B Company in reserve and D Company counter attack company.	O/R
LOW KEEP	13.4.18		The day was spent in improving the front positions. A draft of 7 O.R. joined the Battn.	A/T Coll
MILL KEEP	14.4.18		At 1 a.m. the Battalion was relieved by the 26th Battn. Royal Fusiliers, and moved to CARTE KEEP and MILL KEEP. Battn. H.Q. was at MILL KEEP. I.5 2 6. At 5 pm the Battn. commenced work on a new line in front of MILL KEEP in front working by Company billets. Battalion strength 32 officers 1084 O.R.	O/R
MILL KEEP GOLDFISH	15.4.18		At 4 pm the Battalion moved to a Camp in the neighbourhood of GOLDFISH CHATEAU H.11.b & H.11.d.	O/R
CHATEAU CAMP	16.4.18		The Battalion took baths at VLAMERTINGHE by Companies. The rest of the day was spent in cleaning up. The Camp area was heavily shelled with H.E. and Gas	O/R
GOLDFISH			The Battalion commenced work on Army Reserve Line trenches V.3 and V.4 from H.12 c 7.6 to H.6 a 2.3. Work from 6 am	O/R
CHATEAU CAMP	17.4.18		Work on Reserve Line trenches V.3 and V.4 was continued. Owing to enemy shelling Battn. H.Q. and B Company moved from Huts at H.11 d 2.3 to H.11 6 6.6	O/R
GOLDFISH CHATEAU CAMP	18.4.18		Work was continued on defensive trenches V.3 & V.4. The Camp was shelled until 2 P.E. & Coy & the Camp had to be evacuated temporarily. Casualties the day O.R. 1 killed 1 wounded	O/R
GOLDFISH CHATEAU CAMP	19.4.18		Work on defensive trenches V.3 and V.4 was continued. The Camp and its neighbourhood was shelled	O/R
GOLDFISH			Work was continued on defensive line trenches V.3 & V.4 by 3 Companies. I Company was employed on the defences at ST JEAN. The C.O. reconnoitred the ground in the vicinity of N.E. REMMEL. The following officers reported	O/R
CHATEAU CAMP	21.4.18		for duty: 2/Lt J.C. CARVER, 2/Lt F.W. CROFTER, 2/Lt F.E. ELLS, 2/Lt C.H. FRISCHLING, 2/Lt O.R. GEORGE, 2/Lt W.G. GREENHILL, 2/Lt J.S. K. LAWTON, 2/Lt R.M. MERDAWS, 2/Lt E.S. REYNOLDS, 2/Lt J.C. WALLER, 2/Lt L.A. WAITE. Strength 6 Battn 1087 O.R.	O/R

WAR DIARY
12th Battalion East Surrey Regt.
INTELLIGENCE SUMMARY
(Erase heading not required)

Army Form C. 2118.

Instructions regarding War Diaries and Intelligence Summaries are contained in F.S. Regs., Part II. and the Staff Manual respectively. Title pages will be prepared in manuscript.

Place	Date	Hour	Summary of Events and Information	Remarks and references to Appendices
GOLDFISH CHATEAU CAMP	22.4.18		Work was continued on the defended localities V.3 and V.14 by 3 Companies and one Company worked on the defences at ST JEAN. The Camp and neighbourhood were heavily bombarded with gas shells during the night 22/23rd.	A/IP
GOLDFISH CHATEAU CAMP	23.4.18		Work on the defended localities V.3 and V.14 and at ST JEAN was continued. The C.O. reconnoitred the line in front of VOORMEZEELE. 2/Lt W.P. SELBIE proceeded to join the 8th Batt. East Surrey Regt on transfer A/05718 authy A.G./21158/1239 (0) A/18 7/18	A/IP
GOLDFISH CHATEAU CAMP	24.4.18		The Battalion continued work on the defences V.3 and V.14 and at ST JEAN. Major Williams and Company Commanders reconnoitred the country in the neighbourhood of RIDGEWOOD	A/IP
GOLDFISH CHATEAU CAMP	25.4.18		The Camp and neighbourhood was heavily shelled with gas shells from 3 p.m. to 8 a.m. Working parties went out and all were recalled at 12 a.m. and the Battalion were ordered to stand by by Brigade at short notice. At 6.15 p.m. the Batt. moved to DAMBRE CAMP, B2g+c arriving at 9 p.m. Casualties the day 2 killed 21 wounded, 1 of the wounded (2/Lt. YOUNG) died in addition, 9/15 F.C. ELLIS and 2/26 C.A. GEORGE and 20 O.Rs were slightly gassed, remaining with Batt.	A/IP
DAMBRE CAMP	26.4.18		At 12 noon the Battalion moved to the Brigade rendezvous at H.11.6.255 near GOLDFISH CHATEAU. The day was spent in the field. At 4 p.m. the Battalion returned to DAMBRE CAMP.	A/IP
DAMBRE CAMP	27.4.18		From 8 a.m. to 8.30 a.m. the Camp neighbourhood was shelled by a H.V. gun, with disastrous results. The GREEN LINE from H.3.a.central B.14.B.4 was reconnoitred by the C.Os. and Company Commanders. 2/Lt. D.WALNER and another officer for duty. Casualties this day 10 O.R. wounded.	A/IP
DAMBRE CAMP	28.4.18		The Battalion was standing by all day. The strength of the Battalion is 43 officers 1037 other ranks.	A/IP
	29.4.18		Battalion standing by. Companies carried out musketry by platoons during the afternoon. There was Recon artillery fire from 3 a.m. till 8 p.m.	11.30 p.m.
	30.4.18		During the morning Companies carried out Musketry Instruction. At 1.20 p.m. a working party of 2 Offrs & 150 ORs. Per company paraded for work on the GREEN LINE. The remainder of the Battalion carried recreational training. 2nd Lieut W.D. MUTCH, M.C. rejoined the Batt." from English leave this day. Capt. H. WALKER, M.C. M.B. was wounded & evacuated this day.	10 p.m.

A.L. Brown Lt Col.

12th East Surrey's

April 1918

Opn Orders

12th Bn. East . Surrey Regt

OPERATION ORDER No.141.

Reference Map. Sheet 28 Ed 3 and 28 N.E.

1. The Battalion will relieve the Battalion holding the right front position of the left Brigade Sector of the right Division VIII Corps Front on the 7th April 1918, and will proceed by trains leaving QUINTIN at 6 p.m. and 6.15 p.m..

2. The Battalion will parade at 4.45 p.m. on the road in the following order :-   B.Coy, D Coy, C Coy, A Coy.
    Dress :-   SOMME Fighting Order with Greatcoats.

3. Disposition of Coys in line.
    "B" Company   Left Front.
    "D" Company   Right Front.
    "C" Company   Left Support
    "A" Company   Right Support.

4. Officers Trench Bundles, Mess Kit for line &c will be stacked outside Quartermasters Stores by 11 a.m.
    Spare Mess Kit, Blankets in bundles of 10, men's packs &c of men going into the line will be dumped in Canteen Hut by 12 noon.

5. All Aeroplane photographs, Defence Schemes, S.A.A., Grenades, and all Trench Stores including reserve rations, Policy of work, and Intelligence Notes, will be taken over and lists forwarded to Battalion Headquarters by the 8th inst

6. Completion of relief will be reported to Battalion by wire using the Company Commanders name as code word.

7. 2nd Lieut. A. E. Bell will act as Town Major at Post 23S.

8. Personnel not proceeding to the line will parade on road in full marching order ready to move off at 5 p.m.

9. Transport Lines will be situated at H.7.c.3.3.
    Small standings are allotted to the Battalion at I.9.a.2.9.

Issued at 10.30 a.m.
Date. 7th April 1918.
                    (sd)   H.S.Walker   Capt & Adjt.
                            12th Bn East Surrey Regt.

SECRET.   Copy No. 1.

13th Bn EAST SURREY REGT.

WARNING ORDER No. 1.

1. On arrival in MONDICOURT AREA the Battalion will be in G.H.Q. Reserve, and will be prepared to entrain at 24 hours notice at MONDICOURT.

2. The Battalion will entrain as follows; times of departure of the trains will be notified later.
"D" Company will entrain with Brigade Headquarters on No.1 train, and will take one cooker and team.
The remainder of the Battalion and Transport will entrain on No. 4 train.
All personnel and transport will report at Entraining Station three hours before the scheduled time of departure of the respective trains.

3. Each train will consist of the following vehicles :-
   30 Covered Trucks.
   17 Flat Trucks.
   1 Officers Coach.

4. The Battalion will entrain with the unexpired portion of the day's rations plus rations for the day subsequent to entrainment on the man. The O.C. Divisional Train has been detailed to arrange on receipt of orders, to load supply vehicles from Supply Column in sufficient time for the Supply wagons to entrain full.

5. Baggage and supply wagons will entrain with the Battalion. Baggage wagons will join the Battalion on receipt of warning wire.
Supply wagons will join the Battalion as soon as they are loaded with rations for the second day subsequent to entrainment (vide para 4) or, in case of lack of time, will proceed direct to the entraining station.

6. In the event of a move at short notice all surplus kit will be sent forthwith to the D.A.D.O.S. Store.
The Officer in charge "Crumps" has been instructed to leave behind sufficient personnel to receive and guard all surplus kit.
No responsibility will be accepted for damage to or loss of kit deposited in this store.

7. It is hoped that lorries will be available to carry blankets to the station. In the event of lorries not being available one blanket will be carried on the man.

                              (sd) H.S.Walker,
                                   Capt & A/Adjt,
                                   13th Bn East Surrey Regiment.

Issued at..........

           Copy No. 1. File.
            "   No. 2. War Diary.
            "   No. 3. C.O.
            "   No. 4. 2nd-in-Comd.
            "   No. 5. Adjutant.
            "   No. 6. O.C. A Coy.
            "   No. 7. O.C. B "
            "   No. 8. O.C. C "
            "   No. 9. O.C. D "
            "   No.10. Transport Officer.
            "   No.11. Quartermaster.
            "   No.12. Medical Officer.
            "   No.13. Intelligence Officer.

12th Bn. East Surrey Regt.

OPERATION ORDER No. 139.

Reference Map. LENS 11 1/100,000.

1. The Battalion will parade this evening as follows :-
   Starting point. at E in HALTE South of POMERA.
   Time. Head of column to pass starting point at 4 p.m.
   Route. HALLOY - MONDICOURT Station.
   Order of March. Headqrs, A Coy, Band, B Coy, C Coy, Drums, D Coy.
   Dress. Marching Order, Caps will be worn.

2. The Transport will move independently under the Transport Officer.

3. Officers Trench Bundles, Mess Kit etc., will be ready for collection at Quartermasters Stores at 2.30 p.m. The Transport will take these to MONDICOURT Station and place them in charge of the Guard there.
   In the case of B Coy., the Transport will collect Kit from B Coy. at 2 p.m.

4. O.C. Companies are responsible that all billets are left scrupulously clean.

5. The Officer i/c of train is Lieut. Col. R. PENNEL, D.S.O.

6. The Battalion may be called upon to move at very short notice on arrival in the new area.

                (sd)   H.S.Walker   Capt & Adjt.
                          12th Bn East Surrey Regt.

12th Bn East Surrey Regt.

OPERATION ORDER No. 140

Reference Map. Sheet 57d.

1. The Battn will entrain on Train No.3 at FREVENT Station at 6.30 p.m. tomorrow 3rd April 1918, and will embus at embussing point - MARIEUX-THIEVRES road-head of Brigade at THIEVRES facing North - at 9 a.m.

2. The Battn. will parade on the AMPLIER - ORVILLE road in column of threes facing East at 6.45 a.m., head of column to be at "A" Companys Billet.
   Order of march. H.Q., A, C, Band, B, Drums, D Coys.
   Starting Point. Cross Roads south of ORVILLE - H.10.a.2.8.
   Time. Head of column to pass Starting Point at 7.22 a.m.
   Dress. Marching Order, caps will be worn. Blankets will be carried on the man.
   Embussing. The Battn will be in position on the embussing point 30 minutes before time of embussing.

3. Officers Valises, Company Mess Boxes etc. will be ready for collection by Regtl Transport at 5.45 a.m.
   It is probable one lorry will be available for Brigade H.Q., 12th E.Surrey R. and 122 T.M.B. Packs of the Band and Drums will be carried on this lorry. They will be dumped at the Quartermastrs Stores by 6 a.m. The Quartermaster will detail one man to meet this lorry at Brigade H.Q. at 7 a.m. The guide, and one man from the orderly Room only will be left in charge of these Packs etc., and they alone will be allowed to travel on the lorry.

4. The Battn. Transport will be brigaded, and march to entraining station as a group under the Orders of O.C. No.2 Company 41st Divl Train, and will pass starting point at Cross Roads H.10 a.2.8. by 7 a.m.
   In the case of the Battn not entraining for some time after arrival in the entraining area, Transport will join the Battn in rest billets and proceed to entraining Station under orders of the Commanding Officer.

5. Supply Wagons will entrain loaded and will join the Battn. Transport as soon as loaded with the Rations with which they will entrain.

6. Personnel will report at entraining station one hour and transport three hours before scheduled time of departure of train.

7. A Billeting Party of One Officer and 2 O.R's, to be detailed by the Adjutant, will proceed by first train leaving FREVENT at 3.20 p.m.

(sd) H.S.Walker   Capt & Adjt.
12th Bn East Surrey Regt.

SECRET.

File

41st Div.
G. 170.
67/1.

122nd Infantry Brigade.
123rd Infantry Brigade.
124th Infantry Brigade.
No. 41 Bn. Machine Gun Corps.
C. R. E.
19th Middlesex Regt. (P).

As the Division is likely to take part in a more open form of warfare, the Divisional Commander wishes the following points to be impressed upon all ranks.

1.— Both in an advance and during a withdrawal no opportunity should be lost for making use of covering fire of rifles, machine guns and Lewis guns; such fire may be direct overhead or enfilade according to the nature of the ground. There should be no movement without fire when troops are in touch with the enemy. Well directed fire causes the enemy to keep his head down and to fire high and wildly, it therefore saves casualties to our own troops.

2.— In open warfare it is unlikely that units will be in a continuous line, and, so long as the intervening ground is covered by fire from one or the other or by cross fire from both, there is little danger of the enemy penetrating.
At night or in foggy weather such places must be patrolled continually, or standing patrols must be posted to prevent small parties of the enemy working through.

3.— In defence, every approach by which the enemy may advance against the position, must be securely guarded. A definite unit must be made responsible for the defence of each approach. Roads, railways, pathways and bridges must be blocked by strong obstacles; the question of whether these should be destroyed by demolition depends on the likelihood of their being required for future use by our troops.
All bridges, culverts, roadways and trees, however, which are behind the line of defence, should be prepared for demolition.
The order for exploding the charges will only be given by an Officer specially detailed for this duty.

4.— Local resources must be made use of for construction of obstacles, such as :—
  (a) Barricades of timber or other material.
  (b) Felled trees.
  (c) Wire obtained from local fences or supplied by R.E.
  (d) Wire gates or knife rests.
  (e) Upturned carts filled with earth.
Whatever form the obstacle takes, it should be securely picketed so that it is difficult to remove.

/ If

If there are forward troops who require to use the approach which has been blocked, the obstacle can be made with a passage which can be quickly closed by a gate.

```
              Enemy's line
              of advance.
                   ↓
             ┌──────────┐
             │ Obstacle │
             │ ▓▓▓▓▓▓▓▓ │
      Gate →       ▓▓▓▓▓▓▓▓
                  │ Obstacle │
                  └──────────┘
```

All obstacles must be under direct fire of a post in the vicinity.

5.- Cross roads should be avoided, the enemy will shoot by map and halts must not be made, or obstacles constructed, at cross roads.

6.- Troops should not halt or bivouac in a village when in close proximity to the enemy.

7.- If it is desired to defend a village, troops should be kept clear of the outskirts; when possible, ground should be held on either flank of the village from which the approaches can be covered by fire.

If the enemy gets among the buildings, he can be shelled out.

8.- In enclosed country the enemy will make every endeavour to gain tactical points by infiltration, pushing forward individuals or small parties along hedges and ditches.

Every hedge and ditch which is perpendicular to the line of defence should be covered so that it is impossible for anyone to work along them unseen.

9.- The defended line must always be covered by outposts :-
    (a) To give due warning of the enemy's approach.
    (b) To break up his attack.

Under no circumstances should troops occupying a defended line allow the enemy to make a reconnaissance of the position, and to then bring up his troops and develope an attack in his own time.

Outposts must be alert and imbued with the offensive spirit. They should only withdraw if forced to do so by superior numbers, they will then have carried out their role, which is to :-
    (a) Obtain information.
    (b) Give the defence time for preparation.
    (c) Force the enemy to disclose his intentions.

10.- Attention is directed to G.H.Q. letter O.A. 185 dated 13th April 1918, forwarded under 41st Div. G. 105 (39/2) dated 15th April 1918.

E a Beck.
Lt. Colonel. G.S.

17th April 1918.

SECRET

12th East Surrey Regt.
15th Hampshire Regt.
18th Kings Royal Rifle Corps.
122nd Trench Mortar Battery.

B.M. 746.

264/W/18

For information.

G.H.Q. letter quoted in para.10 of attached, was forwarded to 3 Battalions only, under this office B.M.725 dated 16-4-18.

The principles contained in these instructions must be explained by all Officers to their men.

L R Hogg
Lieut.
A/Brigade Major
122nd Infantry Brigade.

17-4-18

1 to each Coy
BM

264/WV/18

Confidential.

12th East Surrey Regt.

The Officer Commanding "A" Coy (12th East Surrey Regt.) informed the Divisional Commander yesterday that he had not had a copy of 41st Division G.170 (6/1) dated 14th April.

Two copies of the above letter, for distribution down to Companies, were forwarded under this Office B.M. 746 dated 17-4-18.

Will you please investigate and report for the information of the Divisional Commander.

G.R. Hogg
a/ Lieut.
BRIGADE MAJOR,
122nd INFANTRY BRIGADE.

21st April 1918

C.9.a.
C 30

Headquarters
122nd Inf Bde

Herewith copy of
war diary for month of
May.

[signature]
Lieut Col
Comdg 12th Bn East Surrey Regt

3-6-18.

Army Form C. 2118.

12 East Surrey Regt

WAR DIARY
INTELLIGENCE SUMMARY.
(Erase heading not required.)

Place	Date	Hour	Summary of Events and Information	Remarks and references to Appendices
CAMP? H.A.a.]	1918 May 1st		REF MAP SHEET 28. Casualties posted of 2 OFFS at 150 ORS. Per company paraded this day for work on the Green Line behind VLAMERTINGHE. Our own & enemy artillery were exchanging action throughout the morning mostly on ROOST CALNE. Remarks Two OFFS Gassed	
	2nd		Coys. as before throughout the day. Usual morning instruction. The Battalion opened at 8 p.m. to YPRES SECTOR to take over OUTPOST Position from the 2nd ROYAL FUSILEERS 123rd Brigade on a line stretching from I.14.c.3.4. to T.10.c.1.6. Two Companies in Front Line & Coys in Support each with 2 Platoons in reserve. Dispositions were carried out during the night. Casualties reported a Counter preparation shoot from 3 to 4 pm 3.5.15 whilst though heavy was very light retaliation from the enemy. Casualties 1 OR.	
YPRES	3		Enemy artillery quiet on this Sector from 8 am until noon and it the exception of Bde are Shells during the afternoon our own & artillery lines were heavily shelled causing 12 casualties 2 Killed 10 Wounded. Our own & enemy aircraft active throughout the day. Lt N HOLT & Mc WALTER rejoined this day from Eng. Corps School.	
	4		Our artillery carried out a counter preparation shoot during the morning. Our own & enemy artillery carried out Harassing Fire in the afternoon during the day. Our own & Supports Lines were heavily shelled during the evening causing 15 casualties. At about 11 am the Bn Battn HQ was shelled during the evening. Total Strength 40 OFFS 1050 ORS. R.E. on Strength 30 OFFS 848 ORS	Lally 25C gassed

WAR DIARY or INTELLIGENCE SUMMARY

Army Form C. 2118.

Place	Date	Hour	Summary of Events and Information	Remarks and references to Appendices
YPRES	1918 May 5		Artillery fairly quiet throughout the day but Area active owing to enemy shelling the PETITE 9 MENIN Rd Junction the afternoon. BD GOC visited Battalion HQ this day & presented our Commanding Officer Lt Col C.R.R. Barnes with a memorandum list of gallantry awards on May 24th 1918. Ribbons 1.O.R front.	
"	6		Battalion quiet throughout the day. Reconnoitring parties began examining shell guns our Bn frontage. OC 9 Rif. Bde B.D. sent out a raiding party of one officer to JAMES FARM for identification purposes but found from enemy. Casualties NL wounded.	
"	7		Battalion quiet for the day. Reliefs between us & the Germans carried out. OC 9 Rif. BDE. GOC 18 BDE the evening 18 Battn came in to line relieved us relieving the 1st Bn HANTS Regt & the one extra Company from 1347? to 2167? new position 12 NW & camp? + 106? found 9h w GREENHILL Range	
"	8		Artillery quiet throughout the day. A lot of traffic on the part of the enemy. Aeroplane activity throughout the day. Enemy machines bombed our aerodrome & YPRES. Our aeroplanes retaliated the firing line. En casualty nil.	

WAR DIARY
or
INTELLIGENCE SUMMARY.
(Erase heading not required.)

Army Form C. 2118.

Place	Date	Hour	Summary of Events and Information	Remarks and references to Appendices
YPRES	1918 May 9		Artillery fire throughout the day becoming quiet at times during the evening. Enemy's snipers & M.G.s active in front line but were driven back by machine gun fire. Several attempts at sniping by an Austrian Scout Group but counter measures taken.	
"	10		Artillery quiet with the exception of a few rounds into Potijze Street. YPRES on two nights [illegible] the Battalion became front line & relieved the 116th Bde. on the right. Relieving own Bn. of the Front Line by 16/18th Bn. King's Royal Rifles, also 50th of 116th Front Bn by the YORKS & LANC'S REGT. The Battalion were relieved from this line & went back to 116th of Industrial Regt. Relief completed at 2 AM 11-5-18	
"	11		Artillery fairly quiet. Enemy shelling River & also YPRES [illegible]. But the day was [illegible] aircraft. Several fine shoots for our aircraft. YPRES 2nd Lieut. C.C. Simpson joined the Battalion. Also 2nd Lieut J.W. Barton & [illegible] 38 Officers 1910Rs	
"	12		Artillery on both sides [illegible]. Enemy shelling YPRES & Vlamertinghe own forces area. Aircraft quiet. Several fine [illegible] & [illegible] shoots by our aircraft. [illegible] & aeroplane co-operation.	
"	13		Artillery over YPRES and Vlamertinghe & all other and intense activity with [illegible] the Steen, Enemy Aircraft was active during the attention on enemy back areas arranged for own also a clear sky at night	

Army Form C. 2118.

WAR DIARY
or
INTELLIGENCE SUMMARY.
(Erase heading not required.)

Instructions regarding War Diaries and Intelligence
Summaries are contained in F. S. Regs., Part II.
and the Staff Manual respectively. Title pages
will be prepared in manuscript.

Place	Date	Hour	Summary of Events and Information	Remarks and references to Appendices
YPRES	1917 Aug 14		Bn. proceeded by rail to YPRES arriving [illegible] Regiment [illegible] Bn PA area detrainment. Journey to YPRES being made DEAD END camp. Reserve casualties including 3 O.R.s (Other ranks) killed and one O.R. died of wounds. Enemy shelling current rest day. A draft of 5 O.R.s reported. Enemy dropped bombs at observation Post area Casualties 3 for Battalion Commencing [illegible] Aug 3rd line into front line by reliefs. O. comdg Pnrs. at Obs. was wounded for a billeting area billet at [illegible]	
"	15		H.W. Capt R. Lavallie M.R.C. Ord. man Jenkin [illegible] after noon YPRES accounts of [illegible] Kaiser Thursday [illegible] Armand of Gunners at with Heavy Barrage in [illegible] a reply to our attack on vicinity HINDEL O. Cambrai [illegible] slight was selecting and lay in artillery during the evening Concentrated artillery fire 6 pm - 2/Lt F.C. Fuss found	
"	16		One [illegible] from shelling YPRES a Back Area which was anticipated to [illegible] by enemy also a few bases a few hours been [illegible] from the area of attack after was carried out from battle point of evening A.Ram enter of Gunnery. Buried the Battalion were relieved by 1/8 K. Liv [illegible] Regt relief	
"	17		complete 1-30 am Batt. marched [illegible] and arrived there at B.45 a.m. march at 2:30 PM extreme quiet during the [illegible] Remain D.H.Q.	

Army Form C. 2118.

WAR DIARY
or
INTELLIGENCE SUMMARY.
(Erase heading not required.)

Instructions regarding War Diaries and Intelligence Summaries are contained in F. S. Regs., Part II, and the Staff Manual respectively. Title pages will be prepared in manuscript.

Place	Date	Hour	Summary of Events and Information	Remarks and references to Appendices
CAMP H.30.c	1915		Batteries employed during the morning in escorting fresh supply of R.E. bodyskin [?] down for new pits for 2nd Bty during the evening & night 17/18th June in vicinity of Roest.	
			Battery received hours that fresh Enemy trench Mortar Battery arrived 18th.	
			At Rien o'karuff. 3 Offrs & 1034 ORs National streigth 21 Offrs 740 ORs. Rations being drawn for Reinforcts. The Divisional Park [?] rear afford are to dumour [?] dispose of for funer [?] complete change of underclothing was one issued & all men taken to Rikey Baron [?] Bracks [?] [illegible] along [illegible] every night — Every aircraft was seen about trailing Rail Broas [?]	
	20		Batteries employed during the morning in instructing Officers & other ranks in latest systems for Officials were again sent to H.Q. Conclany the army as experts during the evening and Night patrols were sent to Perryshu [?] the caves in [illegible] being [illegible] ReR ant in a most adjunning [?] [illegible] a slabby Transport [illegible] the residue [?] caused the unwal [?] come as it was [?] Both protoo. Nits to the East.	
	21		Battery employed during the morning in instructing for first Squad Drill Aiming Drill & quiet during the day. But increased Rangers [?] to arming & laying Canon of garrating [?] gunnery. Family Parade Breaches [?]	

Army Form C. 2118.

WAR DIARY
or
INTELLIGENCE SUMMARY.
(Erase heading not required.)

Instructions regarding War Diaries and Intelligence Summaries are contained in F. S. Regs., Part II. and the Staff Manual respectively. Title pages will be prepared in manuscript.

Place	Date	Hour	Summary of Events and Information	Remarks and references to Appendices
CAMP H30C	1918 Sept 22		Whilst Battalion Physical Drill was carried out during the day. During the evening the camp was subjected to machine gun fire from enemy planes & camp was ordered to carry on Plan for moving to Reserve in the field	
	23		Battalion paraded at 10.30 P.M. for C.O.'s inspection & march to Reserve area carried out. The Battalion was left in Reserve in the L area to await further orders. Enemy activity normal during day & later.	
	24		Enemy aeroplanes flying about in evening on harassing expedition dropped string of bombs near camp during Battle Orders operations in the vicinity. In the evening the Divisional Concert Party gave one of its concerts to the men of the Battalion. Casualties 10R.	
YPRES	25		Companies paraded at the disposal of Company Commanders at 8.30 A.M. Battalion marched to YPRES. Baths & relieves the Royal Berks in Brigade Reserve at a bn strength from 1.10.40 to 6.55. It was S.B.O. H Coy Railway Dugouts, G Coy Plateau Dugouts D Coy in Dugouts & B Coy in reserve with remainder at 2.30 A.M. Casualties 9 R. Rations Strength 38 OFF's 1033 O.R's Ration Strength 25 OFF's 922 O.R's Capt. W.O. SEARLE joined the Bn. this day	

WAR DIARY
or
INTELLIGENCE SUMMARY.
(Erase heading not required.)

Army Form C. 2118.

Place	Date	Hour	Summary of Events and Information	Remarks and references to Appendices
YPRES	1918 May 26		Artillery quiet throughout the day. Enemy trench mortars were fairly active and completion of communication trench at ECOLE SWITCH when in the vicinity of the Church, Our Snipers claimed a few also a trifle more enemy snipers during the morning. Enemy aircraft exceedingly active. Visibility good. Major C.E. WILLIAMS proceeded to 18 RES. Bn. on the day. Casualties: 1 O.R. killed, 10 O.R. wounded.	
	27		Our artillery and enemy artillery active. A H.E. shell on a bomb emplacement was placed in vicinity of HEADQUARTERS A Support Company was employed during the morning on new trench to the building up of parapets & improving same. During the evening 6 fatigue parties 1 off 2 O.Rs was sent out to support R.E. ifford & Lamb, to officer in command. Pgt. J. PENNISON T/Cpl. J. W. ADDIS KIA. 9 Lt. T. THORNTON & Lt. R. GRAVES joined 25 Sup. Co. during the day	
	28		Artillery normal. Quieter active. Support between companies during the night diggers 3 trench from G. ECOLE SWITCH front 2 Platoons took up positions in BRIT Line, returned left on Enemy at 1.15 am. No casualties. Good news that 2nd R. FUSION Lines have penned off during the day, enemy H Battalion.	
	29		W.P. early. Artillery day and one of enemy artillery was exceedingly active. Delivery active. Brickfield Guns to our trenches. Also the unions Our artillery was ordered very extensively. In self defence casualties 1 60 Amm. & officer on Ecole switch	

Army Form C. 2118.

WAR DIARY
or
INTELLIGENCE SUMMARY.
(Erase heading not required.)

Place	Date	Hour	Summary of Events and Information	Remarks and references to Appendices
YPRES	1918 May 30		Artillery fire was quiet at Bn Headquarters and mopping up. This are trenches Both units were out for review of Battalion Headquarters. 2/Lt. J. Rodger and the Battalion from the public the day. Major C.E. Williams rejoined the Bn for duty from leave. 2/Lt. C.C. Simpson proceeded on short leave to England this day.	
	31		Artillery & enemy aircraft extremely active throughout the day. 16 casualties for Bn front. All available men employed on front line trench which has been greatly improved during the past few days.	
			Riband Awards for the Month of MAY 1918	
			D.S.O. Lt. Col. G.L. Brown	
			Bar to M.C. Capt. H.S. Walker M.C., Capt. J.A. Rogers M.C.	
			M.C. Capt. F.B.B. Dowling, Lieut C.C. Davenport, Lieut H.F. Copp 13 Bn Essex Surry Regt	
			D.C.M. No 16320 L/c Philpott, No 17177 Pte Sherborne H.J.	
			M.M. 16041 Pte T. Chappell, Pte 12222. T. Moore, 14256 Pte J. Hester, 5383 Pte A. Beck, 2203 Sgt J. Lewis	
			18522 Pte A.E. Dinnington, 7197 Sgt A.W. Thompson, 33266 L/c W.E. Smith, 17641 Sgt E. Davey, 9581 Sgt R.E. Newble	
			242677 Cpl W.N. Mann, 11415 Pte W.A. Smith	

A.W. Burn Lt. Col.

12th East Surrey Regt.
15th Hampshire Regt.
18th Kings Royal Rifle Corps.

1.- It has been decided by the Commander-in-Chief that the system of employing large numbers of Officers, and men extra to Establishment with various Headquarters, is to cease.

2.- The G.O.C. wishes you to go into this matter and take steps to ensure that no Officer, N.C.O. or man is employed in any manner not provided for by Establishment for an Infantry Battalion, forwarded under this office B.M.83 dated 11-3-18.

3.- Please certify by 6 p.m. to-morrow, 4th instant, that this has been done.

If any men not on the Establishment laid down for Battalion Headquarters are considered indispensable, particulars and numbers of such personnel should be stated.

Captain.
Staff Captain.
122nd Infantry Brigade.

3-5-18.

Secret

DIGT
Operation Order No 2
Map Ref 28. N.W.

(1) The Battn will be relieved in the Outpost line by the 15th Hampshire Regt on the night of 7/8th. No movement will be made before 9pm. relief to be complete by 2am 8th inst.

(2) Disposition of Coys will be as follows:—

15th Hants	12 E Surreys	Sector
B Coy will relieve	A Coy	Right Front
A " "	D "	Left Front
D " "	C "	Right S.R.
C " "	B "	Left S.R.

(3) Guides one per platoon will meet the incoming platoons at 9.30pm at the House in SAVILLE RD I.8.c.2.0. (50ˣ from Bn HQ) and will guide them into position.

(4) 1 Officer, 1 NCO and 2 runners per Coy and 2 runners for Bn HQ from 15th Hants will report to their opposite numbers tonight 6/7th and will remain in the line for 24 hours to learn dispositions etc.
In addition Coy Commanders of 15th Hants will visit the line tonight 6/7th.

(5) Defence Scheme, scheme of Counter-attack, photograph maps and Trench stores will be handed over on relief. Copies of receipts will be forwarded to Bn HQ of all trench stores.

(6) Companies will report relief complete by wiring the word "PONGO".

7. On relief the Battn will occupy the line of YPRES Defences vacated by the 15th Hants as follows:—

12th E Surreys	15th Hants
A Coy will occupy position of	B Coy
D " " " "	C Coy

12 E Surreys   15th Hants

   C Coy will occupy position of D Coy.
   B "   "   "   "   A   "

(8) Each Coy will send 1 N.C.O and 4 men (1 per platoon) to report to HQ 15th Hants at DEAD END tonight 6/7th. They will live with the 15th Hants tomorrow and will report back to their own Coy Commanders tomorrow night 7/8th and will guide their Coy into the new positions when relief is complete.

(9) The men of the 15th Hants living with the East Surreys for 24 hours will be rationed by East Surreys and vice-versa. No rations will therefore be required to be taken.

(10) Acknowledge.

Copy no 1 A Coy
       2 B
       3 C
       4 D
       5 W? ?
       6 ?
       7 ?
       8 File
       9 War Diary

(Sd) D Walker
Lieut A/Adjt
D.C.L.I.

Issued at 9 pm

6.5.18

SECRET   Copy No. 11.

Battalion Operation Order No.95 by Lieut. Colonel. C. MURDOCH.
Commanding "DINGLE".
Dated 7th. May. 1918.

Reference Map Sheet 28 N.W.

1. The Battalion will relieve "DIGIT" in the right sub-sector of the Outpost Line on the night 7th/8th May 1918.

2. All Trench Stores, Defence schemes, Schemes of Counter Attack and plans will be taken over on relief. Trench Stores held by Companies in YPRES DEFENCES will be handed over to the N.C.O. of "DIGIT" at present with Companies.
   All Trench Papers and maps, and Defence Schemes of this Sector will be forwarded to Orderly Room by 4 p.m. today. A List of the Stores handed over and taken over will forwarded to Orderly Room as soon as possible.

3. All movements will be by platoons at 100 yards interval.

4. Companies will relieve Companies of "DIGIT" as under:-

   Coy. of "DINGLE" to relieve Coy. of "DIGIT" : LOCATION.
   "B"   "A"   Right Front.
   "A"   "D"   Left Front.
   "D"   "C"   2 Platoons in Right Support.
                                                    2 Platoons in Right Reserve.
   "C"   "B"   2 Platoons in Left Support.
                                                    2 Platoons in Left Reserve.

5. One guide per platoon of "DIGIT" will be at house at SAVILE ROAD I.5.c.2.0. at 9.30 p.m. 7th. May.
   The leading platoon of Companies will meet guide at above reference at times as under:-
       "B" Company.   9.30 p.m.
       "A"   do.   9.50 p.m.   9.40 P.M.
       "D"   do.   10.10 p.m.   9.50 P.M.
       "C"   do.   10.30 p.m. 10. 0 P.M.
   Battalion Headquarters will march off at 10 p.m. and proceed to "DIGIT" Battalion Headquarters at I.9.c.15.80.

6. DRESS. Fighting Order with greatcoats rolled round the haversack.

7. Relief complete will be reported by wire by the following phrase:-
       "Have got Dixies"

8. Report centre will be at Battalion Headquarters at House at I.9.c.15.80.

9. ACKNOWLEDGE.

Issued at 10.A.M. 7th. May 1918.   Capt. & Adjt.
                                                          DINGLE.

               Copy No. 1.   Commanding Officer.
               do.   2.   Second in Command.
               do.   3.   Filed.
               do.   4.   War Diary.
               do.   5.   O.C. "A" Company.
               do.   6.   O.C. "B" do.
               do.   7.   O.C. "C" do.
               do.   8.   O.C. "D" do.
               do.   9.   Transport Officer.
               do. 10.   Quartermaster.
               do. 11.   DIGIT.
               do. 12.   L.S.R.

ADMINISTRATIVE INSTRUCTIONS
Reference
Battalion Operation Order No. 95.

1. RATIONS.
   (a). The next ration for consumption on the 8th instant, and during the time the Battalion is in the Outpost Line will be cooked daily at the Transport Lines. Rations for consumption on the 8th inst. will be carried up to the Outpost line on the men. Rations will be delivered at Ration Dumps in the YPRES DEFENCES before 8.30 p.m. on the 7th inst.
   Rations for the 9th inst. and future days' will be brought to Ration Dump at I.3.c.1.2. by limbers at 10 p.m. daily. Ration parties will be at Dump for rations at that hour.
   (b). "D" Company will supply daily a ration party of 20 Other Ranks for "B" Company and "C" Company a similar party for "A" Company.
   (c). The following will arrive with rations each night commencing 7th inst.
        Each Company. 10 Petrol Tins of Tea and
                        9 Petrol Tins of Water.
        Battn. H.Q.   6 Petrol Tins of tea and
                        8 Petrol Tins of Water.
   (d). A supply of solidified alcohol will arrive with the rations daily.

2. GUARD.
   "D" Company will supply a guard for Battalion Headquarters of 1 N.C.O. and 6 men. This guard will report to the R.S.M. at present Headquarters at 9 p.m. today.
   "D" Company will also take over the Anti-Aircraft guard at I.9.a.2.9.

3. MEDICAL.
   Regimental Aid Post at Battalion Headquarters.

4. ACKNOWLEDGE.

7th. May. 1918.
                                        (Sd). S.P. WIGMORE.
                                              Capt. & Adjt.
                                              DINGLE.

Copies to all recipients of Battalion Operation
Order No. 95.

12th Battn East Surrey Regt.
Operation Order No. 3

1. The Battalion will relieve the 18th K.R.R. Corps on the night of 10/11th May 1918. in the YPRES DEFENCES and RAMPARTS. Battalion H.Q will be at I.8.d.1.6

2. Dispositions of Companies will be as follows:-
   A Coy on Right D Coy on Left will relieve B Coy 18th K.R.R Corps in the RAMPARTS.

   C. Coy.
   2 Platoons will relieve 1 Platoon of A Coy 18th K.R.R Corps
   2 Platoons will relieve 1 Platoon D Coy and 1 Platoon C Coy 18th K.R.R.C

   B Coy.
   3 Platoons will relieve 2 Platoons C Coy 18th K.R.R Corps and
   1 Platoon detached (Guide from C Coy K.R.R.C.)

3. Guides will be allotted as follows:-
   A Coy 2 Guides from B Coy K.R.R. Corps
   D " 2   "   " B "   "   "
   C " 1   "   " A "   "   "
   C " 1   "   " D "   "   "
   C " 1   "   " C "   "   "
   B " 2   "   " C "   "   "
   B " 1   "   " C "   "   "   for detached Platoon

4. Companies will march out in the following order:-
   A Coy D Coy B Coy and C Coy.
   Times of departure will be notified later
   Guides will meet the Companies before moving off.

5. Companies will send this evening 1 Officer and 1 man to their New Line to reconnoitre. Also B & C Coys will send a N.C.O to reconnoitre the detached Sector of their Line.

6. All Trench Stores, Gas rattles and Flappers and S.O.S. Rockets will be handed over to the incoming Unit of the 9th Battn Royal Inniskillen Fusiliers

7. Rations except Tea, will come up cooked tonight and will be issued before moving off. Ration arrangements for to-morrow will be notified later.

8. Completion of Relief will be wired using the name of the Company Commander respectively.

9. The 9th Battn Royal Inniskillen Fusiliers will take over from the Battn in its present position in the following order:-
   B Coy will be relieved by No 2 Coy R.I.F.
   C   "   "   "   "   "   1   "   "
   D   "   "   "   "   "   4   "   "
   A   "   "   "   "   "   3   "   "
   Guides 1 per Platoon will report at Battn H.Q at 11.45 pm tonight

10. All Company Stores &c will be stacked at Coy. Dumps at 8-30 p.m and will be loaded on empty limbers. They will be taken as far as the New Battn H.Q.

11. Acknowledge.

        Copies to   O.C. A. Coy
                    O.C B "
                    O.C C "
                    O.C D "
                    O.C. 18th R.R.R.C
                    122nd Inf Bde   (Sd) D Walker
                    File   Capt & a/Adjt
                    War Diary   DIGIT

10. 5. 18
                                    Issued at 8.30 PM

SECRET

12th East Surrey Regt.
15th Hampshire Regt.
18th Kings Royal Rifle Corps.

S.C.D.445

At a Conference held at 123rd Infantry Brigade Headquarters on 8th inst., the following modifications in the Establishment laid down for an Infantry Battalion forwarded under this office B.M.83 dated 10-3-18, were made.

1.

	No. of Horses.	Personnel.
Transport Sergt.	1	1
Officers Mess Cart.	1	1
2 Water Carts.	4	2
Maltese Cart.	1	1 (a)
3 S.A.A.L.W.G.S.	6	3
1 Grenade L.W. G.S.	2	1
2 Tools " " " "	4	2
4 Lewis Guns " " "	8	4
4 Travelling Kitchens.	8	4
6 Pack Animals.	6	6
4 Spare Animals.	4	2
Spare Drivers.	-	2 (b)
Officers Chargers less Tpt.Offr. and Qr.Mr.	8	5 (c)
Officers Chargers. Tpr.Offr. & Qr.Mr.	2	1 (d)
Pioneer.	-	1 ø
18 vehicles.	55 Horses	36 N.C.Os & men.

(a) One of M.Os orderlies. (b) Trained as Cold Shoers.
(c) C.Os groom and 4 Coy. Commanders Grooms. (d) Tpt.Offr. and Qr.Mr. use their two batmen as 1 servant and 1 groom.
ø Saddler.

In addition to above a proportion of Battalion H.Q. personnel will always be with the Transport and are available for duty on the March, brakesmen must be found from personnel whose duties permit of, or necessitate their accompanying vehicles. There is no objection to the employment of fatigue parties at the Transport lines from time to time when specially required

2. It was decided that 2 cooks mates per company were required in addition to the two shown on establishment, also that a Company storeman was essential, and that the above might be employed extra to establishment.

P.T.O.

-2-

Units will at once re-organise existing Transport Establishment to conform to above.

If any difficulty is experienced, it should be reported in detail by 8 p.m. 13th May.

11-5-18

Captain.
Staff Captain.
122nd Infantry Brigade.

12th Battn East Surrey Regt
Operation Order No 11

1. On the night 11/12th of May the Battn will extend its Right Flank to include the HORN WORKS I 9 d 6.6 and the fortifications around them at present occupied by 2 Companies of the 2nd Battn Yorks Lancs. One Company in RAMPARTS and One in HORN WORKS

2. Dispositions
   C Coy will relieve C Coy Yorks Lancs in HORNWORKS
   A Coy will relieve A Coy Yorks Lancs in RAMPARTS
   B Coy will re-organize 2 Platoons in Front Line and 2 Platoons in Area vacated by C Coy I 8 b 6.2
   D Coy will occupy RAMPARTS as far as Battn HQ I 8 d 1.6

3. The Dispositions of the Battn will then be:-
   B Coy Left Front (2 Platoons in rear)
   C Coy Right Front
   D Coy Left Support in RAMPARTS
   A Coy Right Support in RAMPARTS

4. A. C Coys will send an Officer to reconnoitre and one man per Platoon to the new Sector. They will return to their Coys and act as guides

5. Coys will move into new positions at dusk. No movement of greater parties than 5 before that time.

6. All Trench Stores, Gas appliances etc will be taken over and lists forwarded to this Office

7. Completion of Relief will be reported by Runner to Battn HQ

8. Acknowledge

Copies to   O C A Coy
            O C B Coy   (Sd) D Walker
            O C C Coy   Capt a/Adjt
            O C D Coy   D 16/11
            O C Yorks Lancs
            122nd Inf Bde   Issued at
            File
            War Diary   11-5-18

Secret   p 33.

12th Inf Bde
OC D Coy D/3/T

Dispositions of Companies

1. "C" Company will reinforce your 2 platoons in the YPRES DEFENCE LINE by one platoon from the RAMPARTS at 10pm tonight, taking over from the platoon of the 15th Hampshire Regiment which moves forward. You will keep in touch on the left with the 1st Inniskilling Fusiliers.

2. All arrangements will be made between Company Commanders concerned.

3. Acknowledge.

D Wellesley
Capt & Adjt
12th Bn East Surrey Regt.

15/5/18

OC A Coy
OC B Coy
OC C Coy
OC D Coy
2nd Lt Bae
OC Queen

Secret

Operation Order No 5

Dispositions of Companies

1. Platoons of 16th KRR Coys occupying the Sector between YPRES-POTIJZE Road and the Cemetery will move forward tonight 16/17th May.
3 Platoons of A Company 12th East Surrey Regt in the RAMPARTS will reinforce the line and take over that Sector together with a portion of Front at present occupied by 1 platoon of B Coy

2. Each Coy will re-organize 3 platoons in Front Line and 1 in immediate Supports as follows:—
Support platoon of A Coy will move from the RAMPARTS into Area I.8.b.4.4.
Support platoon of B Coy into Area I.8.b.6.0.
"   "   of C   "   "   I.8.b.6.0.
leaving RAMPARTS vacated except for Battn HQrs and guard on SALLE PORT which will remain as at present.

3. Company Boundaries will be as follows

D. Coy. from left to T.8.b.8.7.
A Coy T.8.b.8.7 to T.9.a.2.3.
B. Coy T.9.a.2.3 to T.8.a.8.6
C Coy T.8.a.8.6 to Right boundary.
4/ No movement will be made before 10pm.
5/ Acknowledge.

A Walker
Capt. Adjt.
1/4th Bn East Surrey Regt.

16/5/18

S E C R E T.

12th East Surrey Regt.
15th Hampshire Regt.
18th K. R. R. Corps.

B.M. 331.
25/.

  For information and necessary action.

  Please take special steps to ensure that these instructions are made known to all concerned.

              Lieut,
             A/Brigade Major,
17th May 1918.   122nd Infantry Brigade.

To all Coys

Operation Order No 6
by
Lieut Col [?] Bower DSO
Comdg 1/4th Bn East Surrey Regt

1. The Bn will be relieved on the night of 17/18th May by the 23rd Bn Middlesex Regt in the YPRES DEFENCE LINE commencing at 11.30pm. Relief to be complete by 2am 18th.

2. Companies will take over letter for letter.

3. Guides 1 per platoon will report at Bn HQrs at 10.30pm to receive instructions.

4. Trench Stores, SOS Rockets and water tins both in the line and at the Transport will be handed over and receipts forwarded to Bn HQ. Any Defence Schemes, or schemes for counter attack etc in possession of Coys will also be handed over.

5. On relief Coys will proceed to FOSTER CAMP H.1.c.5.8. for training, taking over the Camp letter for letter as vacated by 10th R.W.Kents. 1 Officer for HQ and 1 NCO per Coy will proceed immediately to take over from the 10th R.W.Kents in Camp and will report to HQ at 12 noon. Companies will choose their own route. The village VLAMERTINGHE and the main road should be avoided.

6. Lewis gun ammunition will be dumped inside the RAMPARTS just south of MENIN GATE each team leaving one man with the guns. At 1am Transport will collect the ammunition and take them to the new Camp.

7. Trench [?] will be [?] stacked [?] Bn HQ by 10pm.

8. Completion of relief will be reported to HQ by wiring name of Coy Commander.

9. Acknowledge

(Sd) D Walker
Capt & Adjt
1/North East Surrey Regt

17/5/18

SECRET.

13th Bn. East Surrey Regt.

OPERATION ORDER No. 7.

Ref. Map :- Sheet 28 N.W. 1/20,000.

1. The Battalion will relieve the 26th Bn. Royal Fusiliers in the line on the night 25/26th instant, in the left sub sector.

2. <u>Dispositions in line.</u>   I.9.c.6.2
Battalion Headquarters will be situated at ECOLE ~~xxxxxxxxx~~

  <u>Front Line.</u>   "A" Coy 13th E.S.Regt will relieve   Coy 26th R.F.
<u>Immediate Support.</u> "C" Coy 13th E.S.Regt will relieve   Coy 26th R.F.
  <u>Support.</u>   "D" Coy 13th E.S.Regt will relieve   Coy 26th R.F.
  <u>Reserve.</u>   "B" Coy 13th E.S.Regt will relieve   Coy 26th R.F.

3. <u>Move off.</u>   The Battalion will march off in the following order:-
                  Headquarters   8.30 p.m.
                  "A" Company   8.36 p.m.
                  "C" Company   8.42 p.m.
                  "D" Company   8.48 p.m.
                  "B" Company   8.54 p.m.
Platoons will march at 100 yards interval.

4. <u>Route.</u> ROME FARM TRACK - MACHINE GUN FARM H.6.c.9.9. to MENIN ROAD. Leading platoon will pass Machine Gun Farm at 9.45 p.m. The Battalion will be clear of Machine Gun Farm by 10.15 p.m.

5. Companies will each detail 1 Officer, 1 N.C.O. and 2 Runners to report to 2nd Lieut. Mutch at Battn. Headquarters at 5 p.m. today. They will proceed to the line and remain attached until the relief.

6. <u>Trench Stores.</u> All Defence Schemes, Schemes of Counter Attack, Plans, Aeroplane Photographs, Trench Stores, Patrol rnos etc will be taken over and ~~xxxxxxxx~~ lists thereof forwarded to ~~————~~ B.H.Qrs.

7. <u>Transport arrangements.</u> Company Stores, Trench Bundles etc., will be dumped at Battn. Headqrs at 8 p.m. tomorrow 25th inst.
Lewis Guns and ammunition will also be sent to Battn Headqs by 8 p.m., and one man per team will be left with each gun. They will be taken by Transport as far as the Ramparts - I.8.a.95 where each team will pick up its own gun as they pass and proceed to the line.

8. <u>Guides.</u> Arrangements re Guides will be notified later.

9. <u>Relief complete.</u> Completion of relief will be wired to Battn. Headquarters by sending Company Commander's own name.

10. <u>Details.</u> Companies will only leave 6 Lewis Gunners and 1 Lewis Gun N.C.O. per Company for traing at Details Camp.

11. ACKNOWLEDGE.

24th May 1918.   (sd)   D. Walker.   Capt & A/Adjt.
Issued at 12.50 p.m.
                                              13th Bn East Surrey Regt.

12th East Surrey Regt.

WAR DIARY
or
INTELLIGENCE SUMMARY.
(Erase heading not required.)

Army Form C. 2118.

Place	Date	Hour	Summary of Events and Information	Remarks and references to Appendices
YPRES	1918 JUNE 1		Artillery fairly active on both sides also our own & enemy aircraft. Men employed on Tour Cine Trench & Ecole Switch. Both of which form line greatly improved during the last week. Major A.K. Edgell posted to 1st Bn R.W. Surrey Regt. 23.5.18. Strength 42 Off 1018 OR's Ration Strength 29 Off 1081 OR's	
"	2		Artillery active during the day mostly on rear areas. Our own & enemy planes over sector during the early evening & afternoon. Men employed during the day on Tour Cine Trench & Ecole Switch	OPERATION ORDER
"	3		Artillery extremely active throughout the day on Enemy Lines also on YPRES & Gye [ ]. Gas shells were sent over. The Battalion was relieved this day by 1E Lt Dorse of Wellington 30 Div. Four fourteen Officers were attached to the Battalion the day for instructional purposes. Reld. relief at 11.30 AM. The Battalion marched by Companies to Mission Sidings B2.16 where they entrained for PRO EN GA arriving at the Battalion's arrival to ROAD CAMP Sheet 27 A.2.a.3.7.C at 11am til 1.15 pm when they proceeded to DRAVEN SIDING where they entrained at 12.noon for WATTEN	OPERATION ORDER
WATTEN	5		Battalion arrived at 6.30 AM at WATTEN STATION & marched to Billets at BEVECHEM arriving at 9.30am. The Battalion rested during the remainder of the day. 2/Lt H.J. SHERBOURNE awarded 14 days leave to England.	
"	6		Arrival Capt H.V. REINER Knox from E. ENGLAND on 21 days M.E. leave. Battalion employed cleaning up. 2/Lt Cooney to [ ] Officers Hospital sprung to E. Owen a[ ] & 14 days leave.	
BAYENHEM				

26.C
6 int

Army Form C. 2118.

WAR DIARY
or
INTELLIGENCE SUMMARY.
(Erase heading not required.)

Instructions regarding War Diaries and Intelligence Summaries are contained in F. S. Regs., Part II. and the Staff Manual respectively. Title pages will be prepared in manuscript.

Place	Date	Hour	Summary of Events and Information	Remarks and references to Appendices
Boyelles	1918 June 1		War Diary kept V.L. Clift Warrand for Maj: R. Awl. 15.2.18. Capt (A/Lieut Col) G.L. Brown D.S.O.	
	2		Middlesex Regt. transferred Battalion to 6 Temp Helt Colonel & just whilst in rank 17-3-18. 2nd Lieut (A/Capt)	
			F.R.B. Dowling M.C.R.E. Lieut. 16/2/18. 2nd Lieut A.E. Topham from 1 Battalion the day employ'd as 2nd Lieut.	
			R.B.S. D.P. from [illegible] with 2 240R.I. 28.08.	
			B.R. [illegible] Bn. [illegible] Lieutenants Ferguson [illegible]	
	4		Bgade. O.P. on Croisilles area gone to all Officers N.C.O. & other ranks. H. Thorburn	
			[illegible] of R.B. & Lieut Hed. McInnes & 2nd Lieut J.T. Thornton the June 15	
			[illegible]	
	8		[illegible] on field of A. [illegible] [illegible] Rifle Range [illegible] were R.H.Q. Brown.	
			[illegible] at 3.30 [illegible] were [illegible] of [illegible] & [illegible] B & Skmell in off. 1043. O.R.R. strgh of 27. H.Q. no CT	
	9		Bde. sports at 9.45 P.M. [illegible] [illegible] Capt. & M. Christie B. R.M.A. previous to [illegible] before Friday	
			Bn's [illegible] at 3.30 P.M. to lead to Rifle Range where they were engaged [illegible] [illegible] all day, arrived back at 3.30.	
	10		Major J.Thornton [illegible] Hospital Bethune 9 [illegible] Rest day	
	11		[illegible] [illegible] [illegible] [illegible] B. [illegible] [illegible] M. [illegible] [illegible] J.Thornton [illegible] J.C. Jollowing	
			[illegible] O/[illegible] N.C. B [illegible] [illegible] C.B. [illegible] [illegible] [illegible] [illegible] John N.300 R.Q.M.S.	
			[illegible] N. Le S. L.W. Turner, Girls S. G. W. Turner [illegible] Lieut J.T. Thornton [illegible] Runner Bass	

Army Form C. 2118.

WAR DIARY
or
INTELLIGENCE SUMMARY.

(Erase heading not required.)

Army Form C. 2118.

Instructions regarding War Diaries and Intelligence Summaries are contained in F. S. Regs., Part II. and the Staff Manual respectively. Title pages will be prepared in manuscript.

Place	Date	Hour	Summary of Events and Information	Remarks and references to Appendices
Bastigny	1918 June 12		Battalion employed on training. Coys billeting parties left for Brocourt C.C.	
			Rest of Capt. Altair carried out Coy training for rear day's Battalion brought forward to advance.	
			March Rest of day.	
	13		Inspection of rifles & fighting equipment by Coy Comds. 9.0 am. A Clean-up by 10.0 am. Remainder of day spent on Coy. platoon & Coy drill.	
	14		The day devoted to Musketry & Brigade sports. To happen later if still in area from Hd Qrs.	
	15		The Bn. was this day allotted to the Battalion Bois Roux. Marching was also carried out. Total Battalion	
			Strength 31 Officers. 1024 O.R's. Ration Strength 24 Officers 217 O.R's	
	16		The Battalion paraded at 9 am for Church Service. A Battalion march past followed during the afternoon	
			about 4.30 p.m. 133 Infy Bde Commander. The following Officers, N.C.O's and men received in Medals: 28.5.18	
			Capt (A/L.) Stallard C.F. M.C., Capt J. Maser Williams G.T., T/Lieut. (A/Capt.) Kerr H. G.P.G, 2nd Lt (A/Capt.) F.B. Dowling,	
			A/Lieut R.R. Heide 9379 Sgt (L/Sgt) C. Hammond, 25433 Cpl. Sgt (A/Sgt.) H. Elce, 11273 Cpl (A/L/Sgt.) W. Hall, 12332 Pte. A.E. Pennington.	
		2.53.83 pm	J. M Sweeney (TMC)	
	17		Training this day included Musketry Att Battalion H.Qs took part in the divisional platoon Rifle Competition &	
			Coy. Coy. by 3 Coy. It to the 18th Hampshire Regt. A. Competition were finally won by the 18th King's Royal Rifle Corps	

Army Form C. 2118.

WAR DIARY
or
INTELLIGENCE SUMMARY.
(Erase heading not required.)

Instructions regarding War Diaries and Intelligence Summaries are contained in F. S. Regs., Part II. and the Staff Manual respectively. Title pages will be prepared in manuscript.

Place	Date	Hour	Summary of Events and Information	Remarks and references to Appendices
BRINCKEM	1918 June 18		Training to day included the firing of Bayonet on Cotton Butt. The G.O.C. expressed satisfaction at the general standard of efficiency of the Bayonet Company which was off "B" Coy, 1st Battalion.	
"	19		Training to day included a Battery of Exercises in Advance. The Battalion was inspected by Brig. Gen Burn.	
"	20		Lt. Col. R. Buchanan D.S.O. & Lieut. C.C. Simpson proceeded to lecture on Factory Certifi. GRANTHAM. The Battalion had Paxton a Brigade Field day. The object of the Advance being to push in pickets on Ruyley district. The direction was carried on through the EPERLEQUES WOOD.	
"	21		The Battalion carried out a practice attack culminated the day in EPERLEQUES WOOD. The Troops moved at 10am but for a performance to the Battalion Band.	
"	22		The Battalion paraded at 8.30am & marched to Divisional Sports when all ranks were present. Strength 31 Offrs 1013 ORs. At 2.00 pm Lieut. [illegible] won the nomination steeplechase for officers. Battalion Strength 31 Offrs 1013 ORs.	
"	23		Battalion Church Parade at ORFS Sgts ORs. The Battalion paraded at 7.30am & marched to "A" Range where musketry firing was carried out. Strength as above. Returning to billets at 12.30pm. Divisional Service was held at 5.30pm.	
"	24		Training to day included Companies in attack on strong point, Battalion School Platoon commanders firing on the open Butts. Evening the Battalion Hockey Team scored a win from "B" Coy 36th.	

Army Form C. 2118.

WAR DIARY
or
INTELLIGENCE SUMMARY.
(Erase heading not required.)

Instructions regarding War Diaries and Intelligence Summaries are contained in F.S. Regs., Part II. and the Staff Manual respectively. Title pages will be prepared in manuscript.

Place	Date	Hour	Summary of Events and Information	Remarks and references to Appendices
BAYENGHEM	1918 JUNE 26		The Battalion paraded at 8.30 AM & marched to RUBROUCK where the 10th Bn Battalion for the 38th arrived at 3 pm.	
			Capt C.H. BISHOP D.S.O rejoined the Battalion this day from Base & assumed command this day 23.6.18	
RUBROUCK	27		The Battalion paraded at 9am & continued march to BEUVOORDE where billets were alloted.	
BEUVOORDE	27		Companies disposed of company stores on arrival in Coys & platoon Comdrs reconnoitred Bn Coy & Platoon Training Areas in the vicinity for training of units.	
	28		Companies placed at disposal of Company Commanders. Major C.F. WILLIAMS rejoined the Battalion this day from leave.	
			The Coys & platoons were inspected by Lt Col R.C. KNOX and by the G.O.C. Brigade.	
	29		Weather fair. Disposal of Company Commanders. Battalion Strength 38 Off. 994 O.R.	
			Return 35 Off. 27,026 Y.11. O.B.S	
	30		Company placed at disposal of Company Commanders. 2nd Lieut C.R. WATTS joined the Battalion this day.	
			Casualty's during the Month of June 3 Killed 19 wounded	

R.C. Knox Lt Col
Comdg 10th Bn E. Surrey Regt

SECRET.

12th. East Surrey Regt.
15th. Hampshire Regt.
18th. Kings Royal Rifle Corps.

    The attached memorandum on the Organisation, Training and tactical handling of Lewis Guns, is forwarded for your consideration. The 4 Anti-Aircraft guns have not been taken into account.

    The notes are compiled with a view to leading up to a system which may meet present requirements.

    Would you kindly give your views and any suggestions you may wish to add, by last D.R. 3rd. instant.

                                Lieut.,
                            A/Brigade Major,
2.6.18.   122nd. Infantry Brigade.

Secret   Copy No. 9.

Operation Order No. 9.
by
Lieut. Col. L.L. Brown D.S.O.
Comdg. 12th Bn East Surrey Regt.

Reference:- Sheet 28. N.W. 1/10.000.

2nd June 1918.

1. The Battalion will be relieved by the 6th Duke of Wellington's on the night of the 3rd/4th June 1918, commencing about 10.30 pm.

2. Companies will be relieved as follows, and in the following order:-

   Our
   Coy.   Front Line   Theirs
   A   Front Line   D Coy.
   B   Support   A
   D   ECOLE Support   C
                       Reserve   B

3. Each Company will detail one guide per platoon and one N.C.O. or Signaller for Coy H.Q. Headquarters will detail 3 guides. These will report at Bn H.Q. with rations for the day, before dawn on the 3rd inst.

4. The following personnel of the incoming Battalion will be attached from to-night until relief:-
   Battn H.Q.   1 Officer & 6 O.R.
   Each Company   1 Officer & 4 O.R.

5. All maps, aeroplane photographs, Defence Schemes, Schemes of Counter attack, Trench Stores, and 20 petrol tins per company will be handed over as Trench Stores, and receipts forwarded to this Office as soon as possible after arrival in Billets.
   All Anti Aircraft L.G. positions will be handed over.

6. Each Company will leave behind one Officer for 24 hours after Relief, or until their services are dispensed with. Transport arrangements for these officers will be notified later.

7. All Company Stores, trench kindlers, mess tins etc. except that which can be carried, will be sent down to-night by the Ration parties, to return in empty limbers. Any of the above not sent down to-night should be sent down to Machine Gun Siding H.12.a. as soon as possible after dark on the night of the 3rd.

P.T.O.

Contd:

8. On relief the Battalion will entrain at Machine Gun Siding, H.12.a. Central, and will move into rest at Road Camp, Sheet 27 L.2.a.2.8. Details of train arrangements will be notified later.

9. Completion of Relief will be notified to Bn H.Q. by wiring Company Commander's own name.

10. Acknowledge.

(sd) D. Walker,
Capt & adjt,
/2nd East Surrey Regt.

Issued at 5 pm

Copies to:-
- No. 1 C.O.
- 2 OC A Coy.
- 3 OC B Coy.
- 4 OC C Coy.
- 5 OC D Coy.
- 6 OC. 6th Duke of Wellington's.
- 7 Quartermaster & Transport Officer.
- 8 War Diary.
- 9 File.

Operation Orders No. 10.
by
Lt Col. G.J. Brown D.S.O.
Comdg 12th Bn East Surrey Regt.

1 The Battalion will move to 2nd Army Training Area by train today.

2 The Battalion will parade at 5.45 pm ready to move off by that hour in the following order
    Headquarters
    A Coy
    B "
    C "
    D "
100 yds interval will be maintained between Coy's on the march

3 The Battalion will entrain at PROVEN for WATTEN arriving at WATTEN about 12.30 am 5.8.18. Not more than 40 men will travel in each truck

4. On arrival at WATTEN the Battalion will march to Rest Billets at BAYENGHEM.

5 Transport will move independently arriving at entraining Station PROVEN at 7 pm.

— CONTINUED —

Transport will proceed to ST OMAR. where they will be met by a Guide
6. Supply Railhead will be at WATTEN from 5 June inclusive
7. Officers Mess Kit will be ready for collection at 5pm. The QMR will make the necessary arrangements

(Sgd.) D. Walker
Captr & Adjt
8th East Surrey Regt

Issued at 1 pm
4-6-18.

Copy

SECRET.

Headquarters,

    41st. Division "G".

    Reference G.307 (62/6) dated 30th. May 1918.

    At a Brigade Conference held on 4th. June 1918, the memorandum on the organisation of Lewis Guns was discussed.

1.   The opinion was, that the arrangement outlined in para 1. would be unsatisfactory and would only result in the loss of Lewis Guns and ammunition.

2.   Though, against the recent instructions as regards Specialising and also against the opinion expressed at the last Divisional Conference, that the Lewis Guns should be treated as an automatic rifle, the Commanding Officers were of opinion that to get good results with the present quality Platoon Commanders, who are constantly changing, it is necessary to group the guns of each Company to-gether under one officer, for training and in action.

3.   The following organisation of the Company is suggested:-

Lewis Gun Platoons with 8 guns in each Company, organised into 4 Sections, each with 2 guns.
Each section as follows:-

    2 guns.
    1 N.C.O.
    8 Lewis Gunners (2 Nos. 1.
                   (6 Ammunition carriers.
    2 Scouts.

Total 11 O.R.

Ammunition carriers would each carry:-

    Rifle.
    50 rounds S.A.A. only.
    8 full drums i.e. 48 filled drums in each Section.

The Lewis Gun Platoon would then be organised as follows:-

    8 guns.
    4 Sections, each 11 O.R. = 44 O.R.

  In each Company there would then be only enough men to form 2 rifle platoons.

4.   The following suggestion was made, but opinion was not unanimous:-
That every rifleman carried a full drum in place of the Entrenching Tool, and less 1 bandolier of ammunition.

                                (sgd) F.W. TOWSEY,
                                  Brigadier General,
5.6.18.   Commanding 122nd. Infantry Brigade.

SECRET.   -2-

12th. East Surrey Regt.
15th. Hampshire Regt.
18th. Kings Royal Rifle Corps.

    For information.
    Reference line 3 of the above letter, Memorandum on the Organisation of Lewis Guns was forwarded to you under this office B.M.574 (62/-) dated 2.6.18.

                                    Captain,
                                  Brigade Major,
7.6.18.   122nd. Infantry Brigade.

Operation Order No. 15
by
Lieut. Col. F.L. Brown D.S.O.
Comdg 12th Bn. East Surrey Regt.

5th July 1918.

1. The Battalion will relieve the 15th Bn Hampshire Regt in the front line and one Company of the 2nd Yorks Lancs Regt in Squares N.8.a and b, on the night of the 5th/6th July 1918, in the following order:-

12th E. Surrey Regt.   15th Hants Regt.
B Coy. H.Q. will relieve one platoon of   B Coy (front line)
  "   "   "   "   "   "   "   "   D Coy   "
  "   "   "   "   "   "   "   "   B Coy in Close support
  "   "   "   "   "   "   "   "   C Coy in Support.

A Coy   will relieve   A Coy.
D Coy   will relieve 2 platoons of   D Coy in front line,
                                                        and one platoon in close support.
  "   "   "   one platoon of   C Coy in Support.

C Coy will relieve Support Company of 2nd Yorks Lancs
         in Squares N.8.a and b.

2. Guides. Guides for A B & D Coy one per platoon will be at Hogers.
15th Hants Regt at 10.45 pm. Guides for C Coy as arranged.

3. Platoons will march at 100 yds. interval.

4. Trench Stores. Defence Schemes, Maps and Trench Stores will be taken over, and a copy of receipts forwarded to Battn H.Q.

5. Completion of relief will be wired by using Company Commanders own name.

6. Trench Bundles etc. Trench Bundles, Cooking Utensils, Company Stores etc. will be stacked at present Battn H.Q by 10 pm and will be taken by limber to the new Battn H.Q.

7. Rations. Rations for 6th will be dumped at new Bn H.Q. and one platoon from each Company will draw rations, water, and tea in petrol tins as it passes that point.

8. Acknowledge.

(sd) W Walker
Capt & Adjt
12. East Surrey Regt.

S E C R E T

O.B./1919

Second Army.
----

1.   In accordance with G.H.Q. letter No. A.G./4176(O) dated 8th April 1918, British Infantry Battalions will not for the present be maintained at a higher establishment than 900 Other Ranks.

2.   Table A attached shews the lower establishment drawn up to meet the requirements of this temporary reduction.   The general organisation at present existing will remain unchanged, except that each Platoon will consist of two Rifle Sections and one Lewis Gun Section of two guns.

3.   The organisation, as explained in the attached memorandum and detailed in Table A., will be put into force in all British Infantry Battalions forthwith.

4.   Instructions will be issued very shortly with regard to the transport of the additional Lewis Guns and ammunition.   In view of the increased number of weapons, Lewis Gun ammunition will be reduced by about 1,000 rounds per gun.

5.   Special attention is drawn to the principles upon which the organisation of the double Lewis Gun Section has been based; (attached memorandum, para.3).

6.   The fighting strength of the Battalion will always be based on the minimum strength laid down for rifle and Lewis Gun Sections, and no more than the minimum.

General Headquarters,   (sd) G.F.DAWNAY, M.G.
14th June 1918.   For Lieut.General,
                                              C. G. S.

SECRET.   Copy No. 1

12th Bn EAST SURREY REGT.

WARNING ORDER No. 2.

1.   In the event of the Division being required, the Battalion will be prepared to move to another area by rail.

2.   The Battalion will entrain as follows ;- times of departure of the trains will be notified later :-
   A Coy. will entrain with Brigade Headquarters on No 1. train, and will take one cooker and team.
   The remainder of the Battalion and Transport will entrain on No. 4 train.
   All personnel must report at the Entraining Station one hour, Transport 3 hours, before scheduled hour of departure of the respective trains.
   Probable entraining stations will be :- ST.OMER, ARQUES, or WIZERNES.

3.   Baggage and Supply Waggons will entrain loaded with the Battalion.
   Should the Battalion entrain before 3 p.m. rations for the day of entrainment will be carried on the man, and for the following day on the Supply Waggons.
   Should the Battalion entrain after 3 p.m. rations for the following day in addition to the unexpired portion of the current day's rations will be carried on the man, and the rations for the day after on the Supply Waggons.

4.   Entrainment states will be handed in to Orderly Room one hour before the notified time for parade.

5.   If the journey is of less duration than 18 hours horses will be entrained with saddles and harness on, girths will be loosened and bits removed.

                                   (sd) D. Walker,
                                        Capt & A/Adjt,
                                   12th Bn East Surrey Regiment.

Issued at 6 pm
16th June, 1918.

            Copies to:-
                     No. 1 File.
                     No. 2. O i/c Headquarters.
                     No. 3. O.C. A Coy.
                     No. 4. O.C. B Coy.
                     No. 5. O.C. C Coy.
                     No. 6. O.C. D Coy.
                     No. 7. Transport Officer.
                     No. 8. Quartermaster.

Secret.

12th East Surrey Regt.
12th Hampshire Regt.
18th K.R.R. Corps.

BM 895 / 46 /

J57 / O / 18

Herewith one copy of G.H.Q. O.B. 1919 dated 14th June 1918 — new "ORGANISATION OF THE INFANTRY BATTALION", which will come into force forthwith.

The Brigade Scheme will be carried out under the existing organisation, on 20th inst.

Almont.

R. ———
Captain,
for Brigade Major,
122 Infantry Brigade.

15.6.18

Copy No....1....

OPERATION ORDER No.11
by
LIEUT.COL.G.L.BROWN, D.S.O.,
Comdg 12th Bn EAST SURREY REGIMENT.

Reference. France 27 A. N.E. 1/20.000.

1. The Battalion will take part in a Brigade Field Day to-morrow, 30th June, 1918.

2. The object of the scheme is to practise Units in keeping direction, maintaining touch in a wood, and to illustrate the necessity of close formation in wood fighting.

3. GENERAL IDEA.

   1. On the day previous to the exercise, British Troops have gained a line of Railway WATTEN - AUDRICQ on a broad front, and have pushed through into the Eastern edge of EPERLECQUES WOOD.

   2. The 122nd Infantry Brigade, with other Units on Right and Left, is ordered to continue the advance.

   3. The enemy has retired leaving a series of strong points in the Wood.

4. SPECIAL IDEA.

   1. The frontage of the Brigade will be from K.11.b.0.2 on the Right to K.17.b.5.2, cross roads, on the Left.

   2. The Brigade will advance on a true bearing of 278°, and the objective will be on the road running from K.9.a.5.8 to K.14.b.3.8.

   3. At 9.30 a.m. the Brigade will be disposed as follows:-

   16th Bn. King's Royal Rifle Corps.   On Right.
   15th Bn. Hampshire Regt.   On Left.

   The dividing line being K.11.d.2.2.
   The dividing line at the objective will be K.8.d.9.9.
   The 12th Bn. East Surrey Regt. will be in reserve on the roads in K.12.c. and K.17.b.
   Brigade Headquarters will be at the bend of the road at K.12.b.2.6.
   The 122nd Trench Mortar Battery will be on the road immediately in rear of Brigade Headquarters.
   A Machine Gun Company will be at the disposal of the Brigade and will be situated in square K.18.b.

   4. Zero hour will be 10 a.m.

5. The Battalion will form up for the exercise by 9.30 a.m. as explained to Company Commanders.
   Battalion Headquarters will be at K.18.b.9.6, Dressing Station at K.18.b.0.3, Advanced Brigade Headquarters K.18.a.0.9.

6. The Battalion will parade at 6.45 a.m. in the following order:-
   Headquarters.
   C Company.
   D Company.
   A Company.
   B Company.
   head of column at bend in road K.1.a.9.5 facing East.
   Dress:- Fighting order without Steel Helmets.

P.T.O.

Contd.

7. Each Company will detail 5 O.Rs. to parade outside Battalion Orderly Room at 6.45 a.m. under a Sergeant to be detailed by O.C. D Company. This party will report to Brigade Headquarters, they will draw 30 rounds of blank ammunition per man from the Quartermaster.

8. Lewis Gun Limbers and all Pack Ponies will parade with Companies, Lewis Guns etc. must be loaded over night.

9. Cookers and Mess Cart will meet the Battalion in field at K.13.d.5.2 at 1.15 p.m.

10. Each Company will draw 350 rounds of blank ammunition.

11. No ball ammunition will be taken on parade.

12. Each Company will carry two stretchers.

13. Watches will be synchronised on the ground at 9 a.m. The Signalling Officer will send a N.C.O. to Brigade Headquarters at K.1c.b.5.6 for that purpose.

14. ACKNOWLEDGE.

           (sd) D.Walker,
            Capt & A/Adjt,
          13th Bn East Surrey Regiment.

Issued at 4.30 p.m.
19th June, 1918.

Copies to:-

  No. 1. File.
  No. 2. War Diary.
  No. 3. C.O.
  No. 4. 2nd-in-Command.
  No. 5. Adjutant.
  No. 6. O.C. A Company.
  No. 7. O.C. B Company.
  No. 8. O.C. C Company.
  No. 9. O.C. D Company.
  No.10. Transport Officer.
  No.11. Quartermaster.
  No.12. Medical Officer.
  No.13. Intelligence Officer.
  No.14. Signalling Officer.
  No.15. R.S.M.

13th Bn. East Surrey Regiment.
BATTALION EXERCISE
for 21/6/18.

1. **OBJECT.**   To practice 3 Companies in the attack and 1 Company in withdrawal in close country.

2. **GENERAL IDEA.**   The line held by our troops runs along the road from K.16.d.6.8. to K.15.a.3.7., thence to edge of wood at K.8.c.1.7.

3. **SPECIAL IDEA.**   The Battalion is ordered to advance in conjunction with other Units, clear the wood and consolidate on the edge of the wood, on a line from K.3.c.9.0 to K.9.b.6.8.

4. **INSTRUCTIONS.**

    (1) "A", "B", and "D" Companies will form up as follows on a line from K.14.b.7.7. to K.15.a.5.5. at 9 a.m. "B" Company on left, "D" Company on right, "A" Company in support.

    (2) The Reserve Company will be imaginary.

    (3) The dividing points between the two front Companies will be K.15 a.1.7. south of bend in road, and K.9.b.2.9.

    (4) "C" Company will represent the enemy under special instructions issued separately to O.C. "C" Company.

    (5) Zero hour will be 9.30 a.m. Approximate direction of advance 26°.30' true.

    (6) Battalion Headquarters will be at the bend in the road K.15 a.1.7.

    (7) <u>Parade.</u> "C" Company under orders of O.C. "C" Company H.Q., "A", "B", and "D" Companies will parade at 7.30 am Head of column near Battalion Orderly Room facing West.
    <u>Order of March.</u> H.Q., "D", "B", "A" Coys.
    <u>Dress.</u> Fighting Order without steel helmets.

    (8) Lewis Gun Limbers and pack animals will be with their Companies.

    (9) The Commanders of "A", "B", and "D" Coys will meet the Commanding Officer at cross roads K.14.b.2.5. at 8.30 am.

                                    (sd)   D. Walker   Capt & A/Adjt.
                                              13th Bn East Surrey Regt.

12th. BN. EAST SURREY REGT.

OPERATION ORDERS No. 12.

1. The Brigade will move to-morrow to the RUEBROUCK AREA Transport will accompany Units.

2. All packs and Officers valises will be stacked outside the Quartermasters Stores by 7.30 a.m.
Officers Mess kits etc. will be placed the various Compy H.Qs. for collection by the Mess cart at 7.30.a.m. The Transport Officer will arrange to collect these.

3. The Battallion will parade on the road at 8.30.a.m. with head of column at K.31.a.9.6. facing N.E.
   ORDER OF MARCH.   H.Q. Band D. Coy C. Coy Drums B. Coy A. Coy. Distances to be maintained on the march will be 100 yards between Companies. and 500 yards between Battalion.
   DRESS.   Fighting Order   Caps will be worn.

4. 2nd. Lieut. Frischling and I N.C.O. per Compy. including H.Q. will report at Btn Orderly Room at 7.30. a.m. to-morrow morning as Billetting Party. They will proceed to RUEBROUCK on cycles and will report to 2nd. Lieut. Edgar at the Church at 9.30.a.m.

5. One N.C.O. and one man per Compy including H.Q. will be left behind as rear party and will inspect all billets after they have been vacated. They will proceed under 2nd. Lieut Hall to the new aera.

6. One lorry is allotted to the Battallion for the conveyance of packs.   O.C. C. Compy will an Officer to Supervise the loading of packs etc.   O.C. Compys. will eaxh detail one man as a guard.   He will report at the Quartermasters Stores at 7.30.a.m.

7. O.C. Compys. are responsible that all their Compy. billets are left in a scrupulously clean cindition and that all claims for damage are paid before leaving. A certificate will be rendered to Orderly Room by 8. a.m. that this has been done.
The certificates which are issurd to Compys. with these orders will also be renered to Orderly Room by 8.a.m.
This certificate must be signed by the owner of each billet

(Sgd) D. Walker
Capt & A/Adjt.
24m 6. 18.   12th. East Surrey Regt.

12th Bn. East Surrey Regt.

OPERATION ORDER No.15.

Refce :- Sheet 27., 1/40,000 & Hazebrouck 5a 1/100,000.

1. The Battalion will move into the Reserve Area today 26th inst.

2. The Battalion, with Transport, will parade on the road in column of threes at 9 a.m. with head of column at H.14.a.9.1., Sheet 27, facing South in the following order :-
   H.Q., Drums, A Coy, B Coy, Band, C Coy, and D Coy.
   The usual distances will be maintained between Companies etc., after the Battalion has marched off.
   Dress :-   Fighting Order; caps will be worn.

3. Company Commanders will hand over their Company to their 2nd-in-command, and will report at Brigade H.Q. in the village (H.13.b.9.6) at 7.30 a.m. They will proceed by Lorry to reconnoitre a part of the East Poperinghe Line which the Battn. will be required to occupy on receipt of orders.
   A guide from the 3rd Battn. 52nd Regiment will meet the above Officers on the main STEENVOORDE - ABEELE Road just S.E. of the 2nd E. in BEAUVOORDE.

4. A lorry will convey Packs to the new area.
   Each Company will detail one man to mount guard over Packs.
   2nd Lieut Watts is detailed to supervise the loading etc.
   The above will report at the Quartermasters Stores by 6.30 a.m.
   The lorry will be loaded, and will proceed as soon as possible to STEENVOORDE where it will dump the first load which will be left under a guard to be detailed by O.C. Loading party.
   A Guide will meet the lorry after the 2nd journey & will guide same to the new Billets.

5. Officers Mess Kit, Valises, etc will be stacked outside Company H.Q. Billets by 8 a.m. The Transport Officer will make all necessary arrangements to collect same.

6. 2nd Lieut. Frischling and 1 N.C.O. per Company including H.Q., will form Billeting Party. They will report at Battn Orderly Room at 6.45 a.m. and will proceed to the Church ARNEKE where they will report to Lieut. Edgar at 7.30 a.m.
   The Quartermaster will detail a N.C.O. for the purpose of guiding supply wagons. He will proceed with the above party at 6.45 a.m.

7. As the march will be a long one, meals will be had en route, place and hour of which will be notified on the march.

8. O.C. Companies are responsible that their Company Billets are left in a scrupulously clean and sanitary condition.

                                        (sd) D.Walker   Capt & A/Adjt.

Issued at 4 a.m.
26th June 1918.   12th Bn East Surrey Regt.

SECRET.   Copy No......1......

12th Bn East Surrey Regt.

OPERATION ORDER No. 14.

Reference Maps. Sheets 27 and 28.

1. The Battalion will relieve "C" Battalion 103rd Regiment in Reserve on the night of the 1st/2nd July, 1916.
   The Battalion will move off in the following order:-
   "B" Coy, "A" Coy, "D" Coy, "C" Coy, H.Q.
   The 1st Platoon of "B" Coy will pass the point K.36.d.0.6 at 10 p.m. Distances as follows will be maintained:- 100 yards between Coys, and 50 yards between Platoons and H.Q.

2. Guides. 1 Officer, 1 N.C.O. and 4 men per Company and 1 Cycle Orderly for Battn.H.Q. will meet the Battalion at L.33.d.9.5. Sheet 27. 1 Officer per Company and 1 N.C.O. per platoon should reconnoitre the route to this point.

3. All copies of aeroplane photographs, defence schemes, and plans for counter attack will be taken over on relief and copies of receipts for same forwarded to Battn.H.Q.

4. Completion of relief will be wired by using the Company Commander's own name.

5. The S.O.S. Signal = 3 White stars now used by the 7th French Divn. will remain in force until 3 a.m. 2nd July, after which the 2nd Army S.O.S. Signal - red over red over red will be used. Arrangements have been made to take over a number of French Pistols and S.O.S. Signals. These must be returned to Battn.H.Q. by 6 a.m. 2nd July.

6. Water. The supply in the forward area is reported to be badly contaminated and must not be used for drinking purposes. For cooking it must be carefully chlorinated and boiled. All water for drinking purposes will be brought up in Petrol Tins at 20 per Company and 10 for Battn.H.Q.

7. Lewis Guns. Each Company will have one Lewis Gun Limber for the conveyance of Lewis Guns and ammunition. One gun per Company will be left out for instructional purposes.

8. Cooking. Cooking can only be done at night, and every care must be taken that all fires and lights are properly screened. Cooked meat and dry tea will be brought up with rations. 1 cook and 1 assistant cook per Company will be left with the cookers for this purpose.

9. Great Coats will not be taken into the line. Only 120 rds S.A.A. will be carried.

10. Advance Parties. Advance parties consisting of the Company Commander, 1 N.C.O. and 2 guides per Platoon and one guide per Battn.H.Q. will go forward to the position to be taken over, and reconnoitre sub sectors. These parties will remain in the line and rejoin the Battalion on relief.
    Guides from "C" Battalion, 103rd Regiment, will meet the above party at L.29.c.9.2. Sheet 27. at 9 a.m. 1st July.
    Lorry arrangements will be notified later.

11. Transport. Transport will take over sites now occupied by opposite number on relief, which is disposed in 2 Echelons as follows:-
    "A" Echelon.   LAPPE   L.34.c.9.4.
    "B" Echelon.   BEARVOORDE WOOD K.33.& 34.
    Any rearrangement in the disposition of transport will be made after relief.

12. Rear Parties. The following personnel of the 7th French Division will remain in the line for 24 hours after the relief.
    1 Officer per Company.
    1 Officer per Battn.H.Q.

Contd.

13. **Special precautions.** Absolute silence, no lights, and strict adherance to distances as laid down on the march.

There should be one Officer and 1 N.C.O. per Company always on duty to ensure that the men do not expose themselves unnecessarily and that sentries are posted to give warning of approaching aircraft.

Excess of smoke must be avoided.

The reason for such special secrecy is to prevent the enemy from obtaining indications of a relief of the French by the British is in progress. This should be explained to all ranks.

14. Arrangements re dumping packs. Company Stores etc. will be notified later.

                                       (sd) D.Walker,
                                          Capt & A/Adjt,
                              12th Bn East Surrey Regiment.

Issued at 4 p.m.
30th June, 1918.

Copy	No. 1.	File.
"	No. 2.	War Diary.
"	No. 3.	C.O.
"	No. 4.	2nd-in-Command.
"	No. 5.	Adjutant.
"	No. 6.	O.C. A Company.
"	No. 7.	O.C. B Company.
"	No. 8.	O.C. C Company.
"	No. 9.	O.C. D Company.
"	No.10.	Transport Officer.
"	No.11.	Quartermaster.
"	No.12.	Medical Officer.
"	No.13.	Intelligence Officer.
"	No.14.	Signalling Officer.
"	No.15.	R.S.M.

ORGANISATION, TRAINING AND TACTICAL HANDLING OF LEWIS GUNS.

Points to be considered in deciding upon the re-organisation of Companies, owing to the increase in Lewis Guns, and suggestions for consideration in the Tactical Training of Lewis Gun Sections.

1. Up to the present, with 16 Lewis Guns per Battalion, 25% of the Company enter the fight as Lewis Gunners, and cannot therefore be looked upon as available in the assault, although all the section except Nos. 1 and 2 are armed with rifle and bayonet and are trained to their use.

With 32 Lewis Guns per Battalion, only 50% of a Company can be considered available in the assault, if Lewis Gun Sections are kept at their present strength.

Though this present strength is one N.C.O. and nine men, two men, only, are sufficient to work the gun in action, provided that there are a sufficient to work the gun supply of drums alongside them.

Provided then that the ammunition can be got to the guns, there is sufficient personnel with a section to work two guns in action.

On this assumption, it is suggested that each Lewis Gun Section remains as at present constituted but that one extra gun (with its ammunition) for each section be carried by supporting troops.

This extra gun is then available for sending forward, either to replace a damaged gun, or to give increased fire power when required.

It is considered necessary to carry 60 drums of ammunition for each Lewis Gun, 30 must be carried by the Lewis Gun Section, and the remaining 30 must be distributed among the rifle sections whose S.A.A. carried on the man would then be proportionately decreased. A form of carrier to be devised which will contain one Lewis Gun drum and which can either be slung or attached to a waist belt.

2. The method of handling Light Machine Guns adopted by the enemy, makes it very apparent that Lewis Gun Sections must be brought to such a high state of efficiency as to be able to act independently, if required.

To train Lewis Gun Sections separately and to operate them independently dislocates the platoon of which the Lewis Gun Section forms part, and, if the Platoon Commander who is responsible for the Training of his platoon, devotes sufficient time to the training of his Lewis Gun Section, the training of his remaining sections is bound to suffer. Further, every Platoon Commander is not sufficiently trained himself to undertake the task.

With the situation as it is at present, opportunities for training are confined to brief periods during which Brigades are in Divisional Reserve. During this period, Platoon Commanders have to devote their time to general training, with the result that the Lewis Gun Sections are probably handed over, mostly to the care of Battalion Lewis Gun Officers. In any case Lewis Gunners and riflemen alike only receive the divided attention of their Platoon Commander.

3. The conclusion arrived at then, is that Companies should be organised into 3 Platoons of riflemen, and 1 Platoon of Lewis Guns.

The Lewis Gun Platoon, subdivided into 4 Sections would be commanded by an officer who is expert in the mechanism as well as in the tactical handling of the Lewis Gun. Though every Platoon Commander does not possess this knowledge or the natural aptitude for acquiring it, there is every hope of finding one officer in each Company who does.

4. From a training point of view this organisation offers the following advantages:-
(a) The training of Lewis Gunners in each Company would be in the hands of a specially selected officer.

The Commanders of the 3 remaining Platoons would be relieved of instruction in the Lewis Gun and would then be able to concentrate on the training of the riflemen.

(b) A higher standard of efficiency both in Lewis Gun Teams and in Rifle sections would be reached.

(c) When Battalions are in Brigade Reserve a Lewis Gun Platoon could be sent back to train without dislocating the organisation of platoons.

5. Tactically, the disadvantage appears to be that the system destroys the idea of the platoon being a tactical unit.
The following points however, claimed as advantages would seen to outweigh this objection:-

(a) Rifle platoons would learn the real use of the rifle and not to rely almost entirely for fire effect on the Lewis Gun.

(b) The Lewis guns would mutually support one another.

(c) The fire of the Lewis Guns would not be used on targets which should be dealt with by re riflemen and their ammunition would be available when suitable targets do appear.

(d) Lewis Guns, working independently, would be under the supervision of their Platoon Commanders and the fact that they were taken from Companies would not mean that the remaining platoons are disorganised by their withdrawal.

6. In considering the tactical Training of Lewis Gun Sections, the chief point to keep in mind appears to be the lesson learnt in recent operations about BAPAUME.
The outstanding feature of the enemy's method of advance was the part played by his light machine guns.
These guns he pushed forward by sections, each section working on its own initiative, controlled only by general instructions and guided by the general line of attack. Organised in depth and taking advantage of available cover, rifle sections followed the Lewis Gun sections. By this means, fire positions were built up with a minimum exposure of personnel, gaps were penetrated by light machine guns working singly or in pairs and resistance overcome as much by this skilful method of "infiltration" as by actual weight of numbers.

7. To use our Lewis Guns, as the Germans use their Light machine guns, sections must be trained in scouting, in the use of ground and in the selection of fire positions as well as in the selection of targets and the principles of "mutual support".
Formations suitable for this system of advance require to be carefully studied. As a guide, diagrams or a suggested formation used at a recent Demonstration are given.
The two scouts per section are not more than sufficient to keep touch laterally with the scouts of neighbouring gun sections, the other members of the section are required therefore, one to act as directing file to the section, one to act as connecting file between the scouts and the section commander, and one to connect with a neighbouring section.
With the section commander would be the remaining members of the section and one or two Lewis Guns according to circumstances.
(vide Diagram 1)

Diagram No.1.

No.4. Section.
(left section)   o..................Directing File (No.4.)

                    o...................o.Flank Scouts (Nos.5 & 6.)

Lateral connecting file.
   o (No.8)   o.............Connecting File (No.7).

                              o.............Section Commander.

                              1/1..............Nos. 1 & 2.

                              o.............No.3.

8.   It is claimed for this method of advance, that with well trained Lewis Gun Sections who can keep direction and select fire positions, the remainder of the infantry do not require to be so highly trained in moving warfare.

   The reason being that each Lewis Gun Section is followed by sections of riflemen, each of which in turn occupies all fire positions selected by the Lewis Gun scouts.

   As each fire position is occupied by the rifle sections, the Lewis Gun section again moves forward. It is further claimed that by such a formation, fire positions can be built up with a minimum exposure of personnel.

   Diagram No.2. shows a Company advancing on a 2 Platoon front covered by a Lewis Gun Platoon.

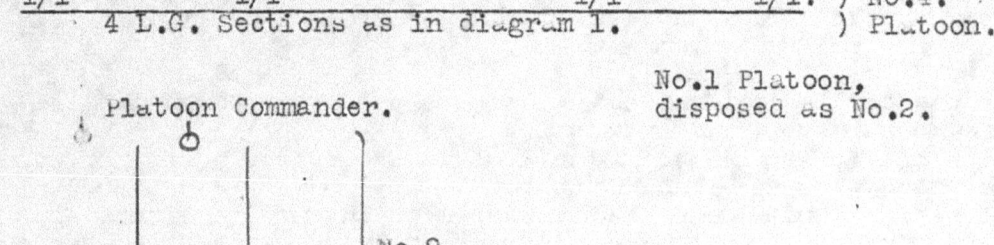

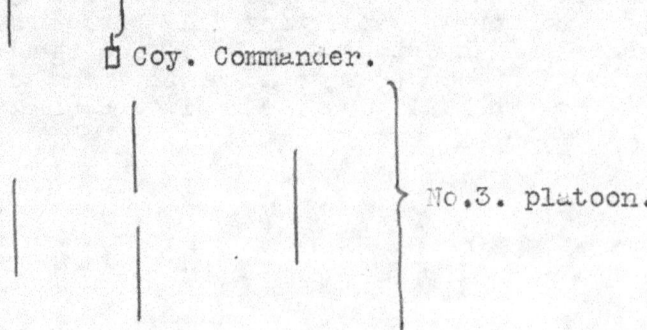

General Staff,
    41st. Division.
        31st. May 1918.

Headquarters
41st Division

Herewith original
War Diary of the
battalion under
my command,
from 1st to 31st July
inclusive.

H.S Walmesley Brown
Major
Comdg. 12th East Surrey Rgt.

12th Battn. East Surrey Regt.

WAR DIARY
or
INTELLIGENCE SUMMARY
(Erase heading not required.)

Army Form C. 2118.

July 1918

Vol 27

27.C
3 sheet

Place	Date	Hour	Summary of Events and Information	Remarks and references to Appendices
RENINGHELST	1/7/18		Bn moved to Bn WOODS at RENINGHELST & took over Brigade Reserve to La CLYTTE Rue Train	
"	2/7/18		103rd French Regiment arrived 1.30am. 2/Lt Foster to England on leave	
"	3/7/18		Bn. relieved C Bn 103rd F.Rgt. in WESTOUTRE LINE 2.30am. No casualties. 2/Lt R.W. Davis joined Battn.	
"			Bn. quiet during day. Moved active at night on La CLYTTE - RENINGHELST ROAD. Five casualties by looking party rear roads.	
"	4/7/18		Bn. quiet during day. Wiring parties active at night. 2/Lt Roberts + Lewis Mackenzie return from English leave. Capt J A Regan MC to Puris on leave	
LA CLYTTE	5/7/18		Bn. relieved 15th Hants in front line. B+C Coys in front line. A+D Coys in support. First line Battn. punch our night, battalion posts on left. Relief complete 2am 6/7/18. Casualties 1 wounded	
"	6/7/18		Normal Bn act. By day Bn. HQ. VIERSTRAAT. OR to cay ? Telephonist on ops Reninghelst F 27.7.22	
"	7/7/18		Normal LA CLYTTE - RENINGHELST ROAD & vicinity of Bn HQ received extra heavy shelling. Return parties on Battn. find on 2 horses wounded. Battn. relieved Cavalier 2.O.R. wounded	
"	8/7/18		En. act. action day. En. H.Gs. active. C+D Coys wired Brigade on front	
"	9/7/18		Normal Bn act + H.Gs action during night. Police point driven off by a succession of wind one casualty. 2 O.R wounded	
"	10/7/18		Enemy artillery action during day. T.Ms on front + support line. Barrage night.	

12th Battn. East Ann. Regt.

Army Form C. 2118.

July 1918

WAR DIARY
or
INTELLIGENCE SUMMARY
(Erase heading not required.)

Instructions regarding War Diaries and Intelligence Summaries are contained in F. S. Regs., Part II. and the Staff Manual respectively. Title pages will be prepared in manuscript.

Place	Date	Hour	Summary of Events and Information	Remarks and references to Appendices
LA CLYTTE	11/7/18		Battn. relieved by 18th K.R.R.C. & retired to support line	
"	12/7/18		Normal routine. Relief at night. Conference held at night under R.E. supervision	
"	13/7/18		Artillery active, mostly fairly active. Conference work as before. Telegraph 40 946. Return strength 26 762	
"	14/7/18		Artillery fairly active in evening. Conference work as before. Lieut-Col Brown D.S.O. to transit Base	
"			Joined on English team Major C.T.H.Hudson assumed temporary command	
"	15/7/18		Battn. relieved by 18th K.R.R.C. & returned to 16th Hants. in reserve line	
POPERINGHE	16/7/18		Quiet. Baths. Lectures. Work at night under R.E.	
"	17/7/18		Full inspection. Church service and lecture on competitive shoots during night Several ?	
"	18/7/18		20 "Other ranks" rejoined the Battn. N.C.O. Humett, Qur. Augur IV. presented 15th Platoon Colours Cups & Certificate to Championship	
"	19/7/18		Company inspection. Sports. Interviews arranged with Rev W. Engels at Base	
"			Lectures & operation at H.G. Battn. aid of E at night. Training periods altered	Coll. Roads
"			Interviews from Lectures & 2/Lt. Foster from English Base	
"			Coy training relative lectures. Conferences with Brigade & Battn. Staff. Some games	
"	25/7/18		Battn. relieved 12th Hants. on live ? at night from 1.30 a.m. & Coys received	
			Telegraph 40 923. Return strength 29 761	

12th Bn. East Surrey Regiment

WAR DIARY
INTELLIGENCE SUMMARY
(Erase heading not required.)

July 1918

Army Form C. 2118.

Place	Date	Hour	Summary of Events and Information	Remarks and references to Appendices
LA CRÈCHE	21/7/18		Situation normal. Enemy could possibly have shortened his line very little hereabouts.	
	22/7/18		Our snipers [...] active. Our officers patrols active but no enemy encountered.	
	23/7/18		Could [...] [...] obstacles than we have [...] one post [...] Enemy Encountered.	2/Lt R.W. Davy wounded
	24/7/18		Relief carried out by 15th Hants to clean identification. [...] obtained his casualties [...]	
	25/7/18		Rest & [...] [...] casualties known 7 killed & 3 wounded.	
	25/7/18		Very quiet. On aircraft active. Baths [...] by 18th KRRC & look over subject [...] from 15th Hants. Very quiet evening.	
	26/7/18		Chiefly devoting to England in Gas.	
	26/7/18		Normal. Snipers [...] [...] shorts. [...] dull & heavy [...] [...] [...].	
	27/7/18		Bombardment carried out [...] [...] front line. 15th KRRC and [...] failed to obtain identification but one [...] obtained. Total shells 85 OR. [...] 59 OR. Returns left 25 1/1 Lieut H Parrs [...].	No.
	28/7/18		Situation normal. Continued work on battle positions & strong front C.W.T.R. [...] & [...] [...].	
	29/7/18		Got active at night. Conferences work on battle positions [...] [...].	
	30/7/18		Bn moved by 13th KRRC & took over from 15th Hants in reserve [...] lines.	
RENNINGHELST	31/7/18		Situation normal. Continuous working to WESTOUTRE Line.	
			Draw [...] [...] [...] [...] [...] held [...] Aug 1st, 2nd & 3rd to [...] be held in Div. Summary on [...]	
			[...] A.C. /4/5/1218 (6) Connection & [...]	O.R. 2 1 31

Crittenden/Major
Ch. 12th East Surrey Regt

12th Bn East Surrey Regt.

In continuation of Operation Order No.14 d/30.6.18.

1. Transport, B Echelon, and Details under Captain Cooper will be at K.28.d.4.8, and not as stated in para.11 of above.

2. Officers Kits etc. ~~All Officers Kits and~~ Company Stores etc. and Trench Bundles, will be stacked outside Company Billets at 8.30 p.m. The Transport Officer will make arrangements to collect these.

3. Transport. The Transport Officer will arrange to send to Companies at 8.30 p.m. one limber and to Headquarters two limbers.
   The above will be loaded with 20 petrol tins for Companies and 10 for Headquarters, also Lewis Guns, Ammunition, Trench Bundles, Company Stores etc.
   Any stores surplus to above will be notified and will be collected by H.Q. limber.

4. Officers Valises etc. Officers Valises, Mess Kit etc. Surplus Stores, will be collected by the Transport Officer at 9 p.m. commencing with B Company.

5. Ammunition. The Transport Officer will arrange to draw to-day from the Divisional Ammunition Dump 50,000 rounds S.A.A. This will be taken to the line on G.S. wagon which will proceed with Headquarters.

6. Rations. Rations for to-morrow will be issued and taken to the line on the man.

(sd) D.Walker,
Capt & A/Adjt,
12th Bn East Surrey Regt.

Issued at 11.30 a.m.
1st July, 1918.

Issued to all recipients of Operation Order No.14 s/30.6.18.

Operation Order No 24
by
Major C T Gillman
Commdg. 12th East Sussex Regt

1. The Battalion will relieve the 4th Bn Canadian Mounted Rifles in the front line during 2nd August 1918.

2. Order of relief and dispositions is as follows
   - B Coy Front Line System
   - D   Jolie Schuppen burg – Breikenbrueck Switch Line
   - C   Centre with 1 platoon in close support to front line
   - A   Right

3. Guides and HQ Platoon and one Lewis Gun HQ from the Mounted Rifles will meet their opposite numbers at Front line Bn HQ (N.1.c.4.1.). Transport platoon of B Coy will reach this point at 10.30 pm.

4. Companies will parade and march off from present billets at the following times.
   - B Coy 8 pm
   - D   8.15 pm
   - C   8.30 pm
   - A   8.45 pm

   Lewis guns and ammunition will be carried. Movement will be by platoon at 200 yds interval.

5. Ration. The Dry portion (meat) will be carried on the man. The Transport Officer in Coy will make the necessary arrangements to have tea and water dumped at front line Bn HQ at 10.15 pm where each platoon will collect same as they pass.

6. Officers kits, trench bundles, Coy stores etc. will be dumped outside Coy billets not later than 6pm the Transport Officer will make arrangements to collect these. Coys will ensure that kit not required in the line is put in separate dump and collected by respective limbers. Kits, Coy Stores proceeding to the line will be dumped at the forward Bn HQ at 10.15 pm.

7. Captain Searle and 1 NCO per platoon will be sent in advance and will report at the front line Bn HQ at 9 pm. They will join their opposite numbers at Ullock to take over all trench stores etc, receipts to be

forwarded to Bn HQ by dawn 4th inst.
The above will proceed from here under Coy arrangements.

8 Advance parties from the 4th Bn Canadian Mounted Rifles will report to Coy today. All trench Stores defence Schemes Schemes for Counter attack will be handed over to senior Officer or NCO in charge copies of receipts to be forwarded to Bn HQ by dawn 4th inst as in para 7.

9 Relief to be completed by 12 midnight, Completion to be noted Company Commanders own name.

10 Acknowledge.

3-Aug 1916

(Sd) D Woulka
Capt & A/Adjt
Root.

Operation Order No 25
by
Major C.T. Williams
Commanding "ROOT"

1. The Battalion will be relieved on night of 7/8 Aug by 18th K.R.R.C. as follows:-
   B Coy. will be relieved by A Coy 18th K.R.R.C.
   A "   "   "   "   " C   "   "   "
   C "   "   "   "   " B   "   "   "
   D "   "   "   "   " D   "   "   "

   On relief the Battalion will occupy positions in the Supports vacated by 18th K.R.R.C. as follows:-
   B Company — Left Front at present C Coy K.R.R.C.
   A   "   — Right   "   "   "   B "   "
   C   "   — Left Rear "   "   "   D "   "
   D   "   — Right "   "   "   A "   "

2. Guides for incoming Units 1 per Platoon and 1 per Company HQ will report to Battn HQ not later than 10.30pm on night of 7th inst.

3. Advance parties from 18th K.R.R.C. will report to opposite numbers at dusk on 7th inst as follows:-
   B Coy. 1 officer and 1 representative per Platoon
   A.C.& D Coy. 1 Officer.

   The above will take over all trench stores, defence schemes etc, copies of receipts to be forwarded to Bn HQ by dawn 8th inst. Hot Food Containers and Tommy Cookers will also be handed over both at Coys Stores and in the line. Those in the line will be handed over at Bn HQ. Containers mentioned in para 2 will bring the above to Bn HQ's
   The Quartermaster will forward receipts by 12noon 8th inst

4. Each Coy will detail advance parties of 1 NCO per Coy and 1 representative per Platoon to report to Battn HQ tomorrow Tues by 3am. They will proceed to opposite numbers and take over all trench stores etc which must be carefully checked. Copies of receipts to be forwarded to Bn HQ by dawn 8th inst as in para 3. The above with exception of NCO's will rejoin their Coys before relief and will guide their respective Platoons to Support Areas.

5. In view of forthcoming Operations, D Coy will on relief take over Strong Point Garrison of 2 platoons vice 1 Platoon of C Coy and one of D. which will take up the position in Support Line vacated by the Platoon of D Coy.

6. The Transport Officer will arrange for the transport of kits, trench bundles, Coy Stores etc from front line Bn HQ where Coys will have above dumped by 10pm 7th inst. They will be carried to Support Bn Ration Dump.

7. Rations for Feb inst will be carried to Support Bn Rations Dump as usual by transport.

8. Relief complete in both cases will be reported by wire using Coy Commanders own name.

9. Acknowledge.

Aug 6th 1918

(Sd) D. Walker
Capt a/Adjt
Root

S E C R E T.

12th. East Surrey Regt.
15th. Hampshire Regt.
18th. Kings Royal Rifle Corps.

        With reference to G.H.Q. letter No. O.B.1919 dated 14.6.18. "Organisation of the Infantry Battalion", forwarded under this office B.M.895 (46/-) dated 18.6.18.

1.   It has been ruled that, as an attack may be expected at any time against this front, the strength of Battalions in the line will be maintained at the minimum (O.R. only) as described in the above quoted letter.

2.   As regards Officers, Battalions will leave with the men, who are out of the line, all Officers in excess of 20.

3.   The O.R's to be left behind must be in accordance with para. 7 of O.B. 1919.
        The actual number of fighting men in the line must in no case be below 400, made up as follows :-
        32 Rifle Sections   @ 7 each   =   224.
        16 Lewis Gun Sections @ 11 each   =   176.
                             Total :- 400.
    The difference between the above (which is the minimum), and the maximum establishment is 192. From this must be allowed sick, leave, courses, Bde. and Divl. employ etc. the remainder representing the details to be left behind, which should be approx. 100 O.R.

4.   Details of Battalions left out of the line will be formed into composite Brigade Companies, each company commanded by an Officer to be detailed by the Brigade concerned, and will work on rear defences under arrangements to be made by the C.R.E.

5.   In order that the same Officers, W.O's, N.C.O's, and men should not be always away from their Battalion, Brigade will arrange for each Battalion, when it moves back into reserve, to exchange such personnel as were left out of the line during the previous period, with the exception of permanent specialist instructors.

6.   Please report, by last D.R. 11th inst., if it will be necessary to send down, or bring up, any men to comply with these requirements, and if so, how many.

                                          Captain,
                                    A/Brigade Major,
                               122nd. Infantry Brigade.

Coy 12th B. East Surrey Regt

July 7th 1916

No 1 The Battalion will be relieved on the night of the 10/11th July 1916 by the 18th K.R.R.C. in the following order:—
Headquarters
D Company
B
C
A

No 2 On relief the Battn will take up the position vacated by the 15th Hampshire Regiment in the support line. In each case the relief will be letter for letter respectively.

Guides. Guides 1 per platoon and 1 for Company HQ will report at Battn HQ at 10.45 pm [10 ch int] The above will be practised on the route tonight and will report at Battn HQ with a chit which will be signed and the guide will be sent back to the Company.

1 NCO per Company. and one man per platoon will report at Battn HQ tonight. They will proceed to the Support Battn there they will remain for 24 hours. They will rejoin their own Companies tomorrow night before relief and then into the new positions.

No 4 Trench Stores etc. S.O.S Rockets Defence Schemes Maps, details, for working parties and trench stores will be handed over and certificates forwarded to Battn HQ.
Solidified alcohol and S.O.S. containers will also be handed over.

No 5 Advance Parties. Advance Parties of 1 officer per Company and 1 NCO per Platoon from 18th K.R.R.C. will report to their respective Company's tonight and will live with their opposite numbers until relief.

No 6 Rations. Rations for 11th inst. will be dumped at the new Battn HQ M.6.d.4.4.

and will be in position by 11pm. Coys
will arrange to draw rations from Batt HQ
as soon as possible

No 7. Completion of relief will be wired by
incoming Company Commander over name
which will also be wired when Coys are
settled in the Support Area.

No 8. OC. D Coy. will detail 1 Officer to take over
strong point in. M.6.

No 9. Acknowledge.

(Sd) C Walker
Capt. D/Adjt

No extra transport Root will be provided
for Kits etc.

SECRET

NARRATIVE OF OPERATIONS CARRIED OUT BY THE 122nd INFANTRY BRIGADE
COMMENCING MIDNIGHT 8th/9th AUGUST 1918.

Ref. Map Sheet 28 S.W.1. KEMMEL 1/10,000.

1. The objective of the attack was to straighten the Salient in the existing front line between the LA CLYTTE-KEMMEL Road, and HALKIN FARM N.15.b.1.8.
   The capture of this objective had the following advantages:-
   It established a more suitable jumping off place and simplified the barrage for an assault upon KEMMEL. At the same time it added depth to the defence of the SCHERPENBERG-DICKEBUSCH LAKE LINE.

2. The total frontage to be attacked was 1125 yards and the greatest depth 500 yards.

3. One Battalion of infantry was detailed for the task, assisted by two strong platoons of the 6th Division; 5 platoons of infantry and 1 Field Company R.E., for carrying parties and consolidation, were also attached.

4. The following local factors should be borne in mind:-
   (a) The German defences were not strong, the wire being mostly weak, except around certain known posts and machine gun nests.
   (b) The objective was very limited, especially on the flanks.
   (c) The country was suitable for a night attack, being "open" and providing a certain number of landmarks, as an aid to direction.
   (d) The country, being entirely overlooked by KEMMEL HILL, was not suitable for an attack at dusk, owing to the difficulty of forming up; or at dawn, owing to the impossibility of consolidating such a short front, under direct close enemy observation.
   (e) The weather had been showery for several days prior to the assault, but on Zero night it was fine, but very dark.

5. In order to ensure that the actual frontage and objective should be hidden from the enemy as long as possible, the co-operation of the Brigades on the right and left was arranged for.
   The Right Brigade 41st Division, carried out a raid, supported by the artillery of the Right Group.
   The Brigade on the left carried out a minor operation to seize the high ground at VIERSTRAAT.

6. The Battalion and the Field Company R.E. detailed for the attack were withdrawn from the line on the night of August 1st/2nd and proceeded by lorry to 2nd Army Training Ground.

7. The front was held by the 12th East Surrey Regt., until the night 7th/8th August, when they were withdrawn into Support, the line being taken over by the 18th King's Royal Rifle Corps, who were prepared to take over the captured line 24 hours after Zero.
   The preliminary preparations, wire cutting, establishment of advanced Report Centres, Medical Aid Posts, Forward Dumps, routes and tracks etc., were entrusted to the 12th East Surrey Regt., and completed by the 18th King's Royal Rifle Corps.

8. Zero hour was fixed at midnight, August 8th/9th. This gave approximately 3 hours of darkness to consolidate and wire the new line.

9. Troops detailed for the assault were concentrated in the ZEVECOTEN AREA on the day preceding the operation 7th August.
   On the nights 6th/7th and 7th/8th August a tape line was selected and laid parallel to and across the KEMMELBEEK on which the Infantry were to form up.
   On the night 7th/8th August all the preliminary preparations were complete.

10. The 41st. Divisional Artillery was reinforced by 1 Brigade of the 66th. Divisional Artillery and 1 Brigade of the 6th. Divisional Artillery for the operations.

The reinforcing batteries were brought up during the nights 6/7th and 7/8th. August and were withdrawn during the nights 9/10th. and 10/11th. August 1918.

During the period preceding the attack from August 3rd to August 8th. the 4.5" Howitzers Battery commanded by Major DARE, "D" Battery, 11th. Brigade R.F.A., unobstrusively destroyed the belts of old British wire in the neighbourhood of MILIM WAY (N.14.b.) and WILLESDEN CAMP "B" (N.15.a.) so successfully that it presented no obstacle.

The Heavy Artillery effectively destroyed the Railway Embankment and enemy trench from N.14.b.27.20 to N.14.d.10.80, which was carried out by a 9.2" Siege Battery, with aeroplane observation.

During the night preceding the attack and Zero night, harassing fire was carried on as usual.

11. The attack was carried out under a barrage, which was arranged in "lanes".

The lanes moved forward at 2 minute intervals, commencing from the left, as the infantry advanced, reaching the final barrage line at Zero plus 12 minutes, where it remained as a protective barrage until Zero plus 45 minutes, in order to cover the earlier stages of consolidation.

The barrage was entirely shrapnel. The 4.5" Howitzers and the Heavy Artillery engaged selected targets and formed a protective barrage on the flanks of the attack and the known routes and approaches used by the enemy.

12. The 41st. Bn. Machine Gun Corps co-operated in the attack: 23 guns were employed in the operation. During the actual assault, harassing fire was kept up on all roads, approaches and centres of activity.

After Zero plus 12 minutes, the guns were laid on S.O.S. Lines across the front, reinforcing the artillery barrage.

The S.O.S. barrage (Machine Gun) was not called for and was not fired. The barrage guns were kept in the battle positions for 48 hours after Zero.

13. Prisoners subsequently captured, stated the artillery and machine gun barrage was most destructive, the 5th Coy. 240 R.I.R. 52 Reserve Division suffering very heavy casualties, and practically ceasing to exist.

1st. PHASE.

14. The attack was carried out by the 15th. Hampshire Regt and 2 Platoons of the 2nd. Durham Light Infantry, 6th. Division.

The 233rd. Field Company, R.E. were responsible for consolidating the new line.

One Company of the 12th. East Surrey Regt. was attached, in 4 parties, to the 233rd. Field Company for consolidation.

One Platoon of the 12th. East Surrey Regt. followed behind the attack to dig Supporting Points along the Railway Embankment at N.14.b.55.82 and N.14.b.85.95.

15. The Infantry formed up along the tapes, the 3 centre Companies in 2 waves.

Forming up was completed by 11.30 p.m.

16. The Artillery and Machine Gun Barrage opened to the second and the attack commenced simultaneously, the infantry getting well away immediately.

17. From prisoners' statements, it appears the attack came as a complete surprise.

18. At Zero plus 3 minutes, the enemy artillery barrage came down along the line of the assembly tapes.

19. The enemy quickly realised our intentions and gradually shortened the barrage until it arrived about 200 yards in advance of our objective, where it remained until Zero plus 55 minutes, when all artillery activity was reported to have ceased.

20. On the Right the operation proceeded according to programme. Owing to the entire destruction of the enemy trenches along the Railway Embankment by the heavy artillery (subsequently confirmed by aeroplane photograph) little opposition was met and at 12.22 a.m. the light signal "Objective reached" was seen.
    The centre of the attack met with very stubborn resistance, but after hand to hand fighting succeeded in reaching their objective astride the MILKY WAY about 12.30 a.m.
    The extreme left of the attack, at the junction with the 6th. Division, apparently lost their direction. One section of the 15th. Hampshire Regt. reached the enemy trench at N.15.a.7.6. but found it too strongly held to capture, and eventually dug in at N.15.a.45.91.
    At 12.55.a.m. the enemy barrage ceased, but there is every indication that until dawn considerable hand to hand fighting took place, especially in the centre.

21. Owing to the uncertainty of the situation, the R.E. parties were unable to erect a belt of wire across the front, but a wire obstacle was built across the MILKY WAY and about 100 yards of wire put out on the right.

22. The carrying parties made several journeys and dumped a quantity of R.E. stores near the objective.

23. The 1 Platoon detailed to dig the Supporting Points carried out the task, and dug two posts at N.14.b.60.75 and N.14.b.8.9.

24. Owing to the local fighting, no re-organisation was possible during Zero night, and the Platoon of the 12th. East Surrey Regt. mentioned in paragraph 22, was not relieved, and remained as garrison until the night 9/10th. August.

25. At dawn 9th. instant the situation appeared to be as follows. Posts had been established at :-
    N.14.c.80.95 - N.14.b.05.05 - N.14.b.20.10 - N.14.b.25.30 - N.14.b.45.20 - N.14.b.75.35 - N.14.b.90.40 - N.15.a.10.40 - N.15.a.30.50 - N.15.a.30.75 - N.15.a.85.85.- N.15.b.10.90 - N.15.b.30.80.

    The Post at N.15.a.80.65 had not been established, and the enemy were holding trench at N.15.a.55.55 and N.15.a.70.55.

26. On reaching their objectives the infantry lost no time in digging themselves in, and there is no doubt that this materially assisted them in keeping down casualties and preventing the enemy's counter-attack, on the morning of the 10th. instant, meeting with any success.

27. Touch was not established with the 6th. Division whose right hand post was at N.15.a.85.85.

28. Communications worked exceedingly well throughout the operation.

29. The arrangements for the evacuation of the wounded were complete in every detail, the majority of the wounded being collected and cleared before dawn on the 9th. instant.

30. At dawn /-

30. At dawn a contact aeroplane flew over the new line, calling for flares.
    From this information, together with the reports from the Observation Post sent down by the Brigade Intelligence Officer throughout the day of the 9th. inst., the position of several of the posts, was confirmed.

31. The 15th. Hampshire Regt. were withdrawn during the night 9/10th. August, the new line being taken over by the 18th. Kings Royal Rifle Corps and one Company of the 12th. East Surrey Regt.

32. The total casualties for the first phase of the operation were:-

	Officers.	Other Ranks.
Killed	3.	15.
Died of Wounds		3.
Wounded	3.	121.
Missing	1.	14.
	7.	153.

- 2nd. PHASE -

33. The dispositions of the 122nd. Infantry Brigade on the morning of the 10th. August, were as follows:-
    In the Line. 18th. Kings Royal Rifle Corps, plus 2 Companies of the 12th. East Surrey Regt.
    In Brigade Support. Remaining 2 Companies of 12th. East Surrey Regt.
    In Divisional Reserve
    in KEVECOTEN Area. 1 Battalion (10th. R.W. Kent Regt) 123rd. Infantry Brigade.
    At rest in Area.
    27/L.25. 15th. Hampshire Regt. withdrawn after attack.

34. At 9 p.m. August 9th. enemy opened a hurrican bombardment with Field guns on the new line and Forward Area which ceased at 9.30 p.m. No Infantry action developed. From Prisoners' statements it was subsequently heard that a counter attack had been ordered but had been postponed.

35. The nights of 9/10th and 10/11th. August passed in consolidating and increasing the wire. Hostile Machine Guns were very active being pushed forward very near our new posts.

36. At 3.26 a.m. on the morning of the 11th. instant, a heavy bombardment opened on the front of the 122nd. Infantry Brigade, extending on both flanks. At that time there was a very heavy mist, which did not clear away until 8.15 a.m.

37. At 3.35 a.m. 41st. Divisional Artillery was asked to fire on the Counter Preparation lines along the fronts of the 122nd. and 123rd. Infantry Brigades.

38. At 3.40 a.m. the 41st. Divisional Artillery and the Heavy Artillery were firing on their Counter Preparation Lines.

39. At 4.15.a.m. the enemy barrage had ceased. Our artillery was asked to stand down but to be ready to resume if required.

40. Owing to the mist, no further information was received at Brigade H.Q. until 6 a.m. when the S.O.S. was reported from the centre of the new line. The Support and Reserve Battalions were ordered to "Stand to".
    From subsequent reports and prisoners' statements it appears that the enemy attacked at 3.30 a.m. with 3 companies on the right and the centre of the new front line.

41. Several of the enemy had Megaphones and were continually shouting through them. The attackers appeared to be much disorganised, as many parties were seen wandering about quite ainlessly.

42. No determined effort to advance was made until 4.15 a.m. when the attack developed, not all along the line, but in parties which worked their way forward in the mist.
    The wire and trench consolidation came a complete surprise to the enemy and materially disorganised the attack.
    The right Company, holding the front line from the KEMMEL - LA CLYTTE Road to the MILKY WAY maintained its line intact, although for some hours there is little doubt many of the posts were cut off from each other, and in one case surrounded. The enemy in rear of the latter post were eventually driven out by a counter attack section in a support point in rear.
    The attack on the Left Company, holding from MILKY WAY to the Left Brigade Boundary was better organised but was easily beaten off by Lewis Gun fire about 30 prisoners being taken. A sufficiently large escort could not be spared and the prisoners were therefore sent down with only a few men. They suceeded in escaping and established themselves in the derelict huts at WILLESDEN CAMP "B" and subsequently got back to their own lines, before the Platoon sent forward from the LA CLYTTE Line could round them up.

The Post at /-

The Post at N.15.a.3.4. was overwhelmed before they could be reinforced from the supporting Platoon.

The enemy was assisted in the advance by a contact aeroplane, flying low and dropping red, green and orange lights.

Fighting continued until 8 a.m., during which time 3 Platoons in all were sent forward to reinforce and clear up the situation.

43. At 6.20 a.m. a prisoner, on examination, stated the attack was a local one to get back the front line, which in this Sector was the main line of resistance. It was essential that this line was retaken, as we were now too near the defences of KEMMEL.

44. At 6.22 a.m. 18th. Kings Royal Rifle Corps reported that the enemy was mainly attacking for the LA CLYTTE - KEMMEL Road and astride the MILKY WAY.

45. At 6.24 a.m. 190th. Brigade R.F.A. were asked to reinforce the barrage astride the LA CLYTTE - KEMMEL Road with 1 battery of 18 pounders, which they did. The 123rd. Infantry Brigade were also asked to send a strong fighting patrol from their trench at POMPIER EST. to cross the LA CLYTTE Road and attack the enemy in HIM CAMP (N.14.c.) from the flank, which they did.

46. At 7.15 a.m. there being no enemy artillery fire, our artillery were asked to "Stand down" except for firing at intervals at slow rate.

47. At 7.40 a.m. a message was received from the 18th. Kings Royal Rifle Corps that the Company on the Right held their line intact but the front of the Left Company, the enemy were probably through in small bodies. The 2nd. Durham Light Infantry (6th. Division) also reporting that the enemy had been seen at WILLESDEN JUNCTION N.9.c.

O.C. 18th. Kings Royal Rifle Corps asked permission to carry out a Counter attack in conjunction with the 2nd. Durham Light Infantry who were willing to put in one Company. Permission was given to use one Company from the SCHERPENBERG - DICKEBUSCH LAKE Line, which would form up along the light railway from the MILKY WAY to the hutments at N.8.d.8.4. which would be the junction with the Company of the 2nd. Durham Light Infantry.

Zero was fixed at 8.30 a.m., subject to the mist continuing to allow the troops to get into position without being seen from KEMMEL. The Artillery barrage was to come down on the S.O.S. Lines as a guide to direction in the mist. The Company, thus moved up for the Counter attack, was to be replaced in the SCHERPENBERG - DICKEBUSCH LAKE Line by 1 Company to be moved up from the Support Battalion.

48. At 7.55 a.m. message was received from the 18th. Kings Royal Rifle Corps that the whole front was reported intact.

49. The orders for the counter attack were cancelled.

50. The Support and Reserve Battalions were ordered to "Stand down" and the situation reported to Division at 8.3 a.m.

51. During the day, enemy snipers were particularly active harassing our posts.

52. At 10 p.m. message was received that the enemy was trying to infiltrate through on the front of the Left Company, east of the MILKY WAY from behind the houses at N.14.b.95.25. The 11th. Brigade R.F.A. were asked to fire on the houses, which they did, clearing out an enemy machine gun which had been active from N.14.b.95.30.
The 18th. Infantry Brigade, 6th. Division, were able to send out a strong fighting patrol to help clear up the situation.

53. The 18th. Kings Royal Rifle Corps were withdrawn from the line on the night 11/12th. inst. to the ZEVECOTEN Area, coming into Divisional Reserve.

The 12th. East Surrey Regt. took over the new line, relief being completed at 1.50 a.m. 12th. instant.

54. Total casualties for the Second Phase were 6 Officers and 57 Other Ranks.

Total prisoners taken in the operation were 37 Other Ranks and 2 Machine Guns.

Operation Order No 27
by Major C T Williams
Comdg "ROOT"
Ref Map Sheet 28 SW.

1. On the night of 9/10 the 15th Bn Hampshire Regt will be relieved by the 18th Bn KRRC in the front line. A Company and 1 platoon D Coy 12th East Surrey Regt will move up and take over positions vacated by 1 Company and 1 platoon of the 18th KRRC in the SCHERPENBERG DICKEBUSCH LINE and SUPPORT LINE and will be under the command of the OC 18th KRRC.

2. Advance Parties. A party of one officer detailed by OC A Company and 2 representatives from each of the 5 platoons will report at the Battn HQ of the 15th Hants at 9:30 pm. where they will be met by guides of the 18th KRRC who will guide them to the positions to be occupied. 1 representative per platoon will then return to the 18 KRRC HQ at N.1.C.5.1. where they will meet their respective platoons at 11 pm and guide

2

them to these positions.

3. **French Stores**

French Stores, aeroplane
proper, defence schemes etc will
be taken over and receipts
forwarded to Bn HQ of the 18th
K.R.R.C. at N.1.c.5.1.

4. **Lewis Guns**

Lewis Guns and Ammunition
will be carried to the positions
to be taken over.

5. **Rations**

Rations will be drawn
before moving off and carried to the
line. On the night 10th and
subsequent nights rations for
this party will be dumped at
N.7.a.50.95.

6. Completion of relief will be reported
to Bn HQ 18th K.R.R.C. at N.1.c.5.1.

Issued at 6.45 pm   (Sgd) L D Murdoch
9-8-18   2/L A/Adjt
Copies to OC A Coy   R.o.t.
              B "
              C "
              D "
              122 Inf Bde
              18 KRRC

Operation Order No 28
by
Major C. Williams
Comdg. 12th East Surrey Regt

Ref Map Sheet 28 KEMMEL

1. **SITUATION** At 3.26 am on the morning of 11th inst the enemy put down a heavy barrage on our forward systems. Infantry action followed at 5.30 am but the attack failed. Shortly before 6 am reports were received that the enemy had effected an entry into our lines. Situation remained obscure until 7.55 am when reports were received that the line had been completely regained.

2. **RELIEF** On night of 11/12th the 12th East Surrey Regt will relieve the 18th K.R.R.C. in the front line.

3. **BOUNDARIES** The area between LA CLYTTE–KEMMEL ROAD exclusive and the MILKY WAY inclusive will be taken over by B Company. The area between MILKY WAY exclusive and the Northern Brigade boundary running through N.15.a. Central will be taken over by D Coy. Touch must be maintained with the units on flanks.

4. **DISPOSITIONS**
   RIGHT FRONT B Coy will relieve B Coy 18 KRRC in Right Front Sector the posts in front line of posts nos 1-4 inclusive numbered from right to left. Each post will be manned by 2 Sections. 2 platoons will be in support in the Right Sector of our old front line.

   LEFT FRONT D Coy will relieve D Coy 18 KRRC in left front sector and will hold line of posts nos 5-8 inclusive. Each post will be occupied by 2 sections. The remaining 2 platoons will be in support occupying the posts: 1 at approximately N14.b.80.90 2 in posts near Coy HQ.

   C Coy will relieve C Coy 18th KRRC in the SCHERPENBURG–DICKEBUSCH LINE

   A Coy will remain in their present positions a left of the SCHERPENBURG–DICKEBUSCH LINE

5. **RELIEF** The 10th Royal West Kent Regt will move to positions in the support line vacated by 12th East Surrey Regt.
   A Coy 10th Royal West Kent Regt will relieve A Coy 18th K.R.R.C. in the SCHERPENBURG–DICKEBUSCH LINE.

Cont'd

6. **GUIDES** The following guides will be supplied by 18th KRRC
(1) 1 Guide for each of front line Posts
(2) 2 Guides for each Platoon in support
(3) 2 Guides to Platoon for the Coys in the SCHOPPENBURG - DICKEBUSCH LAKE LINE
(4) 1 Guide for each Coy HQ.

The guides will meet opposite numbers at the HQ. of 18 KRRC as follows:
B Coy — 10 pm
D " — 10.15 pm
C " — 10.30 pm
A " 10th RWK Ret 10.45 pm

7. **ADVANCE PARTIES** Advance parties of 1 Officer and 1 NCO for the two front line Coys will report at the Bn HQ 18th KRRC at 8.45 pm where guides will meet them and take them up to their respective Coys.

8. **RATIONS** Rations will be dumped at Front line Battalion HQ N.1.c.5.1 and will be picked up by Platoons as they pass and carried up to the line.

9. **SAA** OC Coys will issue 50 rounds SAA and 1 Mills Grenade extra to each man before moving off.

10. **TRENCH STORES** All trench stores, aeroplane photos, defence schemes etc will be taken over and copies of receipt will be forwarded to Bn HQ by dawn 13th inst.

11. Advance Bn HQ will be established at N.7.b.8.5

12. **Pass word** for tonight will be RUM.

13. **INSTRUCTIONS** The trench system will be held as an outpost line, and will be held to the last. The garrison of the SCHERPENBERG - DICKEBUSCH LAKE LINE will not be used forward of that line except to meet a penalty locus. Penetration by the enemy, and the flanks shall hold their original line. Active patrolling will be carried out throughout the night.

The double posts are:-
KIM CAMP and hedge from N.14.c.80.70 towards N.14 central. Dead ground from N.14.b.55.05 to sunken road at N.14.b.95.85

S E C R E T.

41st Division "G".
C.R.A. 41st Division.
12th East Surrey Regt.
15th Hampshire Regt.
18th King's Royal Rifle Corps.
122nd Trench Mortar Battery.
"B" Coy. 41st Bn. M.G.Corps.
11th Brigade R.F.A.
233rd Field Coy. R.E.
123rd Infantry Brigade.
19th Infantry Brigade.

Herewith narrative of Operations carried out by the 122nd Infantry Brigade since midnight August 8th/9th 1918.

Brigadier General,
Commanding 122nd Infantry Brigade.

12th Bn. EAST SURREY REGT.
RECEIVED 14.8.18.

Contd!

The Completion of relief will be wired to
Bn HQ by using Coy Comdrs own name
to Acknowledge

Issued at   (Sd) W.D. Mutch
11-8-71   2/L A/maj
    Copies to File   Rovt
        OC A Cy
           B
           C
           D
        18 KRRC
        122 Lt Bn
        123 "   "
        10th RWK
        T.O
        Qms.

Operation Orders
by
Major C. F. Williams
Comdg. 12th Bn. East Surrey Regt.

14th July 1918

1. The Battalion will be relieved by the 18th KRRC. on the night of the 15/16th inst.
   The Battalion will proceed on working parties to be detailed later, at 10 p., after which they will occupy Divisional Reserve Positions vacated by the 15th Hants.

2. Dispositions. Relief will be carried out letter for letter in both cases.

3. The following Advance Parties from the 18th KRRC. will report to Companies to-night
   1 N.C.O. per Company.
   One representative per platoon.

4. Companies will obtain receipts for all trench Stores, Defence Schemes, Programmes of work etc. handed over. Copies of receipts will be sent to Bn H.Q. by noon 16th inst.

5. Companies will send at 12 noon to-morrow, 15th inst. Advance parties to report to the 15th Hants Regt, as follows:-
   1 NCO per platoon.
   1 Officer per Company.
   All trench Stores, defence Schemes, Programmes of work, etc. will be taken over by the officer and one NCO per Coy. will be left in Charge. The remainder will return to their Companies in the evening and will proceed on working parties with their Coys.

6. Completion of Relief will be wired by using Coy. Comdrs. own name.

7. Acknowledge.

(sd) D. Walker.
Capt & Adjt
R.O.C.

O.C. Company.

17th.

Reference Operation Order 17. further instructions:-

1. All Lewis Guns, Ammunition, petrol tins etc., will be dumped with Company Stores at 10pm at M.6.d.7.7. Lewis Guns and Ammunition will be conveyed by limbers to new H.Q. from which place they will be drawn immediately on arrival in new position. Petrol tins will be taken to Transport Lines. Sgt Lattimore H.Q. and party from H.Q. will load and be responsible for L.G's to new H.Q's.

2. Acknowledge.

July. 15. 1918.

Wallsee
Capt. A/Maj'
T Coy.

Operation Order No. 29
by
Major C. T. Williams
Comdg. 12th East Surrey Regt.

Ref. map. Sheet 28 S.W. KEMMEL.

1. The Battalion will be relieved in the Front Line on the night of the 16/17th August 1918. by the 15th Bn. Hants Regt in the following order:-

15th Hants		12th E. Surrey's
D Coy	will relieve	B Coy } Front
A Coy.	" "	D " } Line.
C Coy.	" "	C Coy. Right Scherpenberg-Dickebusch line
B Coy.	" "	A Coy Left " " "

2. On relief the Battalion will move into Reserve Positions vacated by 18th K.R.R.C. Advance parties as detailed in para 5 will take their platoons straight to the new positions allotted.

3. Guides. Guides for the incoming Unit, one per Post in the Front Line, two per platoon in Support, one for Coy. H.Q. also 5 per Coy. for Companies in the SCHERPENBERG - DICKEBUSCH line, will report at Bn H.Q. at 11 pm on night of relief, and guide their respective parties to their posts.

4. Advance Parties of one Officer and 4 NCO's per Company will report to their opposite numbers to night, and will remain until relieved.

5. Advance Parties of one NCO. per Coy. who will take over trench stores, will report at Reserve Bn H.Q. before dawn 16th inst. They will afterwards act as guides to their respective Companies, whom they will meet at G.35.d.90.15, and guide to their respective positions.

6. All trench Stores, defence Schemes, Tommy Cookers etc. will be handed over and receipts obtained, copies of which will be sent to Bn H.Q. together with copy of trench stores taken over in the new position by dawn 17th inst.

All Hot Food Containers will be handed over and receipts obtained. Those in the line will be brought down by the guides as in para 3. and will be handed over at Bn H.Q. The Q.mr. will forward by noon 17th receipt for Tommy Cookers and Hot Food Containers handed over.

Contd.

7. RATIONS. Rations will be dumped at the Reserve Bn HQ. from which place Companies will draw them on arrival in the new position.

8. The Transport Officer will arrange after dumping rations at Reserve Bn HQ. that 3 limbers will collect all Lewis Guns and ammunition, trench bundles etc. which will be dumped on road near Support Bn. HQ. at M.6.d.80.60, and will convey them to the Reserve Bn HQ. where they will afterwards be picked up by Companies.

9. Completion of relief will be wired by using Coy. Comdrs. own name.

10. ACKNOWLEDGE.

(sd) W.D. Mutch
2/Lt & a/adjt.
Root

Issued at 10 pm.
15th August 1918.

Copies to :-
    File.
    O.C. A Coy.
    O.C. B Coy.
    O.C. C Coy.
    O.C. D Coy.
    12 2nd Inf. Bde.
    15th Hants
    18th KRRC.
    10th Rw Kents.
    Quartermaster.
    Transport Officer

12th. East Surrey Regt.
15th. Hampshire Regt.
18th. Kings Royal Rifle Corps.

B.M. 245
46/-.

1. G.H.Q. letter O.B. 1919 dated 14.6.18. "Organisation of the Infantry Battalion" and this office B.M. 70 (46/-), dated 8th. inst. do not appear to be understood.

2. It has been ruled that, as an attack may be expected at any time against this front, the O.R. to be left out of the line by Battalions must be in accordance with para 7 of O.B. 1919.
Under no circumstances will the details laid down be departed from.

3. Battalions should therefore have in the line with them the following :-

32 Rifle Sections of 7 each		224.
16 Lewis Gun Sections of 11 each		176.
		400.

Battalion H.Q.
Sgt. Major. (optional)	1	
Orderly Room Clerk	1	
Provost Sgt & police (optional)	5	
Scout Sgt.	1	
Scout Cpl. (optional)	1	
Signallers and runners up to	30	
Stretcher bearers	9	
Pioneers up to	11	
M.O. orderlies	1	
Sanitary	1	
Batmen up to	7	68.

A.A. Lewis Gun Section   13.

4 Company Headquarters.
C.S.M's	2	
Signallers up to	24	
Stretcher bearers	16	
Gas	4	
Runners	8	
Buglers up to	4	
Batmen up to	8	66.

16 Platoon Headquarters.
Sergeants	16	
Runners	16	
Batmen	16	48.

Minimum Trench Strength :-   595

4. The total strength of 900 is therefore made up as follows :-
(a) Minimum number in the line   595.
(b) At transport lines.
Administrative portion as per O.B.1919
Battalion H.Q.	61
4 Company H.Q.	16
Sgt. Cook and cooks (optional)	11
Sgt. Drummer	1
Drummers and buglers	4

(c) At details camp   100
    Sgt. Instructors   6

(d) Leave, Courses, sick, Bde. & Div.employ   106
                                               900

4. (continued)

NOTE.

If the total of item (d), (106) is exceeded, the excess will come off the 100 left at details, i.e. the minimum trench strength will not in any circumstances fall below 595.

Captain,
A/Brigade Major,
122nd. Infantry Brigade.

12th Bn. EAST SURREY REGT.
RECEIVED 16.7.18.
FILED

Operation Orders No 18
by
Major C. T. Williams
Comdg Roof

1. The Battalion will relieve the 15th Hants on night of 20/21st inst.

2. **Dispositions:-**
The Front System is now held by 3 platoons in the Front Line and 2 platoons in close support. The remainder occupy part of the SCHERPENBERG — DICKEBUSCH — LAKE Line. The relief will be as follows and in the following order:-

Headquarters
A Coy will relieve C Coy 15th Hants with 3 platoons in Front Line and 1 Platoon in close support 14 o 5.9.
B Coy will relieve B Coy 15th Hants — Left.
C " " " A Coy " " — Centre with 1 platoon in support of Front Line in N.8.c.7.7.
D Coy will relieve D Coy 15th Hants — Right.

3. **Guides** 1 per Platoon and 1 per Coy HQ will be at HQ 15th Hants at 10.45 pm 20th inst.

4. **Route** will be overland track to N.1.c.4.1. thence by Railway. Intervals of 200 yds between platoons will be maintained. 1st Platoon will be at Hants HQ by 10.45 pm.

5. **Advanced Parties** of 1 Officer per Coy and 1 representative per platoon will report to HQ 15 Hants at 9.45 pm 19th inst and will remain with their opposite number until relief when they will meet their own platoons and assist guides from 15th Hants.

6. **Rations** will be dumped at 10.45 pm on night of 20th at N1.C.4.1. and each Platoon will collect its own rations as it passes this point for the remainder of the tour. D Coy will supply as well, as their own, carrying parties for the Front Line. Petrol tins and food containers will be returned to B. HQ each night in time to go back with returning ration limbers.

7. **Work** B Coy will supply 100 men each night for work under R.E. in their own trenches. C & D Coys will supply two platoons each for work under R.E. on their own line.

3rd/12/8

P.T.O.

8. **Trench Stores** All trench stores, hot food containers and Tommy cookers will be taken over also Defence Schemes and receipts forwarded to Battn HQ by dawn 21st inst

9. The positions vacated in Divisional Reserve will be occupied by 18th KRRC

10. Advanced parties will report to opposite numbers on 20th inst from whom receipts for trench stores, Defence Schemes etc will be obtained and forwarded to Bn HQ as in para 8.

11. Completion of relief will be wired using Coy Commanders own name.

12. Acknowledge.

(Sd) D. Walker
Capt. & Adjt
Root.

Issued at 6.30 pm
19-7-18

Operation Order No 25
by
Lieut Col. G. L. Brown D.S.O
Comdg 12th Battn East Surrey Regt

1. On the night of the 21/22nd the Battn will move into positions vacated by the 18th K.R.R Corps in the Rest area G 25 and G 30 as follows

     A Company · 9.30 p.m
     B   "   9.40 "
     C   "   9.50 "
     D   "   10. 0 "
     H Q

2. Companies will take over same positions as they occupied the last time the Battalion was in that area.

3. The 10th R W Kents will take over the positions in Reserve vacated by the Battalion.

4. Advance parties from the 10th R W Kents will report to their opposite numbers during the day.

    Companies will each send 1 Officer and one representative per platoon to the new area. They will report to their opposite number of the 18th K.R.R. Corps before 6 p.m.

    The senior Officer or N.C.O in charge of the above parties will take over Defence schemes Schemes of counter attack Trench stores Reserve ammunition etc Copies of receipts in each case to be sent to B.H.Q by dawn on the 22nd.

5. Lewis Guns Ammunition Trench bundles Petrol tins Company stores etc will be dumped at present B.H.Q by 9 p.m on the 21st and will be collected from the new B.H.Q immediately on arrival.

    The Transport Officer will arrange to collect the above at 10 p.m.

    Rations for the 22nd inst will be dumped in the new area where Companies will have their cookers.

    The Quartermaster will arrange to have a hot meal for the Companies as they arrive from the line.

6. Company Commanders will report Relief as they pass present B.H.Q on march out and report their Coys present in the Rest area

7. Acknowledge.

August 20th 1918

(Sd) D Walker. Capt & Adjt
12 Bn East Surrey Regt

12th. East Surrey Regt.
15th. Hampshire Regt.
18th. King's Royal Rifle Corps.

B.M.986.

With reference to the operations carried out by the 41st. Division during the week ending 16th. August, the Army Commander has expressed the opinion that :-

"The operations were well planned and carried out and reflect great credit on all the troops engaged."

The Divisional Commander has already expressed to the troops his satisfaction at the manner in which they performed their share in the operation, which satisfaction, is heartily endorsed by the Brigade Commander.

Captain,
A/Brigade Major,
122nd. Infantry Brigade.

RECEIVED 22.8.18

Battn Order

Reveille 7am   Breakfast 7.30am
Sick Parade 8am

1. Parades for tomorrow are cancelled.

2. Baths at DALLINGTON CAMP are allotted to the Bn tomorrow 24th August as under.

   C. Coy.   8am to 9.30am
   B "   9.30am to 11am
   A "   11am to 12 noon
   HQ   12 noon to 12.30 pm
   D "   1.30 pm to 2.30 pm

   Capacity 60 men per hour. Parties should be marched there every half-hour. There will be a further allotment of baths on the 26th inst. report to Coy as under tomorrow

3. Inspection. The Brigade Gas Officer will inspect Box Respirators

   D Coy.   10am to 10.45am
   C "   10.45am to 11.30am
   HQ "   11.30am to 12.15pm
   B "   2 pm to 2.45 pm
   A "   2.45pm to 3.30 pm

4. Officer Arrival and Postings.   2/Lieut Lewis joined Bn for duty – and posted to C Coy.
   2/Lt Horsley joined Bn for duty – and posted to B Coy.
   (also Lt Johnston 2/Lt Pursley)

5. Drafts

6. Copy of Bn 956.

7. **Accidental Wounds** Several cases of accidents due to careless handling of revolvers have occurred recently and certainly in some cases these appear to be due to want of instruction of men armed with revolvers. Company Commanders will be held responsible that no man is allowed to proceed to the line armed with a revolver who has not received instruction in its use. Coy Commanders will take immediate steps to instruct all men with ~~ar~~ armed with revolvers.

8. **Orderly Room** The afm will attend the Orderly Room
    Sgt Hurt
    Cpl Hurran
    Cpl Church
    Pte Pocock also add any men who have returned from Courses and have the reports which you will send up.

SECRET.   OPERATION ORDER No. 19.
                    by
            MAJOR C. T. WILLIAMS.
         Comdg 12th Bn EAST SURREY REGIMENT.
                                                Copy No......

                                        24th July, 1918.

1. The Battalion will be relieved in the Front Line on the night of the 25th/26th July, 1918, by the 18th K.R.R.C., in the following order:-

   A Coy will be relieved by C Coy K.R.R.C.
   D "   "   "   "   " A   "   "
   C "   "   "   "   " B   "   "
   B "   "   "   "   " D   "   "

2. On relief the Battalion will move into Support positions vacated by the 15th Hants Regt. ~~Guides detailed in para 3 will take their platoons straight to the new positions allotted. Orders of relief~~

3. Guides for the incoming Unit, one per Platoon and one per Coy.H.Q. will report at Bn.H.Q. at 10.30 p.m. on the 25th inst.
   Guides one for Coy.H.Q. and one per platoon to the Support position will be supplied by the 15th Hants Regt. They will report to these Hdqrs. at 11 p.m. where they will meet their opposite number, as they come out of the Front Line.

4. Advance parties from the 18th K.R.R.C. of one Officer per Company and one representative per platoon will report to their opposite numbers to-night, and will remain until relief.

5. Advance parties of one N.C.O. per Company who will take over Trench Stores, will report to these Hdqrs at 12 midnight 24th inst, and will proceed to the Support Battn.H.Q.
   O.C. A Coy will detail an Officer to report as above who will be responsible for the taking over of trench stores in the new position. He will rejoin his Company after relief.

6. All trench stores, defence schemes, Tommy cookers will be handed over and receipts obtained, copies of which will be sent to Bn.H.Q. together with copy of trench stores taken over in the new position by dawn 26th inst.
   All Hot Food Containers will be handed over and receipts obtained. Those in the line will be brought down by the guides as in para.3. and will be handed over at Bn.H.Q.
   The Quartermaster will forward by noon 26th receipts for Tommy cookers and Hot Food Containers handed over.

7. Rations will continue to be cooked at the Transport Lines as usual and will be dumped at the Support Battalion ration dump, from which place Companies will draw their rations on arrival in the new position.

8. The Transport Officer will arrange for one limber to be at front line Battn.H.Q. on night of relief to convey any trench bundles, stores etc, which cannot be carried.

9. Completion of relief will be wired by using Company Commander's own name.

10. A Company of Americans will be attached to the Battalion in Support from the 25th inst, as per Operation Order issued herewith.
    Guides for the incoming Americans @ O.R. A Coy, 1 N.C.O. B & D Coys, will report to these Hdqrs. at 10 a.m. 25 th. They will rejoin the Battalion in the Support area.

11. ACKNOWLEDGE.

                              (sd) D.Walker, Capt B A/Adjt
                                   12th East Surrey Regt.

OPERATION ORDER No. 20.
by
MAJOR C. T. WILLIAMS,
Comdg 12th Bn EAST SURREY REGIMENT.

24th July, 1918.

1. One Company of the 27th American Division will be attached to the Battalion from the 26th to the 31st July, 1918, inclusive.

2. Guides as per para.10, Operation Order No.19, will meet the incoming Americans at 11 p.m. on the 25th inst, on the road junction G.34.d.1.6, from which they will guide them to the Support Battalion H.Q. They will be allotted to Companies as follows :-
   2 platoons A Company.
   1 platoon B   "
   1 platoon D   "
to whom they will report about 2 a.m. on the morning of the 26th inst.

3. Two platoons of A Coy will be withdrawn to the vicinity of the WESTOUTRE LINE. Position to be notified later. These platoons will proceed under one Officer.

4. All ranks must be impressed with the importance of assisting and helping in every way the attached troops.

5. Acknowledge.

(sd) D. Walker,
Capt &A/Adjt,
12th Bn East Surrey Reg.

Ref. Map Sheet 28.

OPERATION ORDER No. 30.
by
LIEUT COL. G.L.BROWN, D.S.O.
Comdg. 12th. Bn. East Surrey Regiment.   Copy No. 1.

25th. August 1918.

1. The Brigades of the Division will be re-distributed on night of 26/27 August 1918, so that the front is held by two Infantry Brigades in the line and one Infantry Brigade in Support. The Divisional Northern and Southern boundaries will not change. The new inter-Brigade boundary will be as follows:- from point Sheet 28.N.13.d.70.2 through points N.7.c.4.0. N.11.b.6.1. to point M.5.d.0.1. The 122nd. Infantry Brigade will be in Divisional Reserve with two Battalions in the WESTOUTRE Line.

2. On night of 26/27 The Battalion will move into Divisional Reserve relieving the 10th. Bn. "QUEENS" (Royal West Surrey Regt.) in the Right Sector WESTOUTRE Line ~~Brasserie~~ G.34.d.4.8
   B.H.Q. Headquarters at ~~Bd B.T.O.~~ RENINGHELST. Sheet 28.M.4.a.7.6.

3. DISPOSITIONS.
   Companies will take over letter for letter respectively and will march out without relief as follows:-

   Headquarters.
   "A" Company   8. p.m.
   "B" Company   8.10p.m.
   "C" Company   8.20p.m.
   "D" Company   8.30p.m.

   Platoons will march at 200 yards interval.

4. GUIDES.
   Guides 1 per platoon, and 1 per Company H.Q. will be supplied by the advance party and will meet companies at cross roads Sheet 28. G.34.d.0.6.

5. ADVANCE PARTIES.
   1 Officer and 1 N.C.O. per company and 1 representative per platoon will report to their opposite numbers before noon 26th. inst.
   The Officer will take over all Trench Stores, Trench Schemes, Schemes of Counter-Attack etc. and copies of receipts will be forwarded to Bn. H.Q. by dawn 27th. inst.

6. RATIONS.
   Rations for the 27th. inst. will be dumped at the new Bn. H.Q. Cooking can be done in the reserve positions, arrangements to be taken over and arranged direct with Quarter-master.

7. TRENCH BUNDLES. ~~Officers Valises~~
   Company Stores etc. will be dumped outside Company billets by 7.45. p.m. 26th. inst. The Transport Officer will arrange to collect the above and convey them to the new Bn. H.Q's.
   Lewis Guns and Ammunition will be carried.

8. PACKS. & Officers Valises
   All packs will be stacked outside company billets by 2. p.m. 26th. inst. The Transport Officer will arrange to collect them and hand them over to the Quarter-master. Also Officers Valises at 8 pm.

9. ACTION.
   While the Battalion is in Divisional Reserve on receipt of order " Occupy WESTOUTRE LINE" companies will occupy portion of the WESTOUTRE GOET MOET MILL LINE. from point M.4.d.8.5. to point M.5.a.65.20. ~~and sectors~~ allotted to them.

10. Completion of relief will be sent. to Bn. H.Q. on using Company Commanders own name

11. Acknowledge.

(Sgd.) D. Walker Capt & Adjt.
12th. Bn. East Surrey Regt.

Issued at ....9 pm 25th June

            Copy No. 1.   File.
                 No. 2.   C.O.
                 No. 3.   War Diary.
                 No. 4.   A. Coy.
                 No. 5.   B. Coy.
                 No. 6.   C. Coy.
                 No. 7.   D. Coy.
                 No. 8.   Quarter-master.
                 No. 9.   Transport Officer.
                 No. 10.   10th. "Queens" (R.W.S.Rgt.)
                 No. 11.   R.S.M.
                 No. 12.   Spare.

SECRET.

INSTRUCTIONS FOR HOLDING THE LINE
Battalion in Brigade Reserve.

1. ACTION IN CASE OF ATTACK.
    a. "C" Company, less one Lewis Gun Section, is placed at the disposal of O.C. Front Battalion. Immediately a hostile attack is imminent, O.C. "A" Company will immediately send an Officer to report to Front Line Battalion H.Q. for instructions and to act as a liaison Officer.
    The Lewis Gun Section of "C" Company above mentioned will in the event of a hostile attack occupy the Lewis Gun Post at N.1.c.7.7. to cover the left flank of Vickers' Guns near that point. They will not go forward with the remainder of "C" Coy, but will remain at that post.
    b. One Platoon of "A" and "B" Coys. under 2/Lieut. C.H.FISHER will hold the strong point in M.6. as a permanent garrison.
    Their role will be :-
        (1) To act as a rallying point on which troops of the SCHERPENBERG LA CLYTTE positions can be reformed and in this way to act as a battle stop.
        (2) To arrest and break up any further attempt of the enemy to advance.
        (3) To assist by fire, the advance of our counter-attacking troops.
    c. "A", "B", & "D" Coys less two platoons are available as Brigade Reserve which will on receipt of orders from Battn. H.Q. be prepared to carry out counter-attacks upon :-
        (1) Any portion of the LA CLYTTE SCHERPENBERG LINE between the Brigade boundaries.
        (2) Farm at N.8.b.35.45.
        (3) Farm at N.14.b.00.65.
        (4) To take up a defensive line from M.12.b.7.4. astride the LA CLYTTE ROAD to the N.Divisional boundary at about N.1.central, in prolongation of the line to be taken up by the Right Brigade from M.12.a.2.2. - M.12.d.3.8. - M.12.b.7.4. in the event of the main line of resistance being taken,
        (5) To form a defensive flank from MILLEKRUISSE to N.1.central in the event of the enemy penetrating the front of the Division on our left.
    Should either or both of "C" and "D" Coys be sent forward their place will immediately be taken by "A" and "B" Coys less the two platoons in Strong point at M.6. which, on no account, will move from their defences.
    "B" Coy. would take up the position of "C" Coy., and "A" of "D" Coy.

2. Immediately a hostile attack appears imminent and no orders are forthcoming, Coys will garrison their battle positions and prepare to hold them at all costs.
Roads will be wired and barricades erected across them immediately.
3. Immediately a hostile attack becomes imminent, all working parties will return to their battle positions in this Sector.
4. All Officers and senior N.C.O's will thoroughly reconnoitre the ground with a view to making any of the counter-attacks enumerated in para 1.
Maps of Dispositions attached.
5. ACKNOWLEDGE.

28th July 1918,

Capt & A/Adjt.,

12th Battn. East Surrey Regt.

Operation Order No 21
by
Major C. T. Williams,
Comdg. 12th Bn East Surrey Regt.

1. The following reliefs will take place on the night of the 30/31st July 1918.
   The Battalion will relieve the 15th Hants Regt in the Reserve Area. Coys will be disposed the same as the last time the Battn was in Reserve.
   The 18th KRRC will take over positions in Support vacated by this Battalion.

2. Companies will move as follows and will pass the point M.6.d.7.7. at the following times:—
   A Coy   10 pm
   B —   10.15 pm
   D —   10.30 pm
   C —   10.45 pm

3. Advance parties of one Officer and one OR will report to their opposite numbers of the 15th Hants by 12 noon, 30th July 1918. They will take over Defence Schemes, all trench Stores etc. which must be carefully checked receipts forwarded to Bn HQ by dawn 31st.

4. Bays of the 27th American Divn. will remain in the Support Line and be handed over to the incoming Company of the KRRC.

5. The Transport Officer will arrange for one limber to collect trench bundles, Coy Stores etc. from M.6.d.7.7. where Coys will have the above dumped by 10 pm. Lewis Guns & ammunition will be carried.

6. Rations for to-morrow will be dumped at the Reserve Bn HQ.

7. Advance parties from 18th KRRC will report to the opposite numbers as follows:—
   1 Officer per Battn. who will take over Defence Schemes work on hand etc.
   1 Sgt per Coy. who will take over Trench Stores, accommodation etc.
   Trench Stores must be carefully handed over and receipts forwarded to Bn HQ by dawn 31st.

8. Completion of relief will be notified to Bn HQ by sending Coy Comdrs. own name.

9. Acknowledge.

(sd) D. Walker
Capt & adjt
12th East Surrey Regt

30th July 1918.

Operation Order No 23
by
Major C. G. Williams
Comdg 12th Bn East Surrey Regt

1. The Battalion will be relieved by the 11th Queens on night of 1st/2nd August, 1918.
On relief the Battalion will occupy billets in the Divisional Reserve vacated by 11th Queens. Hdqrs at L.30.c.8.5.

2. <u>Dispositions</u>. Companies will take over letter for letter.

3. Advance parties of one officer for the Battalion, 1 NCO per Company, and one for Bn H.Q. will report at Bn H.Q. at 8 am. They will proceed to the new area and take over accommodation.

4. Those detailed in para. 3 will take over any Defence Schemes, Schemes for counter attack, and trench Stores, receipts forwarded to Bn H.Q. by noon 2nd inst.

5. Companies will remain in their present positions until relieved and will hand over to the incoming unit, Defence Schemes, Schemes for counter attack, Trench Stores etc, copies of receipts to be forwarded to Bn H.Q. by noon 2nd inst.

6. Companies will march out by platoons at 200 yds interval. Route and points where Coys will meet their guides will be notified later.

7. The Quartermaster will take over cooking arrangements and rations will be brought up accordingly.

8. The Transport officer will arrange to send two limbers to present H.Q. to convey S.G. ammunition, also 3 limbers to carry petrol tins, trench bundles, Coy. Stores.
Coys will have the above dumped at Bn H.Q. by ~~~~~~ 10p 1st Augt 1918. L.G's will be carried.

9. Completion of relief will be notified to Bn H.Q. by sending Coy Comdrs. own name.

10. Acknowledge.

(sd) D. Walker
Capt & Adjt
12th East Surrey Regt

31st July, 1918.

12th Bn East Surrey Regt.

O.C. "A" Coy.
 "   "B" "
 "   "C" "
 "   "D" "
O1/c H.Q.

Organisation of an Infantry Battalion.

1. The general organisation at present existing will remain unchanged, except that each Platoon will consist of 2 Rifle Sections and 1 Lewis Gun Section of 2 Guns.

2. Instructions will be issued very shortly with regard to the Transport of the additional Lewis Guns and Ammunition. In view of the increased number of weapons, Lewis Gun Ammunition will be reduced by about 1,000 rounds per Gun.

3. The Fighting Strength of the Battalion will always be based on the minimum strength laid down for Rifle and Lewis Gun Sections, and no more than the minimum will go into action.
    A reduced establishment has been drawn up as shewn on the attached table "A" (other ranks only) giving sections complete at their minimum, also establishment figures which allows a wide margin for maintenance.

4. It is essential to allow a wide margin between the maximum and the minimum of the Rifle and Lewis Gun Sections so as to ensure as far as possible that the normal deductions from the Fighting Strength can be met without reducing sections below the minimum necessary for tactical efficiency. The maximum represents the War Establishment (as temporarily reduced to 900 O.R's per Battn). The minimum represents the actual Fighting Strength at which a Battalion will go into action, no more and no less.

5. The minimum number necessary for the tactical efficiency of a Rifle Section is placed at 1 leader and 6 men
    The minimum number necessary for the tactical efficiency of a Lewis Gun Section of 2 Guns is placed at 1 leader and 10 men. This latter is less than the number required to fight the two Guns separately, but the principals on which the double Lewis Gun Section must be based are, that the Lewis Guns must be fought in pairs if the utmost tactical efficiency is to be secured : that the section should be able to ensure having one Gun always in action, and that the possession of the second Gun may enable double fire power to be developed when fleeting opportunities offer in specially favourable circumstances.

6. In providing for the indicated increase in the Lewis Gun Sections, and in providing the necessary margin between the maximum and minimum of both Rifle and Lewis Gun Sections it is impossible at present to maintain the existing number of Rifle Sections in a Platoon. It becomes necessary therefore to reduce the Platoon to two Rifle Sections and one double Lewis Gun Section.

7. Allowance for maintenance in the strength of a Bn.
    Average number of men on Command,
        sick etc.   = 50
        Courses, leave etc.   = 90
                            TOTAL   140
of which total 4/5ths may be assumed to be a drain on the strength of a Platoon.

12 E Surrey Regt
August 1918
Vol 28

28 C
4 mins

WAR DIARY or INTELLIGENCE SUMMARY
Army Form C. 2118.

Place	Date	Hour	Summary of Events and Information	Remarks and references to Appendices
RENINGHELST	1/8/18		Battalion in Lines. Billets. Passes forwarded to WIPPENHOEK not received. Reason taking out from 23rd Division.	
WIPPENHOEK	2/8/18		Boys started a training Programme.	
	3/8/18		Estellé des ordres du Dumin. Enemy aeroplanes over the Lines. One of the 30/- Battalions whose Bn. Guard was made (P.M. one of our men).	
LA CLYTTE	4/8/18		Enemy artillery very active – moved Line front to L1 Support RIDGE WOOD area. Shelled during the morning against E ridge. A considerable enemy activity on East W. Front. 2/Lt. H. E. Hamilton & 30 OR wounded. Casualties Killed 1 OR Wd 30. Lt. Bell 1.8.18 2/8/18. Off to OKE 931.	
	5/8/8		Our own Enemy artillery very active throughout the night.	
	6/8/18		2 Bns. 6 Co manned – our artillery carrying out counter preparation shoots.	
	7/8/18		Relieved in line by 18th KRRC with the 2 Bn on the right our left. Battalion artillery activity active by night.	
	8/8/18		Enemy artillery activity active by night.	
	9/8/18		C Coy one platoon DC attacked 4/15 Hants for operations carrying out the night – 4 strength about 20 our post. JCL was met by enemy party – 6 platoon RO by dig, Coy. strength 12 on either side of the MILKY WAY – active at about 6 of 12 men sought all objective taken. Casualties 2 Wd. Lt. 4 NCOs. Returned you relieved later.	
	9/8/18		18 KRRC took our front the together with our Company of 12 E Surrey Battalion on Rt. L. Dames relatively after.	
	10/8/18		The Div. Coy. Counter attacked on the front line Rt. Ch. 13 KRRC & regained 1 Plos post & that hill between night – later old 18 KRRC return the post.	
			CH ORS 5/8/18 placed on duty	
			11 killed	
			2 16 wounded	
			40 926	
			Casualties week ending 10/8/18	
			D of W 6	

Army Form C. 2118.

WAR DIARY
or
INTELLIGENCE SUMMARY
(Erase heading not required.)

August 1918

Place	Date	Hour	Summary of Events and Information	Remarks and references to Appendices
LA CLYTTE	11/8/18		The Battalion relieved the 18th KRRC in the front line - Relief was complete at 3:30 am. Capt Rogers MC returned to duty on Lieut Bundy going to hospital sick. During the day the KRRC approached by the enemy. The posts were lost - In the evening we dug a post midway between 7 CLYDESDALE CAMP & PLUGSTREET posting the	
"	13/8/18		New post was dug out & held during the night by one Section & the Company & 9 pose in the trench which connects the two new posts	
"	14/8/18		Situation normal - Enemy artillery active throughout the night MGSW and lewis gun active in front. Our artillery active in Enl. battery activity throughout the night. Most of our fire was 4 enemy position steamed by our F.A.P.	
"	15/8/18		Situation normal during the day - rather it quiet. During the night the enemy F & E system of posts was attacked by enemy 2 parties. & parties let off by own Lewis gun & Tank guns for 4 bombs. Our attack was beaten off by the Lewis guns & Tank bombs. Our casualties were one killed and two wounded.	
"	16/8/18		Battalion relieved the 18th KRRC & came back to Regt. & moved back to reserve	
KEMMELHURST	17/6/18		Bn in reserve when needed during the night for digging. Cas. 16 or work of the 17/8/16 killed wounded	
"	18/8/18		2 Lt Deering B 17/8/18 Co. OR	
			Comparies Employed in a bombing dump during the day. During the night Battalion finds R.E. Parties.	

Army Form C. 2118.

WAR DIARY
or
INTELLIGENCE SUMMARY
(Erase heading not required.)

August 1918

Place	Date	Hour	Summary of Events and Information	Remarks and references to Appendices
RENINGHELST	19/8/18		Hostile artillery particularly active on our batteries & roads. Bn. HQ shelled. 2 R.W.F. killed. Capt. Dimsdale M.C. & Capt. Gwynne wounded. SOS sent up during the night. Rain in late.	
"	20/8/18		Situation normal. Enemy artillery active on our road. SOS went up early in the morning. Enemy's barrage during the night. Troops taken for showers & fine regime baths in afternoon for cleaning.	
"	21/8/18		Moved from RENING camp to B. Annexe 2 Reninghelst & WIPPENHOEK Camp. Capt. Cox succeeds Lt. Capt. Gilkinson. Remainder rested.	
WIPPENHOEK	22/8/18		Bn. resting & cleaning. Arrangements made in the afternoon. Rain in the afternoon.	
"	23/8/18		Bn. were employed in making a demonstration in the afternoon.	
"	24/8/18		Bn. moved from RENING camp Big Rest line B.12 — 2 BALLINGTON CAMP. Allotted to his Battalion. Guard of 1 Officer & 20 and during the night.	Killed 620 R.D. wounded 1 G.C. missing 1 G.C.
"	25/8/18		Bn. resting. All ranks went to film by pigeon Gun officers. 1 officer per Company & 1 man from each Company attend WESTOUTRE line. Lieut. S. J.W. Booker, relieved to duty. The following Honours have been gazetted to the following on alongside & B/S O.C. T.A. West Australia:— 17729 Sgt Hall W. DCM. M.M. 7523 Cpl Homan J. C.S.M. M.M. 26626 Pte. Goodall A. C.C.M. M.M. 22782 " Curtis D D.C.M. M.M. 29765 " Burke A.E. M.M. W. Corporal Walken L.M.S.	

Army Form C. 2118.

WAR DIARY
or
INTELLIGENCE SUMMARY
(Erase heading not required.)

August 1918

Instructions regarding War Diaries and Intelligence Summaries are contained in F. S. Regs., Part II. and the Staff Manual respectively. Title pages will be prepared in manuscript.

Place	Date	Hour	Summary of Events and Information	Remarks and references to Appendices
RENINGHELST	26/8/18		Rumour from Red Cross WIPPENHOEK to area passed by 10th Divisions in Battle of WESTOUTRE GOLF MOET hill Div.	
"	27/8/18		Companies on hook of perim. Capt Barry returned from leave.	
"	28/8/18		Battalion relieved by 7/11th Queens (35th Brigade). Capt Dowling M.C. proceeding int 6.10 out pant of Regiment	
ABEELE	29/8/18		Battalion entrain at 11 a.m. at ABEELE & detrain at LUMBRES at 7 pm. march to billets at ESQUERDES. Brigade in G.H.Q. reserve.	
ESQUERDES	30/8/18		Cleaning of kit & rifle inspection etc. Remainder of day recreation. Battalion on rest in the Brigade.	
"	31/8/18		Battalion route march 7/Lt in 102 MC proceeded to WISQUES on a course. 7/Lt Wade & Bryant joined B.T.E. 7/Lt Carne also 7/Lt Lt. Col. returns from leave during 31/8/18 - P.R.L.	
			Total casualties for month	

Officers   O.Rs
  1   16 killed
  3   64 wounded
               3 missing

Casualties also during 31/8/18
Officers   ORs
  39   984

R.W. Burn Lt Col
Comdg. 12th East Surrey Regt.

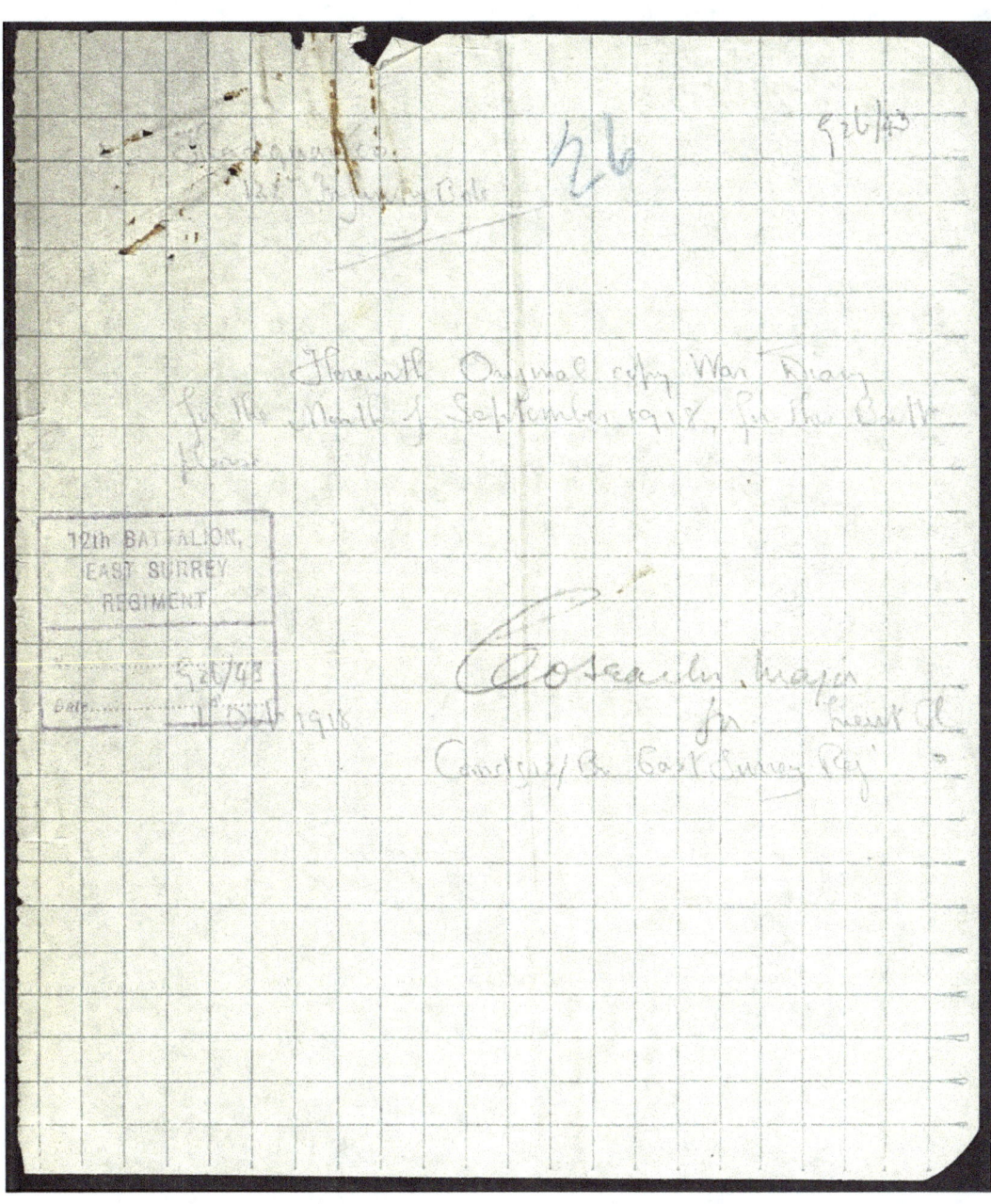

Herewith Original copy War Diary
for the Month of September 1918, for the Battⁿ
please

12th BATTALION,
EAST SURREY
REGIMENT
528/48
Date 1st Oct 1918

Coscaden, Major
for Lieut Col
Comd^g 12th Bⁿ East Surrey Reg^t

12th Gloucester Regiment.
Vol 30 29
122/4

WAR DIARY
or
INTELLIGENCE SUMMARY.
(Erase heading not required.)

Army Form C. 2118.

Place	Date	Hour	Summary of Events and Information	Remarks and references to Appendices
	Sept			
	1		The Battalion paraded at 1:30am and marched from ESQUERDES to LUMBRES where they entrained for ABEELE detraining at 2pm and billeted for the night in the ABEELE AREA. Battn. strength on the day 38 Offrs 884 O.R's	(90)
	2		Battn. moved by Coys to relieve troops of the 27th American Divn. arriving at No 647 on the Vierstraat Road at 10:30 p.m. to the position also cleared the Battn. took up a line with 2 Coys in front from O.7.c.9.8 to O.13.a.O.2 and 2 Coys in the VIERSTRAAT SWITCH LINE (see Diary of operations attached)	(90)
	3		At 1:30 am the O.C. A Coy reported that B & C Coys had proceeded along the VIERSTRAAT- WYTSCHAETE road and had met strong parties of the enemy on either side of the road at N.11.d.9.3. Our casualties were inflicted with M.G. fire. The Battn attacked the flanks of the VIERSTRAAT, Nos 1 & 2 Coys occupied the VIERSTRAAT switch line, B Coy was ordered to advance thru the WYTSCHAETE road as far as possible then dig in. This was completed at dawn. At 3 pm G.O.C. 122 Bde held a conference of Bn Commanders. The Battn. received orders to attack the following morning. No pb stock necessitated making good the line of own Railway from N11b.1.0.7 to N11.c.9.0 when this reached M.G. fire opened up—noted & kept to advance. Our left and right [?]	(90) 29.C 8 struck

WAR DIARY
or
INTELLIGENCE SUMMARY.
(Erase heading not required.)

Army Form C. 2118.

Place	Date	Hour	Summary of Events and Information	Remarks and references to Appendices
	3.		each covered by a Lighting patrol. Mr. G.OC a conference of Commanding Officers was held by G.O.C. 122nd Inf Bde. Details where were then issued for the attack to be delivered at 5.30 am on the 4th. (See Diary of Operations attd.) CAPT. D. WALKER M.C. 2 LIEUT. BELL. CAPT 2N CHRISTIE R.A.M.C. Gassed and evacuated.	[A]¹
	4.		Coys were reported in position for attack at 4 am. C and D coys in front on line of the railway N.12.d.0.7 to N.12.c.9.0. The barrage for the attack commenced at 5.30 am and by 6.15 am C + D coys had reached their objective i.e. line of the road along the Western of BOIS QUSIRANTE and commenced to consolidate. Casualties slight, nil practicer. No opposition to enemy barrage fallen. They were subject to heavy machine gun fire from OAK TRENCH on their right rear and 2 large pill boxes to GRAND BOIS. In endeavouring to keep the men together all officers of the 2 coys with the exception of 2/Lt Reynolds became casualties. A + B coys under Capt Reynolds M.C. moved from Railway and endeavoured to form a defensive flank and fill up gap between C + D coys. And 1/5th Hampshire Regt. About 7.15am the enemy reached our back of objection in the attack and consolidated C + D coys. at the same time filtering through small parties with Light Machine guns. D coy who had suffered severe casualties were driven back to the Rly. and C + a line manoeuvring to the East of Railway in N.12.b. Her positions were held until 1pm when A + B coys who had suffered heavy casualties from hostile M.G. fire fell back to the VIERSTRAAT SWITCHLINE	[B]¹

WAR DIARY
or
INTELLIGENCE SUMMARY.
(Erase heading not required.)

Army Form C. 2118.

Place	Date	Hour	Summary of Events and Information	Remarks and references to Appendices
	Sept 4			
	4		D Coy withdrew to a line of trenches astride the VIERSTRAAT-WYTSCHAETE road from N.11.d.6.7 to N.11.d.4.4, thus leaving 2/Lt Reynolds with C Coy holding forward post East of Pt Cabo. These positions were maintained until handed over to the 18th Bn KRRC's (see Diary of operations attd) Capt A.A. Bright killed in action; Capt Barry ?R wounded and missing; Capt ?SB Dunley MC, Lto ?BM°HARTER, PR Johnstone, and 2/Lts ?E Lewis, OA George, WE Bundy, wounded on this day. Capt J Ferguson RAMC joined the Battalion on this day.	601
	5		The Batt were relieved by the 23rd Middlesex and proceeded to billets in vicinity of HOOGRAAF FARM. Sheet 28 N N.E 70000. HQ at G26.d.6.4. Lt R M MEADONS died of wounds on this day.	601
	6		Batt spent the morning on cleaning clothing equipment etc. The Cooks were allotted the Batts in the afternoon. Capt Ryan returned from leave on this day.	601
	7		Batts training under Coy arrangements. Batts strength 27 O. 679 OR's. Casualties for the week 11 O. 220 OR's	601
	8		Divine service at 11:30 by C of E. Maj Wilkins C.J admitted to Hospital on this day.	601
	9		Batt training under Coy Commanders. CO's conference at 2 pm of Coy Commanders.	601
	10		Batt training under Company arrangements.	601
	11		Batt training according to programme. 2/Lt HALL, W.S proceeded on leave to England.	601

WAR DIARY
or
INTELLIGENCE SUMMARY.

Army Form C. 2118.

Place	Date	Hour	Summary of Events and Information	Remarks and references to Appendices
Lyft	12/4		Lieut. Col. Brown C.L. wounded (gazed.) Batt. training was continued. Companies practised the attack with special reference to "Strong Points" and Machine Gun nests. 2/Lt RODD rejoined the Batt. from duty at the Divisional Reception Camp. The following joined the Batt. 2/Lt ADAMS, C.N. 2/Lt SLEATH, C.W. 2/Lt NORTHWOOD, D.F. 2/Lt SOMERS, W.G.T. 2/Lt SMITH, C.E. 2/Lt SAVILLE, G.S.	[63]
	13.		Training was continued according to programme. Inter-Company attack and defence schemes were carried out.	[63]
	14th		During the day the Batt. paraded by Companies for Baths and fort heatreat Voluntary Church Service for Church of England and Nonconformists were held. The Batt. paraded at 5p.m. and marched to ELLARSYDE SIDINGS where it entrained and proceeded to the VIERSTRAAT SECTOR and relieved the 23rd Middlesex Regt. in a front extending from N.12.d 40.45 to O.1.d 30.65. Casualties Offr. 2 O.R. 13. Battalion strength Officers 33 O.Rs 660.	[63]
	15th		Relief reported complete 1.30 a.m. Enemy artillery was active, especially in the neighbourhood of RIDGE WOOD. Heavy rain had rendered movement difficult.	[63]
	16th		Aerial activity was normal. Enemy artillery was active throughout the day. The posts on our left were advanced to conform to the movement of the 35th Division.	[63]
	17th		2 enemy aircraft flew over our lines at a high altitude. Bombs were dropped near N.12.d 55.75 and an O.lancaster Balloon was brought down in flames behind KEMMEL HILL. A prisoner of the 134th I.R. was captured by one of my new posts. The officer was wounded with the post established at O.7.a 75.65 and O.1.c.00.20 and	[63]

WAR DIARY
or
INTELLIGENCE SUMMARY
(Erase heading not required.)

Army Form C. 2118.

Place	Date	Hour	Summary of Events and Information	Remarks and references to Appendices
	Sept. 18th		The Batt. was relieved by the 16th Hants. Regt. on the night of the 17th/18th Sept. The relief was reported complete at 1 a.m. The Batt. moved into nights support at M.14.3.6. Enemy Artillery was active throughout the day.	901
	19th		Enemy artillery continued active in the nights support area. The whole of the Batt. which was available was engaged on working parties under R.E. officers. 2/Lt. Lieut. C.F.W. proceeded to England to join the R.A.F. The following Officers joined the Batt. 2/Lt. COMBE-CEATON F., 2/Lt. ALDRIDGE, L.H., 2/Lt. JAMES. P.W. 2/Lt. PAVIOUR, T.W. 2/Lt. ADAMS. was wounded and 1 O.R. wounded.	903
	20th		Batt. H.Q. was heavily shelled, a direct hit being obtained. Working parties were furnished for work with R.Es. Lt. A.E. BELL to Batt. from Hospital.	903
	21st		The day was quiet. The Batt. was relieved by the 8th Royal Scots 34th Division. Relief was reported complete at 9 p.m. and the Batt. marched to OVERDOM where it embussed for ABEELE. Batt. strength Offs. 36. O.R. 695. Casualties 1 Off. 6 O.R.	903
	22nd		The Batt. battled from 8 a.m. to 12 noon. Voluntary Church Services were held for Church of England and Nonconformists were held during the afternoon. Evening respectively.	903
	23rd		The remainder of the Batt. battled. Companies did one hour close order drill. Complete inspection of hats, equipment etc. were carried out, and also a thorough medical inspection.	903

Army Form C. 2118.

WAR DIARY
or
INTELLIGENCE SUMMARY.
(Erase heading not required.)

Instructions regarding War Diaries and Intelligence Summaries are contained in F. S. Regs., Part II. and the Staff Manual respectively. Title pages will be prepared in manuscript.

Place	Date	Hour	Summary of Events and Information	Remarks and references to Appendices
	Sept. 24		The Batt. paraded for training under Company Commanders. Special attention was paid to Lewis Gun Instruction & Musketry. Lt Col G.L.BROWN.D.S.O. returned from Hospital and resumed command of the Batt.	(co)
	25		The Batt. practised a scheme of attack, with special reference to strong points and protection of the flanks.	(co)
	26		The Batt. took part in a Brigade operation in the country between GODEWAERSVELDE and MONT DES CATS. the special points practised were keeping direction and dealing with strong points. Both the day received warning order for a move to HOOGRAAF area.	(co)
	27		During the day the rest of the day was free until 7 pm when the Battalion paraded and moved to HOOGRAAF area by march route arriving at 9 pm. Strength Officers 38. other ranks 857.	(co)
	28		The Battn. paraded at 6.20 am and moved to SCOTTISH CAMP from there it moved at 12.30 pm and marched to SWAN CHATEAU 28/J.19.c.4.6. from there it moved at 5.30 pm to RAVINE WOOD J.34.B.	(co)
	29		The Battn. moved at 9 am to Sheet 28/P.14.B.8.95. B Coy furnished Advance Guard. A strong point was met at P.15.c. Central. D Coy was sent forward	(co)

Army Form C. 2118.

WAR DIARY
or
INTELLIGENCE SUMMARY.
(Erase heading not required.)

Instructions regarding War Diaries and Intelligence Summaries are contained in F. S. Regs., Part II. and the Staff Manual respectively. Title pages will be prepared in manuscript.

Place	Date	Hour	Summary of Events and Information	Remarks and references to Appendices
	Sept 29		to deal with it. The Batn. moved forward to the Guentelus area P.15.b. central at 4 pm. Casualties :- 1 officer wounded (Capt. G.S. Sowell) other ranks 4 killed 10 wounded.	607.
	30		A Coy moved forward at 6am in an endeavour to make good a line P.15.c.8.4. to P.16.d.1.4. and to get touch with 35th Div on left. This was done. At 12.45 pm. the Batn. moved to a new concentration area at P.16.c.7.3. A warning Order was received for a move early next morning.	607.

Cockade hern
for Lieut. Col.
Comdg 12th East Surrey Regt.

O.C.
Company

In continuation of O.O.23 Headquarters will be as follows:-
Bn Headquarters   Sheet 27   L.30.a.90.05
A Coy   "   "   "   "   L.29.d.70.35
B   "   "   "   "   "   L.29.b.8.1
C   "   "   "   "   "   L.29.a.96.75
                              (PATRICIA CAMP)
D   "   "   "   "   "   L.29.b.8.9

Reference para 1 of O.O.23 the Battn will relieve 23rd Middlesex Regt. Reference para 6 O.O.23 Guides. 1 per Platoon from 23rd Middlesex will meet their opposite numbers as they pass Cross roads G.32.d.7.3 (Sheet 28). Companies will draw rations for 2nd Aug to be arranged on arrival in new billets.

Working parties for tonight are cancelled.

Sd D. Walker
Capt & Adjt
Rov.

1-8-18

SECRET.

OPERATION ORDER No 32
by
LIEUT.COL.G.L.BROWN, D.S.O.

In continuation of Warning Order issued yesterday.

1. Battalion Orders Nos. 499 and 500 d/31.8.18, are cancelled.

2. The Battalion will parade at 7.30 a.m. this morning, 1st September, 1918, and will form up on the road the same as yesterday, 31.8.18, and will march to LUMBRES where the Battalion will entrain for ABEELE. Packs will be carried.

3. O.C. A Coy will detail an entraining Officer to report at Battn.H.Q. at 7 a.m.

4. TRANSPORT. The Transport will proceed by road and will pass Starting Point (F.1.d.2.5) at 7.10 a.m. en route for new area. Major E.G.WHATELEY, M.C. D.A.A.G. will meet on march and will allot accommodation.
Route:- WIZERNES - BLENDECQUES - ARCQUES - BAVINCHOVE - OXELAERE - STEENVOORDE.
O.C. No.2 Coy. Div.Train will command the column.

5. RATIONS. Rations for the 2nd Septr. will march with column to be delivered on arrival.

6. O.C. C Coy will detail 20 men under a N.C.O. to report to Lieut.G.A.Bettinson, 122nd T.M.Battery at H.Q. 122nd Inf.Bde at 6 a.m. this morning.
The above will report at Battn.H.Q. at 5.30 a.m.

7. All stores drawn from the Area Comdt. ESQUERDES, will be returned to the Area Comdt. by 7 a.m. and receipts obtained.

8. LEWIS GUNS. All Lewis Guns and ammunition will be dumped at Battn.H.Q. at 6 a.m. The Transport Officer will arrange to collect same. Sgt.Lattimore, H.Q. will supervise loading.

9. COMPANY STORES etc. Coy.Stores etc. will be dumped at Qmr. Stores by 6 a.m. 1st Septr. The Qmr. will arrange transport.

10. OFFICERS KITS. Officers Kits will be stacked outside Coy. billets by 6 a.m. The Transport Officer will arrange to collect above.

11. One lorry is allotted to the Battalion. Any surplus stores etc. will be stacked at Qmr.Stores at 6 a.m. and will proceed by lorry under 2nd Lieut, GEORGE, D Coy.

12. On the night of the 2nd/3rd September, 1918, the Battalion will relieve the Battalion in the line of the 106th Infantry Regt. 27 American Division.

13. The Battalion will parade in full marching order.

(sd) D.Walker,
Capt & A/Adjt,
12th Bn East Surrey Regt.

1st September, 1918.

SECRET.

12th East Surrey Regt.
15th Hampshire Regt.
18th King's Royal Rifle Corps.
'D' Coy. 41st Bn. M.G. Corps.
122nd Trench Mortar Battery.

As the Brigade is likely to take part in a more open form of warfare, the Brigade Commander wishes the following points to be impressed upon all ranks:-

1. No opportunity should be lost of making use of the covering fire of rifles, Lewis and Vickers Machine Guns.

2. It is unlikely that Units will be in a continuous line, after an advance, but as long as the tactical features are held, and the intervening ground covered by fire, there is little danger of the enemy penetrating.
   At night, or in foggy weather, such intervening ground must be continually patrolled, and standing patrols put into positions.

3. Commanders should study the use of ground, as giving cover from view and from fire. Good leaders and scouts will pass over an area totally unseen, whereas careless leading would at once expose the whole force.
   The first principle of the advance is to make good each "bound" before commencing the next.
   Advancing platoons and companies will thus keep some sort of "formation", and remain under the control of the Unit Commander.
   The danger is that platoons and companies will get mixed up in the early stages of the advance and thus control&command are lost.

4. In the attack in open and semi-open warfare, fixed objectives for each wave cannot be laid down.
   The Battalion Commander will be given a final objective, between definite Battalion Boundaries, and the time the advance is to commence.
   A creeping barrage cannot be arranged, but the field artillery will probably be employed in engaging certain known strong points, and the heavy artillery will be engaging enemy communications and approaches for reinforcements, and finally a protective barrage well in front of the final objective

5. Battalions must push on to their final objective, whether <u>or not</u> the troops on the flank are advancing or held up.

6. Depending entirely upon the success of each Battalion operation, objectives will be given for several advances in a day.

7. Under such circumstances, active patrolling by day and night is essential.

8. The attention of Commanding Officers is drawn to the danger of getting support and reserve troops all involved in the early stages of an advance. Reserves should be kept well back, and not committed until the situation demands it.
   If reserves are too close up, the only use to which they can be put is to throw them into the fight as reinforcements.

9. <u>Headquarters</u> - Brigade should always be kept in close touch with any move forward, and new Headquarters established should be marked with a small flag. This presents no difficulty as it can always be concealed from the enemy.

para.10/-

10. **Vickers Machine Guns.** - The role of the Vickers M.G's is to assist the infantry by:-
Overhead covering fire on enemy approaches during the advance.
Protection of flanks, if troops on right and left do not get forward.
The Vickers M.G's advance in bounds, always maintaining echelon formation in depth, thus to be ready at any time to repel counter-attacks.
Section commanders must keep in close touch with Battalion Commanders, and should establish their Section H.Q. with, or close to, the Battalion holding the sector in which they are operating.

Captain,
A/Brigade Major,
122nd Infantry Brigade.

12th Bn. EAST SURREY REGT.
RECEIVED
Date 2.9.18.

OPERATION ORDER. No. 33.

Ref. Maps. Sheet 27. 1/40,000
    "   "   28. S.W. 1.1/10,000 (KEMMELL)

1. The situation appears to be as follows :-
    The 106 American Infantry Regiment reached the Line of trenches immediately East of and parallel to VIERSTRAAT - KEMMELL ROAD on the night of the 31st/1st. Septr. 1918.
    On the morning of the 1st, Spetr. 1918, an advance was commenced at 7.a.m. the objective being a general line from VIERSTRAAT to V.C. Road (N.23.b.0.6.) The advance was held up by hostile machine gun fire and the situation yesterday afternoon was obscure.
    Dispositions of the 106th. A.I.R. at mid-day yesterday were approx. in front line (not yet defined) 4 Companies of the 3rd. Bn. and 1 Company of the 2nd. Bn. In the line of trenches parallel and immediately East of VIERSTRAAT - KEMMEL ROAD running through N.11. Central - N.17.a. - N.16.d. 3 Companies of the 1st. Bn. In the original British Front Line N.10.a. - N.9.d.- N.15.a. 3 Companies of the 2nd. Bn. 1 Company of the 1st. Bn.

2. *On night of 2/3rd inst.* The Battalion will relieve the troops holding the left Sub Sector. Brigade Front - Northern Boundary VIERSTRAAT Cross Roads N.11.c.9.9. Inter Battalion Boundary N.16.b.0.3.- N.17.a.0.3.- N.18.a.0.3. Battalion Headquarters at H.32.b.6.6.
    Advance Bn. Hqr's PILLBOX at N.16.d.6.9. Approximately.

3. DISPOSITIONS.
    A. Coy on the left C. Coy on the right will relieve the troops holding the Front Line.
    B. Coy. on the left D. Coy. on the right will relieve the troops holding Support Trenches.
    Inter-Company Boundary will be a line from GODAZONNE FARM N.10.d.2.6. to a point N.17.b.6.8.
    The 15th. Hants Regt. will be on the right of C. and D. Coys.
    A Battalion of the 124. Inf. Bde. on the left of A. and B. Coys.

4. PARADE.
    Companies will parade and march off in the following order:-
    A. Coy. to pass Starting Point Cross Roads Sh.27.L.17.d.6.4 at 7.m
    C. Copy.   "   "   "   "   "   "   "   "   "   at 7.15
    B. "   "   "   "   "   "   "   "   "   "   " 7.30
    D. "   "   "   "   "   "   "   "   "   "   " 7.45
    Movement will be by Platoons at 200 yards interval.

5. OFFICERS VALISES, MENS PACKS ETC.
    Mens Packs and Companies Stores will be stacked outside Coy. Billets at 3.p.m. for collection by Transport Officer.
    Officers Valises Mess Boxes etc. will be stacked at Bn. H.Q's. by 6.30.p.m. The Transport Officer will arrange to collect same.
    The R.S.M. will detail a Guard to be in charge of the above until collected.

6. S.A.A.
    Each man will carry 50 rounds extra S.A.A. this will be issued this afternoon.

7. RATIONS.
    Rations will be delivered this afternoon, cooked in billets and carried to the line on the man.

8. L.Gs. & AMMUNITION.
    One limber will be at the disposal of each Coy. and one for H.Qr's for Lewis Guns etc. they will proceed with the first platoon of each Coy. They will report to Coys this afternoon.
    Company Commanders will decide point where Lewis Guns etc. will be unloaded, and from that point they will be carried by the teams. Limbers will be sent back to the Transport Lines.
    Transport can be taken to any point West of VIERSTRAAT - KEMMEL Road.

- 2 -

9. **WATER.**
   12, Tins per Company and 12 tins for H.Qr's will be issued this afternoon As there may be a scarcity of Water for the first 24 hours, Special care willbe taken to fillall Water-bottles.
   Empty Petrol Tins must be returned to-morrow night, with any taken over or found in the Area

10. **DUMPS.**
    A Reserve Dumps of S.A.A is situated at Bn.H.Qr's.

11. **R.A.P.**
    The R.A.P. is situated near Bn. H.Qr's.

12. **S.O.S.**
    The S.O.S. Signal is a Rifle Grenade, bursting into three stars Red over Red over Red.

13. **GUIDES.**
    1 per Platoon and 1 per Coy. H.Q.will meet Companies at Sheet 28. H.31.a.6.9. at 9 p.m.

14. **TRENCH STORES.** All trench stores etc. will be taken over and copies of any stores in the sector will be forwarded to Bn.H.Q.

15. The Corps Commander wishes to impress on all concerned the importance of operations on a wide fronts and of enveloping tactics on all formations and units down to platoons.

16. A sketch if possible, or a report shewing the line taken up and approximate dispositions of Companies will be forwarded to Bn.H.Q. by 3 a.m. 3rd inst.

17. Companies will get into and maintain touch with/troops on either flank as soon as position is taken up.

18. Completion of relief will be sent to Bn.H.Q. by sending Company Commanders own name.

19. Acknowledge.

                                              (sd) D.Walker,
                                              Capt & A/Adjt,
                                  12th Bn East Surrey Regiment.

2nd September, 1918.

                Copies to:-
                        File.
                        O.C. A Company.
                        O.C. B   "
                        O.C. C   "
                        O.C. D   "
                        Quartermaster.
                        Transport Officer.
                        R.S.M.

Secret

124 I.B.
X.4.

To:- Officer Commanding,
  10th Bn. "Queens" R.W.S.Regt.
  26th Bn. Royal Fusiliers.
  20th Bn. Durham Light Infy.
  12th E.Surrey Regt.
  187th Brigade R.F.A.
  190th Brigade R.F.A.
  'A' Coy. 41st Bn. M.G.Corps.
  'C' Coy. 41st Bn. M.G.Corps.
  101st Infantry Brigade.
  41st Division G. (for information).
  102nd. Infantry Brigade.

On the night 5th/6th October 1918, the 20th Bn. D.L.I. will be relieved in the Right Sub-sector of the Brigade Front as follows :-

(a) From the Right Boundary i.e. Q.10.a.4.8 to the MENIN ROAD (exclusive) probably by the 1/4th Cheshire Regt. (H.Q.Q.3.c.5.6) of the 102nd. Infantry Brigade. From the MENIN ROAD (inclusive) to bifurcation of roads at K.34 c 9.2 by the 4th Bn. "Queens" R.W.S.Regt. 101st Infantry Brigade, and from bifurcation of roads at K.34 c 9.2 to Inter-Battalion Boundary at K.34 c 3.5 probably by the 26th Bn. Royal Fusiliers, who will extend their front to their right for this purpose.

All details of relief will be arranged between Officer Commanding, 20th Bn. D.L.I. and Commanding Officers concerned.

26th Bn. Royal Fusiliers will make the necessary reconnaissances and will be prepared to carry out the relief mentioned above if ordered to do so.

(b) On relief 20th Bn. D.L.I. will either
  (i) Relieve the 12th Bn. E.Surrey Regt. in K.26.central (H.Q. K.27 a 5.9) if orders are received for this Battn. to rejoin the 122nd. Infantry Brigade.
      OR
  (ii) Move to bivouacs in the neighbourhood of K.20.central. Officer Commanding, 20th Bn. D.L.I. will have both these areas reconnoitred.

(c) 10th Bn. "Queens" R.W.S.Regt. may have to move to another area, probably either K.20.central or J.24 b.and d. and K.19.a and c. Officer Commanding, 10th Bn. "Queens" R.W.S.Regt. will have both these areas reconnoitred.

(d) Completion of all moves and reliefs will be reported to Brigade Headquarters.

(e) Relief of Machine Guns will be arranged between Officer Commanding 'A' Coy 41st Bn M.G. and other Company Commanders concerned.

Acknowledge

Captain,
Brigade Major,
124th. Infantry Brigade.

2-10-18.

OPERATION ORDER No. 38
by
LIEUT.COL.G.L.BROWN,D.S.O.
Comdg 12th Bn EAST SURREY REGIMENT.

8th October, 1918.

Reference Maps Sheets 27 . 28. 1/40.000.

Battalion Tactical Exercise to practice following points.

1. Following a creeping barrage.
2. Mopping up by sections specially detailed.
3. Supporting Companies passing through on reaching first objective and continuing to second objective.
4. Communications.
5. Keeping direction on Compass bearing.

---

1. The Battalion will form up by 10 a.m. to-morrow morning 20 yards in rear of the road running through DREEF CROSS ROADS 27/L.34.d.1.3 to 27/L.34.b.1.7 in the following formation :-
    Right Front B Coy.   Left Front A Coy.
    Right Support D Coy.   Left Support C Coy.
right of B Coy to rest at the end of the houses 27/L.34.d.1.4.
    Each of the two front Companies will take a frontage of 225 yards.
    Formation will be as laid down at Company Commanders Conference.
    Zero hour will be 10.30 a.m. at which time the Infantry will advance. Direction of attack 63° true.

2. The first objective will be taken by A and B Companies. Line of the road 27/L.30.c.5.3 to 27/L.30.a.0.0.
    The second objective will be taken by C and D Companies - 28/G.26.a.0.1 to 28/G.25.b.5.7.

3. Barrage. The barrage will be represented by band and drums under Major Searle, provided with flags.
    The barrage will drop 50 yards in front of the forming up line two minutes before zero and at zero will advance at the rate of 100 yards for two minutes until reaching the first objective where it will halt for 15 minutes. During this 15 minute halt C and D Companies will pass through A and B Companies and will form up under the barrage and follow it to the final objective. The barrage will halt 300 yards in front of final objective for 20 minutes.

4. Major Searle will also arrange Strong Points during the advance to be mopped up by sections detailed for this purpose.

5. Dress. The band and drums will wear steel helmets and fatigue dress; all others fighting order and soft caps.

6. Battalion Headquarters. Position of Battalion Headquarters - DREEF CROSS ROADS Sh.27/L.34.d.1.3 until capture of first objective where all messages will be sent.

(sd) G.L.BROWN,
Lieut.Col.
Comdg. 12th Bn East Surrey Regiment.

Issued at 18.00.
8th October, 1918.

Copies to:- Comdg.Officer.   O.C. B Coy.
            2nd-in-Comd.   O.C. C Coy.
            Adjutant.   O.C. D Coy.
            File.   Hdqrs. 122nd Inf.Bde.
            O.C. A Coy.

OPERATION ORDER No.39
by
LIEUT.COL. G.L.BROWN, D.S.O.
Comdg 12th Bn EAST SURREY REGT.

9th October, 1918.

Reference Maps Sh.27 & 28. 1/40.000.

Details for Brigade Tactical Scheme to-morrow
10th October, 1918.

1. The Battalion will parade at 04.15 to-morrow as under head of column where track crosses the road 28/G.26.c.3.7 and will march to assembly area 28/G.33.b.3.8.
    Headquarters
    B Company.
    A Company.
    D Company.
    C Company.
Dress:- Fighting order, steel helmets will be worn, except those detailed for barrage and enemy.

2. Special Idea. The Battalion will attack with the 18th K.R.R.C on right and 15th Bn Hampshire Regt on left to establish line of the Railway from 27/L.23.a.6.6 to 28/G.7.d.0.4. The advance will not be continued to the Railway but will halt on the Red Line (see map) and consolidate and re-organise in depth.

3. The Battalion will form up on a two Company front in two waves of two lines each. The first line composed of six rifle sections per Company as under:-
    A Company Left Front.   B Company Right Front.
    C Company Left Rear.   D Company Right Rear.
Distances and formations after zero willbe the same as practised this morning.
On reaching the first objective - Blue Line - the leading Companies A and B will halt and the two rear Companies will continue the advance passing through A and B Companies forming up under the barrage then to follow up and attack final objective halting on the Red Line.
Battalion boundaries are shown on attached map.

4. Zero hour will be 06.00, 10th October, 1918.

5. True bearing of attack is 314° T.B. A and C Companies on the left will direct.

6. Mopping up parties will pay special attention to all Farms etc.

7. Barrage. There will be a creeping barrage moving by lifts of 100 yards every two minutes. At zero minus 2 minutes barrage will come down 200 yards in front of forming up position when the leading wave will close to within 70 yards. The first lift will be at zero. There will be a pause in the barrage of 15 minutes every 1500 yards.

8. Battalion Headquarters will be at 28/G.35.b.0.6 until the capture of the first objective.

9. Communications. Os. C. C and D Companies will arrange to send a message by message rocket from the final objective to Bn.H.Q.

10. General. There will be a skeleton enemy who will wear soft S.D.Caps and will fire blank. O.C. H.Q.Coy will detail 1 N.C.O. and 10 men from band and drums to report to Lieut.Prince at HOOGGRAAF CAB. 28/G.26.c.4.3 at 05.30 for above, also 5 men each with signal flag for barrage reporting as above to Lieut. Anderson.

No. 2.

At 08.30 all Officers and senior N.C.Os will rendezvous at 27/L.17.d.7.3 leaving the troops to be marched back to billets under juni or N.C.Os.
There will be no smoking or ~~unnecessary noise~~ *talking* while the Battalion is forming up. No lights will be shown.

        (sd) D. Walker,
           Capt & A/Adjt,
        12th Bn East Surrey Regiment.

Issued at 18.30.
    9th October, 1918.

Copies to :-
- File.
- Commanding Officer.
- 2nd-in-Command.
- Adjutant.
- O.C. A Company.
- O.C. B Company.
- O.C. C Company.
- O.C. D Company.
- Intelligence Officer.
- H.Q. 122nd Infantry Brigade.
- O.C. 18th K.R.R.C.
- O.C. 15th Bn Hampshire Regt.

12th. Bn. East Surrey Regt.
OPERATION ORDER No. 40.
by
LIEUT COL G.L.BROWN D.S.O.

less Transport & Details

1. The Battalion will move from present Area into bivouacs J.14.Area. by light railway entraining at REMY North Siding 27/L.23.a.   Parade 11.60 head of the column on road outside B.HQ. in the order H.Qr's A.B.C.D.
Detraining Station STERLING CASTLE J.14. at approximately 15.00

2. On the night of the 12th./13th. inst the Battalion will relieve the 11th. "QUEENS" 123. Brigade in the line.
H.Qr's at K.27.d.2.7.   Dispositions (Subject to alteration)
   - A Company   Left Front.
   - B. Company   Centre
   - D. Company   Right Front.
   - C. Company. Support.

3. Present situation The Front Line is now reported to be as follows (S to N.) points Q.4.c.0.0. - Q.4½.c.4.7. - along MENIN ROAD to Q.3.b.70.15. - K.35.a.5.6. - K.29.c.8.0. K.29.d.0.4 K.29.d.9.5. - K.30.a.00 - K.24.c.95.00

4. Guides 1 per Platoon and 1 per Company H.Qr's will meet the Battalion at 28/K.27.a.6.6. Movement forward of bivouac area will be by platoons at 50 yards distance.

5. A proportion of N.C.O's and men who have actually patrolled the front will be left in the line for 24 hours after relief.

6. Packs, Blankets, Surplus Kit, Officers Valises and Officers Mess Kit will be stacked on Main Road running past B.H.Qr's by 69.30 they will be collected by a lorry and despatched to D.R.C. under arrangements to be made by MAJOR SEARLE. The above will be placed under a Guard supplied from Details.

7. Lewis Gun Limbers. These will report to Companies today and will be loaded. They will proceed with the Transport and will rejoin the Battalion in bivouac area.

8. Relief will be notified at Battalion H.Qr's by wiring Company Commanders own name.

9. On the night of the 13th./14th. inst. the 18th. K.R.R.C. on Right and 15th. Hants, on Left will take over the line outside Battalion Boundary (see Map issued with O.O.No.41.)
A. and B. Companies will close to the Right D. Company will move behind B. and C. Company will move up behind A.
A and B Company will be responsible for a patrol covering the Battalion Front, during assembling.

10. Completion of Assembly will be notified at B.H.Qr's (see O.O. No.41.)

(Sgd) D. WALKER,   Capt & A/Adjt,
12th. Bn. East Surrey Regt.

12th Bn. East Surrey Regt.

OPERATION ORDER NO. 41.

Refce Map. 1/20,000, issued to Companies with this order.

The attack in the North will be continued by the French, Belgians, and 2nd Army on the 14th instant.

The 122nd Infantry Brigade will attack with all three Battalions in the line as follows :-
  18th Bn. K.R.R.C. on the right.
  12th Bn East Surrey Regt in the centre.
  15th Hampshire Regt on the left.

The Brigade will be disposed between the following points :- K.34.c.5.0. to K.29.d.9.8.

The Battalion will attack with two Companies "A" and "B" in the front line; two Companies "C" and "D" in the second line.

The formation for attack will be two waves, each wave consisting of two lines of sections in Artillery formation, 20 yards distance between lines and 50 yards distance between waves, the latter to be increased to 100 yards distance as soon as possible after the attack has started.

The Battalion boundaries are shown on the map which has been issued to Company Commanders today.

The dividing line between Companies will be K.36.a.45.55. to L.32.c.6.9.

There will be two objectives, the blue line and the red line. The blue line will be taken by "A" and "B" Companies; the red line will be taken by "C" and "D" Companies. The blue line will be from point K.36.d.0.90. to K.31.a.10.60. The red line will be from point K.31.d.85.70. to K.32.b.05.2. Both these two lines are situate 200 yards West or in rear of the second pause in the Artillery Barrage.

On reaching the blue line "A" and "B" Companies will halt, and "C" and "D" Companies will pass through them and continue the advance to the red line. "A" and "B" Companies will follow as soon as "C" and "D" Companies are clear. On reaching the red line "C" and "D" Companies will consolidate in depth on their objective, "A" and "B" Companies consolidating in rear of them on the general line L.31.d.1.7. to L.32.a.1.4.

Assembly. Companies will assemble on the line of our front line posts from approximately K.35.a.0.25. to K.35.a.8.95. the dividing point being K.35.a.45.55; each Company attacking upon a front approximately 500 yards long. The lateral bearing of the forming up point is 58½° Magnetic and 238½° Magnetic. The Battalion will be in position 3 hours before "H" hour. "A" and "B" Companies will be responsible for patroling the front during the time the Battalion is assembling.

The day of the attack will be "J" day.
The hour "H" and the Magnetic bearing of the advance will be 107.

Each Company will detail 1 N.C.O. and 3 men to keep touch with units on their flanks. They will send continually reports to Battalion Headquarters that this is being maintained.

Moppers up will be as arranged, two sections of Riflemen in each of the second lines.

O.C. "A" Company will detail one Officer and two Other ranks to march on his left flank and maintain the direction of the Battalion.

Light Signals. One blue smoke Rifle Grenade indicates "we are here". One red smoke Rifle Grenade indicates "we are held-up"

The signal "we are here" will be sent up to indicate :-
  (a) That the first objective has been reached
  (b) That the second objective has been reached.
The red Rifle Grenade will obly be sent up under very exceptional circumstances, i.e. when the situation cannot be held without further Artillery preparation. If this signal is used it must be followed by the blue grenade when the position [resistance] has been overcome.

Communications. A central forward party will be formed as follows :-
  Two Signallers to be detailed by Battⁿ Headquarters,
  Two Signallers to be detailed by O.C. "A" Company,
  One Signalling L/Cpl to be detailed by O.C. "D" Coy.
This party will advance with the second line between the two Companies and on reaching the blue line will continue in the centre of "C" and "D" Companies to the final objective. They will assist Companies to keep in touch with Battalion Headquarters. Any Company which fails to pick up Battalion Headquarters will use this party, who should be permanently in touch as a means of communication.
All Runners should be instructed the line of advance of this party.

Vickers Guns. The first 1200 yards of the advance will be covered by a Machine Gun lifting barrage which will drop approximately 800 yards in front of the advancing Infantry.

Lewis Guns. On reaching the red line, the 124th Brigade will leap-frog the 122nd Brigade and continue the advance. Every opportunity of pushing Lewis Guns forward as far under the barrage as possible should be taken to assist the subsequent advance of this Brigade.

Aeroplane co-operation. Contact aeroplanes will fly along the front one hour after "H", and thereafter every clock hour. Red Flares will be shown in groups of three when called for, by the most advanced troops. The necessity of showing their position by this means, by tin discs, or by any other means must be impressed on all ranks. A counter-attack aeroplane will fly continuously over the front and will signal an impending enemy hostile counter-attack by firing a red parachute light.

Situation Reports. Situation reports will be sent every half hour, or more frequently if necessary.

Synchronisation. Watches will be synchronised at 11.49 on "J" minus one day, and at 84.01 on "J" day.

Artillery. The Artillery are cutting gaps in hostile wire every 100 yards, and if time permits every 50 yards; and are also carrying out destructive shoots on enemy positions.

Barrage, & Time Table of Attack. The attack will be covered by a creeping barrage. It will drop at "H" minus 2 minutes on the line K.36.d.4.65 to K.31.d.8.55 at which moment the Infantry will close up to it as close as possible.
"H"   - First lift of barrage and simultaneous advance of the infantry to the attack.
"H" plus 24 minutes   - Barrage arrives on blue line.
"H" plus 28 minutes   - Barrage arrives at the line of 1st "Pause", where it remains until "H" plus 45 minutes.
"H" plus 45 minutes   - Barrage lifts and advance on 2nd objective commences.
"H" plus 69 minutes   - Barrage arrives on red line.
"H" plus 73 minutes   - Barrage arrives on line of 2nd "Pause", where it remains until "H" plus 90 minutes.
"H" plus 90 minutes   - Barrage lifts and advance of the 124th Infantry Brigade commences.
A proportion of smoke shell will be fired along the flanks of the attack to assist Infantry in maintaining direction.

Two rounds of Thermite shell will be fired at each line of the barrage, one round when the barrage first lifts and one round one minute later.

At the pauses of the barrage one round of Thermite shell will be fired to mark the pause, and one round per minute during the first 5 minutes of the pause.

Battalion Report Centre and R.A.P. will be notified later. It will not move until the final objective is reached.

GENERAL. On the night of the 12th/13th the Battalion will relieve the 11th "Queens" R.W.Surrey Regt in the line, and will hold the entire Brigade front as follows :-
"D", "B", and "A" Companies in the front line.
"C" Company in support.
On the night of the 13th/14th, the two front Companies "D" and "A" will be relieved by the 18th K.R.R.C. and Hampshire Regt respectively, and will side slip inwards and form up within the Battalion boundaries for attack. "C" Company will move from support and also form up. Special orders for this relief will be issued separately.

                    (sd)   G.L.Brown   Lieut. Col.,

                Comdg 12th Bn East Surrey Regt.

Issued at 18.30.
11th October 1918.

--------ooooooOoooooo--------

Distribution.   Copy No.1,   File.
                        2,   War Diary.
                        3,   Commanding Officer.
                        4,   2nd in command.
                        5,   Adjutant.
                        6,   Intelligence Officer.
                        7,   O.C. "A" Company.
                        8,   O.C. "B" Company.
                        9,   O.C. "C" Company.
                      10,   O.C. "D" Company.
                      11,   Medical Officer.
                      12,   Transport Officer.
                      13,   Transport Officer. Quartermaster
                      14,   122nd Infantry Brigade
                      15,   Bde R.F.A.
                      16,   Spare.

12th. BN. EAST SURREY REGT.
ADMINISTRATIVE INSTRUCTIONS IN CONNECTION WITH O.O. No.41.

1. Deatils will parade at present B.H.Qr's at 11.30 to-morrow after departure of Battalion and will be marched under Senior Officer to D.R.C. BRANDHOEK G.12.a & b where they will report to O.C. Brigade Details. 1 Cooker will accompany this party.

2. Transport :- "A" Echelon will be located about J.23.d.
   "B" Echelon will be located about HELL FIRE CORNER I.10.d.
   The above will march Brigaded to HELL FIRE CORNER to-morrow after which they will split up into respective echelons in accordance with Brigade Instructions issued to Lieut McKECHNIE who will pass them to Quartermaster for information.

3. Ammunition etc. has been issued to Companies as under:-
No.34 Egg Bomb	2 per man
No.36 R.G.	32 per Company.
No.31 R.G. Red Smoke	15 per Company
No.31 Blue Smoke	15 per Company
Ground Flare Red	2 per man
Very Lights	50 per Company
S.O.S.	3 per Coy, 8 to Battn H.Qr's
White Tape	1,000 yds to B.H.Qr's
Wire Cutters Large	4 per Coy, 3 to B.H.Qr's
Wire Cutters Small	10 per Coy, 5 to B.H.Qr's
Sandbags	2 per man

   Billhooks 12 per Compy

   S.A.A. and ammunition can be indented for in the usual way but it is most important that Company Dumps are formed to be made up from S.A.A. etc. taken from casualties and salved L.G. Magazines.

4. Rations, for 13th. inst will be delivered to Companies in bivouac area to-morrow. Rations for 14th. will be notified later
   at "H" hour every man must be in possession of 1 days complete ration and Iron Ration.

5. Water. Will be delivered in petrol tins with rations. Every effort will be made to return to Ration Dump all empty tins including any which can be salved. Water bottles must be kept filled from this date.

6. Soft S.D. Caps will not be taken forward but will be left in the pack.

7. Rear Orderly Room will be with "B" Echelon and will proceed with G.S. Waggons to-morrow morning under arrangement to be made by the Quartermaster.

8. Cookers. 3 cookers will proceed with the Transport and will rejoin the Battalion in the bivouac area where they will cook a hot meal for the Battalion; after which they will rejoin "B" Echelon.

11.10.18. (Sgd) D.WALKER Capt & A/Adjt,
12th. Bn. East Surrey Regt.

12th Bn East Surrey Regt.   SECRET

WARNING ORDER.

1. The Battalion will relieve the 23rd Middlesex Regiment in the Left Sub-Sector on the night of the 14th/15th inst.

2. Advance parties as under will parade at Brigade Headquarters (G.14.c.2.4) at 6.15 p.m. to-night ready to proceed to the line and live with opposite number until relief.
   - Battn. H.Q.   1 Officer, 1 N.C.O. & 2 Runners.
   - Each Company.   1 Officer, 5 N.C.O's.

   This party will proceed by transport from Brigade Headquarters and will report at Headquarters 23rd Middlesex Regiment N.4.b.3.3.

3. Advance parties will take over all Defence Schemes, Maps, Plans, Aeroplane photos, and Trench Stores, before relief.
   Rec-eipts for same to be at Battn. Hdqrs. by 6 p.m. 15th Septr, '18

4. On night of relief the Battalion will proceed to the line by train from ELLARSYDE Siding G.21.c. First train will probably leave about 6.15 p.m. Further details will be issued later.

5. Company Commanders & I.O. will attend Battn. Hdqrs. to-night at 8 p.m.

6. All mens packs will be stacked outside Company Headquarters by 7.30 a.m. to-morrow morning for collection by Transport Officer, who will arrange transport.

7. Dispositions in the line will be as follows :-
   - A Coy.   Right Front.
   - B Coy.   Left Front.
   - C Coy.   Right Support.
   - D Coy.   Left Support.

   Each Front Line Company will have three platoons in the front line and one platoon in close support.

(sd) A.C. EDGAR,
Lieut & A/Adjt,
12th Bn. East Surrey Regiment.

13th September, 1918.

Copies to:-
1. A Coy.
2. B Coy.
3. C Coy.
4. D Coy.
5. Quartermaster.
6. Transport Officer.
7. File.
8. H.Q. 122nd Infantry Brigade.
9. War Diary.

Operation Order 32

MAJOR G. O. SEARLE
Comdg 12th Bn. EAST SURREY REGT.

1. The Battalion will relieve the 23rd Bn. Middlesex Regiment in the Left Sub-Sector to-night 14th September, 1918.

2. Companies will move independently to arrive at ELLARSYDE SIDING G.21.d.2.7 by 5.45 p.m.
    The Battalion will then entrain to CAMBRIDGE SIDING N.2.b.9.5 where it will detrain and move off in the following order

    A Coy. B Coy. C Coy. D Coy. Headquarters.

    Companies will proceed to point N.10.b.2.6 where guides of the 23rd Bn Middlesex Regt, will meet them. They will maintain intervals of 200 yards between platoons. Headquarters will move to N.4.c.5.3 where guides will meet them.

3. Dispositions in the Line will be as follows:-

Coys.	Relieving Coys.
Right Front Coy "A"	"C" Coy. 23rd Middlesex Regt.
Left Front Coy "B"	"A" Coy. 23rd Middlesex Regt.
Counter-attack Coy "C"	"B" Coy. 23rd Middlesex Regt.
Support Coy "D"	"D" Coy. 10th R.W. Kent Regt.

4. Copies of Aerial photographs, maps, plans, defence schemes, and trench stores, will be taken over and receipts forwarded to Bn. H.Q. by 6 a.m. to-morrow, 15th Septr, 1918.

5. Completion of relief will be notified by using Company Comdrs. own name.

6. Rations for to-morrow will be carried on the man. Water bottles must be taken up full.
    The Transport Officer will arrange to dump 10 cans of Tea per Company at 9.30 p.m. at DEAD DOG FARM to be drawn under Company arrangements. "C" Coy will draw for "A" Coy.
    In future tea will be made in RIDGE WOOD near R.A.P. and Companies will send Hot Food Containers and sufficient petrol tins there to draw it. The Transport Officer will arrange to deliver tea and sugar for the Battalion in bulk to Battn. Hdqrs. daily on Battn. Hqrs. limber.

7. Lewis Guns and ammunition will be dumped under cover at ELLARSYDE SIDING between 2 p.m. and 3 p.m. to-day. O.C. D Coy will detail a guard.
    They will be collected by Companies on arrival at Siding.

8. Officers Valises and Mess Stores will be dumped outside Company and Battn. Hdqrs. by 4 p.m. to-day. The Transport Officer will arrange collection. Trench bundles will be carried by the Battalion.
    The Transport Officer will detail two limbers to be at Bn. Hdqrs. at 4.15 p.m. to collect Headquarter Stores and rations for to-morrow. These limbers will also take up water for Headquarters and seven gallons Rum.

9. Solidified Alchhol will be issued before moving and will be carried up on the man. Another limber will report to Battn. Hdqrs. at 4.15 p.m. to take Orderly Room stores etc. to Details.

10. Companies will arrange with C.Q.M.S's for dry socks to be brought up nightly, and for corresponding pairs to be sent down for washing and drying.

11. All Details under Capt. J.A. ROGERS, M.C. will report to Major W.P. BRISTOWE, M.C. 18th K.R.R.C. at G.20.a.4.5. by 6 p.m. to-day.
    Not more than four Officers per Company are to be taken into the line. Rolls of details to be at Battn. Orderly Room by 2 p.m.

12. Locations will be as follows:-

New Bn. H.Q.	N.4.b.3.3.
A Coy. H.Q.	N.12.b.80.95. approx.
B Coy. HQ	O.1.c.1.7. approx.
R.A.P.	N.5.a.3.6.

13. All ~~Company~~ Runner *a Relay* Posts will be established at D Coy's H.Q. BRASSERIE. Each Company will keep two runners *there*.

14. Each Company will take up into the line one cook and one bugler. The cook will live at Battn. Hdqrs.

15. ACKNOWLEDGE.

           (sd) A.C. EDGAR,
             Lieut & A/Adjt,
           12th Bn. East Surrey Regiment.

Issued at............
14th September, 1916.

Copies to:-

1. File.
2. War Diary.
3. O.C.
4. O.C. A Coy.
5. O.C. B Coy.
6. O.C. C Coy.
7. O.C. D Coy.
8. Quartermaster.
9. Transport Officer.
10. Intelligence Officer.
11. H.Q. 122nd Infantry Brigade.
12. R.S.M.

VERY URGENT.   ①   Tel/d   SECRET

The 34th Divn. is going to advance tonight to try & establish a line along FRENCH TRENCH North-eastward to SPOIL-BANK.

The division wants us to try & push forward & establish posts at O.7.a 85.80, O.7.B 10.95, O.1.D 35.20, & O.1.D 50.65.

The only enemy post it is thought will be in the way is one supposed to be at O.1.D 1.4.

Zero hour for 34th Divn will be 10.25 pm & whether artillery will be required or not is not at present known.

— You will therefore push out strong fighting patrols to occupy & consolidate posts as near as possible given above.

(2)

I suggest that you push out a fighting patrol of 1 officer + 12 O.R. to seize + establish post at O.1.D.32.20 ~~O.1.D.50.65~~. + that you should push out two small patrols of 1 officer or 1 NCO + 6 men to establish posts at O.7.a.85.80 + O.7.B.10.95. + that your left hand post could advance the short way to O.1.D.50.65 + establish a post nearer the road. If strong opposition is met with this operation is not to be carried on with, but if the supposed post at O.1.D.1.4 can be taken + a prisoner captured it will be very expedient to do so to save our having to make another raid to secure a prisoner.

If a post at O.7.B.10.95 cannot be conveniently established, the ones at O.7.a.85.80 + O.1.D.35.20

(3)

will suffice if they are mutually
supporting.

The remainder of the details I must
leave to you as you are on the
spot, but you must bear in mind
that your company line is part of
the line which must be held.

It is suggested that you should push
out to these posts before 10.28 pm
if you can arrange in time.

I will arrange for D Coy to bring
up your rations.

If you manage it all right send code
'BEER' if your line remains
where it is now send 'WHISKY'
Full report to follow by runner.

Copy No. 5

23rd Middlesex (Operation) Order No. 23.
Ref. WYTSCHAETE 1/10000 Sheet 28.

(1) **INTENTION.** The Battalion less D Coy. plus D Coy Kents. will be relieved tomorrow night 14/15 by the 12th E. Surrey Regt. On relief Battalion will move back by platoons at 100 yds distance to area G.36.a. Coys. will occupy the same billets (approx) as when last in this area.

(2) **DETAILS.** A Coy. MIDDX. will be relieved by B" E. SURREY'S
　　B　　"　　"　　"　　"　　"　　"C"　"　"
　　C　　"　　"　　"　　"　　"　　"A"　"　"
　　D　　" 10th R.W.Fus　"　　"　　"　D　"　"

(3) **ADVANCE PARTY**
(a) The Quartermaster will arrange to take over new positions from 20th R.F. and to supply 5 guides per Coy. & 1 for Bn. Hqrs. to be G.31.b.0.5. at 11.30 P.M. 14th.
(b) E. Surrey advance party will report to O.C. Coys. this evening.

(4) **REAR PARTY.** 1 Officer per Coy. & 1 N.C.O per platoon will be left behind in the line until daylight 15th.

(5) GUIDES. 2 Guides for Bn. Hqrs.
1 Guide per Coy Hqrs. + 1 guide for platoon will meet E. Surrey Regt on the Road at N.10.b.1.9 at 8:30 PM
They will report at Bn. HQ before dawn the 14th

(6) TRANSPORT. 2 Limbers will report to B.Hq. at usual place at 7 PM
1 Limber per Coy. will be at N.10.b.1.9. at 10.30 PM for L. Guns etc.
Empty Petrol Cans and food Boxes will be collected from Coy Hq. and placed on limbers by transplanters.

(7) RATIONS & } will be drawn in
    WATER   } new area

(8) STORES. All defence schemes, work under construction, trench stores will be handed over, receipts obtained + copy sent to this office by 8 PM 15th inst.

10/XII/   12th East Surrey Regt.
                OPERATION ORDER NO.

            Ref Maps 28SW 2 1/10000
               "   27 x 28   1/20000

1   The 12th East Surreys will be relieved
    by 8th Scottish Rifles in support
    positions on night 21/22 Sept.

2   Advance parties of 8th Scottish Rifles
    will report to Coys tonight

3   The following rear parties will be left
    in the line after relief for 24 hrs
        1 Officer   for Batt HQ
        1 Officer   per Coy
        1 NCO   per platoon

4   Coys will arrange guides for the
    relieving Units 1 per platoon & 1 per
    Coy HQ to be at KRRC present HQ
    N 10 B 2.8 at 9.0 pm 21st inst

5   Defence Schemes Plans Aerial photos
    & all trench stores, including petrol tins
    and solidified alcohol, will be
    handed over
        Receipts in duplicate will be forwarded

Batt HQ by 6pm 22nd inst

all Tprt Stores at transport lines
will be handed over & receipt sent to
Batt HQ with the following exceptions
1. Water carriers
2. Pack Saddlery
3. Sgts Cook Gal
4. Tents which will be handed to
DADOS & receipt obtained

7. On relief Coy will march by
platoons at 200yds interval to a
point about 28/G35 B 28 on OUDERDOM
– ZEVECOTEN Road via HALLEBAST
CORNER & OUDERDOM.
At this point they will embus to
new location I/L 21.0.C. (LYNN HOUSE)
NAVAL FARM — huts between road
& railway.
Lorries will be ready at embussing
point at 11.30pm & each lorry proceed
as soon as loaded — Each lorry
will carry 25 men.

8. Coy will dump Lewis Gun
Magazines, Mess Tins & Trench Rounds
at H4 c 53 (where fatigue party from
Batt HQ will meet Head)

as they march out

Each Coy will post a guard to see
these stores are properly loaded
TO will arrange limbers for these
Stores at 10 pm

9. Capt D WALKER. MC will arrange for
Billetting parties to report to Area
Commandant ABEELE Area at
CARSO FARM. 27/L31d.0.5 at 2.15 pm
26 inst
    He will arrange guides to meet
Coys at a suitable point in main
road running through L 21 c

10. TO will arrange to deliver rations
at new locations tomorrow night

11. Lorries will report at HENGIST
CROSS 28/G 27 d. 30. 61 at 8 am 26th inst
to move surplus stores from
Transport Lines to new position

12. In case of stores handed over
at Transport Lines if not taken over
before Transport moves the Quarter-
Master will be responsible that an
NCO remains behind and obtains
receipts

13. Coy will report completion of Relief by Runner to Bn HQ on passing.

14. Acknowledge

1-4   Copies A B C D Coys
5-6   TO & QM
 7   Details
 8   Brigade
 9   War Diary
10   File

20/9/18

Ajayi PAWU   Lieut

Ref. 12th East Surrey Regt
Sheet 29   Operation Order No   22-10-18

(1) 123 Inf Brigade will continue the advance
tomorrow to the final objective as laid down
in yesterdays Oper orders line of BOSSUYT —
AVELGHEM Road within the Brigade Boundary

(2) 29th Div will be on left, 124 Brigade on Right

(3) Brigade will attack as follows
    12th Surreys Right Front
    15 Hants   left   "
    18 KRRC.   Support

(4) Inter-Battalion Boundary will be a line drawn
through O.17.c.0.4 to V.8.6.0.4
Brigade Boundary same as yesterday

(5) Battalion will form up at 05.30 as follows
    B. Coy Right Front from O.22.b.9.3 to O.16.d.5.0
    A "   Left   "   " O.16.d.5.0 to O.16.d.9.4
    D "   Right Support
    C "   Left   "
Dividing Point between Coys O.16.d.5.0

(5) same formation as for yesterday

(6) True Bearing of attack 124° taken from left of A Coy which will direct

(7) There will be an intermediate objective on line O.30.c.1.3 to p.19 central where barrage will halt for 20 minutes. On reaching this line the two rear Coys will leap frog A & B Coys & the four Coys will continue to final objective. There will be no barrage after intermediate objective

) Zero Hour will be 09-00 at which hour the advance will commence

) On reaching final objective D Coy will send forward one platoon to seize Bridge Head at V.10.c.1.5

( ) Artillery
09.00 barrage opens on line O.23.c.8.4 to O.18c.4.6 when infantry will close up under it

DIARY OF OPERATIONS, 21st. & 22nd. October, 1918.

At 03.00 on the 21st. October, the Battalion moved from billets in COURTRAI and took up a position in artillery formation along the line O.7.d.31 - O.13.a.5.4. Battalion Headquarters was situated at N.12.d.8.2.

The advance was commenced at 07.15. and little opposition was met until the line O.21.b - d. was reached. After sharp fighting the enemy retired behind a strong belt of wire covering the tunnel in O.22.d. Here the Battalion was forced to halt by very heavy machine gun fire.

At 03.00 on the 22nd. orders were received to form up on the eastern bank of the CAMBRAI - BOSSUYT CANAL, in preparation for an attack at 09.00.

A, B, & D Companies crossed the canal at 04.00 and C. Company followed later, having suffered casualties in a previous attempt.

In spite of every effort the attack was halted by very heavy machine gun fire.

At 16.30 another attack was launched and an advance of 400 yards was achieved. The Battalion remained in this position until 23.45 when it was relieved by the 23rd. Middlesex Regt. 123rd. Brigade.

---oOo---

DIARY OF OPERATIONS, 26th. October 1918.

The Battalion moved from billets in O.16.d. at 07.00 and marched to the concentration area in P.31. b & d. Battalion Headquarters being at P.31.a.5.6. At 09.00 orders were received to send out fighting patrols into AVELGHEM and get touch with the enemy.

The village was reported clear of the enemy at 11.40 by signal. The damaged bridgehead was seized and a post established at P.34.a.3.7.

Fighting patrols were sent out to the villages of WAFFLESTRAAT and RUGGE and an enemy patrol was met and dispersed. Posts were established on the road at P.34.a.9.7. and P.34.a.8.4. and in WAFFLESTRAAT and RUGGE.

The village of AVELGHEM was shelled during the day and more heavily during the night

SECRET.

12th East Surrey Regt.
15th Hampshire Regt.
18th King's Royal Rifle Corps.
122nd Trench Mortar Battery (For information).

B.M. 396.
(27/-)

1. S. A. A. can be delivered by aeroplane:
    (a) according to previous arrangement at selected points.
    (b) to H.Q. of companies in the front line who find thems[elves]
        short of S. A. A. and in a situation where they cannot
        get it up.

2. In the case of a previously arranged dropping point, the letter V will be put out at the point selected and the amount of S. A. A. previously agreed on will be dropped there.   This is by far the most satisfactory method.

3. In the case of ammunition being required in a place not previously arranged, the letter V will be put out and will be reported by the contact machine to the O.C. No.10 Squadron R.A.F., who will arrange to drop 6 boxes at the place marked.
    It will take at least 2 hours after the V is seen before ammunition can be delivered, if previous arrangement has not been made.
    One aeroplane can deliver 2 boxes only at a time, so that the length of time before the delivery of the 6 boxes has been completed depends on the number of planes available.
    Each journey will take about 1 hour.

4. Two strips about a foot wide and 6 feet long will be issued for each company headquarters to make the V Signal in question.
    These strips can also be used to indicate position to contact patrols, but in that case must not be laid out in V shape.

5. As absolute accuracy in dropping is impossible, a place at least 200 yards behind the line should be selected.   Dead ground for putting out the V is necessary so that the S. A. A. can be recovered when dropped.
    It is absolutely essential that the parachutes should be returned to the squadron at once.

24th September 1918.

Captain,
A/Brigade Major,
122nd Infantry Brigade.

OPERATION ORDER No.
by
LIEUT.COL.G.L.BROWN,D.S.O.
Comdg 12th Bn EAST SURREY REGIMENT.

25th September,1918.

Ref.Map Sheet 27. 1/40.000.

A Brigade exercise will be carried out to-morrow, 26th September, 1918, with a view to training in the following points.

(a) Operating on a wide front, and enveloping tactics, and maintenance of direction.
(b) Fire and movement.
(c) Action of Scouts and Patrols.
(d) Action of Lewis Gunners in forming "Offensive Points" and bringing enfilade fire to bear on strong points etc.
(e) Map reading and use of compass.
(f) Message writing and situation reports.
(g) Use of, and movement of, reserve Companies and Battalions.
(h) Exploitation of success.
(i) Communications.
(j) Supply and Medical Arrangements.
(k) Collection of ammunition etc., from casualties.
(l) Practice for Battalion and Company Commanders in forming "Local" defensive flanks from troops in rear, thereby not losing momentum for the general advance.
(m) Use of prisoners of war for examining dugouts etc.

1. General Idea. At 6 a.m. the Nth Corps attacked, and established the general line Hill 140, R.15.a. - Aerodrome L.31.c, along the ABEELE - STEENVOORDE ROAD to point K.33.d.6.3.- thence along the Western edge of BOIS de BEAUVOORDE, to K.33.a.
   Little resistance was met, and our Reserve Brigade was pushed on to MONT DES CATS, R.20.c., which was reported captured at 9.30 a.m.
   It was decided by the Higher Command to exploit the success.

2. Special Idea. The 122nd Infantry Brigade is ordered to concentrate in area R.7.c. and continue the advance, covered by an advance, and a Right Flank, guard, and establish the line THIEUSHOUK Q.35.b., to COTTA CROSSING Q.22.c.7.1., and establish touch with troops of the "Y" Corps (who are advancing through STEENVOORDE), in Square Q.22.c.

3. The 122nd Infantry Brigade Group, consisting of the following :-
   12th E. Surrey Regt.
   15th Hampshire Regt.
   18th K.R.R. Corps.
   122nd T.M. Battery.
   "B" Coy, 41st Bn. M.G.C.
   Light Echelon, 138 Field Ambulance,
will concentrate in area R.7.c., in accordance with attached March table; concentration to be completed by 9.30 a.m. Brigade H.Q. will be established in huts at Cross Roads R.1.d.0.0.

4. The 18th K.R.R.Corps will attack on the right,
   The 12th E.Surrey Regt. will attack on the left.
   The 15th Hampshire Regt. will be in Brigade Reserve, and will detail an Officer to report at Brigade Headquarters for Liaison duty.

5. There will be no troops operating on either immediate flank, during the advance.

6. Boundaries. Inter-Battalion boundary on the objective is Culvert at Q.28.d.8.3.

No. 2.

7. __Zero Hour__. For the general advance to commence will be 10 a.m. 26th inst.

8. __True bearing of the attack__, is 230°.

9. __Directing Flank__. The Right Flank of the Right Battalion will be the Directing Flank.

---

1. The Battalion will parade on the Main Road in Fighting Order to-morrow, 26th September, 191 , at 7.30 a.m. in the following order :-

    Headquarters.
    A Company.
    B Company.
    C Company.
    D Company.

    head of column to be at house on right of road L.26.c.3.0 facing S.W.
    Route:- L.31.c.6.5, R.1.b.8.2. R.1.d.0.0 to R.7.b.central.
    The Battalion will form up in artillery formation of platoons 50 yards interval, 50 yards distance, at R.7.c.5.3.

    Left Front "A" Coy.   Right Front "B" Coy.
    Left Support "C" Coy.   Right Support "D" Coy.

    One platoon each from C and D Companies will be held as Battalion Reserve under 2nd Lt.SKELLET, D Coy., and will form up with Battalion Headquarters in rear of the Battalion.

2. __Exercise__. The Battalion will advance at 9.30 a.m. on a two Company frontage, A and B in Front line, C and D in Support.
    The advance of each Company will be covered by scouts supported by one platoon.
    The remainder of the Battalion will advance in artillery formation of sections until forced to deploy by enemy opposition.
    The first objective will be the Blue Line from Q.30.d.0.7 to Q.23.d.8.0. This objective will be taken and consolidated by "A" and "B" Coys, and will be the limit of their advance.
    When the Blue Line is taken C and D Companies will pass through and will advance against the final objective (Red Line) which is as follows :- The village of THIEUSHOUK inclusive, Q.35.b. along the line of the road to Q.28.d.7.4., where touch will be maintained with the 18th K.R.R.Corps.
    This objective will be consolidated in depth.
    C and D Companies during the advance will be covered by their own Scouts supported by rifle and Lewis Gun sections, as for A and B Coys in the first phase.

3. __LIAISON__. O.C. A and B Coys will each detail one section under an Officer to be permanently responsible for watching the outer flanks of the Battalion throughout the whole operation, and keep in touch with other troops.

4. __Machine Guns__. When the final objective is reached the village of THIEUSHOUK will be covered by Vickers Machine Guns.

5. __Stokes Mortars__. One Stokes Mortar will be with Battn.Hdqrs. and will be sent up to Companies if required.

6. __Aeroplane Co-operation__. A Contact Aeroplane will call for tin discs. These will be flashed by the most forward troops of both Companies.
    Battn.Hdqrs. will call for ammunition by displaying a White

7. __Light Signals__. 3 White Very Lights will be the signal "objective reached", which will be fired when the Blue and Red lines are reached by the respective Coy.Commanders.

3.

8. **Communications.** Message carrying rockets will be used to send messages from the Final Objective back to Battalion Headquarters. These will be carried by C and D Companies.

9. **Action of Artillery.** There will be no creeping barrage, but the Artillery will be bombarding the following suspected strong points at the times stated:-

Buildings	Q.18.a.7.2.	10.0 a.m. to 10.10 a.m.
Cottages	Q.18.d.7.0	10 a.m. to 10.10 a.m.
CANTA CORNER	R.19.a.4.2.	10.0 a.m. to 10.10 a.m.
Level Crossing	Q.23.b.6.3.	10.10 a.m. to 10.30 a.m.
KRUYSTRAETE	Q.24.a.1.3.	10.10 a.m. to 10.30 a.m.
Trenches	Q.24.c.9.5.	10.10 a.m. to 10.30 a.m.
Trenches	Q.24.d.8.9.	10.10 a.m. to 10.12 a.m.
HILL 85.	Q.30.b.	10.10 a.m. to 10.30 a.m.
Railway	Q.23.c.2.9.	10.30 a.m. to 11.15 a.m.
Copse	Q.29.a.8.4.	10.30 a.m. to 11.15 a.m.
CLAIM FARM	Q.30.c.0.5.	10.30 a.m. to 11.15 a.m.
Final Objective	-	11.15 a.m. to 11.30 a.m.

    After which it will form a protective barrage 500 yards in front of the final objective from 11.30 a.m. to 12 noon.
    The H.A. will be engaged on distant targets, approaches, and counter battery work.

10. **Headquarters.** Battalion Headquarters on commencement of the operations will form at Fork Roads R.14.c.0.9. It will remain there until Blue Line is captured when it will move forward and re-open at Q.30.c.7.9.

11. **Skeleton Enemy.** O.C. D Coy will detail one Officer, 1 N.C.O. and 9 O.Rs to report to 2nd Lieut. LLOYD, M.C. at Cross Roads, ABEELE, L.26.c. at 8 a.m.

ADMINISTRATIVE INSTRUCTIONS.

1. **TRANSPORT.** Transport will be Brigaded in two Echelons, "A" Echelon under Capt. J.A.MOWAT, M.C. 15th Hampshire Regt., 2nd Lieut. E.J.P.ORRETT, 18th K.R.R.Corps, and "B" Echelon under Lieut. R.McKECHNIE, 12th East Surrey Regt.
    (a) "A" Echelon will concentrate by 9.30 a.m. in field at R.1.d.25.25 and will be composed of Pack Animals as under:-
    6 animals loaded with S.A.A. per Battn.
    2   "   "   "   R.G's.   "   "
    1   "   "   "   Very Lights per Battn.
    1   "   "   "   Tools   "   "
    2 spare Pack Animals from Brigade Hdqrs.
    4 Lewis Gun Limbers per Battn. And
    1 Limber of Brigade Signal Section will join A Echelon when concentration has taken place.
    (b) B Echelon will be located in ABEELE.
    (c) 2 Orderlies from B Echelon will accompany Capt. MOWAT, one of whom will return when position of A Echelon is located.
    (d) 2 Orderlies from A Echelon one of whom will return will report to Brigade Hdqrs. at 9.30 a.m.

2. **AMMUNITION.** Replenishment of ammunition will be made :-
    (a) From casualties.   (b) From any dumps in forward area.
    (c) From A Echelon, by indent on Bn.H.Q.
    To replace any ammunition sent forward A Echelon will demand from S.A.A. Section.

3. **SUPPLIES.** These will be delivered to A Echelon by limber and taken forward by Pack animal.

4. **WATER.** All water bottles will be filled, supplies thereafter will only be obtained from water brought up by rations.

No. 4.

5. **MEDICAL.** Aid Post will be at Bn.H.Q. and Field Ambulance near Brigade Headquarters.

6. **R.E.MATERIAL.** Enemy material will be used as far as possible; otherwise it will be obtained on indent through Bn.H.Q.

GENERAL. The signal for the recall will be the note "G", upon which Officers and senior N.C.Os will assemble at GADGET CROSSING, Q.23.b.5.9. (which will be about 1 p.m.), and troops will march home independently under their junior N.C.Os.

At 10.30 a.m. it will be assumed that an aeroplane has dropped a red parachute flare on the left flank about Square Q.31.

NOTE. The Blue Line is from point Q.30.d.6.4 through point Q.30.c.5.9 to Railway at ΣxΝΩ Q.23.a.8.3. The Red Line is from THIEUSHOOK Q.35.b., inclusive, along road to Q.28.b.3.2 to Q.2 COTTA CROSSING at Q.22.c.7.1. from which point patrols will be sent to find touch with the Corps on flank.

(sd) D.WALKER,
Capt & A/Adjt,
12th Bn East Surrey Regiment.

Operation Order

1. The Battn will attack this afternoon in conjunction with 18th KRRC on left and 15th Hants on right.
2. Intention To capture the village of AVELGHEM
3. Objective To establish and consolidate general line from P.34.a.8.9 — P.34.c.8.8 — P.34.c.7.3.
4. Forming up line from P.32.b.5.9 to P.32.d.5.3. Inter Coy Boundary line drawn from P.32.b.5.1 to P.34.b.0.1
5. The Battn will concentrate at P.31.b.d Concentration to be complete by 08.30
6. Battn will attack on a two Coy front.
7. Zero hour will be 14.00 today 26th inst.
8. True bearing of attack 90°.
9. The Bn will be directing flank, smoke will be used, compass parties will be necessary.
10. Mopping up must be thoroughly done by the two rear Coys of the Battn.
11. Barrage Barrage will come down

at H-10mins (13.50) on a start line
V.2.d.5.5 to P.26.b.5.5. At 14.00
it will lift and advance at the rate
of 100 yds every 2 mins, there will be
3 pauses at 400 yds, 800 yds, 1200 yds
respectively. The first and second
pauses will be each of 7 mins, the 3rd
pause 10 mins. The Barrage will cease
at 15.00, there will be certain
artillery fire on ~~other~~ selected
targets commencing at 13.25. but
the real barrage will not come
down until 13.50.

12 Smoke and thermite will be used

13 Stokes Mortar. 1 gun will be
attached to the Bn in concentration
area.

14 Vickers Gun. 2 Section are at the
disposal of the Battn.

15 Synchronisation. watches will
be synchronised before Zero.

16 Boundaries as follows:- P.32.b.5.9.
"Left" P.32.d.5.3 "Right" Inter Coy
Boundary P.32.b.5.1.

17. Time Table of attack:-
    13.45. Battn will move forward in Artillery formation.
  - 13.50. Battn will reach general line P.32 a 5.9. P.32 c 5.3.
    13.50 - 14.00. Battn will close up under the barrage
    14.00. First lift of Barrage and Inf advance begins
    14.06. Barrage arrives in first pause
    14.13   "   lifts.
    14.19   "   arrives in 2nd pause.
    14.26   "   lifts.
    14.32   "   arrives at 3rd pause
    14.42   "   lifts.
    15.00   "   ceases.
18. Front line is reported to be as follows.
    V.2 c 7.5, V.8 b 3.7, V.2 c 6.1, V.2 a 4.1,
    P.32 d 0.3, P.26 b 0.3, P.13 central
    P.8 central.
    1/23 and 1/24 Inf Bns, will push forward patrols to
19. Battn HQ will be at P.31 d 0.8
20. Disposition of Coy will be as follows
        C Left Front   A Left Support
        D Right Front   B Right "

March Table
21. The Batt. will march from this area in the following order
C. D. A. B. Coy. HQ
at intervals of 100 yds between Coy. Starting Points "now as" at O.23.a.0.8 where Coy with the exception of C Coy will be ready to move off at 06.55. C. Coy will at O.23.a.6.8 by 07.00

22. Routes O.23.a.7.6 — O.30.e.14 — O.36.a.94 — P.31.a.7.5.
A — C Coy by road to P.31.b.6.8
B — D Coy by road to P.31.d.7.3

23. Companies will be responsible for their own protection.

24. C Coy will provide Advance Guard for the Batt.

Operation Order by
Lt Col G L Brown DSO C/O 1 Advance Guard.

1. The 41st Div will advance on MENIN preceded by an Advance Guard of 1st East Surreys At

2. Van Guard will be composed of A & B Coys under CAPT ROGERS MC. 2 Plats B Coy under Lt. EDGAR will form point & screen of scouts 800 yds broad with centre on road of advance. 2 Lt Lloyd & RODD will accompany the scouts also Observers. The scouts will pass Starting point at 5.15 am At ½ mile distances the remaining 2 Plat B Coy and 1 sec MGC Followed at 200 yds distance by A Coy

3. At ½ mile distance from Van Guard HQ MAIN GUARD composed of C & D Coys with 200 yds distance between Coys accompanied by 1 sec FA also Div Cavalry & pyhts which will be operating on Flanks.

4. MAIN BODY follows at ¾ mile distance.

5. Route Starting Point CROSSROADS TENBRIELEN 28/P17 a 0595 thence to P12 c09 - P12 c97 CROSSROADS P12 a80 - Q7 685 - Q7 688 - Q1 d 61 - Q1 d 7.4 - Q2 c 15 - Q2 d 4.9 - Q3 d 0.4 - Q4 c 1.9 - GHELEWE

6. Dawn will be stand aired from rear to front.

7. Fire signallers will accompany Van Guard. Flap will not be used.

8. Halts. Usual hourly halts will be observed.

9. Messages must be sent to report centre at head of MAINGAURD at least every half hour.

10. Officers Dress. Officers will as far as pos' be attired like the men. Sticks will not be taken into action.

11. General Idea 41st Div continues the advance with 29th Div on left & 35th Div on right. The ultimate note of the Div is to hold the line of RIVER LYS from MENIN on the extreme E to WEVELGHEM exclusive on left.

12. All units will be responsible for their own protection.

13. The above is in continuation of verbal orders issued to Coy Cmdrs.

R. Russell
Major
12 E. Surr.

O.C. Coy.

(1) The Battalion will be reorganised in depth on the Red Line at once within the Battalion Boundaries.

(2) Frontages will be as follows

Left Front. C. Coy. from L.32.a.9.3.
  to L.34.c.4.9.
Right Front. D Coy. from L.34.c.4.9.
  to L.31.D.9.7.
Left Support. A. Coy. from L.31.b.7.4
  to MURATTI FARM (Exclusive)
  L.34.B.4.0.
Right Support. B. Coy. MURATTI
  FARM (Inclusive) L.34.B.4.0.
  to L.31.9.7.

(3) The B⁺⁰ is at present mostly in the Hants area and the G.O.C. wishes this corrected.

(4) Touch must be gained with 15th Hants on left and 18 KRRC

on right. There is at present a
gap of 400 yards between our
Right and KRRC.

(5). Companies must be reorganised
into platoons as soon as possible
and one party from each Coy
Isn't along the line of 15th Hants
and 18th KRRC to collect stragglers.

(6) 124 I.B. Have proposed till
and hold Brown line.

(7). Report compliance and give dispositions
as soon as possible.

(8) Acknowledge. By Bearer.

14/10/18.
16.35

~~Secret~~ Operation Orders
12th East Surrey Regt.

(1) The Bn will be relieved tonight by the 17th Royal Scots. Regt. as follows:
D Coy by 2 platoons of W. Coy
C " " 2 " " W. " one of which will hold forward post in WAFFELSTRAAT. The other platoon will occupy a front line from P.34.a.8.2. to P.34.a.9.8.
A Coy by 2 platoons of Y. Coy
B " " 2 " " Y. "
The two platoons of A attached to C will consider themselves relieved with C Coy.

2. On relief Coy will march independently to junction of roads N.18.d.5.2. where guides will meet them and lead them to their respective billets.

3. Route P.31.a.5.5. — O.36.a.3.7 — O.23.c.23 — O.28.a.4.4. — O.21.a.6.7 — O.20.6.20. — O.13. central to N.18.d.5.1.

4. Companies will report relief complete by runner.

5. M.G.C. One section A Coy M.G.C. and one section B Coy M.G.C. both now in line will move out with B Battalion without waiting relief. They will march independently to rest area at N.18.d.5.2. where they will meet guides from their own Units.

6. Lewis Guns. 2 limbers are waiting at Bn HQ. Lewis Guns will be loaded as Coys pass. Coy will not wait but will leave two gunners in charge. Limbers will follow last Coy to N.18.d.5.1.

7. All wounded will to be brought in before relief.

8. Acknowledge by bearer.

Issued at
26-10-18

McB Kurtih
2Lt A/Adjt
T/Acton

OPERATION ORDER No. 36
by
Lieut. Col. G.L. Brown D.S.O.
Comdg 12th Bn East Surrey Regiment.
27th Septr 1918.

1. In continuation of preliminary instructions issued verbally, the Battalion will parade as under and will march to the HOOGRAAF area, starting point opposite 18th Hants Regt H.Q.

   Headquarters to pass starting point at 7.15 p.m.
   "A" Company   "   "   "   "   "   7.18 p.m.
   "B"   "   "   "   "   "   "   7.21 p.m.
   "C"   "   "   "   "   "   "   7.24 p.m.
   "D"   "   "   "   "   "   "   7.27 p.m.

   Transport will join the Battalion on the road.
   200 yards distance will be maintained between Companies. 200 yards distance will be maintained between the Battn and Transport; also 20 yards between each 6 vehicles of transport.
   Dress.   Fighting Order.

2. RATIONS.   Rations which have been issued to Companies today will be carried on the man.

3. Lewis Gun Limbers will report to Companies at 6 p.m. today. They will be loaded and will proceed with their Companies.

4. COOKERS   Cookers will proceed with the Battn to the new area.

5. ACCOMMODATION. The Battn will be accommodated in the new area G.26.c., with Headquarters in PLEASURE COPSE G.26.d.6.3.

6. BILLETING PARTIES. Billeting parties will meet Companies at HOOGRAAF Cabt on the march.

7. PACKS AND BLANKETS. The Packs and Blankets have been collected and will be dumped under a Guard at the Divisional Reception Camp.
   Officers Kits and Mess Baskets etc will be stacked outside Company Billets by 6.30 p.m. The Transport Officer will arrange to collect these.

8. AMMUNITION.   Ammunition on the scale as laid down has been issued to Companies with the following exception :-
   Very Lights. The establishment will be 120 per Company.

9. L.G.MAGAZINES.   16 Lewis Gun Magazines will be taken into action. The remainder will be left under company arrangements at "B" Echelon which will remain at HOOGRAAF.

10. WATER.   Companies are reminded that Water Bottles must be kept filled. In addition, each Company will be issued when in the new area with 1 Petrol Tin per section, which will be filled and taken into action. There will be difficulties experienced in returning Petrol Tins, but Companies must understand that unless Petrol Tins are returned, it is impossible to keep up the supply.

11. DETAILS.   Details will be accommodated at the Divl Reception Camp and will parade under Company Officers who will report to Major Searle at 7.30 p.m.

12. STRENGTH.   Companies will render to Battn H.Q. by 8 p.m. a Trench Strength return.

   The Battalion must move absolutely mobile.

   (sd) D. Walker. Capt & A/Adjt.
   Issued at 5.30 p.m.   12th Bn East Surrey Regt.

SECRET

OPERATION ORDER No. ~~36~~ 37
by
Lieut. Col. G.L.Brown DSO.
Comdg 12th Bn East Surrey Regiment.

28th Septr 1918.

1. The Battalion will parade today 28th inst on the road, and march off in the following order passing the Starting Point as under :-

   Battalion Headqrs. 6.20 a.m.
   "A" Company 6.23 a.m.
   "B" Company 6.26 a.m.
   "C" Company 6.29 a.m.
   "D" Company 6.32 a.m.

   Starting Point 28/G.32.a.7.8. distances to be maintained will be as on the march from the ABEELE area.
   Route:- CONDIMENT CORNER - RENINGHELST - G.34.b.3.0 - G.29.b.5.6.

2. Lewis Gun limbers will accompany the Battalion. They will be unloaded on arrival and returned to B Echelon. Cookers will remain with B Echelon.

3. Soft Caps. No soft caps will be taken into action. These will be collected and placed in sand bags by sections and will be clearly marked and handed in to Quartermaster Stores by 5.30 a.m.

4. Advance Party. One N.C.O. per Company will report to 2nd Lt.RODD at Battn.Hdqrs. at 5.30 a.m. They will proceed on advance to the new area.
   While in the new area the Battalion will be prepared to move at a moments notice.

5. ACKNOWLEDGE.

(sd) D.WALKER,
Capt & A/Adjt,
12th Bn East Surrey Regt.

Issued at 0001.

VERY SECRET.

1. The hour "H" is 5.30 a.m.
   The day "J" is September Twenty-eighth.

2. During operations Battalions will report whenever there appears an opportunity for the employment of Cavalry.
   In order to avoid any misunderstanding all troops will be warned that French Cavalry may be operating.

3. The S.O.S. Signal remains the same GREEN OVER GREEN OVER RED.
   With reference to Very Light Signals i.e. "Hold up" "We are here" - these are now cancelled. No light signals will be used by the 41st Division.

4. ACKNOWLEDGE.

(sd) D.WALKER,
Capt & A/Adjt,
12th Bn East Surrey Regiment.

28th Septr,1918.

SECRET.   15th Batt Hampshire Regiment.   COPY NO. 2.
                 Operation Order No 145.
         Reference Map Sheet 20.   1/40,000.
         ++++++++++++++++++++++++++

1.   The 122nd Infantry Brigade will relieve the 106 Infantry Brigade
     35th Division on night Oct 31st/Novr 1st., between points
     M.9.a.00 and P.29.b.9.8. Inter Battalion Boundary is P,34 centr
2.   The 15th Batt Hampshire Regiment will relieve the 18th H.L.I.
     and 17th. Royal Scots in the right sub-sector of the front line.
     The 18th K.R.R.C. will be on the left.
3.   "A" Company will relieve left front Company.
          "B" Company will relieve right front Company.
          "C" Company will relieve left support Company.
          "D" Company will relieve right support Company.
     Arrangements re guides will be notified as soon as possible.
4.   The Battalion will parade in fighting order, jerkins to be worn,
     at 16.25 tail of column at N.24.c.5.6., and march to the line
     via. KAPELLE – HILEANE – KNOKKE – HOSKE.
     All water bottles will be filled.
     100 yards interval between Companies.
5.   Order of march, "A", "B", "C", "D" Companies, Headquarters.
     Details will report at present Battalion H.Q., at 17.10 where
     they will remain.
6.   Completion of relief to be notified by code, "Reference your L.20
     Nil."
7.   Location of Battalion H.Q., and R.A.P. will be forwarded as so
     as available.
8.   ACKNOWLEDGE.

     ISSUED at 11.30, 31st October 1918.

                              (Signed) G.F.I. SCHWERDT,
                                       Major,
                                       for Capt & Adjt.
                              15th Batt Hampshire Regt.

     Copies to :-No 1. Commanding Officer.
                  2. File.
                  3. O.C. 12th E. Surrey Regt.
                  4. O.C. 18th K.R.R.C.
                  5. O.C. "A" Company.
                  6. O.C. "B" Company.
                  7. O.C. "C" Company.
                  8. O.C. "D" Company.
                  9. Transport Officer.
                 10. War Diary.
                 11. Signalling Officer.
                 12. Medical Officer.
                 13. R.S.M.

12th East Surrey Regt.
122/41

Army Form C. 2118.

WAR DIARY
or
INTELLIGENCE SUMMARY.
(Erase heading not required.)

Instructions regarding War Diaries and Intelligence Summaries are contained in F. S. Regs., Part II. and the Staff Manual respectively. Title pages will be prepared in manuscript.

Place	Date	Hour	Summary of Events and Information	Remarks and references to Appendices
1.10.18	1.10.18	5 a.m.	The Battalion moved at 5 a.m. as Advance Guard for the Division in the direction of MENIN via GHELUWE. 1000 yards East of GHELUWE the Battalion was held up by a strong line of M.G. Posts. Attempts to advance only partially successful and the Battalion suffered casualties. Lt. Edgar and 2/Lt. Target, 2/Lt. James, Lt. Bell, 2/Lt. Topham, 2/Lt. Paviour were wounded.	C/17
	2.10.18	7 a.m.	At 7 a.m. the 15th Hants and 18th KRRC advanced through our lines and attacked the position. At 10 a.m. Capt. Rogers was detailed to mop up part of GHELUWE with his Company. A counter-attack on the Right flank of the Brigade front at 6.30 p.m. was repulsed.	C/17
	3.10.18		The Battalion was relieved during the early morning by the 11th Hertford Regt. and the 17th Cheshire Regt. of the 34th Division and moved to the area Sheet 28/J 34. The Battalion was attached to the 124th Brigade as Reserve but remained in same area.	C/17
	4.10.18	5 p.m.	The Battalion in reserve to 124th Brigade moved at 5 p.m. to area Sheet 28/K 21.C. The move being completed at 9 p.m. The Battalion area was heavily shelled during the night 4/5.18.	C/17
	5.10.18		Battalion in reserve to 124th Brigade remained in area K 21.C. during the days orders were received that the Battalion was again under 122 Brigade. The Adjutant – Capt. Drinkwater went forward to arrange for taking over the line from 26th R. Fusiliers. Casualties – 4 O.R's wounded. The casualty officers were 2/Lt. Savage, 2/Lt. Cockayne, 2/Lt. B.E.C. Walker. Total Strength 32 officers 792 OR. Ration Strength 23 officers 611 OR's.	C/17
	6.10.18	1 a.m.	At 1 a.m. a Warning Order was received for the Batt. to move to Res 27/L 29.6.2.7. At 1 p.m. the Batt. paraded and marched to YPRES where it entrained for L 27. 4. 2. 7. The Batt. was settled in billets at 8.15 p.m.	C/17
	7.10.18		The day was spent in cleaning up, kit inspection and re-organisation. The following officers joined Brev. Rect. E L Morley, 2/Lt. R Stephens, 2/Lt. R.C. Latham, 2/Lt. C.L. Smith.	30. C 5 sheets

Army Form C. 2118.

WAR DIARY
or
INTELLIGENCE SUMMARY.
(Erase heading not required.)

Instructions regarding War Diaries and Intelligence Summaries are contained in F. S. Regs., Part II. and the Staff Manual respectively. Title pages will be prepared in manuscript.

Place	Date	Hour	Summary of Events and Information	Remarks and references to Appendices
	8.10.18		Parades under Company arrangements. Lt. W.H. Robinson rejoined Batn.	appx
	9.10.18		The Batn. paraded for a tactical exercise under the C.O. practising the following of a creeping barrage and mopping up by cleaners specially detailed.	appx
	10.10.18		The Batn. paraded for a Brigade Tactical Scheme for practising an attack with a diagonal advance and moving under a creeping barrage.	appx
	11.10.18		The Battalion rested and prepared for moving into the line. The following Officers joined Batn:- Lieut J.H.A. Lauds, 2/Lieut F.G. REED, 2/Lieut W.D. BAYLIS, 2/Lieut K.E. BANCROFT.	appx
	12.10.18		The Batn. entrained at RENYSIDING (WIPPENHOEK) at 11.30 am, arriving at CLAPHAM JUNCTION at 3pm where it rested for Dinners. The Batn. then resumed the march to K.29.35 (Sh.28.N.E.) where they relieved the 11th Queens Regt. in the front line. Relief completed at 1.30 am. Strength: 43 Officers 795 O.R. Ration Strength 35 Officers 893 O.R's.	appx
	13.10.18		The Baen. of occupied shelling the day passed quietly. Casualties 1 Officer 30 O.R's.	appx
	14.10.18		The enemy carried out a counter preparation shoot at 4.15am which lasted for 45 minutes. At 2.30am the Batn. in conjunction with the Hants Regt on Left and 18th KRRC on Right formed up on a line extending from K.35.a.0.1.6. K.35.a.8.9 on a two Company front. At 5.32am our barrage opened and the Battalion pushed forward under it towards the Blue Line, which was reached at 7.45am. The advance was then continued to the Red Line. The two front companies reached the point at 8.30am, followed closely by the two support companies. The Batn. reached its objective at the time laid down, although an extremely dense fog prevailed throughout the advance and great difficulties experienced in keeping direction with their flanks. Our casualties were light although the line forward was held by numerous concealed MG posts and machine guns. Casualties 3 Officers and 50 O.R's (approx). Prisoners taken by the Batn. amounted to our 250 together with a large amount of machine guns and trench mortars. At 10am the 12th Bde passed through our lines and pushed forward to a distance of 1500 yards. All men of the Batn. fought splendidly and great credit was due to the Btn. Colonels NCOs who kept direction in spite of the Block fog which prevailed.	appx

WAR DIARY
or
INTELLIGENCE SUMMARY.
(Erase heading not required.)

Army Form C. 2118

Place	Date	Hour	Summary of Events and Information	Remarks and references to Appendices
	15.10.18.		The Battn. still in position extended in depth from L.31. & 32.(Sheet 28). Shelling practically Nil. General fire observed in MENIN. Enemy evacuating the town.	A/A
	16.10.18.		At 10.30am the Battn. moved up to MOORSEELE arriving at 11.45am. At 3.15pm resumed the march to BULLEGHEM where they went into billets to do 123rd Brigade being the front line around COURTRAI.	A/A
	17.10.18.		The Battn. still in support to the 123rd Brigade men received a Pack and a change of clothing. Village intermittently shelled during the day. Several enemy aeroplanes flew over by night dropping several bombs. The following Officers join Battn. 2nd Lt. POTTOCK. 2.Lt. T.C. HYDE. 2nd Lt. R.F. BROWNE.	A/A
	18.10.18.		The Battn. still in Support. Several Gas Shells fell in village during the evening causing several casualties. Situation normal.	A/A
	19.10.18.		Battalion moved to Area G.36.d. where Bivvies were allotted. The Battn. reached Hd. Qtrs. at 2.30pm on Map Sheet 28. Posn. Bttn. yd 22 approx. 792 on Ratan Extn. yd 22 approx. 526 on.	A/A
	20.10.18.		The Battn. moved to COURTRAI where they rested in billets during the day.	A/A
	21.10.18.		The Battn. moved to forming up Area in O.7a. and attacked at 0715. C&D Coys front line. A&B Support. A&C on Left. B&D on right. The attack reached a Line O.22.a.3.2. to O.22.c. Central. Battn. H.Q. at H.21.C.2.2. 9/Lt. E.H. SAVAGE Killed.	A/A
	22.10.18.		Orders were received for the Battn. to Cross the CAMBRAI-ESSUYT CANAL and prepare to attack at 0900. A B&D Coy crossed the Canal. C Coy was held up by M.G. fire. Captn. RYAN being killed. The Battn. was relieved at 23.59 by 23rd Middlesex and moved to Area O.9.a. and O.8.c.	? COURTRAI A/A

WAR DIARY
or
INTELLIGENCE SUMMARY.
(Erase heading not required.)

Army Form C. 2118.

Place	Date	Hour	Summary of Events and Information	Remarks and references to Appendices
	23.10.18		The Battn. moved from Area O.9.C. and O.8.B. to Area O.11.B and C. Battn in Divisional Reserve.	O/st
	24.10.18		The Battn. moved to Area O.3.a. Move completed at 6 p.m.	O/st
	25.10.18		The Battn. received orders at 1.30 to move to Area P.19.d. En route this was changed and Battn. halted in P.7.a. At 9.30 pm the Battn. moved to Area O.16.d.	O/st
	26.10.18		At 5am orders were received to concentrate in Area P.31. & d in readiness for an attack on AVELGHEM. The concentration area was reached at 0830. At 1000 patrols were sent into the village and reported that the enemy had evacuated. A patrol was then sent out to secure bridge head across ESSCHYT River. This was done and posts established. The village was heavily shelled during the night. Lieut. W.G. ROBINSON was wounded. Yest Steregt: 38 Officers 677 OR's. Rolds Strength 22 Officers 4930 Res. 35 & Devon Poley Complete The Battn. was relieved by the 15th Royal Scots.	O/R
	27.10.18		5am. On relief the Battn. moved to Area N.18.C N.17. & .d. The Battn. rested during the day. 2/Lt. SUMNERS. W.G. was wounded.	O/st
	28.10.18		The day was devoted to clearing up. 200 Companies 2H.Q. bathed.	O/st
	29.10.18		Training was carried out during the morning under Coy arrangements. The afternoon was devoted to Sports.	O/st
	30.10.18		Training was continued under Company arrangements.	O/st
	31.10.18		Church parade was held during the morning. At 4 p.m. the Battn. marched to WIERKEERHOEK Sheet 29/0.2.L. into Brigade Support. Total Casualties for month:- Killed 4 Officers 58 OR's. Wounded 10 Officers 257 OR's. Missing 19 OR's.	O/st

LT.-COL,
COMDg. 12th BATT. EAST SURREY REGT.

12th East Surrey Regiment

Army Form C. 2118.

WAR DIARY
or
INTELLIGENCE SUMMARY.
(Erase heading not required.)

Vol 31

Place	Date	Hour	Summary of Events and Information	Remarks and references to Appendices
	1.11.18		Battn in support in area sheet 29 P.19 & O.24. The line was reconnoitred by Coy comdrs. Orders were issued at 18:00 to move to area O.17 but these was cancelled at 22:10	108
	2.11.18		The day was quiet. Coys carried out musketry & L.G. training in billets.	
	3.11.18		Training was carried out under coy arrangements	
	4.11.18		Battn moved to area O.10. C.O & coy comdrs reconnoitred line of river Escaut in Q.10	
	5th		Battn moved to billets in HARLEBEKE	
	6th		Training under coy arrangements	
	7th		Battn bathed during morning. Training under coy arrangements	
	8th		Divine Service at 08:45. At 11:00 Battn practised crossing of river by foot bridge. Crossing was followed by an attack. At 15:00 all Battn assembled in area H.25.a ; A & B coys sent 40 men across river to foots. Remainder of Bn crossed by means of two foot bridges. Whole operation was carried out in the dark	
	9th		Bn moved from HARLEBEKE to area J.34 & d	
	10th		Bn continued move over R.17 crossing near ESCAUT at BERCHEM	
	11th		Signing of armistice was announced at 10:30; divine service held at 15:00	31.c 3sheets

12th East Surrey Regiment

WAR DIARY
or
INTELLIGENCE SUMMARY.
(Erase heading not required.)

Army Form C. 2118.

Instructions regarding War Diaries and Intelligence Summaries are contained in F. S. Regs., Part II. and the Staff Manual respectively. Title pages will be prepared in manuscript.

Place	Date	Hour	Summary of Events and Information	Remarks and references to Appendices
	12.11.18		A quiet day; sports & a concert were arranged	
	13th		Batt'n moved into area S2a LOUISE-MARIE	
	14th		Batt'n continued march at 11.26 and reached EVERBECQ at 17.30	
	15th		Training under Coy arrangements. H.Q drew with C coy in foot ball match 4-4.	
	16th		Short route march in morning. B coy beat D coy 4-1	
	17th		Divine Service at 10.30. Replay between H.Q & C coy ended in a win for H.Q 5-2. Two officers posted to 2nd Lt WALKERS and 2nd Lt WILKINS A.R. they were posted to B & A coys respectively	
	18th		Batt'n continued march and was billeted in BIEVIN	
	19th		Training under Coy arrangements. Semi-final inter coy competition – H.Q. v rear B coy 3-0	
	20th		Division was replaced by 9th Div and Batt'n moved back to EVERBECQ. Award of M.C. to Capt E & Lt J. RYAN (Rifles in action)	
	21st		Coy training & cleaning up.	
	22nd		C.O's inspection at 10.00	
	23rd		Short route march at 10.00. Final of inter coy competition H.Q. beat H coy 3-1. Following awards were announced. 2nd Bar to M.C. Capt J.H ROGERS M.C. Bar to M.C. 2nd Lt W.D. MUTCH	
	24th		Divine Service at 10 am on the parade ground	

12th East Surrey Regiment

Army Form C. 2118.

WAR DIARY
or
INTELLIGENCE SUMMARY.
(Erase heading not required.)

Place	Date	Hour	Summary of Events and Information	Remarks and references to Appendices
	25th		Training under coy arrangements. LT H.D. GOLD & LT A.W. ENGLAND joined Bn and were posted to D & B coys respectively	
	26th		MAJOR toA over command of Bn during absence of C.O. (on Brigade) SEARLE. Sports committee was appointed composed of : LT GOLD, LT BROWNE, 2nd LT SLEATH & 2nd LT ALDRIDGE	
	27th		Coy training & short route march. Concert given by B & D coys was held at 17.30	
	28th		Training under coy arrangements. Concert given by A & C coy at 17.30	
	29th		Coy training and inter platoon football	
	30th		MAJOR C.T. WILLIAMS rejoined battn and took over command. Football :- Probable beat possibles 11-0	

Graham L.
COMDG 12th BATT. EAST SURREY REGT.

Army Form C. 2118.

WAR DIARY
or
INTELLIGENCE SUMMARY.
(Erase heading not required.)

32.C

Place	Date	Hour	Summary of Events and Information	Remarks and references to Appendices
EVERBECQ	Dec 1		Battalion paraded for Divine Service. Officers thereafter were pictured in two groups with C. of E. & Major C.F. Williams reformed the Battalion. Northern Command G.H.Q.	
	2		Battalion paraded at 9.30 A.M. & proceeded on Battalion Route March out ending 12.30 P.M.	
	3		Railway warrants were issued under Company arrangement. Lieut. GEHEAD joined the Bn for duty this day.	
	4		Battalion was allowed Bath this day 1 P.M.	
	5		Training two continuous sides day arrangement 1 P.M.	
	6		Training carried out on Coy arrangement 1 P.M.	
	7		7/p C.O. inspected the Battalion. The Coy. A. Horry, P. Rt. arranged since on our Bn. 7/p Battalion Rout Route Party the 18 R.P.R.C. Sent down of Pt. Brigade Town annual training by 3 double 2 P.M.	
	8		7/p Battalion Paraded for Divine Service 10 A.M.	
	9		Training was carried out under Coy arrangement 10 A.M.	
	10		7/p Coy moved section to Bn Tactic Exerc 10. Training included Company & Coy man Drill. The Division is commanded following included Platoon Ribbons to 18 following NCO's was 712 Cpls Stewart 375166 C/pl. Lewis D.S.M. M.M. 36123 L/Cpl Brunlies S.E. M.M. 24260 A/c Gerge O.T. 23469 Cpl Bailey F.S.I. 25309 Pte. Delot W.M.M. W.M.M.	

Army Form C. 2118.

WAR DIARY
or
INTELLIGENCE SUMMARY.
(Erase heading not required.)

Instructions regarding War Diaries and Intelligence Summaries are contained in F. S. Regs., Part II. and the Staff Manual respectively. Title pages will be prepared in manuscript.

Place	Date	Hour	Summary of Events and Information	Remarks and references to Appendices
EVERBECQ	Dec 12		The Battalion continued the march towards the Frontier arriving at HERINNES where they billeted for the night. WDh	
HERINNES	13		Battalion continued march to BIERGES WDh	
BIERGES	14		March continued to WANTHIER – BRAINE WDh	
WANTHIER – BRAINE	15		Battalion rested throughout the day, there future march in future. WDh	
"	16		March continued to VIEUX – GENAPPE WDh	
VIEUX GENAPPE	17		March continued to TILLY. The Batt. was congratulated by H.E. G.O.C. on its turnout. WDh	
TILLY	18		March continued to LIGNY WDh	
LIGNY	19		March continued to BELGRADE WDh	
BELGRADE	20		March continued to PONTILLAS WDh	
PONTILLAS	21		March continued to WARNANT WDh	
WARNANT	22		Battn. enjoyed their first Holiday during the trip. WDh	
	23		Parades made for arrangements WDh	
	24		Parades today, later on Xmas Eve in future. WDh	
	25		Battalion paraded for Divine Service. WDh	
	26		The Battalion paraded 09:30 Route March Point Maral. WDh	

Army Form C. 2118.

WAR DIARY
or
INTELLIGENCE SUMMARY.
(Erase heading not required.)

Instructions regarding War Diaries and Intelligence Summaries are contained in F. S. Regs., Part II. and the Staff Manual respectively. Title pages will be prepared in manuscript.

Place	Date	Hour	Summary of Events and Information	Remarks and references to Appendices
HARANT	1918 Dec 27		Parade under Coy arrangements. Sport during the afternoon.	nil
	28		Parade under Coy arrangement. Bath now erected to R.E. 8".	nil
	29		Church service in Pavilion at Recreation Room	nil
	30		7th G.O.C. inspected 1/0 Battalion arrayed during the morning	nil
	31		Parade under Coy arrangement. Each Company was served out during the afternoon.	nil

C. Clark Major
COMDG. 12th BATT. EAST SURREY REGT.

SECRET.   12th. Bn. East Surrey Regt.   Copy No. 1

OPERATION ORDER No. 150.

Ref. Sht. 29.1/40,000

Information.   The Battalion will be relieved to-night by the 2/14 London Regt.

Instructions.
1. On relief, Companies will march independently to new Area O.17.
2. Guides which are detailed from Battn. H.Q. will meet Companies at O.18.c.3.5. and lead them to their respective billets.
3. Lewis Guns etc. will be carried.
4. Ration Parties will report to Battn. H.Q. on arrival at new area.
5. **Relief.** Completion of relief will be notified by using Company Commanders name.
6. Acknowledge.

                           (Sgd)   W.D.MURCH, 2/Lt. & A/Adjt.
                                  12th. Bn. East Surrey Regt.

1st. Nov. 1918.
Issued at 16.45.

SECRET.

12th East Surrey Regiment.
15th Hampshire Regiment.
18th K.R.R.Corps.
122nd. T.M.Battery.
"A" Coy., 41st. Bn., M.G.C.
"B" Coy., 41st. Bn., M.G.C.
138 Field Ambulance.
41st. Division, "G". (For information).

Ref. Map, Sheet 29.
1/40,000.

1. The next task devolving on the XIXth. Corps is the passage of the L'ESCAUT.
   The XIXth. Corps will attack and force a passage on a date to be notified later, in conjunction with the Xth. Corps on the right and the French on the left.
   All preparations are to be completed by the 7th. instant.

2. On the XIXth. Corps front the 35th. Division will attack on the right, and the 41st. Division on the left.
   The 41st. Division will cross from Q.20.a.8.8. to Q.10.Central. on a two Brigade front, the 124th Infantry Brigade on the right and the 122nd. Infantry Brigade on the left; the inter-brigade boundary will be approx. Q.15.b.1.2.
   The 122nd. Infantry Brigade Group, consisting of:-
      12th. East Surrey Regiment.
      15th Hampshire Regiment.
      18th K.R.R.Corps.
      122 T.M.Battery.
      One Company, 41st. Bn., M.G.C.,
   will be disposed for the attack as follows:-
      18th K.R.R.Corps.   On right.
      12th. East Surrey Regt.   On left.
      15th. Hampshire Regt.   In reserve.
   Each Battalion will attack on a two Company front.

3. The objective will be approximately the general line drawn through W.5.a.0.0. to R.26.Central, which is the limit of range of the Field Artillery (now on the left bank of the river), supporting the attack.
   The 122nd. Infantry Brigade will be responsible for the capture of the general line approx. Q.36.Central-R.25.d.0.0.

4. Assembly positions will be reconnoitred and notified later, but will probably be between river bank and the main road between KERKHOVE (Q.14) and KWAADESTRAAT (Q.5).
   Efforts will be made prior to the assault to draw the enemy's fire to ascertain his barrage line.
   The assembly positions will be marked out by tapes.

5. The attack will probably take place at dawn.

6. The plan of the attack is as follows:-
   I. The crossing will be effected under cover of:-
      (a) The utmost possible artillery support, including the use of smoke shells.
      (b) The concentrated fire of Medium and Stokes' 3" Trench Mortars, and Machine Guns.
      (c) A smoke screen from captured German smoke generators in position on the left bank of the river, provided the wind is favourable.
   II. The actual means of passage may be divided into two phases:-
      (a) <u>Infantry</u>, i.e. Foot bridges of the German type, floats, cylindrical floats, rafts, etc., the policy being to develop all available means so that the passage may be effected simultaneously by the Infantry at the maximum number of points. If possible, five foot bridges will be built for each brigade.
      (b) <u>Other arms</u>. Pontoon bridges to take Field Artillery and Horse Trasport.

III/-

III. Eight boats will be at the disposal of the Brigade, i.e., four for each Battalion, i.e., two per front line Company. Crossing places for boats will be selected.
Each boat will hold twelve men.
About 40 men per Company will cross in these, and endeavour to reach the line of the road through Q.16.C.3.0. to Q.17.a.4.5. in order to clear the houses in MEERSCHE and to cover the erection of the foot bridge.
Covering parties on the left bank will be found from the reserve Battalion (15th. Hants Regt.).
The foot bridge will be erected in 30 minutes, after which the assaulting Battalions will cross, form up, again on a two Coy. front, along the line of the railway running through Q.22.a. and Q.17.c.
Bridge Police and Control Posts will be found by the reserve Battalion, 15th. Hants Regt., and strict discipline enforced.
The advance from the railway embankment will commence at a later hour (probably 2½ hours after Zero), and will be protected by a creeping barrage.
The barrage will lift 100 yards in three minutes, and there will be pauses of 5 minutes at 500 yards and 1,000 yards, and a pause of 30 minutes at 1,500 yards, to enable the rear Companies to leapfrog and continue the advance to the final objective.

7. Owing to the number of small groups of farms and hamlets, special mopping up parties will be detailed by each assaulting Battalion.

8. O.C., 122 T.M.Battery will select positions on the left bank from which to engage the houses in MEERSCHE, and the isolated houses at Q.15.d.85.80.-Q.16.c.1.4. and Q.16.c.6.1., and will get in touch with O.C., 124 T.M.Battery (H.Q. at O.18.a.2.4.) to arrange for dumps of ammunition, if necessary placing his G.S. Waggon at the latter's disposal.

9. O's. C. "A" and "B" Coys., 41st. Bn., M.G.C. will reconnoitre positions from which the crossings can be covered by direct overhead fire.

10. Brigade Signal Officer will arrange for all means of communication to be used, including visual, pigeons, and message carrying rockets.

11. Battalions will arrange for Officers to reconnoitre the assembly positions etc., and the forward area as soon as possible, but all Officers must be impressed with the necessity of secrecy in this reconnaisance, in order that the actual points of crossing shall not be revealed to the enemy.

12. ACKNOWLEDGE.

Captain,
Brigade Major.
3rd. November, 1918.   122nd. Infantry Brigade.

OPERATION ORDER No.146
by
LIEUT COL. G.L.BROWN DSO.

Ref. Sht. 29 I/40,000

1. The Battalion will move to new area (H.12.) to-morrow 5th. inst.

2. <u>Route.</u> Road Junction O.4.c.7.8. - O.4.b.5.0. - H.12.

3. <u>Order of March.</u>   Battn H.Q.
   C. Coy.
   D. Coy.   Intervals of 100 yards between
   B. Coy.   Coys, will be maintained.
   A. Coy.
   Transport.

4. <u>Starting Point.</u> O.10.c.4.7. with the exception of B and A Coys. who will join the Battalion at the following point at ~~O.9.4.6.~~ 09.40
   B. Coy. O.4.c.7.8.   A. Coy. O.4.b.5.0.

5. <u>Time</u>   From starting point (O.10.c.4.7.) ~~09.3.0.~~ 09.40

6. <u>Baggage.</u> Officers valises and blankets will be stacked outside Coy. billets by ~~xxxxxxx~~ 08.15 from where they will be collected by G.S. waggons.

7. <u>Lewis Guns.</u> will be collected by limbers.

8. The Transport Officer will arrange for 2 limbers to collect Coy. Lewis Guns and 1 limber for Battn. H.Q. After collecting Lewis Guns they will follow A. Coy. on road running East from O.4. at xxx. 09.50.

9. <u>Cookers.</u> will follow their respective Coys.

10. <u>Billetting Party.</u> consisting of:- 1 N.C.O. per Coy. and Pte. TROUT of C. Coy. who will report to 2/Lt. COWLIN at Battn. H.Q. by 07.15. Dress Fighting Order.

11. <u>Chargers.</u> Officers chargers will be at Battn H.Q. and Coy. H.Q. by 09.30. for the following Officers:- C.O. 2nd. in Command, Adjutant, M.O. and Coy. Commanders.

12. Companies will report location of their H.qr's on arrival in new area.

Issued at 23.45.   (Sgd) W.D.MUTCH, 2/Lt. & A/Adjt.
   4.11.18.   12th. Bn. East Surrey Regt.

12th Bn. EAST SURREY REGT.

WARNING ORDER NO.101.

1. The Battalion will proceed by march route tomorrow 9th November 1918. to relieve a Battalion of the 123rd Infantry Brigade in the line.

2. "A" Company will proceed by Bus as far as VOSSENHOEK J.25.d.9.5., at a time to be notified later.

3. Probable time of departure for the remainder of the Battn. will be about 12.00. There will be a halt for Teas on the road. Cookers will proceed with Companies.

4. All kit not being taken into the line will be ready by Companies for collection at 10.00.

                    (sd)   J.D.Mutch.   2nd LT & A/Adjt.

Issued at 16.15.   12th Bn. East Surrey Regt.
8th Novr 1918.

OPERATION ORDER No.149.
by
LIEUT.COL.G.L.BROWN,D.S.O.
Comdg 12th Bn. EAST SURREY REGT.

1. The Battalion will continue the march to-morrow, 10th November, 1918.

2. <u>Starting Point.</u> Bend in road at P.5.c.0.7, head of column to be at Starting Point at 8.45 a.m.
   Order of march:- Headquarters, Band, C, D, Drums, A, B.
   Dress:- Fighting order.

3. Officers Valises will be ready for collection outside various Headquarters at 7 a.m.
   Blankets will be ready for collection outside various Headquarters at 6 a.m.
   The Transport Officer will arrange to collect Blankets and dump them at the Qmr.Stores. The Qmr. will detail a G.S.Wagon to collect Officers Valises.
   All surplus kit other than above which cannot be carried on the Regtl.Transport will be dumped at Bn.H.Q. by 6 a.m.
   The Transport Officer will arrange for one limber to collect this and take it to the Qmr.Stores. The Qmr.Stores will dump packs and any other kit which they cannot carry and will leave one man to look after it.
   Two Regtl.Police will be detailed by the R.S.M. to report at the Qmr.Stores at 6.15 a.m. to remain in charge of this baggage.
   Baggage should be put under cover.

4. Destination of the Battalion will depend on the result of operations on the Divisional front.

5. Battalion Transport will march in rear of B Company.

6. Divisional Boundaries now run as follows :-
   North Q.10. central due East.
   South Q.30.d.0.0 due East to R.27.c.4.0 thence R.21.c.4.0 thence due East.

                                    (sd) W.D.Mutch,
                                         2nd Lt & A/Adjt,
                                    12th Bn East Surrey Regiment.

Issued at 23.40.
9th November, 1918.

12th. Bn. East Surrey Regt.

OPERATION ORDER No.

1. The Battalion with Transport will move from present area to the vicinity South of GRAMMONT to-morrow and will parade in the following order:- H.Qr's, Band, B. C. Drums A. D. Head of column outside D. Coys billet at 09.30 facing S.W.
Dress - Fighting Order.
Attention is drawn to March Dicipline Orders issued recently.

2. Blankets tied in bundles of 10, mens packs, Coy. stores etc. will be stacked by A. B. D Coys. in village square by 08.30 H.Qr's & C. Coy. will stack the above outside their own billet at same hour.

3. Lorries are allotted as under:-
    A & B. Coy.   1 Lorry
    C & D. Coy.   1 Lorry to collect D. Coy. then C Coy
    H. Q. Canteen etc. 1 Lorry.
    Quartermaster   1 Lorry
O.C. A. Coy. will detail an Officer in charge of lorries, who will superintend loading and proceed with the lorries.
Coys. will each detail 1 man, sick or unable to march if possible as loading parties. The above will report to Bn. H.Qr's at 08.15.

4. Officers valises will be collected/by G.S. waggon, 6 from H.Qr's 5 from each Coy. The remainder will be loaded as in para. 3. Mess kit will be collected at 08.30.

5. Billetting Party under 2/Lt. A.C.COWLIN, have proceeded. An N.C.O. from A. B. & D. Coy. will report to head of column at starting point, they will guide their respective Coys. to billets on arrival.

6. The Battalion will remain in new area for two days.

7. Watches will be synchronised to-night and again at the Brigade starting point.

8. Supplies for 19th. inst. will proceed with column. Empty waggons will be returned to Brigade H.Qr's.
This will apply throughout the march.

9. STRAGGLERS. The rear Company will detail an Officer to be in charge of stragglers to march in rear of the Battalion and collect all stragglers.

10. Acknowledge by bearer.

(Sgd) D. WALKER. Capt. & A/Adjt.
12th. Bn. East Surrey Regt.

Issued 19.00
17th. November 1918.

Copy No. 3

122nd INFANTRY BRIGADE OPERATION ORDER No. 253

Ref. Map Sheet - TOURNAI 5. 1/100,000.

1. The 41st Division will be replaced by another Division, in the Line tomorrow 20th instant.

2. 122nd Inf. Bde. will proceed to EVERBECQ - GOEFFERDINGE Area in accordance with attached March Table.

3. Usual billeting parties will meet the Staff Captain at VIANE Church at 0800; 12th East Surrey Regt., 15th Hampshire Regt., and 138th Field Ambulance representatives will await the Staff Captain on the Bridge, LES-DEUX-ACREN at 0830.

4. Brigade Signal Officer will synchronise watches.

5. Brigade Report Centre will close at VIANE at 0830 and will re-open at EVERBECQ on arrival.

6. ACKNOWLEDGE.

Issued to Signals at 2330.
19th November 1918.

Major,
A/Brigade Major,
122nd Infantry Brigade.

Copy No. 1. File.
2. 41st Division "G".
3. 12th East Surrey Regt.
4. 15th Hampshire Regt.
5. 18th King's Royal Rifle Corps.
6. 11th Army Brigade R.F.A.
7. 228th Field Coy. R.E.
8. 138th Field Ambulance.
9. No. 2 Coy 41st Div. Train.
10. Staff Captain.
11. Brigade Signal Officer.

Administrative Instructions follow

12th. Bn. East Surrey Regt.

OPERATION ORDER, No.151.

Ref. Map. Sht.-
TOURNAI. 5. 1/100,000.

1.

1. The 41st. Division will be replaced by another Division, in the Line to-day 20th. inst.

2. The Battalion will move from present area to EVERBECQ-GOEFFERDINGE area, and will parade in the following order:-

        Headquarters,
        Drums.
        D. Coy.
        B. Coy.
        Band.
        C. Coy.
        A. Coy.
        Transport.

Head of column to be on Village Cross Roads at 08.15. 20th. inst.
Dress - Fighting Order as laid down.

3. Blankets and packs will be stacked in the vicinity of Coy. Billets by 07.45. ready for collection by lorry.

4. Officers valises, 6 for H.Qr's and 4 per Coy. will be collected at 07.30, the remainder will be stacked as in para. 3. Mess Kit will be collected at 07.30.

5. O.C. B Coy. will detail an Officer to be in charge of lorries he will report at Battn. H.Qr's at 07.30.

6. In confirmation of Warning Order the billetting party will proceed under 2/Lt. Hall at 07.30. and will meet the Battalion and guide it to new billets.

Issued at 03.30.
20th. November 1918.

(Sgd). D. WALKER Capt. & A/Adjt.
12th. Bn. East Surrey Regt.

OPERATION ORDER No.150.
by
MAJOR C.T.WILLIAMS,
Comdg. 12th. Bn. East Surrey Regt.
------------ooo------------

1. The march will be recommenced on Thursday 12th. inst. The first stage will be 3 days march, then 1 days rest.

2. The Battalion with Transport will parade at 08.12 on 12th. inst as under.
   H.Qr's - Band - C. A. Coy. - Drums - D. B. Coy.
   Head of column opposite village church facing E.
   Dress - Full Marching Order. Jerkins carried as for inspection on 7th. inst. Tin mugs will be carried <u>inside</u> pack or haversack.
   Attention is drawn to March Discipline Orders and Fourth Army Notes on March Disipline.

3. The Battalion will be located night 12th./13th. inst. in HERINNES Area and 13th./14th. inst. in BOIS de HAM Area.
   Billetting Parties of 1 N.C.O. per Company, 1 from H.Qr's and 1 from Transport and Quartermaster's Stores will report on 12th. inst at 07.00 to Lieut. W.D.MUTCH, MC Battn. H.Qrds. They will rejoin their respective Companies on the march to guide them into billets. The above will meet the Staff Captain who will allot billets at HERINNES CHURCH at 09.30 12th. inst.

4. Two lorries are allotted to the Battalion to carry blankets and surplus kit. O.C. C. Company will detail an Officer in charge of lorries to report to Battn. H.Qr's at 08.00 12th. inst.

5. Blankets will be stacked by 07.30 in bundles of 10 outside Company billets.

6. Officer's valises, Mess kits etc. will be stacked by 07.30 ready for collection by Transport. Only 5 valises per Company will be placed on G.S. Waggon, remainder will be stacked as in para. 5.

7. Supplies will be delivered by A.S.C. to the Battalion on arrival in new area.

8. Companies are individually responsible that no damage is done to billets, and certificates - pro forma to be issued - to this effect will be obtained for each billet before moving to new area.
   This will be observed throughout march and certificates will be retained by Companies.

9. <u>Foot Inspection</u> - The Medical Officer and the Battalion Chiropodist will inspect feet of the men of the Battalion to-morrow at times to be arranged. The following points must be attended to:-
   All corns to be prepared by the Chiropodist.
   Socks must fit correctly.
   No man to start the march with socks which have holes in them.
   Particular attention is to be paid to the fitting of boots. During the line of march a feet inspection will be held at the end of each day's march. All men should wash their feet before and after each day's march, and must ensure that they are thoroughly dried. Socks should be changed frequently

10. The Signalling Officer will arrange synchronisation of watches the evening before each move.

11. Acknowledge.

Issued at 16.00   (Sgd) D. WALKER, Capt, & A/Adjt.
10th. Dec. 1918.   12th. Bn. East Surrey Regt.

12th Bn EAST SURREY REGIMENT.

1st AMENDMENT TO OPERATION ORDER NO.152.

Para. 3.   Billeting parties will consist of one Officer per Company, one officer and one N.C.O. from Bn.Hdqrs, one N.C.O. from Transport and Qmr.Stores. They will report to Lieut.W.D.MUTCH, M.C. at Bn.H.Q. at 0600 to-morrow, 12th inst,

Para 6.   Officers Valises, Mess Kits, etc. will be stacked at 0700 ready for collection by Transport.

Para 8.   All billets must be left in a scrupulously clean condition, and will be inspected at 0700 by the Orderly Officer, who will report at Bn.H.Q. at that hour.

There will be a halt from 1150 to 1300 for dinners. A and B Companies will cook dinners for Brigade Headquarters, and C and D Companies for Bn.H.Q.   Company Q.M.S's will arrange to draw rations for the above to-night.

(sd) D.Walker,
Capt & A/Adjt,
11.12.18.   12th Bn East Surrey Regiment.

12th. East Surrey Regt.
15th. Hampshire Regt.
18th. King's Royal Rifle Corps.
138th. Field Ambulance.
228th. Field Company, R.E.

No.2.Coy. 41st. Divl.Train.
11th Army Brigade, R.F.A.
Transport Officer.
Q.M.S. CASS.
O.C. 122nd. Bde. Signals.

AMENDMENT TO ADMINISTRATIVE INSTRUCTIONS ISSUED WITH
122ND INF. BRIGADE ORDER NO.257 dated 7.12.18.

Para 2. "SUPPLIES"

(a) Railhead.

after "B" to "F" Day both inclusive, delete ENGHEIN and substitute BRAINE LE CONTE.

Captain,
Staff Captain,
122nd. Infantry Brigade.

OPERATION ORDER No.153
by
MAJOR C.T.WILLIAMS.
Comdg 12th. Bn. East Surrey Regt.

1. The Battalion with Transport will parade to-morrow 13th. inst. at 10.28 as under:-
   H.Qr's - Drums - A. D. Band - B. C. Coys.
   Head of column where Main Road meets village Square Facing S.
   Dress - Full Marching Order.

2. The Battalion will be located night of 13th./14th. inst. in BOIS de HAM Area, distance about 11 kilos.
   Billeting Parties as laid down in OO 152 will report to 2nd. Lt. W.S.HALL at the Village Church at 08.00 to-morrow.
   The above will meet Staff Captain at Road Junction STEENKUP at 09.00.

   2/Lt A.C. Cowlin is detailed

3. Lorries will be the same as to-day. ~~O.C. A. Coy will detail an~~ Officer in charge of lorries to report to Battn. H.Qr's at 09.00 also, when lorries arrive in the new area

4. Blankets will be stacked by 09.00.

5. Officers valises Mess kits etc. will be stacked as to-day ready for collection at 09.00.

6. ACKNOWLEDGE.

(Sgd) D. WALKER Capt & A/Adjt.
12th. Bn. East Surrey Regt.

Issued at 18.10
12th. Dec. 1918.

OPERATION ORDER No.154
by
MAJOR C.T.WILLIAMS.
Comdg. 12th. East Surrey Regt.

1. The Battalion with Transport will parade to-morrow 14th. inst. at 08.10 as under:-
    H.Qr's - Band. - D. B. Drums.- C. A. Coys.
    Head of column at Road Junction ENGHIEN - HAL Road, between Kilos 25 & 26 Facing E.
    Dress - Full Marching Order.

2. The Battalion willbe located on night 14th./15th. inst in WANTHIER-BRAINE Area. where it will remain for the days rest. Billeting parties as usual eecept only 1 N.C.O. will be supplied from Transport & Q.M.Stores, will repprt to LT. W.D.MUTCH, MC. at Battn. H.Qr's at 06.30 sharp to-morrow.
    The above will meet the Staff Captain at Station WANTHIER BRAINE at 08.30.

3. Lorries will be the same as to-day. 2/Lt. A.C.COWLIN is detailed as Officer i/c lorries, he will report ay Battn H.Qr's at 07.45. Afte r collecting blankets etc. they will meet M.T.Officer at Main Cross Roads SAINTES at 12.00.

4. Blankets will be stacked by 07.15 outside Company billets.

5. Officers Mess kit etc will be stacked ready for collection as under:-
    A. Coy.   06.25.
    C. Coy.   06.45.
    D. & B. Coys.   07.00.

6. Acknowledge by bearer.

Issued at 21.10
13th. Dec. 1918   (Sgd) D. WALKER, Capt & A/Adjt.
                              12th. Bn. East Surrey Regt.

S E C R E T. B.M. 664. Copy No. 2

122nd. INFANTRY BRIGADE WARNING ORDER NO. 111.

The 122nd. Infantry Brigade Group will be prepared to move at short notice.

All working parties will be recalled forthwith.

ACKNOWLEDGE.

Major,
A/ Brigade Major,
122nd. Infantry Brigade.

Issued to signals at 1415.
13.11.18.

Copy No. 1. File.
2. 12th. East Surreys.
3. 15th. Hampshire Regt.
4. 18th. Bn., K.R.R.Corps.
5. 122nd. T.M.Battery.
6. "B" Coy., 41st. Bn., M.G.C.
7. 140th. Field Ambulance.

SECRET.   Copy No... 5.

122nd. Infantry Brigade Operation Order Number 250.

Ref. Map, Sheet 30, 1/40,000.

1. The 122nd. Infantry Brigade will march to area in squares O 14, O 20, and O 26, in accordance with attached march table. tomorrow 14th inst.

2. Brigade Signalling Officer will arrange to synchronise watches.

3. Locations of Units will be notified to Brigade Headquarters, at once, on arrival in new area.

4. There will be a halt from 1250 to 1400 for a meal.

5. Brigade Report Centre will close at present position at 0945, and re-open on arrival at new billet.

6. Rations for 15th. will be delivered to Units by 0900. Wagons will accompany Units.
   Wagons will report direct to Brigade Headquarters, and 15th. Hampshire Regiment; wagons for 12th. East Surrey Regt. and 18th. K.R.R.Corps will report to, and accompany, Brigade Headquarters, joining above Units on route.
   When rations have been unloaded, wagons will be instructed to return to road junction at SCHOORISSE, 30/N.11.c.1.0., where guide from No. 2 Coy., 41st. Divisional Train will conduct to new location of latter near SCHOORISSE.
   No. 2 Coy., 41st. Divisional Train will be moving to NEDERBRAKEL on 15th. Guides for rations for consumption 16th. will be at road junction, N.24.a.40.05. at 1000 on 15th. instant.

7. BAGGAGE. Lorries to make one journey are allotted to Units as under for march:- Each Battalion - 2.   Bde. H.Q. - 1.
   Guides from Units for lorries will report to Brigade H.Q. at 0945 tomorrow.

8. The usual billetting parties will report to the Staff Captain at road junction, PARICKE, O.26.c.5.3. at 1300.

9. TRAFFIC CONTROL. 18th. K.R.R.Corps will arrange traffic controls in LOUISE-MARIE, who will be responsible that there is no congestion of traffic.

10. MEDICAL. O.C., 140 Field Ambulance will collect sick from Units by 0830 tomorrow morning.

11. ACKNOWLEDGE.

Issued to signals 2340..
13th. November, 1918.

Major,
A/Brigade Major,
122nd. Infantry Brigade.

Copies to 1. File.
2. War Diary.
3. 41st. Division "G".
4.   do.
5. 12th. East Surrey Regt.
6. 15th. Hampshire Regt.
7. 18th. K.R.R.Corps.
8. 122nd. T.M.Battery.
9. "B" Coy., 41st. Bn., M.G.C.
10. 140th. Field Ambulance.
11. No. 2 Coy., 41st. Divisional Train.
12. D.A.P.M., 41st. Division.
13. A.D.M.S., 41st. Division.
15. Staff Captain.
16. Brigade Signalling Officer.

March Table to accompany 122nd. Infantry Brigade Operation Order Number 250.

Serial No.	Unit.	From.	To.	Starting Point.	Time.	Route.	Remarks.
1.	18th. K.R.R.Corps.	LOUISE-MARIE.	New area.	S.3.b.5.9.	1150.	LOUISE-MARIE - COCAMBRE - Cross roads S.11.a.4.3. - N.17.c.5.2.	100 yards between Coys. 200 yards between Battalions.
2.	12th. East Surreys.	do.	do.	do.	1145.	do.	
3.	15th. Hampshire Regt.	do.	do.	do.	1210.	do.	
4.	Brigade Headquarters.	do.	do.	do.	1225.	do.	
5.	122nd. T.M.Battery.	do	do.	do.	1229.	do.	
6.	"B" Coy., 41st. Bn., M.G.C.	do.	do.	do.	1232.	do.	

Troops not to enter LOUISE-MARIE before 1100, and to be clear by 1200.

S E C R E T   Copy No... 10 ......

R.A.M.C. OPERATION ORDER No. 75.
---------by---------
COLONEL L.W.LLOYD, C.M.G., D.S.O., R.M.S.,
A.D.M.S., 41st DIVISION, COMMANDING ROYAL ARMY MEDICAL CORPS.

                                        14th November 1918.

1.   138th Field Ambulance will move on the 15th instant from .... to GLAGEONT and will billet West of the River Londre, and will come into the 123rd Infantry Brigade Group.

2.   Billeting party will be sent on in advance to select suitable billets and site for the Field Ambulance.

3.   On 138th Field Ambulance establishing at GLAGEONT, Officer Commanding will arrange to collect the sick of the 123rd Infantry Brigade Group.
    Cases not likely to be fit for duty immediately will be transferred by D.R.S. (138th F.A.) DENBRAEL.

Issued at 9.0.p.m.

                                     Colonel,
                                     A.D.M.S., 41st Division.

    Issued to all recipients of R.A.M.C. Operation Order No. 74 dated 13.11.18.

OPERATION ORDER NO.50
by
LIEUT?COL. G.L. BROWN, D.SO.
Comdg 12th Bn EAST SURREY REGIMENT.

14th November, 1918.

1. The Battalion will move from the present area to 30/O.20. about 14,000 yards, to-day, and will parade as under :-
    Headquarters.
    Band.
    C Company.
    A Company.
    Drums.
    B Company.
    D Company.
    Transport.

   Head of column to be outside C Company's billet at 1125 facing East.
   Distance of 200 yards between Battalions, and 100 yards between Companies, will be maintained after marching off.
   Dress:- Full marching order.

2. There will be a halt from 1250 to 1400 for a midday meal.

3. Blankets tied in bundles of 10, Company Stores etc. will be stacked outside Company billets with loading party by 1000.
   Two lorries are allotted to the Battalion for the march, and will report to Companies on arrival.
   Officers Valises, Mess Kit etc. will be stacked by 1100. The Transport Officer will arrange to collect these.

4. 2nd Lieut. HALL and a N.C.O. from Bn.H.Q. will proceed by bicycle and report to the Staff Captain at Road Junction, PARICKE, O.26.c.5,8 at 1300. The remainder of the billeting party - one N.C.O. per Company - will proceed to the new area by the first lorry.

5. Rations for the 15th inst. will accompany the Battalion on the march. Waggons when unloaded will be instructed to return to Road Junction at SCHOORISSE 30/M.11.c.1.0. where they will meet guides to new location of train.

(sd) D.Walker,
Capt & A/Adjt,
12th Bn East Surrey Regiment.

Issued at 0240,
14th Novr, 1918.

OPERATION ORDERS No.155
by
MAJOR C.T.WILLIAMS
Comdg. 12th. East Surrey Regt.

1. The march will be continued to-morrow 16th. inst.
   The Battalion with Transport will parade at 10.20 in the following order:-
   H.Qr's - Drums - B. C. Band. A. D. Coys.
   Head of column to be where the railway crosses the road WANTHIER BRAINE Facing N.
   Dress - Full Marching Order.
   Route - RUE - BRAINE l'ALLEUD - La MAISON du ROI.

2. The Battalion will be located on night 16th./17th. inst at PLANCENOITE MARANSARTE Area.

3. The Billeting party as for last days march will repprt to 2/Lt. W.S.HALL in the village square at 07.30. They will meet the Staff Captain at road junction S. of A in PLANCENOITE at 09.00.

4. Lorries will be as usual. 2/Lt. A.C.COWLIN is detailed as Officer in charge of lorries. He will report at Battn. H.Qr's at 09.00. After collecting blankets etc. lorries will meet M.T. Officer at 12.00 at road junction on BRAINE LE CHATEAU -RUE Road.
   It is possible that a portion of the third lorry will be allotted to the Battalion to-morrow to carry leather jerkins. In the event of this being confirmed, jerkins will be stacked by sections with the blankets and O.C. lorries will arrange to collect.

5. Blankets will be stacked by 09.00 outside Company billets.

6. Officers valises, Mess kit etc. will be stacked outside Compy. billets ready for collection as under:-
   H.Qr's   09.00
   A.B.C.D.Coys.   09.15.

7. Each Company will detail 5 men who are unable to march in the column, to parade at 09.00 under an Officer to be detailed by O.C. A. Coy. They will proceed by devious routes to the new area avoiding route as laid down in para. 1.

8. Attention of Company Commanders is drawn to the various points raised at the Conference this morning, re. March Discipline etc.

9. Acknowledge by bearer.

Issued at 19.15.   (Sgd) D. WALKER. Capt & A/Adjt.
15th. Dec. 1918.   12th. Bn. East Surrey Regt.

OPERATION ORDERS No. 156
by
MAJOR C.T.WILLIAMS.
Comdg. 12th. Bn. East Surrey Regiment.

1. The Battalion with Transport will parade at 09.50 to-morrow in the following order:-
   H.Qr's - Band - C. A. - Drums - D. B. Coys.
   Head of column outside Battn. H.Qr's Facing E.
   Dress - Full Marching Order.
   Route - GENAPPE - STATION - QUATRE BRAS to PETIT MARBAIS to TILLY.

2. The Battalion will be located on night 17th./18th. at Glassworks TILLY.

3. Billeting party as detailed for to-day will reprrt to Lieut. W.D.MUTCH,MC at Battn H.Qr's at 07.30. sharp. They will meet the Staff Captain at QUATRE BRAS at 08.00.

4. Lorries will be as usual. 2/Lieut. A.C.COWLIN is detailed as Officer in charge of lorries. He will report at Battn. H.Qr's at 09.00. After collecting blankets etc, lorries will meet M.T. Officer at 12.30 at GENAPPE Station.

5. Blankets will be stacked by 09.00.

6. Officers valsies, Mess kit etc. will be stacked outside Company billets ready for collection at 08.30.

7. Each Company will detail 5 men who are unable to march in the column to parade at 09.00 under an Officer to be detailed by O.C. C. Coy. They will proceed by devious routes avoiding route as laid down in para. 1.

8. The undermentioned men are recommended to travel by lorry to-morrow
   Pte. Wheeler   H.Qr's. Sigs.   Pte. Sharp.   H.Qr's
   Pte. Tugwell   H. QR's   CQMS. Haynes C. Coy.
   Pte. Wade   D. Coy.   Pte. Bennett D. Coy.

Acknowledge.

Issued at 21.15.   (Sgd) D. WALKER, Capt & A/Adjt.
16th. Dec. 1918.   12th. East Surrey Regt.

BATTALION ORDERS
by
MAJOR C.T.WILLIAMS.
Comdg. 12th. East Surrey Regt.   16th. Dec.1918

Reveille 07.00   Breakfast 07.30
        Sick Parade 08.00
Orderly Offr. to-morrow. 2/Lt J.C.Carver -Next for duty 2/Lt WALLER
Orderly Sgt. to-morrow Sgt MEST, B.Coy -Next for duty Sgt HILL B.Cy
----

707 SPECIAL. The Commanding Officer wishes it to be made known to all ranks his satisfaction on the turn out of the men when marching past the G.O.C. to-day and expects that this standard will be kept up.

708 FIELD CASHIER. The Orderly Officer for the 18th. inst. is detailed to attend Field Cashier at Div. H.Qr's MAZY on that date between 12.00 & 14.00. Advance Cash Books to be in Orderly Room by 20.00 to-morrow night.

(Sgd) D.WALKER, Capt & A/Adjt.
     12th. Bn. East Surrey Regt.

"12th E. Surrey Regt"

ADMINISTRATIVE INSTRUCTION No. 1.
REGARDING MARCH OF THE 41st DIVISION TO GERMANY.

16th November 1918.

1. ACCOMMODATION.

The following procedure will be adopted as regards billeting.

The operation order for each day will detail roughly the area in which the group will be accommodated for the night and will fix the rendezvous where Staff Captains of Brigades and billeting parties, including those of Units in Divisional Headquarters Group will meet the D.A.A.G.

At the rendezvous the exact delimitation of areas will be given to Brigades etc., together with all available details regarding accommodation and any special instructions or administrative matters.

For composition of billeting parties see Appendix "A".

Usual billeting certificates will be given by units on A.F. W.3401 or in manuscript if forms not available.

2. SUPPLY.

(a) The Divisional Train will refill daily on conclusion of the day's march, will march loaded, delivering to units for consumption the following day on arrival in new billets.

Arrangements must be made to notify O.C. Train Company as early as possible of position of units in Group areas, guides to be sent if necessary.

(b) Two trucks of supplies will be attached to Corps Troops Pack Train for the feeding of civilians and released Prisoners of War, which will be drawn on when required under instructions to be issued to S.S.O.

(c) Fuel will be sent up on Pack Trains as demanded by the Division.

3. TRANSPORT.

Unauthorised vehicles are not allowed.

Additional Transport for carriage of blankets, packs of Infantry Battalions, and surplus kit, will be allotted as shown in Appendix "B".

As the Railway situation may render the employment of two echelons of M.T. essential lorries shown in the Appendix are liable to recall under orders from Divisional Headquarters at any time, when, if the march is continued packs must be carried on the man, forage by Artillery wagons until those lorries are again available.

(2)

3. TRANSPORT (continued).

Lorries will remain with the Units for which they are working, during the night; units will be prepared to ration and accommodate the drivers.

At the periodical two days halt of the Division, lorries will return to the Divisional M.T. Company for inspection and overhaul, rejoining the units to which they are allotted by 4.0.p.m. the day previous to resumption of march.

Officer Commanding Divisional M.T. Company will detail an officer or senior N.C.O. who will live with the Train Company of each group to be in charge of lorries allotted to that group.

During the march after loading up, all lorries in the Group will move under orders of the M.T. Officer or N.C.O. in charge in rear of both groups using the road. On no account are baggage lorries to pass troops on the march.

4. MARCH DISCIPLINE.

March discipline must be the object of special attention. The following points require particular notice :-

(a). Halts will take place from 10 minutes to every clock hour to the clock hour, whatever time units may have passed the starting point.

Unit and Company Commanders should synchronise their watches so that men are ready fallen in at the clock hour, and the whole column stops off together.

(b). At the halts the road must be cleared instantly, all men falling out on the right of the road.

(c). In Artillery and units marching with transport, a warning will be given a few minutes before each halt to ensure that all vehicles are well into the side of the road when the order to halt is given.

(d). No officers or other ranks will march alongside the Column but must be in the intervals. If they have occasion to pass from front to rear of a portion of a column they will do so on the right hand side.

(e). Any personnel marching with transport will be in formed bodies.

(f). No arms or equipment may be placed on transport and no man may ride on a transport vehicle except driver and mate without the permission of an officer.

(g). On pave roads lorries and cars must be given way to and not turned off the pave.

(h). Troops will march with rifles slung over one shoulder, arms will be sloped on the command "March at Attention", but this command will only be given on arrival in billets and as a compliment on passing the Brigade, Divisional, Corps, or Army Commanders for the first time on any day.

Marching through towns and large villages troops will be given the command "March to Attention with Arms Slung" when all rifles will be slung on the left shoulder, marching in all other respects as when marching at "Attention".

MARCH DISCIPLINE

There are no restrictions as to smoking when marching "At Ease".

5. RELEASED PRISONERS OF WAR.

Any released Prisoners of War should be directed to Divisional Headquarters where arrangements will be made for their despatch to Railhead by empty supply lorries.

6. DRESS.

Uniformity of dress throughout units will be ensured. Leather and Webbing equipment should as far as possible be standardised in Companies, Platoons Sections, as may be possible.

Leather Jerkins may be worn UNDER THE EQUIPMENT, or carried rolled on the belt at the discretion of the Brigade Commanders.

The waterproof sheet will be carried on the man, ready to put on in the event of rain.

7. CANTEEN.

An Advanced Divisional Canteen will open daily after the march is completed at Divisional Headquarters from where units can draw.

The stock available is of course limited by the question of transport.

8. BATHS.

Baths will be opened in each group area during each halt period. Clean clothes will be supplied as transport permits.

9. HEALTH AND SANITATION.

The health and sanitary precautions to be observed by troops on the line of march are given in Appendix "C".

10. LEAVE.

Returning Supply lorries will be used until further notice.

11. REINFORCEMENTS AND PERSONNEL.

These will be sent up to Supply Railhead and brought on by lorry. No reinforcements from overseas will be sent up at all.

[signature]
Lieut Colonel,
A.A. & Q.M.G.
41st Division.

November 16th 1918.

122nd Inf. Brigade.	123rd Inf. Bde.	124th Inf. Bde.
19th Middlesex.	Machine Gun Bn.	Divisional Train.
A.D.M.S.	Signal Co.	Camp Commandant.
41st M.T.Company.	D.A.P.M.	D.A.D.O.S.
D.A.D.V.S.	"G"	52nd M.Vet Section.
Employ Company.	Baths Offr.	Canteen Offr.
IInd Corps "Q".	Senior Chaplains.	C.R.A.
C.R.E.	French Mssn.	Belgian Mssn.

APPENDIX "C".

MEDICAL ARRANGEMENTS TO BE CARRIED OUT DURING AND PRIOR TO THE MARCH.

FEET INSPECTIONS.

During the few days prior to the Division moving off, each man must have his feet inspected; the Company Commander, the Regimental Medical Officer and the Battalion Chiropodist should attend this inspection and the following points must be attended to :-

(a). All corns to be prepared by the Chiropodist.
(b). Socks must fit correctly.
(c). No man should start the march with socks which have holes in them.
(d). Particular attention to be paid to the fitting of boots.

DURING THE LINE OF MARCH.

(a). A foot inspection will be held at the end of each days march.
(b). All men should wash their feet before and after each day's march and they must ensure that they are thoroughly dried.
(c). Socks should be changed daily.
(d). All blisters should be treated with Road's Plaster.
(e). Two pairs of socks should be carried by each man, in addition to the pair he is wearing.

LATRINES.

Long straddle latrines should be made in each billeting area, based on equivalent of three seats per 100 men, and filled in and marked prior to moving off.

At each long halt a latrine should be dug and places marked for urinating and should be correctly indicated as such before moving off.

Promiscuous dropping of dejection must be stopped.

Private latrines and urinals will not be used.

WATER SUPPLY.

All water supplies must be carefully guarded.
Suspicious water supplies will be examined and all water will be boiled or chlorinated.

PACKS.

All packs should be carried high up on the back.

SICK PARADES.

Sick parades should be held twice daily, viz., 1 hour before moving off and 1 hour after arrival in billets.

INFECTIOUS DISEASE.

Medical officers and Interpreters must make enquiries directly on entering any village or town where troops are going to be billeted for the prevalence of any infectious disease. This information will be obtained from the Burgomaster or local doctor.

Any house in which there is infectious disease must be marked "OUT OF BOUNDS" at once.

PREVENTION AGAINST CHILLS, etc.

After arrival in billets, Company Commanders should look to the comfort of the men.

Men should not be allowed to hang about and get cold; after arrival in billets they are to be encouraged to wear their overcoats.

During halts on the line of march, men should take off their packs and be encouraged to rest.

P.T.O.

(8)

MARCHING.

On the line of march each man should be given as much space as possible so as to give him freedom of movement and breathing room.

The pace should be carefully regulated on gradients and when marching on roads with overhanging trees.

==============================

APPENDIX "A".

Composition of Billeting Parties.

Billeting parties will consist of the following members :-

Unit.	Offrs.	N.C.Os.	Men.
Divl H.Q.	1	1	2
Inf Bde H.Q.	-	1	1
Inf & Pioneer Bns.	1	6 N.C.Os and men.	
H.Q.M.Gun Br.	1	1	-
Each M.Gun Co.	1	1	1
R.F.A.Bde H.Q.	1	1	-
Each Battery.	-	1	1
H.Q.D.A.C.	1	1	-
Section D.A.C.	-	1	1
Field Co.R.E.	-	1	1
Sig Co.R.E.	-	1	1
Field Ambulance.	1	1	1
Train Company.	-	1	1

One representative for Headquarters R.A., R.E., Divl Train M.V.S., or any other unit.

Billeting parties will always either be mounted or on bicycles and will be fully armed and equiped.

The Officer or N.C.O. in charge should be in possession of a map.

Sheet 2. Appendix "3".

GROUP.	SUPPLIES FOR.	No of Lorries.	Total.	No of G.S. Wagons.	Total.
Support Brigade Group.	Brigade Headquarters. Packs Blankets & Stores	1		1	
	do. Horse Rugs for the Group.			1	
	3 Battalions at 4 per Battalion. Packs Blnkts Stores	12			
	1 Bde F.Artillery. Forage & Stores.	2		1	
	Field Co. R.E. Stores.			1	
	Field Ambulance.		15		3
	Gross Total.		68		20

The following lorries are liable to be recalled or Double lorry supply Echelon is required. These lorries must be sent to 41st M.T. Company Park immediately on receipt of a wire from this office :-

Each Infantry Battalion 2 = 18
19th Middlesex 2 = 6
Each F.A.Bde. 2 = 2
Cartoon 1 = 1
Total. 27.

Replacement of lorries broken down will be arranged through the M.T.Officer or N.C.O. attached to the group.

Lorries will not be instructed to do double journeys without permission first being received from this office.

*=

APPENDIX "E"

Issued with 41st Division Administrative Instruction No.1.

GROUP.	SUPPLIED FOR.	No. of Lorries.	Total.	No. of G.S. Wagons.	Total.
Divisional Troops Group.					
Divisional Headquarters.	Blankets Packs and Stores.	8.			
C.R.A.	Blankets and Stores.	1		1	
C.R.E.	Blankets and Stores.	1		1	
D.A.D.O.S.	Ordnance Stores.	4		1	
Posts.	Postal Services.	2		1	
Canteen & Crumps.	Canteen and Troops Stores.	2		1	
Baths.	Baths and Clothing.	2		1	
19th Middlesex.	Blankets Packs and Stores.	4		1	
M.G.Bn.H.Q.&2 Companies.	Blankets Packs and Stores.	1		1	
Machine Gun Bn.	To replace Train Supply Wagon.	1			
Divisional Signal Co.	Stores.			1	
			23		5
Each Forward Brigade Group.					
Each Bde Headquarters	Packs Blankets and Stores.	1		1	
- do -	Horse Rugs of Bde Group.	12		1	
3 Battalions 4 per Bn.	Packs, Blankets and Stores.	2		1	
1 Brigade F.Artillery.	Forage and Stores.			2	
Machine Gun Company.	Blankets and Packs.			1	
Field Ambulance.	Blankets and Stores.			1	
Field Co. R.E.	Blankets and Stores.			1	
2/1st Yorkshire Dragoons.	To Divl Train for Supplies.		15		6
	2 Groups at		30	2 Groups at 6	12

TABLES SHOWING COMPOSITION OF GROUPS, ROAD SPACES AND TIMES REQUIRED TO PASS A FIXED POINT, ON WHICH ALL CALCULATIONS FOR THE 41st DIVISION WILL BE BASED.

Composition of Groups.	Road space occupied (in yards).	Time (in minutes) required to pass a fixed point.
Headquarters Group.		
1. Divl. H.Q. (including H.Q.R.A. and R.E., H.Q. and No. 1 Section 41st Divl. Signal Coy.)	300	3
1A. 1st Line Transport of D.H.Q.	300	3
2. 19th Middlesex Regt. (Pioneers) with 1st line Transport.	850	10
3. 41st Bn. M. G. Corps (less 2 Companies).	800	10
4. D.A.C. and A.F.A.B.A.C.	3080	35
5. H.Q. and No. 1 Coy. Divl. Train.	950	10
6. 52nd Mob. Vety. Section.	100	1
TOTAL.	6380	72
122nd Infantry Brigade Group.		
7. 11th Army Brigade R.F.A.	1800	20
8. 228th Field Coy. R.E.	470	6
9. 122nd Infantry Brigade (with 1st line transport).	2300	24
11. No. 2 Coy. Divl. Train.	500	5
12. 138th Field Ambulance (less motor vehicles).	450	5
TOTAL.	5520	60
123rd Infantry Brigade Group.		
13. 190th Brigade R.F.A.	1800	20
14. 233rd Field Coy. R.E.	470	6
15. 123rd Infantry Brigade (with 1st Line Transport).	2300	24
16. 1 Coy. M. G. Corps.	320	4
17. H.Q. and 1 Coy. 1/1st Yorks. Cyclist Regt.	200	2

Composition of Groups.	Road space occupied (in yards).	Time (in minutes) required to pass a fixed point.
18. No. 3 Coy. Divl. Train.	500	5
19. 139th Field Ambulance (less motor vehicles).	450	5
TOTAL.	6040	66

124th Infantry Brigade Group.

20. 187th Brigade R.F.A.	1800	20
21. 237th Field Coy. R.E.	470	6
22. 124th Infantry Brigade (with 1st Line Transport).	2300	24
23. 1 Coy. M. G. Corps.	320	4
23A. 1 Coy. 1/1st Yorks Cyclist Regt.	200	2
24. No. 4 Coy. Divl. Train.	500	5
25. 140th Field Ambulance (less motor vehicles).	450	5
TOTAL.	6040	66
TOTAL FOR DIVISION.	23980	4 hours 24 mins.

OPERATION ORDER No.158
by
MAJOR C. T. WILLIAMS,
Comdg 12th Bn EAST SURREY REGT.

1. The Battalion with Transport will parade at 0815 to-morrow, 19th inst, in the following order :-
   H'Qrs - Band - D - B - Drums - C - A.
   head of column where main road through village meets road to Hdqrs Mess Facing EAST.
   Dress:- Full marching order.

2. The Battalion will be located on the night of the 19th/20th in BELGRADE. area.
   Distance 23 kilos

3. Instructions re billeting parties will be issued later.

4. Lorries will be as usual. 2nd Lieut. A.C. COWLIN is detailed as Officer i/c Lorries. He will collect blankets from Companies commencing at 8 a.m.

5. Blankets will be stacked on main road outside Company billets by 0730.

6. Officers valises, mess kit etc., will be stacked outside Coy. H.Q. ready for collection by 0700.

7. Each Company will detail 5 men who are unable to march in the column to parade at 0700 under the Orderly Officer to-morrow. They will proceed by devious routes avoiding the main road.

8. Aknowledge.

(sd) D. Walker, Capt & A/Adjt,
12th Bn East Surrey Regiment.

Issued at 21.15.
18th December, 1918.

41st DIVISION ADMINISTRATIVE INSTRUCTION No.3.
REGARDING MARCH OF DIVISION INTO GERMANY.

12th East Surrey Regt

December 18th, 1918.

1. AREAS.

(a) The permanent area to be occupied by this Division is as shown in the attached sketch map, and is divided for administrative purposes into various sub-areas as shown.

(b) Brigadier Generals Commanding Infantry Brigades and Brigadier General, Divisional Artillery, are responsible for the administration of their respective areas for seeing that the various administrative orders issued from time to time by the Divisional Commander are put into effect, and that improvements in accommodation and sanitation are initiated; any assistance required being asked for from Divisional Headquarters.

(c) Area Commandants have been appointed in each sub-area. They are under the direct orders of the G.O.C. administrative sub-area as regards allocation of accommodation, and will assist him in the carrying out of any orders issued by the Division with regard to the improvement of their various areas.
Detailed orders regarding duties of Area Commandants are published separately.

2. ACCOMMODATION FOR MEN.

(a) The best possible sleeping accommodation for men will be secured.
Where bunking will improve this, application for necessary material will be made on C.R.E. together with any skilled supervision required.
Bunks when decided on should be so arranged as to be removable and not to damage the buildings they are placed in.

(b) Whenever possible dining halls will be arranged so as to keep food out of the living billets.
If these can be found they go far to solving the provision of Recreation and Educational Rooms.

(c) In addition to Company or Battery etc. dining rooms, Units will where possible establish a Central Recreation Room which can form a centre for all forms of recreation and instruction which may be initiated by the unit.

(d) Funds for the provision of equipment, etc. for such rooms, must be considered generally to be found from the funds of the unit. Any special cases, however, may be put forward to Divisional Headquarters who will try and assist in the most urgent cases.

(e) Y.M.C.A. Institutes are being established at —

   HUY.
   LATINNE.
   MARNEFFE.

3. ACCOMMODATION FOR HORSES.

Every effort will be made to so locate troops in the area that the maximum number of horses may be got under cover, or at least on hard standings.

It should not be necessary for any horses to be standing in fields or orchards, causing thereby considerable damage to permanent pasture.

The Divisional Artillery area has a disused railway running through the whole length which affords ample opportunities for horse standings, wagon parks, and watering places, without causing great damage to the agricultural community.

/4.

4. **SANITATION AND WATER.**

(a) Rules regarding sanitation to be observed in the area are being published by the A.D.M.S., also instructions regarding the supply of sanitary material.

These rules and instructions will be rigorously enforced.

(b) All water used for drinking or cooking will be either boiled or efficiently chlorinated.

The A.D.M.S. will arrange with Area Commandants for all sources of drinking water to be marked with degree of chlorination which may be necessary; only such authorised sources will be used.

(c) Horse watering points will be properly organised in each unit.

Canvas troughs will be erected in the first place, to be replaced by permanent troughs as they become available.

Special care will be taken in selection of sites to avoid the damage to property incidental to large numbers of animals moving across pasture or cultivated land.

5. **MANURE DUMPS.**

G.Os.C. Areas in collaboration with Area Commandants will select sites for central manure dumps, where all manure will be properly stacked and covered with earth.

The necessary labour will be supplied daily by units using the dump.

6. **ROADS.**

Lorry traffic in the area is to be restricted to the lowest possible limits and will not be available for supplies, for which in certain cases a double echelon of M.T. will be necessary; this will be found from the Divisional Artillery in accordance with the special orders which are being issued on the subject.

7. **TRAINING.**

Recreation Grounds, Drill Grounds, Ranges, etc., required by Units will be hired under arrangements to be made with the local civil authorities by the Area Commandant concerned, who will go into the matter with the G.O.C. the sub-area, and notify arrangements and terms to Divisional Headquarters.

It is not proposed to hire ground for manoeuvre purposes.

8. **BATHS.**

It is intended to have one spray bath in each sub-area where change of underclothing will be given under Divisional arrangements. Baths are now located at -
WANZIN. HOUDEN. OTEPPE.
HUY & LATINNE
Applications for allotment will be made to Divisional Baths Office, D.H.Q.

In addition units will make such arrangements as are possible to give Baths to their men in their own areas

9. **CANTEEN.**

The Divisional Wholesale Canteen will be located at Divisional Headquarters, and will open there on the 20th inst.

(3)

10. **DIVISIONAL RECEPTION CAMP.**
   The Divisional Reception Camp is moving to HUY under arrangements to be notified later. HUY will become both Supply and Personnel Railhead for the Division at an early date.

   Arrangements as to men proceeding or returning from leave, or on duty or demobilization will be published when known.

11. **SALVAGE & ENEMY STORES.**
   Any of our own stores etc. which may be salvaged by units will be delivered to Area Commandants, who will start a Salvage Dump at their Office in each area.

   Enemy stores found in the area will be safeguarded and reported to Divisional Headquarters.

12. **DAMAGE AND TREATMENT OF INHABITANTS.**
   All ranks are to be impressed that their good or bad behaviour whilst occupying an allied country in which they are regarded as deliverers from a hateful oppression, reflects directly on the credit and honour of the British Army and Nation.
   Officers will take steps to check all willful and careless damage to civilian property.
   The Orders regarding, tying horses to trees, breaking down fences, riding and exercising over permanent pasture or growing crops, are well known and must be strictly enforced. Officers commanding units should see that men of their unit recognize when they are doing damage to the land, and the unnecessary character of the majority of such damage.

[signature]

Lieut.-Colonel.
A.A. & Q.M.G.
41st Division.

Distribution:-
122nd Infantry Brigade.	123rd Infantry Brigade.
124th Infantry Brigade.	19th Middlesex (P).
41st Bn. M.G.Corps.	41st Divisional Artillery.
C.R.E.	Divisional Signal Coy.
A.D.M.S.	Divisional Train.
Divisional M.T.Coy.	Camp Commandant.
52nd M.V.S.	239th Employment Coy.
"G"	Xth Corps (Q)
D.A.P.M.	D.A.D.O.S.
D.A.D.V.S.	Divl. Baths.
Education Officer.	Divisional Reception Camp.
Divisional Canteen.	French Mission.
Belgian Mission.	All Area Commandants.

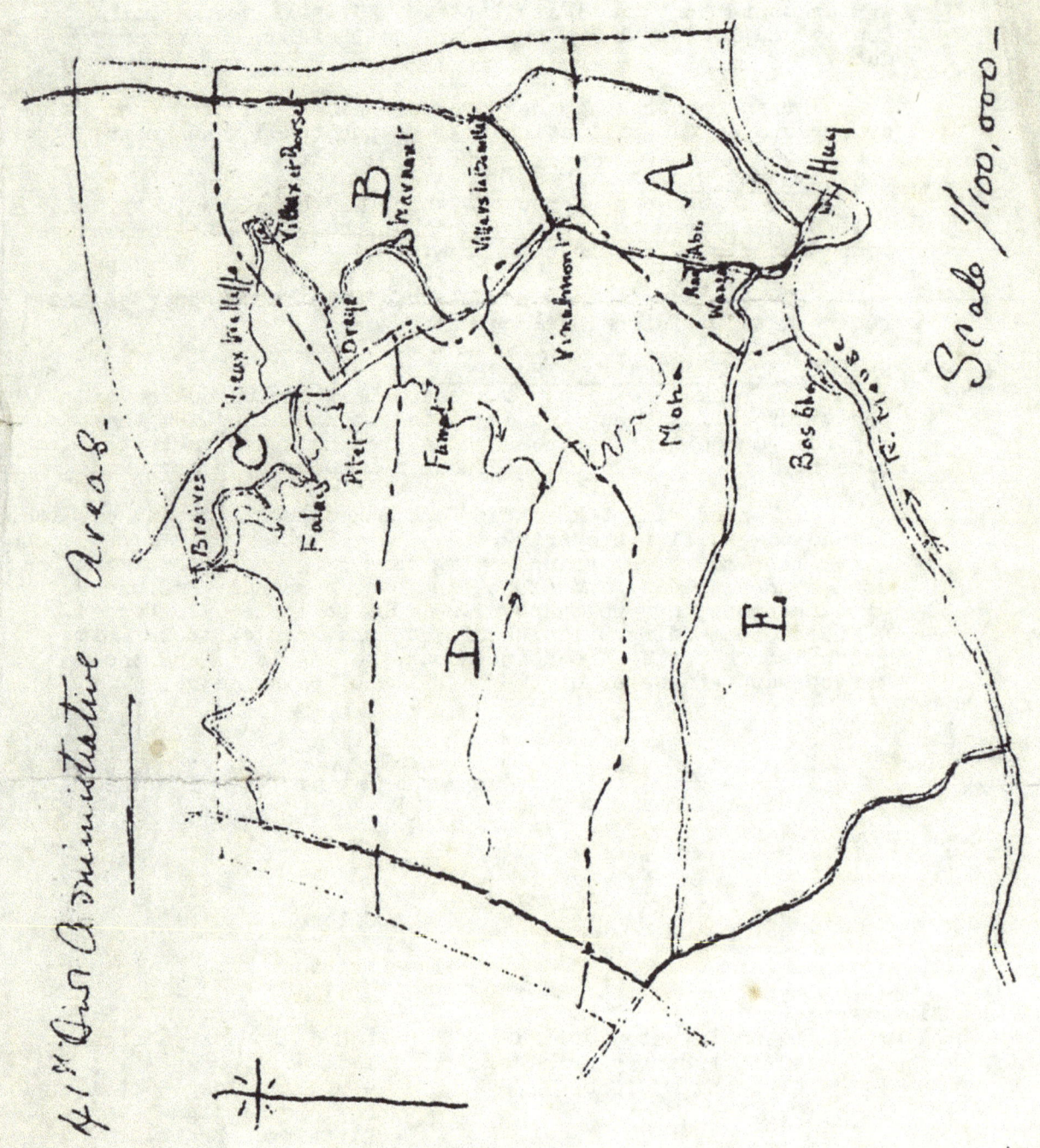

Issued in connection with
41st Division Administrative
Instruction No 3

OPERATION ORDERS No. 159
by
MAJOR C.T. WILLIAMS.
Comdg. 12th. Bn. East Surrey Rgt.

1. The Battalion with Transport will parade at 08.35 to-morrow 20th. inst. in the following order:-
    H.Qr's - Drums - B - C - Band - A - D Coys.
    Head of column to be outside Battn. H.Qr's in column of route facing E.
    Dress. - Full Marching Order.

2. The Battalion will be located on night of 20th./21st. in the BIERWART - HERON Area.

3. Instructions re billeting parties will be issued later.

4. The lorries will be as usual. 2/Lt. A.C. COWLIN is detailed as Officer in charge of lorries. He will collect blankets from Companies commencing at 08.15.

5. Blankets will be stacked on main road outside Company billets by 08.00.

6. Officers valises, Mess kit etc. will be stacked outside Company H.Qr's ready for collection by 08.00. 0730.

7. Each Company will detail 5 men who are unable to march in the column, to parade at 07.30 outside Orderly Room under the Orderly Officer for 21st. inst. They will proceed by devious routes avoiding the main road.

8. Acknowledge.

Issued at 20.00   (Sgd) D. WALKER Capt & A/Adjt.
Dec. 19th. 1918.   12th. Bn. East Surrey Regt.

OPERATION ORDERS No. 160.
by
MAJOR C.T.WILLIAMS.
Comdg. 12th. East Surrey Regiment.

1. The Battalion with Transport will parade at 08.25, to-morrow 21st. inst. in the following order:-
    H.Qr's - Band - C. - A. - Drums - D. - B Coys.
    Head of column 100 yards N.E. of junction of third class road from PONTILLAS with main road facing N.E.
    Dress - Full Marching Order.

2. To-morrow is the final days march. The Battalion will be billetted in WARNANT.

3. Billeting parties have proceeded to-day in advance.

4. Lorries will be as usual. 2/LT. A.C.COWLIN is detailed as Officer in charge of lorries. He will collect blankets from Companies commencing at 08.00 and will report to M.T. Officer at Cross Roads at Kilo. 9. on HERON - WANZE Road at 12.00.

5. Blankets will be stacked outside Company billets by 08.00

6. Officers valises, Mess kit etc. will be stacked outside Company H.Qr's ready for collection by 07.00.

7. Each Company will detail men who are unable to march in the column to parade at 07.30 at Starting Point under the Orderly Officer for to-morrow. They will proceed by devious routes avoiding the main roads.

8. Acknowledge.

(Sgd) D.WALKER, Capt & A/Adjt.
12th. Bn. East Surrey Regt.

Issued at 20.15.
20th. Dec. 1918.

LONDON DIVISION
(LATE 41ST DIVISION)
122ND INFY BDE

12TH BN EAST SURREY REGT

JAN - MAR 1919

Army Form C. 2118.

1/5 East Surrey Regt

WAR DIARY
or
INTELLIGENCE SUMMARY.
(Erase heading not required.)

Instructions regarding War Diaries and Intelligence Summaries are contained in F. S. Regs., Part II. and the Staff Manual respectively. Title pages will be prepared in manuscript.

33.C
Entries

Place	Date 1919	Hour	Summary of Events and Information	Remarks and references to Appendices
WARRANT	Jan 1		Companies under Coy. Commanders. w.o.p.	
	2		Companies under Coy. Commanders. do.do.	
	3		Battalion paraded & inspected by Commanding Officer. Remainder of day Company Drill was carried out w.o.p.	
	4		Route march was carried out during the morning. Football was carried out during the afternoon w.o.p.	
	5		Battalion paraded for Divine Service. Warning order received to relieve the Canadian Division in Germany w.o.p.	
	6		Battalion employed throughout the day preparing for move into Germany. w.o.p.	
	7		Battalion entrained at Huy Station enroute for Germany. w.o.p.	
	8		On train. Germany w.o.p.	
	9		Battalion detrained at HOFFNUNGSTHAL marched to MARIALINDEN when they relieved a Batt. of Canadian Division 1 Company & 2 Platoons in the Outpost Line w.o.p.	
MARIALINDEN	10		Companies now on Outpost duty under Coy. Commanders. Ceremonial Parades w.o.p.	
	11		2nd Lt. G. L. WHITE awarded Military Cross w.o.p. Companies under Coy. Commanders. Inter Battalion Competition (Football) was carried out during the day. w.o.p.	
	12		Companies under Coy. Commanders. w.o.p.	
	13		Companies carried out duties & Inter Coy. Prize Competition w.o.p.	
	14		Companies carried out details & Inter Coy. Prize Competition. Battalion Boxing Competition was carried out in the evening. w.o.p	

Army Form C. 2118.

WAR DIARY
or
INTELLIGENCE SUMMARY.
(Erase heading not required.)

Instructions regarding War Diaries and Intelligence Summaries are contained in F. S. Regs., Part II. and the Staff Manual respectively. Title pages will be prepared in manuscript.

Place	Date 1919	Hour	Summary of Events and Information	Remarks and references to Appendices
MARIALINDEN	Jan 15		Parade under Coy Commander with—	
	16		Parade under Coy Commander with—	
	17		Companies under Coy Commander. The following educational Classes were held with— Bookkeeping, Shorthand & French. The Winners of the Battalion Boxing Competition were cheered on during the evening with	
	18		Companies under Coy Commander. with—	
	19		Battalion paraded for Divine Service with—	
	20		Companies under Coy Commander with—	
	21		" " " "	
	22		" " " "	
	23		Inter Coy Competition was carried out, it was judged by the Commanding Officer with—	
	24		Companies under Coy Commander with—	
	25		" " " "	
	26		Battalion Paraded for Divine Service, 8 men of the Battalion proceeded on Demobilization with—	
	27		The C.O.C. judged the winners of the Inter Company Competition with—	
	28		Companies under Coy Commander. 7 men proceeded for Demobilization with—	
	29		" " " "	
			An Arms Company drill was carried out in the outpost line with—	

Army Form C. 2118.

WAR DIARY
or
INTELLIGENCE SUMMARY.
(Erase heading not required.)

Instructions regarding War Diaries and Intelligence Summaries are contained in F. S. Regs., Part II. and the Staff Manual respectively. Title pages will be prepared in manuscript.

Place	Date 1919	Hour	Summary of Events and Information	Remarks and references to Appendices
MARIALINDEN	Jan 30		Companies under Coy Commanders WD	
"	31		" " " WD	

A.W.Barr LT.-COL,
COMDg. 12th BATT. EAST SURREY REGT.

SECRET

O.C. 12th East Surrey Regt.
 "   15th Hampshire Regt.
 "   18th King's Royal Rifle Corps.
 "   "B" Coy. 41st Bn. M.G.Corps.

B.M. 143.

For information.

26th January 1919.

Captain,
Brigade Major,
122nd Infantry Brigade.

SECRET.   Copy No. 5

122ND. INFANTRY BRIGADE OPERATION ORDER NO.252.

Reference Maps 2 K and 2 L. 1/100,000 GERMANY.

1. The Xth Corps (less 66th Division) is relieving the Canadian Corps in the COLOGNE BRIDGEHEAD.

2. The 41st. Division will relieve the 1st. Canadian Division in the left sector, Xth Corps Front.
   The 122nd. Infantry Brigade Group will relieve units of the 1st. Canadian Division, in accordance with the attached table of relief.

3. The move will be carried out by stragetical trains commencing on the 6th. instant in the following order:-

   124th. Infantry Brigade will move on the 6th January 1919.
   122nd.   "   "   "   "   "   "   7th   "
   123rd.   "   "   "   "   "   "   8th   "

4. Advance parties of 5 per Battalion and 3 for Brigade H.Q. will move on the 5th in accordance with orders already issued.

5. On arrival in the Canadian Corps area, Units of the 41st. Division will come under the command of the 1st. Canadian Division, until command of the sector passes to G.O.C., 41st. Division.
   Command of the Infantry Brigade Sub-sectors will pass on completion of the Infantry relief.

6. All guards, posts, orders and defence schemes will be taken over.

7. ACKNOWLEDGE

12th Bn. EAST SURREY REGT.
RECEIVED | FILED
         | No. 547
Date | Date 9/1/19

Issued at 2300
4th January 1919.
                                                 Captain,
                                              Brigade Major,
                                          122nd. Infantry Brigade.

   Copy No. 1. File.
        2. War Diary.
        3. 41st. Division "G".
        4.   "
        5. 12th. East Surrey Regt.
        6. 15th. Hampshire Regt.
        7. 18th. King's Royal Rifle Corps.
        8. No.2.Coy. 41st. Divisional Train.
        9. 123rd. Infantry Brigade.
       10. 124th. Infantry Brigade.
       11. Staff Captain.
       12. O.C. Signals.
       13. Spare.

TABLE OF RELIEF TO ACCOMPANY 122ND.INF.BDE. O.O. NO.258.

Unit.	In relief of.	At.
122nd Inf. Bde. H.Q. (Centre Sub-Sector).	2nd Can.Inf.Bde.H.Q.	ROSRATH.
12th.E.Surrey Regt.	8th Can.Inf.Battalion.	MARIALINDEN.
15th.Hampshire Regt.	7th Can.Inf.Battalion.	OVERATH.
18th.K.R.R.Corps.	5th Can.Inf.Battalion.	VOLBERG.
1 Bty.11th A.F.A.Bde.	1 Bty.2nd Can. F.A.	OVERATH.
228th Field Coy. R.E.	1 Coy. 2nd Bn. C.E.	EHSEN.
1 Field Ambulance.	No.2.Can.Field Ambce.	URBACH.
1 Coy. 41st Bn.M.G.C.	1 Coy. 1st Bn Can.M.G.C.	MENZLINGEN.
No.2.Coy. Divl.Train.	No.3.Coy. 1st Can.Divl Train.	ROSRATH.

SECRET   R.A.M.C., WARNING ORDER NO.76   Copy No. 9
---------------by---------------
COLONEL L.N.LLOYD, C.M.G., DSO., A.M.S.,
A.D.M.S., COMMANDING ROYAL ARMY MEDICAL CORPS
41ST DIVISION

4th January 1919

1. The 41st Division will relieve the 1st Canadian Division at the Cologne Bridgehead.

2. The Division will move by strategical trains.

3. The order of move will be 124th Infantry Brigade, 122nd Infantry Brigade, 123 I.Bde; Artillery & Div'l Troops later; moves will commence on the 6th instant.

4. Orders for moves of Field Ambulances will be issued later.

5. All Field Ambulances will hold an advance party in readiness to move at sudden notice.

6. O.C., 140th Field Ambulance will detail 1 Medical Officer with sufficient personnel, medical and surgical equipment and 3 cars (2 large and 1 Ford) and one D.R., to proceed by road to act as Detraining Medical Officer at COLOGNE.
The day on which this move is to take place will be notified later, also detraining Stations.
On arrival at COLOGNE, Medical Officer detailed will get into touch with the nearest British or Canadian Medical Units and will arrange for the reception of sick of the 41st Division at the COLOGNE Bridgehead both during the detraining period and until such times as the Field Ambulances 41st Division arrive in the new area and are able to open.
He will also get into touch with the A.D.M.S., 1st Canadian Division.

7. Officer Commanding, 140th Field Ambulance will take steps to have the cars detailed for the detraining Medical Officer placed in proper running order in order to obviate as far as possible, their liability to break down on the journey to COLOGNE.
Rations and petrol for 4 days will be taken.

8. Details for Entraining Medical Officer and personnel will be notified later.

9. ACKNOWLEDGE (Field Ambs only)

Issued to Signals at 1.0.p.m.

J Jackson Maj

Colonel. A.M.S.,
A.D.M.S., 41st Division.....

41st Division Headquarters.
4th January 1919.
JMS.

DISTRIBUTION
Copy No.			
1.	"G"	24.	O.C.19 M'sex Regt.
2	"A"	25.	O.C.41 Div'l Train.
3	O.C., 138th Field Amb.	26	C.R.E.
4.	O.C., 139th Field Amb.	30.	C.R.A.(27 - 30)
5 & 6	O.C., 140th Field Amb.	31.	D.A.P.M.,
7.-10	H.Q., 122nd Inf.Bde.	32	O.C.,11 Bde.A.F.A.
11-14	H.Q., 123rd Inf.Bde.	33.	D.D.M.S., 1st Can.Div.
15-18	H.Q., 124th Inf.Bde.	34 - 35	War diary.
19.	D.M.S., Fourth Army.	36.	File.
20.	D.M.S., Second Army.	37 & 38.	SPARE.
21.	D.D.M.S., X Corps.		
22	O.C., 41st Signal Coy.		
23.	O.C., 41st Bn.L.G.C.		

**41ST DIVISIONAL MEDICAL ADMINISTRATIVE
INSTRUCTIONS RELATIVE TO THE MOVE
TO GERMANY.**

Copy No. 8

46/3

5th January 1919.

1. Herewith copy of 41st Divisional Order No.287 and Administrative Instruction No.4, together with Train schedule. (Field Ambulances only)

2. 1st Field Amb to move - 140 F.A., Date 7.1.19.
   2nd " " " " - 138 F.A. " 8.1.19.
   3rd " " " " - 139 F.A. " 10.1.19.

3. The 138th Field Ambulance will move from MOHA on the morning of the 7th, and take over buildings etc., at HUY occupied by 140 F.A., and function that place till a Canadian Field Ambulance arrives.
   The Canadian Field Ambulance is expected to arrive during the 7th : the two Field Ambulances will arrange to "double up" for the night.
   In the event of the Canadian F.A., not arriving before the 138th Field Ambulance are due to leave by train, the O.C., 138th F.A., will leave a small holding party behind which will follow on by car.

4. Reference R.A.M.C., WARNING ORDER No.76 dated 4.1.19 ; the party detailed in para' 3 to act as Detraining Medical Staff will leave 140th Field Ambulance as early as possible on the 6th inst. by ambulance cars.
   The detraining Stations are shewn on the bottom of the train schedule.
   ADDRESS H.Q., 1st Canadian Division is 5, PARKSTRASSE, MARIENBURG, COLOGNE.

5. In addition to this party an advance party of a maximum of 10 will proceed by the same cars to take over from the 3rd Canadian Field Ambulance at COLNVINSST. Rations as for detraining party.
   (COLNVINSST is just due EAST of COLOGNE.)

6. Field Ambulances requiring extra M.T. transport for conveyance to Entraining Station will apply to A.D.M.S., office by wire, stating the number of lorries required.

7. The 139th Field Ambulance will close at MOXHE on 8th and march on the 9th instant, staying for the night at WANZE. The Area Commandant, 124th Inf.Bde, has been instructed to provide accommodation. O.C.139th F.A., will get into touch with this Officer and arrange.

8. Officers Commanding, 139th and 138th F.A's will arrange to send advance parties - maximum 10, with 140th F.A., leaving on 7th instant to take over their location.

   138th Field Ambulance to URBACH.
   139th Field Ambulance to WAHN.

9. Officers Commanding F.A's at present collecting the various areas will instruct all Units in those areasm who are remaining behind after the F.A's have moved, I.E., Artillery, Pioneers, Machine Gunners etc., that a Canadian Field Ambulance is expected to arrive at HUY on 7th or 8th instant and will be located in HUY, present site of 140th Field Ambulance, and that application for collection of sick etc., should be made to them direct
(See para 9 Administrative Instruction No.4.

10. Officer Commanding Field Ambulances will be responsible for entraining medical arrangements of their brigades and will arrange

that a Medical Officer with medical personnel stays till the last
train of the Brigade has left. This party will rejoin their Unit
by train, or by car, in the new area.

11. All M.T.Ambulance cars will proceed by road under
arrangements to be made by Officer Commanding, Field
Ambulances concerned.

41st Divisional H.Q.,
5th January 1919.
JES.

J.E.Jackson Maj.
Colonel.AMS.
A.D.M.S.,41st Division.

Issued to all recipients of R.A.M.C.,Warning
Order No.76 dated 4th January 1919.

ADMINISTRATIVE INSTRUCTIONS IN CONNECTION WITH
122ND. INF. BRIGADE O.O. 258 dated 4.1.19.

1. The Brigade will entrain for Germany in accordance with attached schedule (A).
    Trains will be stragetical Trains composed of:-

    1 Officers Coach.
    32 Covers (Each truck is registered to carry 50 men but trains have been arranged at about 40 men per truck)
    15 Flats.

    Baggage and supply wagons will travel loaded with Units, reporting to Units by 4 p.m. the day before entrainment.

2. Transport will be at the Station three hours, and personnel one hour before scheduled time of departure of train. As the Canadian Division will be detraining from the same trains, care must be taken to leave approaches to trains clear.
    No loading will be commenced until the Canadian units are clear of the train and approaches, and the trucks cleaned out.

3. Entrainment will be supervised by the D.A.Q.M.G.
    Detrainment will be supervised by the A/D.A?A.G.

4. Loading parties.
    Parties of 4 Officers and 100 O.R. will be detailed by 19th Middlesex Regt. to report at each entraining station three hours before the scheduled time of departure of each train for cleaning out trucks and loading of vehicles and animals. 19th Middlesex will provide shovels and brooms for cleaning out coaches.

5. Before arriving at the Detraining Station, Os.C. all trains will tell off a party of 2 officers and 50 O.Rs. to detrain vehicles. Detrainment will not commence until R.T.O. or Detraining Officer has been consulted.

6. SUPPLIES.
    Units will entrain with the unexpired portion of the days rations plus one days rations on the man. Supply wagons will contain a further days rations.
    Water Carts will be filled before entrainment.
    On arrival in the new area, Units will draw rations from 1st. Canadian Divisional Train until 41st. Divisional Train arrives.
    Canadian Units arriving in this area will draw from 41st. Divisional Train.
    Railhead in new area will be ROSRATH.

7. Area Commandants in present area will remain until 1st. Canadian Division have completely taken over their areas.
    They will be rationed by 1st. Canadian Division after troops of the 41st. Division have left.

8. In both this and the 1st. Canadian Division Area, the nearest Field Ambulance of either Divisions will accept sick and casualties until reliefs are complete. Canadian Field Ambulances are situated as follows:-
    No.1. Canadian Field Ambulance.   TANN.
    No.2.   "   "   "   URBACH.
    No.3.   "   "   "   COLNVINECT.

9. Mobile Veterinary Sections in either area will accept sick horses of either formation until relief is complete.

10. GUARDS.
The following guard on dump of enemy material will remain after the Battalion has left, and will be relieved by Canadian troops on arrival. On relief they will report to R.T.O. HUY and proceed to rejoin their units.

1 N.C.O. and 3 men - guard on enemy material at VILLERS le BOUILLETS (Liege C.D.6.) found by 18th. K.R.R.C.

All guards and parties at present employed by R.S.O. HUY, R.T.O. HUY, O.C. HALTE REPAS, HUY, and on enemy stores in HUY, will be relieved by 56th Division by 1800 hours on 6th instant.

11. DIVISIONAL RECEPTION CAMP.
Divisional Reception Camp will remain at HUY until further orders, but any personnel arriving at HUY will be despatched as early as possible to COLOGNE Area.

12. BATHS.
All baths will close down on the 9th. instant and re-open as early as possible on arrival in the new area.
Baths Officer will be at WAHN.

13. DIVISIONAL CANTEEN.
Divisional Canteen will close on the 9th. instant and re-open on 13th instant in the new area at WAHN Barracks.

ENTRAINING TABLE.

Date.	Train No.	Unit.
7.1.19.	6	12th. East Surrey Regt.
8.1.19.	7	15th. Hampshire Regt.
"	8	18th. King's Royal Rifle Corps.
"	9	T.H.Q. 122nd. Inf. Bde. & 138th. Field Amblce.

5.1.19.

[Stamp: 12th Bn. EAST SURREY REGT. RECD Date 9/1/19 Sub]

2/Lieut.
A/Staff Captain,
122nd. Infantry Brigade.

Issued to all recipients of O.O.258 and 138th. Field Amblce.

1ST. ADDENDUM TO ADMINISTRATIVE INSTRUCTIONS IN CONNECTION WITH 122ND. INF.BRIGADE O.O.258 dated 4.1.19.

1. Reference para 1. for:- "attached schedule (A)" read "Entraining Table on reverse". Entraining Station will be HUY.

2. TRANSPORT.
   2 Lorries will report to units at 8 a.m. on the day they entrain to carry surplus baggage etc.
   15th Hampshire Regt. will detail 1 lorry to report to Brigade Headquarters, without party, to make a second journey.

3. DETRAINMENT.
   13th. East Surrey Regt. will detail 1 officer who will be responsible for detraining the Brigade, name of officer selected to be forwarded to this office by 1800 hours 6th instant.

4. MOBILE RESERVE OF S.A.A.
   Mobile Reserve, S.A.A. will remain at Brigade Dump and be taken over by Canadian Infantry Brigade. Ammunition of Canadian Infantry Brigade will be taken over by units of this Brigade on arrival in new area.
   15th. Hampshire Regt. will supply a guard to report to Brigade Headquarters at 1800 7th. instant, bringing two days rations.

5. Stores under O.R.O. 3084 may be taken. All other stores and R.E. material will be left behind as Area Stores.

6. TIMES OF DEPARTURE.
   No.6. Train probably 14.40 on 7th. instant.
   Exact times will be notified by wire as soon as received.

6.1.19.

2nd. Lieut.,
A/Staff Captain,
122nd. Infantry Brigade.

18th K.R.R. Corps.

Ref OO 258 and Administrative Instructions.

18th KRRC will proceed by train No 11. (eleven) on 9th inst.; time of departure will be notified later. This cancels previous orders.

11th Queens R.W.S. Regt will replace 18th KRRC and proceed by train No 8 on 8th inst.

18th KRRC will appoint their own entraining officer.

ACKNOWLEDGE
6-1-19.
Copies to:- 12 E.Surrey Regt.
138 Fd Amb.

12th Bn. EAST SURREY REGT.
RECEIVED
Date ....
FILED
No. ...551
Date 7/1/19

Lieut.
a/Staff Capt.
122nd Inf. Bde.
15 Hampshire Regt.
123rd Inf. Bde.

12th. East Surrey Regt.
15th. Hampshire Regt.
18th. King's Royal Rifle Corps.
No.2.Coy. 41st. Divl. Train.
138th. Field Ambulance.

S.C.H.324.

Reference Administrative Instructions issued in connection with 122nd Inf.Bde. O.O. 258 dated 4.1.19.

Supply wagons will join their respective units at the Entraining Station 3 hours before departure of the train and not the day previous.

Times of departure of trains are as follows:-

Date.	Train.	Time of departure.	Unit.
Jan.7th.	6.	14.34 hours.	12th. E.Surrey Regt.
" 8th.	7.	11.40 "	15th. Hampshire Regt.
" 8th.	9.	14.40 "	Bde H.Q. & 138th Fld.Amb.
" 9th.	11.	13.03 "	18th. K.R.R.Corps.

This office wire L.300 to 12th. East Surrey Regt and No. 2 Company, 41st. Divisional Train will be amended as above.

6.1.19.

2nd. Lieut.,
A/Staff Captain.
122nd. Infantry Brigade.

SECRET.   Copy No. 6

122nd INFANTRY BRIGADE OPERATION ORDER No. 259.

Reference Maps 2 K and 2 L - 1/100,000 - GERMANY.

In continuation of 122nd Inf. Bde. Operation Order No. 258 dated 4th January 1919.

1.   The 12th East Surrey Regt. will relieve the 10th Canadian Infantry Battalion in the Outpost Line <u>on the day of detrainment</u>.

2.   The 7th and 5th Canadian Infantry Battalions at OVERATH and VOLBERG respectively are moving from their areas without awaiting reliefs.

3.   In all marches from Detraining Stations to Destinations the only roads that can be relied upon are those marked as first class roads on the 1/250,000 GERMANY, COLN, Sheet 10.

4.   On arrival, the following guards will be taken over by Units in accordance with attached Table. Great care will be taken to ensure that all orders and duties are properly understood.

5.   All details of the relief of the Outpost Line will be arranged between Commanding Officers concerned.
       Defence Schemes, Plans and Maps will be taken over.
       Command of the Outpost Line will pass to Officer Commanding 12th East Surrey Regt., on completion of relief, and reported to this Office.

6.   122nd Infantry Brigade Headquarters will close at present location at 1000 hours on the 8th instant, and will re-open on arrival at ROSRATH.

7.   Completion of moves and locations of Headquarters will be reported on arrival.

8.   A C K N O W L E D G E.

Issued at 2100.   Captain,
6th January 1919.   Brigade Major,
                                                   122nd Infantry Brigade.

12th Bn. EAST SURREY REGT.
RECEIVED / FILED
No. 549
Date 9/1/19

Copy No. 1 File.
         2 War Diary.
         3 41st Division "G".
         4   do.
         5 12th E. Surrey Regt.
         6 15th Hampshire Regt.
         7 18th K. R. R. Corps.
         8 No. 2 Coy 41st Divl. Train.
         9 123rd Infantry Brigade.
       10 124th Infantry Brigade.
       11 A.D.M.S. 41st Division.
       12 Brigade Major.
       13 Staff Captain.
       14 O.C. Signals.
       15 Spare.

NOTE. The 10th have relieved the 5th Can. Infy. Bn. in the Outpost line, hence the alteration above.

TABLE OF PERMANENT GUARDS FOUND BY 122nd INF. BDE.

Guard No.	Found by	Party.	Detail.	Remarks.
1.	18th K.R.R.C.	2 N.C.O's 12 Men	Bridge over the SULZ River between VOLBERG and HOFFNUNGSTHAL.	
2.	do.	2 N.C.O's 6 Men	URBACH Town Guard. (Main Road junction in URBACH)	
3.	15th Hants Regt.		Railway Bridges - Ten posts (each double sentry) on the railway line between point where River AGGER crosses BURG Road and where it crosses the SIEBURG Road, 1 mile N. of D of WAHLSCHEID.	
4.	18th K.R.R.C.	1 N.C.O. 4 Men	HOFFNUNGSTHAL Station.	
5.	do.	1 N.C.O. 3 Men	Guarding Railway Bridge over Road South of HEUMAR.	At present found by 1st Canadian Engineers at KALK. To be relieved by the 11th January. 19th Middlesex Regt.(F) will, on arrival, take them over from the 18th K.R.R.C.
6.	do.	2 N.C.O's 6 Men	Factory, HEIDELBURGER Strasse.	
7.	do.	1 N.C.O. 7 men	Permanently attached to A.P.M. COLOGNE.	

No. 161
OPERATION ORDERS
by
LIEUT COL. G.L.BROWN, D.S.O.
Comdg. 12th. Bn. EAST SURREY REGIMENT.

1. The Battalion with Transport will proceed by train to-morrow 7th. January, 1919 into GERMANY, relieving the 5th. Canadian Battalion 1st Canadian Division, in the COLOGNE Bridgehead.
Entraining Station, HUY.   Detraining Station, HOFFNUNGSTIL.

2. The Battalion, less Transport will parade at 11.00 in the following order:-   H.Qr's - Band - A. - B. - Drums - C. - D. Coy.
Head of column outside Battalion Headquarters facing S.W.
Dress - Full Marching Order.

3. The Transport will proceed under its own arrangements to arrive at the Station at 11.40.

4. Advance parties have proceeded and will meet the Battalion on arrival.

5. 2 Lorries have been allotted to the Battalon to transport surplus stores etc. to the station.   They will do 2 journeys and will be in charge of an offider to be detailed by O.C. "A" Coy. who will repor t at Orderly Room at 08.00 for instructions.

6. Blankets will be stacked outside Company Billets by 08.00.   All blankets Company stores etc. not colæcted for the first journey will be stacked outside Battn. H. Qr's by 10.00 from which place the lorries will collect their second load.

7. Blankets will be stacked in bundles of 10 ties tightly about a foot from each end and labelled.

8. Officers valises will be stacked outside Company H. Qr's ready for collection by ~~10.00~~ .08.30
Mess kit etc. will be stacked as above by 09.30.   The Transport Officer will arrange to collect these.

9. <u>Supplies.</u> - Each man will carry the unexpired portion of the days ration, plus one days ration.
The Transport Officer will arrange for watercart to call round Companies before they move off, when all waterbottles will be filled, also, watercarts will be loaded on the train full.

10. <u>Loading & unloading parties.</u> - O.C. "D" Coy. will detail 2 Officers and 50 O.R's to detrain vehicles on arrival at destination O.C. "A" Coy. will detail 1 N.C.O. and 8 men to proceed with the lorry as in Para. 5.   They will proceed in full kit and remain at the station to load blankets etc. on the train.

11. <u>Dinners</u> - Cookers will proceed with the Transport and dinners will be served out at the station before the Battalion entrains.

12. Attention is drawn to train discipline.   No man will be allowed to leave the train without permission and no man is allowed to travel on an open truck.   An N.C.O will be placed in charge of each truck.   Numbers for each truck will be notified at the station when parties will be told off.

Issued at 19.20   (Sgd) D.WALKER, Capt & A/Adjt.
6th. Jan. 1919.   12th Bn. East Surrey Regt.

S E C R E T.   41st Div. G.769/38/2.
****

122nd Infantry Brigade.
123rd Infantry Brigade.
124th Infantry Brigade.
C. R. E.
C. R. A.
41st Bn. Machine Gun Corps.
19th Middlesex Regt. (P).
" Q ".

1.- The primary object of the Bridgehead position at present held by the Second Army is to secure the passages of the RHINE so as to enable a sufficient force being brought forward and concentrated East of the RHINE without interference by the enemy at the point of passage.

2.- With this object in view the Commander-in-Chief has directed that arrangements should be made to put the defended areas now held into a proper and efficient state of defence with the least possible delay.

3.- Brigade Commanders, assisted by the O.C. Field Coy. R.E. and O.C. Machine Gun Coy. affiliated to their Brigade, will carry out reconnaissances as soon as possible and prepare schemes for the construction of defences of the Outpost Zone and Main Line of Resistance in their Brigade Sectors.

In order to strengthen the resistance of the small and scattered garrisons of the Outpost Line, and enable them to carry out with success the role of delaying an enemy advance until such time as the garrison of the Main Line of Resistance is in position, Machine Guns will have to be largely relied upon, a defence to which the ground in question particularly lends itself.

4.- These schemes, together with a map shewing proposed sites for the defences, will be submitted for the approval of the Divisional Commander and after final approval, the work will be put in hand at once.

5.- It is possible that it may be necessary to hold these defences for a considerable period. They should therefore be capable of covering all possible lines of approach on the Divisional Front and should consist of a line of mutually supporting defended localities.

6.- Care must be taken that, at the junction of Brigades and Divisions, the siting of defensive works are co-ordinated. Arrangements as regards the flanks of the Division will be made by Divisional Headquarters.

7.- Work, after schemes have been approved, will be carried out in the following order :-

    (a) Wire.
    (b) Spitlocking of trenches.
    (c) Digging, draining and revetting of trenches.

The construction of concrete pill-boxes should be carried out simultaneously with the other work.

/8.-

8.- As, owing to the winter billetting scheme, troops are much scattered and a long way from the positions selected for defence, the work will be carried out without unduly taxing the men and making them uncomfortable.

9.- ACKNOWLEDGE.

General Staff.
41st Division.
25th January, 1919.

E.A.Beck
Lieut.Colonel,
General Staff.

Copies to -
  29th Division.
  34th Division.
  Xth Corps.
  Canadian Corps.

"C" FORM.
MESSAGES AND SIGNALS.

Army Form C. 2121
(In books of 100.)
No. of Message ....

Prefix	Code	Words	Sent, or sent out.	Office Stamp.
Received from B	By	At ... m.	ESh
Service Instructions		To ...	
		By	

Handed in at **Bde** Office **30** m. Received **36** m.

TO **12 Coat Survey Regt**

*Sender's Number.	Day of Month.	In reply to Number.	AAA
L300	6		

Ref obtaining table aaa Provisional obtaining station no 61 from HOFFNUNGSTIL aaa Time of departure from HUT 1240 hours

FROM PLACE & TIME: **12 Dif RE**

* This line, except A A A, should be erased, if not required.

"C" FORM.
MESSAGES AND SIGNALS.

Army Form C. 2121.
(In books of 100.)
No. of Message ....

Prefix 9M	Code 2153	Words	Sent, or sent out.	Office Stamp.
Received from ZLB	By Britton	At .... m.	ESL 3.1.19
Service Instructions ZLB		To / By	

Handed in at Bde Office 2153 m. Received 225 m.

TO 12th E Surrey Rgt

*Sender's Number.	Day of Month.	In reply to Number.	AAA
R375	3	—	

Warning Order aaa 122 Inf Bde will move to GERMANY by tactical train on 7th inst aaa acknowledge aaa Advanced parties to be held in readiness to move at a moments notice.

FROM 122 Inf Bde

PLACE & TIME

* This line, except AAA, should be erased, if not required.
(3287) Wt. W54/P738. 691,000 Pads. 3/18. A.P.Ltd. (E3013)

"C" FORM.
MESSAGES AND SIGNALS.

Army Form C. 2121.
(In books of 100.)
No. of Message ....

Prefix **9M**	Code **2120**	Words **84**	Sent, or sent out.	Office Stamp.
Received from **ZLB**	By **Bettott**		At .... m.	**ESL**
Service Instructions			To	
ZLB			By	**4.1.19**

Handed in at **Bde** Office **2120** m. Received **2130** m.

TO **12th E Surreys.**

*Sender's Number.	Day of Month.	In reply to Number.	AAA
L286	4		

1 Off 4 ORs from each Battalion advanced party will proceed to 1st Canadian Div. COLOGNE by train leaving HUY 0915 tomorrow STOP guides will meet at other end aaa 12th E Surreys take over from 5th Bn Canadians 15th Hants 7th Bn 18th KRRC 10th Bn Bde No from 2nd Can. Bde Extra 2 days rations to be carried aaa 12th E Surreys will send

FROM ....

PLACE & TIME ....

* This line, except A A A, should be erased, if not required.

"C" FORM.
MESSAGES AND SIGNALS.

Army Form C. 2123.
(In books of 100.)
No. of Message..........

Prefix	Code	Words	Sent, or sent out.	Office Stamp.
Received from ZB	By Betts		At........m.	ESL
Service Instructions			To........	4·1·19
			By........	

Handed in at **Bde** Office **2120** m. Received **21** m.

TO _____ (Cont'd). _____

*Sender's Number.	Day of Month.	In reply to Number.	AAA
	One officer	to take over	
	billets for	Bde Hq.	
	2 Off		
	5 R.W.		

FROM
PLACE & TIME   **122 Inf Bde**

* This line, except A A A, should be erased, if not required.

Army Form C. 2118.

1/5 Surrey Regt

WAR DIARY
or
INTELLIGENCE SUMMARY.
(Erase heading not required.)

Instructions regarding War Diaries and Intelligence Summaries are contained in F. S. Regs., Part II. and the Staff Manual respectively. Title pages will be prepared in manuscript.

Sh. C
2 sheet

Place	Date	Hour	Summary of Events and Information	Remarks and references to Appendices
MARIALINDEN	1919 Feb 1		Companies under Coy Commanders 18 OR's were demobilized the day WBn	WBn
"	2		Battalion Parade for Divine Service. 16 "	"
"	3		Battalion relig cancelled. Coy under Company Commander. WBn	
"	4		Companies under Coy Commander. WBn	
"	5		A Pl. was of Guard of Colours was carried during the morning. Inspected by the Divisional Commander. WBn	
"	6		Companies under Coy Commander. 11 OR's were demobilized the day. WBn	
"	7		Companies under " " 16 off + 7 OR's " " WBn	
"	8		Companies " " " 7 OR's " "	
"	9		Church and camp during the morning. 8 OR were demobilized. WBn	
"	10		Battalion paraded for Divine Service. 9 OR's were demob the day. WBn	
			Battalion paraded for Snow Release of Prisoners of Germany. Te Journey Officers from S. Rome. 2/Lt A J Ropp, 12/38 Sgt Bayas B.E	
			11896 Pte E H Fox, 14950 Cpl 7 Goss L.Cpl	
"	11		Coy were air paraded the day. WBn	
"	12		Te Army Comander visited te Galaxie to te Battalion on te way an OVERATH 10 Off + 13 OR's were demobilized the day. WBn	
"	13		Companies under Company Commander. WBn	
"	14		Te Battalion was relieved by te 18 WRC in te quarter-town. Afte marching te Battalion	

Reserve to Pioneers at HOFFNUNGSTHAL. WBn

(30540) Wt W5300/P713 750,000 3/18 E & S.S. D, D. & L., London, E.C. Forms/C2118/16.

Army Form C. 2118.

WAR DIARY
or
INTELLIGENCE SUMMARY.
(Erase heading not required.)

Instructions regarding War Diaries and Intelligence Summaries are contained in F. S. Regs., Part II. and the Staff Manual respectively. Title pages will be prepared in manuscript.

Place	Date	Hour	Summary of Events and Information	Remarks and references to Appendices
HOTT HUNGSTHL	1919 Feb 15		Corporeus under Coy Commander 14 O.R.'s own demobilized the coy total	
	16		Battalion parade for Divine service. 2 Officer + 24 O.R.'s were demob. total	
	17		Company under Coy Commander. Parade including Grenadier & M.G. crew & rifle total	
	18		Company under Coy " total	
	19		" " " total	
	20		A Police and Visitation coy under the Bn coy total	
	21		A Police inspection carried out under the normal " total	
	22		Parade to coy under the Inspection of the man & rifle total	
	23		Battalion parade for Divine service in the Kings Place total	
	24		Parade under Coy Commander total	
	25		Parade under Coy Commander total	
	26		Parade " " A Lecture was given the Battalion on Discipline total	
	27		A Foot inspection was carried out under the normal total	
	28		Company under Coy Commander total	

Duncan Capt. for O.C.
Comdg. T/12 East Surrey Regt.

OPERATION ORDER No. 162
by
LIEUT. COL. G.L.BROWN, D.S.O.
Comdg. 12th. Bn. EAST SURREY REGIMENT.

1. The Battalion will be relieved by the 18th. K.R.R.C. in the Outpost Line as under on the 4th. February, 1919.
   C. Coy... will be relieved by C. Coy 18th. K.R.R.C.
   D. Coy.   "   "   "   "   "   "   "
   A. Coy.   "   "   "   "   "   "   "
   B. Coy.   "   "   "   "   D. Coy.   "

   On relief the Battalion will move to VOLBERG - HOFFNUNGSTHAL Area where it will be in Brigade Reserve.

2. Defence Schemes, Iron Rations, Washing Bowls, Soyer Stoves, etc. will be handed over, and receipts signed by an Officer will be rendered to Orderly Room together with list of stores taken over, by 18.00 4th. inst.

3. Six lorries are allotted to the Battalion to convey C. Company and the two outpost platoons of D. Company to the new area after they have been relieved.
   Two platoons of C. Company will embus at GRABEN ERHOHE, the remaining two platoons of C. Company will embus at Company H.qr's.
   Company Stores etc. will be taken on these lorries.
   The two platoons of D. Company holding outpost will embus at MARIALINDEN.

4. The remainder of the Battalion will parade at 09.00 outside Battn. H.Qr's MARIALINDEN as under:-
   Headquarters.
   Band.
   A. Company
   2 Platoons of D. Coy.
   Drums.
   B. Company.
   Transport.
   Head of the column western side of village facing WEST.
   Dress - Fighting Order.

5. The above will stack packs, blankets, Officer valises, Mess kit, Company Stores etc. outside Quartermaster Stores by 08.30. They will be taken by lorry to the new area.
   O.C. B. Company will detail an Officer in charge of lorries.

6. Advance parties of one Officer from H.Qr's. one Officer per Company, and one man per platoon will report to Battn. H.Qr's at 10.00 on the 3rd. inst. and will proceed to take over billets. They will remain with opposite numbers until relief.
   Similar parties from the 18th. K.R.R.C. will report to their opposite numbers on the 3rd.

7. Companies will arrange for dinner and tea rations to be on the cookers.   Dinners will be served immediately on arrival in new area.

8. ACKNOWLEDGE.

Issued at... 1800
1st. Feb. 1919.

(Sgd) D. WALKER,
Capt & A/Adjt.
12th. Bn. East Surrey Regt.

Secret.   Copy No. 5

122nd INFANTRY BRIGADE OPERATION ORDER No. 262.

1. The 15th Hampshire Regt. will relieve the 18th King's Royal Rifle Corps in the Outpost Line on the 24th instant, under arrangements to be made by Battalion Commanders concerned.

2. The 18th King's Royal Rifle Corps will on relief, move to billets vacated by the 15th Hampshire Regt., and will then be the Garrison of Main Line of Resistance.

3. Defence Schemes and Maps etc., will be taken over on relief.

4. The permanent Guards and Picquets found at present by the 15th Hampshire Regt. will not be relieved by the 18th King's Royal Rifle Corps, but will remain until the 26th instant, when they will be relieved by the 1/7th Middlesex Regt.

5. Command of the Outpost Line will pass to Lieut-Colonel ..., PUTTICK, ..., Commanding 15th Hampshire Regt., on completion of relief, which will be reported to this Office.

6. The 1/7th Middlesex Regt. (less Transport and Horses) will detrain at OVERATH on the 26th instant, to relieve the 18th King's Royal Rifle Corps and the remaining guards and picquets of the 15th Hampshire Regt.

7. The 18th King's Royal Rifle Corps (complete) will move from OVERATH by march route or train on the 26th instant, to a destination to be notified later.

8. A C K N O W L E D G E.

Issued to Signals at 22:00.
22nd February 1919.

Captain,
Brigade Major,
122nd Infantry Brigade.

---

1. File.
2. War Diary.
3. 41st Division.
4. do.
5. 12th East Surrey Regt.
6. 15th Hampshire Regt.
7. 18th King's Royal Rifle Corps.
8. 1/7th Middlesex Regt.
9. C.R.E. 41st Division.
10. A.D.M.S. 41st Division.
11. D.A.P.M. 41st Division.
12. 138th Field Ambulance.
13. 228th Field Coy. R.E.
14. "B" Coy. 41st Bn. M.G.C.
15. 2/B Battery 126th R.F.A.
16. 123rd Army Bde. R.F.A.
17. 123rd Inf. Bde.
18. 124th Inf. Bde.
19. No.2 Coy. 41st Div. Train.
20. Brigade Major.
21. Staff Captain.
22. Bde. Signal Officer.

ADMINISTRATIVE INSTRUCTIONS REFERENCE 122ND INFANTRY
BRIGADE O.O. 262 DATED 22nd FEB. 1919.

1. Units will move with baggage and supply wagons, but will not take R.A.S.C. horses, harness, or personnel.

2. Units will entrain with the current day's rations and supply wagons full.

3. Times of arrival and departure of trains:-
   TU No.2 Nord with 1/7th Middlesex arrives OVERATH 1200 26th.
   Train for 18th K.R.R.C. departs OVERATH 1141 27th inst.

4. The 18th K.R.R.Corps will arrange to accommodate the 1/7th Middlesex at OVERATH 26th/27th instant. (Strength 24 Officers, 124 other Ranks, 0 horses).

5. 18th K.R.R.Corps will arrange to have guides to meet incoming unit and conduct them to their billets.

6. The horses of the 20th Durham L.I. which are not proceeding with the unit will be taken over at OVERATH by 122nd Infantry Brigade, under arrangements to be made by Capt. J.A.MOWAT, M.C. 15th Hampshire Regiment, and handed over to 1/7th Middlesex on the morning of the 27th instant. Transport personnel detailed by 124th Infantry Brigade will remain with these horses until replaced by personnel from the 1/7th Middlesex Regt.

7. 18th K.R.R.Corps will arrange to have 2 cookers with hot water at OVERATH on arrival of 1/7th Middlesex Regt.

8. 18th K.R.R.C. will send transport with loading party of 2 officers and 100 O.R. to OVERATH Station 3 hours before scheduled time of departure of train.

9. Personnel of 18th K.R.R.Corps will be at Station 30 minutes before the scheduled time of departure of train. 18th K.R.R.Corps will hand in to the R.T.O. an entraining state in duplicate.

10. All extra regimentally employed officers and other ranks of Units moving from the Division will be returned to their units as soon as they can be replaced.
    18th K.R.R.C. will forward a nominal roll of all such officers and other ranks showing where employed and if possible quoting authority, to this office as early as possible.

11. A/D.A.Q.M.G. 41st. Division will act as Entraining and Detraining Officer.

12. 18th K.R.R.Corps to ACKNOWLEDGE.

Lieut.,
A/Staff Captain,
122nd. Infantry Brigade.

25.2.19.

Copies to:-
1. File.
2. 18th K.R.R.Corps.
3. 1/7th Middlesex Regt.
4. 12th E.Surrey Regt.
5. 15th Hampshire Regt.
6. 124th Infantry Brigade.
7. Capt. J.A. MOWAT, M.C.
8. No.2.Coy. 41st. Divl. Train.
9. 133th Field Ambulance.

17th Earl Surrey Regt.

Army Form C. 2118.

WAR DIARY
or
INTELLIGENCE SUMMARY.
(Erase heading not required.)

Instructions regarding War Diaries and Intelligence Summaries are contained in F. S. Regs., Part II. and the Staff Manual respectively. Title pages will be prepared in manuscript.

Place	Date	Hour	Summary of Events and Information	Remarks and references to Appendices
OLBERG	1919 MAR/1		Companies employed under Coy. Commanders. W.D.	
	2		Battalion paraded for Divine Service. W.D.	
	3		Companies under Coy. Commanders. The funeral of Divisional Chpr. Connolly ran took place this day. Hearer as follows:- 2nd 12th East Surrey Regt, 2nd/20th D.L.I. W.D. 1 Field Ambulance. W.D.	
	4		Companies under Coy. Commanders. During the coming season no leave in the Batt. Lower Hole W.D.	
	5		Companies under Coy. Commanders. No. 17637 Cpl. J.M. Rogers awarded Bar to M.M. W.D.	
	6		Companies under Coy. Commanders. W.D.	
	7		The 9/13th East Surrey Regt. moved into Volmers Area this day. W.D.	
	8		All Officers & men of the 12/13th East Surrey Regt. due for Reduction in the Army of Occupation are transferred from this unit to the 9/13th East Surrey Regt. which is now transferred to the 123rd Infantry Brigade. The 12/13th now consists of the Cadre Establishment, men due for Demobilization. W.D.	
	9		Battalion attended Divine Service in Kinzr Church W.D.	
	10		The Cadre personnel together with men for Demob: moved to and billeted the old Vacated Butts, 9.00 a.m., of 9th Bn. East Surrey Regt. W.D.	

Army Form C. 2118.

WAR DIARY
or
INTELLIGENCE SUMMARY.
(Erase heading not required.)

Instructions regarding War Diaries and Intelligence Summaries are contained in F. S. Regs., Part II. and the Staff Manual respectively. Title pages will be prepared in manuscript.

Place	Date	Hour	Summary of Events and Information	Remarks and references to Appendices
VOLBERG	1919 Jan 11		Men employed cleaning up alone etc W.D.L	
	12		" " " " " W.D.L	
	13		" " " " " W.D.L	
	14		" " " " " W.D.L	
	15		" " " " " W.D.L	
	16		Men attended Divine Service this day at Volbergs Church W.D.L	
	17		Men employed cleaning up alone etc. The following Officers proceeded to Concentration Camp for Transport this day. L. G.E.HEAD, L. R.N.HAINE, 2nd LIEUT C.W.SPELLETT, 2nd L. G.BAKER. W.D.L	
	18		Men employed cleaning up alone etc. MAJOR C.T.WILLIAMS proceeded to England this day for transfer to Reserve Camp. W.D.L	
	19		Men employed cleaning up alone etc. The following Officers proceeded to concentration Camp for transport. Capt H.G.EDGAR, Lieut H.S.HALL, 2nd LT A.R.DUTTON, 2nd LT A.J.RODD. W.D.L	
	20		Men employed cleaning up alone etc W.D.L	
	21		" " " " " W.D.L	
	22		" " " " " W.D.L	
	23		" " " " " W.D.L	
	24		" " " " " W.D.L	
	25		" " " " " W.D.L	

Army Form C. 2118.

WAR DIARY
or
INTELLIGENCE SUMMARY.
(Erase heading not required.)

Instructions regarding War Diaries and Intelligence Summaries are contained in F. S. Regs., Part II. and the Staff Manual respectively. Title pages will be prepared in manuscript.

Place	Date	Hour	Summary of Events and Information	Remarks and references to Appendices
VOLBERG	1919 MAR 26		Men emp[loyed] cleaning up Lines etc. The following Officers proceeded to concentration camp for Demob[ilization] 2nd Lt R. NORTHWOOD, 2nd Lt H.C. CONLIN. Lieut Col G.L. BROWN relinquished comd of Batt this day & proceeded to Eng[land] and Capt D. WALKER assumed command of same from this date to Bn.	
	27		" " " " " to Bn.	
	28		" " " " " to Bn.	
	29		" " " " " to Bn.	
	30			
	31		The Cadre, together with remaining men for Demobilization moved to 41st Divisional reception camp, COLOGNE near this day. WDn.	

[Signature] Lt. Col.,
COMDg. 12th BATT. EAST SURREY REGT.

12th BATTALION,
EAST SURREY
REGIMENT.
No.............
Date.............